Go

Oregon

The *Complete* guide to Oregon's golf facilities

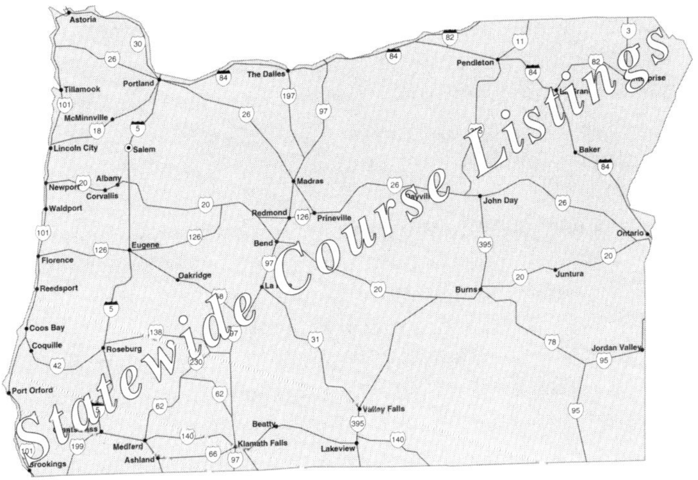

Twelfth Edition by Daniel MacMillan

Published by:

MAC Productions

Golf Guides Since 1986

MEMBER NGF NATIONAL GOLF FOUNDATION ®

Warren Miller

Waiver on Accuracy
We have gone to great lengths to provide the golfer with an up-to-date, accurate and comprehensive guide to golfing facilities in the state of Oregon; nevertheless, we all slice it out of bounds from time to time. Each course reserves the right to change their prices and policies at any time and we will not be held liable for any inaccuracies presented in this book.

Library of Congress Cataloging-in-Publication Data
MacMillan, Daniel E.
Golfing in Oregon; The complete guide to Oregon's Golf facilities (Twelfth edition)
1. Golf course guide-Oregon state
2.Travel-golf-related in Oregon state

Printed in USA at Valco Graphics, INC, Tukwila Washington.

Cover photos appear courtesy of:
Langdon Farms Golf Club (Front cover), Aurora, Oregon
Photographs by: Rick Schafer, Rick Schafer Photography ©
Sunriver Resort (Back cover), Sunriver, Oregon
Photograph by: Rick Schafer, Rick Schafer Photography ©

First Edition, April 1990
Second Edition, January 1992
Third Edition, March 1993
Fourth Edition, March 1994
Fifth Edition, March 1995
Sixth Edition, March 1996
Seventh Edition, April 1996
Eighth Edition, March 1998
Ninth Edition, March 1999
Tenth Edition, March 2000
Eleventh Edition, March 2001
Twelfth Edition. March 2003

ISBN 1-878591-59-2 $12.95

Published by:
MAC Productions P.O. Box 84; Duvall, Washington 98019 USA
Phone: (425) 844-8406; Fax: (425) 844-9245
Web-Site: www.macproductionsgolf.com
e-mail address: mac.productions@gte.net

Preface

In this the twelfth edition of "**Golfing in Oregon**" I hope it will be the most complete golf guide in the state published to date. The size is designed with the idea that the book will more easily fit in your glove box or golf bag. We have also provided small map inserts along with the driving directions to help you get to the golf facilities. As always you will find new courses, par 3's, and ranges just opened or due to open later in the season. Layouts, prices and yardage have been revised to reflect any changes that have occurred since last year. I hope you enjoy the book, see you on the links!

Acknowledgements

A special thanks to all the pros, owners and course managers who have been so helpful in providing us access to their courses and current information.

Thanks to the Oregon Department of Transportation for the endless supply of maps needed in doing this project.

Thanks to Bob (the big picture) Valentine and his personal touch on these projects over the years, Thanks Robert!!

Thanks to the staff at Valco Graphics for the special touch they put on every cover of our golf guides. You guys are the best!

Thanks to Brian and Christie Kruhlak for the endless stream of phone calls that have to be made to keep the information current.

To my children Joshua Daniel, Sarah Gene and Christian Rogers for showing me what really is important in life.

Thanks to my loving wife Kristi Gene. Words cannot express the love and support she has given me on this project. I feel blessed to have a wife whom provided a loving, caring, Christ like atmosphere in which to produce this book in. Thanks Kristi Gene. Most importantly my Lord Jesus, for his gentle hand and firm grip with my life and this company.

Daniel

GOLF COURSE LISTINGS

DRIVING RANGES & LEARNING CENTERS

Daniel MacMillan has been an avid golfer for the past 18 years. He enjoys researching and playing the various golf courses of the Pacific Northwest (if it were only that easy!!). ***Golfing in Washington*** was the brainchild of Daniel and his previous partner Mark Fouty who, one day while playing a round at Snohomish Golf Course, discussed finding a guide to use themselves. When no such guide was available this one was written. The book has taken on many stages. It was originally called ***Golfing in Western Washington***, which encompassed only the more populous half of the state. In 1988 it expanded to ***Golfing in Washington*** (now in it's 17th edition). Meanwhile Mark pursued a career in New York so Daniel bought out Mark's share of the company. The company has therefore become a real family operation. Daniel drags his wife Kristi and their three children throughout the west coast seeking information on new courses and facilities for upcoming publications. We hope all the thousands of miles and endless phone calls have paid off. This guide is designed to have all the information a golfer wants and needs to know about playing a course, and as a golfer Daniel has done just that.

Golfing in Oregon is the second book published by MAC Productions and written by Daniel. Now in its 12th edition it also is published on an annual basis. This book too has taken many forms it was originally called ***Golfing in Oregon & Idaho***. In 1992 the book was changed to reflect the new format and now only includes the state of Oregon.

Golfing in Idaho & Montana is the third book published by MAC Productions and written by Daniel. The first edition of this book was called ***Golfing In Idaho*** and was published in 1994. Now in it's 3rd edition ***Golfing In Idaho & Montana*** was published in spring of 2003. Look for it in a pro shop or book store near you.

The Birdie Book is another one of MAC Productions titles that was first published in November of 1998. It is a coupon book that offers the golfer over $3000.00 worth of savings at many of Oregon, Idaho and Washington's finest golf facilities, stores and learning centers.

New territories are always being explored for writing golf course guides such as this. It takes many man hours and attention to detail to produce books of this nature. From start to finish a new book takes about two years to produce. Currently four more are in the works and will be released in 2003. **Arizona**, **British Columbia**, **Hawaii** and **Nevada** are slated to hit the shelves soon. Look for the new publications at a pro shop or book store near you. Daniel's hope is that you will find this to be the best golf guide of its kind on the shelf. Visit us at our web site to look for new titles and the availablity of the region that you are interested in.
Our web site address is: **www.macproductionsgolf.com**

Abbreviations, Explanatory Notes and Disclaimers

Executive Course-An executive golf course is usually longer than a typical par 3 short course but shorter than a regulation course.
Private Course- A golf course that is not open to public play.
Semi-private- golf courses that are closed to the public at certain times during the week. Best to call ahead to reserve tee-times.
Tees: T-Tour; **C**-Championship; **M**-Men; **F**-Forward; **W**-Women.
W/D-Weekday; **W/E**-Weekend; **Hol.**-Holidays. **N/A**-Not available.
Course rating-This rates the degree of difficulty of course in the northwest and refers to the average number of shots per round a scratch golfer ought to shoot. It is figured by rating teams who factor in terrain, length and hazards of each course. The higher the rating the more difficult the course. Course ratings appear courtesy of the ***Pacific Northwest Golf Association, Idaho Golf Association*** and the ***Oregon Golf Association***.
Slope-This is similar to the course rating but it considers other factors as well. The slope rating takes into consideration the playing difficulty of a course for handicaps above scratch. The higher the number, the more difficult the golf course. Slope ratings courtesy of the ***Pacific Northwest Golf Association, Idaho Golf Association*** and the ***Oregon Golf Association***.
Green fees- prices are subject to change at any time. Because a number of Eastern Oregon courses close for the winter, the prices may reflect those of last year. When two prices are given, the first refers to the 18 hole fee, the second to the 9 hole fee. "Reciprocates" refers to the practice of private courses allowing members of other private courses to play their courses. However, because some courses only reciprocate with a limited number of other courses, it's best to call first.
Trail fee- the fee a course charges an individual to use their own power cart on the golf course.
Reservation policy- This refers to the maximum number of days the course allows reservations to made in advance under normal circumstances.
Winter condition- Dry, damp, wet refers to the club pro's opinion of the course's condition in rainy conditions. Also whether or not the course is closed during the winter months.
Terrain- Flat, flat some hills, relatively hilly, very hilly.
Tees- All grass or mats are the alternatives for tees.
Spikes- many of the area golf courses are going to a soft spike policy during the peak golfing season. Be sure to check each course prior to play as the policies vary a great deal from course to course.
Course layouts/yardage- My intent is to show tees in relation to greens, obvious hazards and other holes. Some hazards may not be adequately represented, nor are trees shown. Use these layouts as a reference at the kind of golf course you are planning to visit. The more the hazards the more difficult the golf course will play.

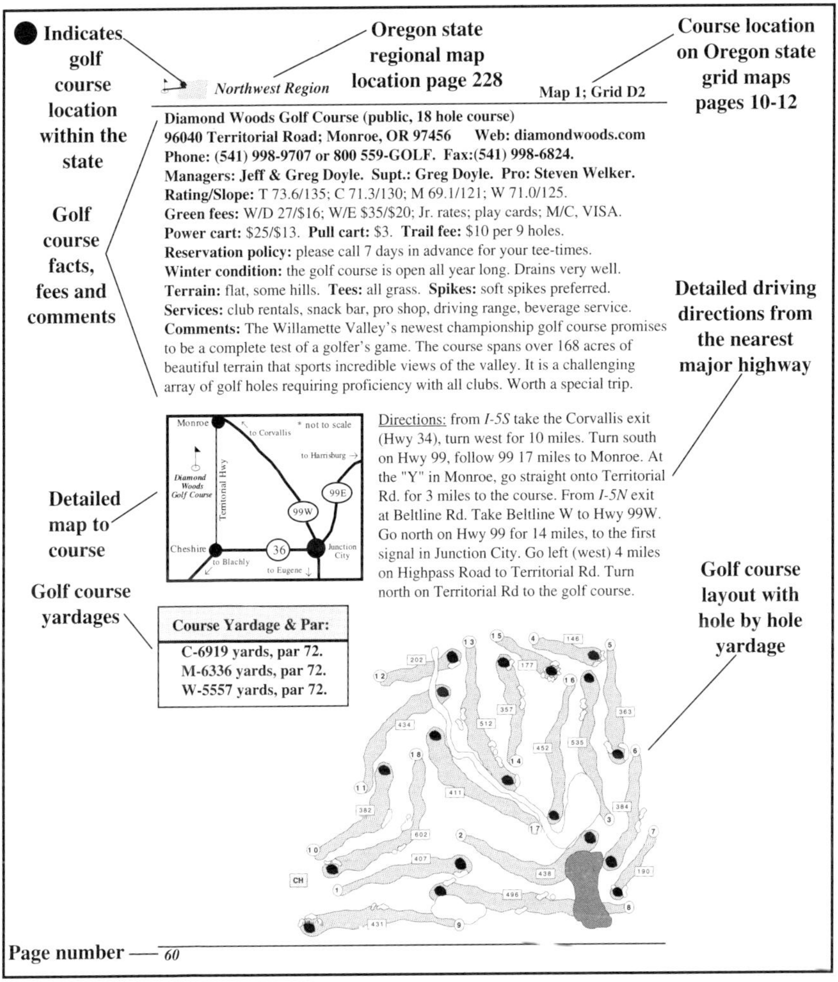

All **MAC Productions** golf guides are alphabetically arranged by golf course name for easy use. You can also find the golf course locations by using our geographical index located on pages 225-227. Simply look up the nearest city or town to the location you will be visiting and the courses are listed accordingly.

In addition to this feature we also include a geographical index that is arranged by ten regions within the state of Oregon. If you are visting the southern Oregon coast, for example, you would look in the geographical index by region on pages 229-234. Then find the southern coastal region in this section and it will tell you the names of the golf courses located in that region.

The state maps on pages 10-12 coincide with the map and grid numbers listed on the top right corner of each course page. These maps are intended for approximate location within the state only. The detailed map grid and driving directions are provided on the listing page for accurate course or range locations.

Map 1 (1) Donotes approximate Golf Course Location.

Numbers on map correspond with golf course page numbers.

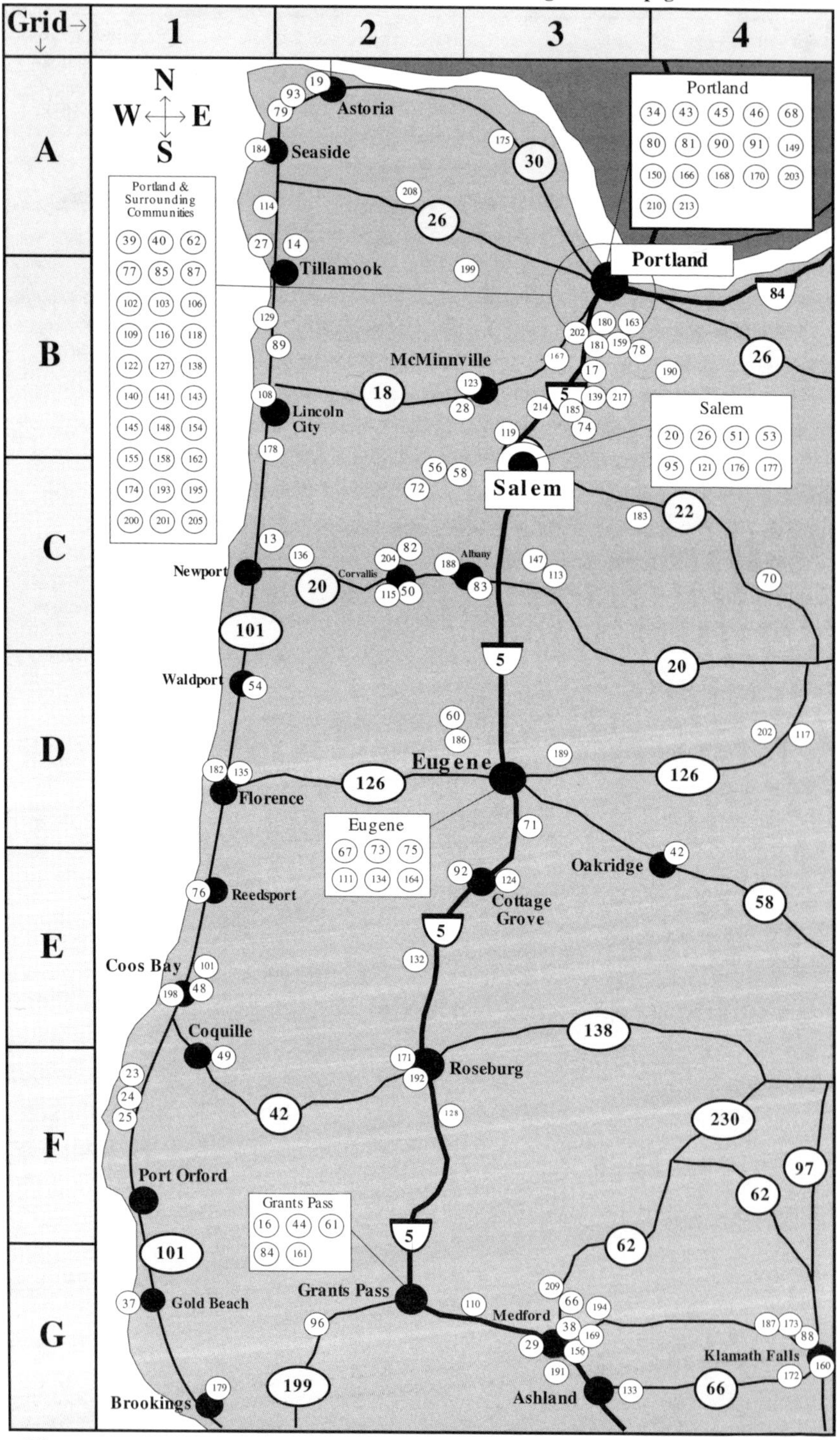

Map 2 ① Donotes approximate Golf Course Location.

Numbers on map correspond with golf course page numbers.

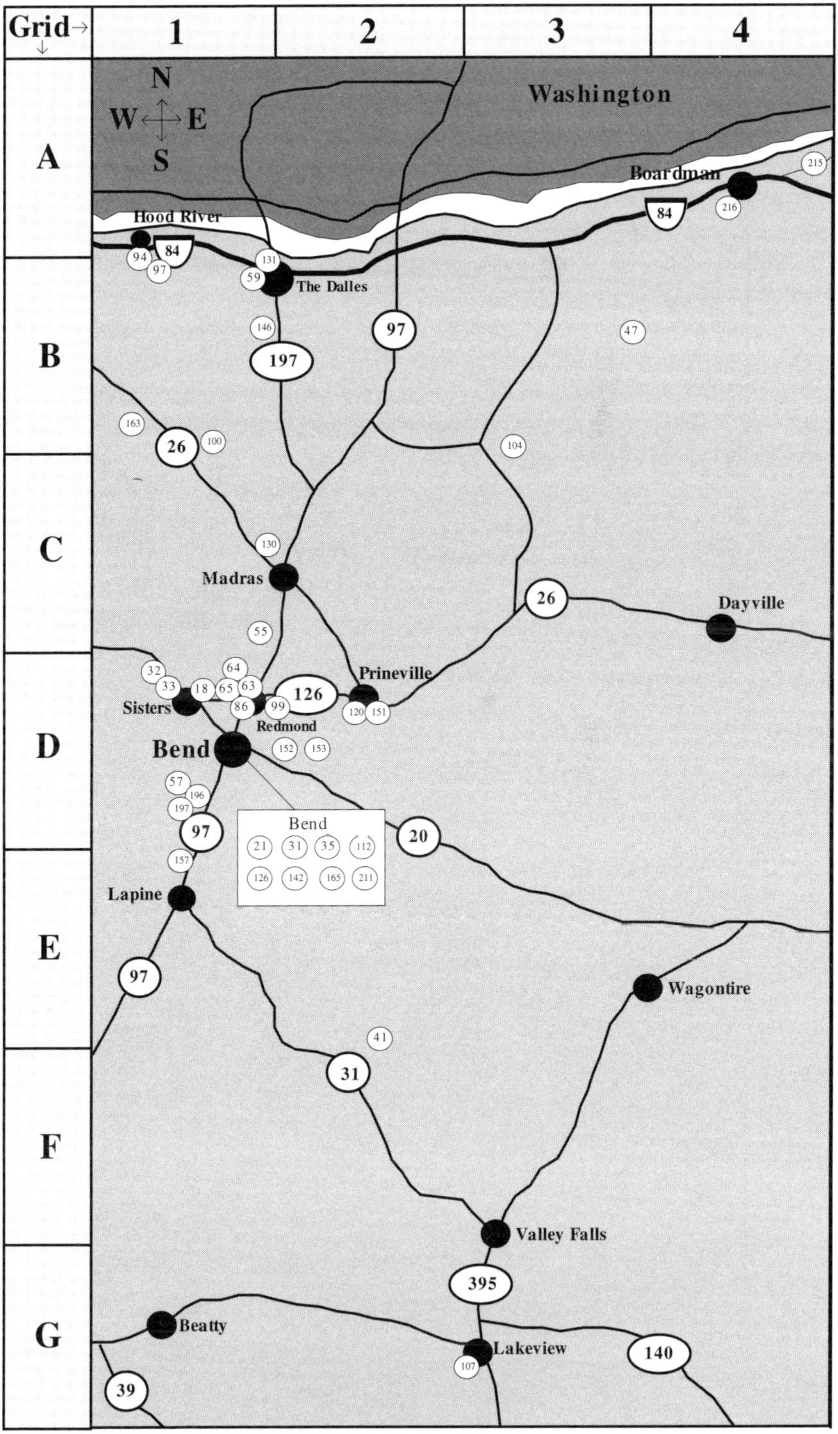

Map 3 ① Donotes approximate Golf Course Location. Numbers on map correspond with golf course page numbers.

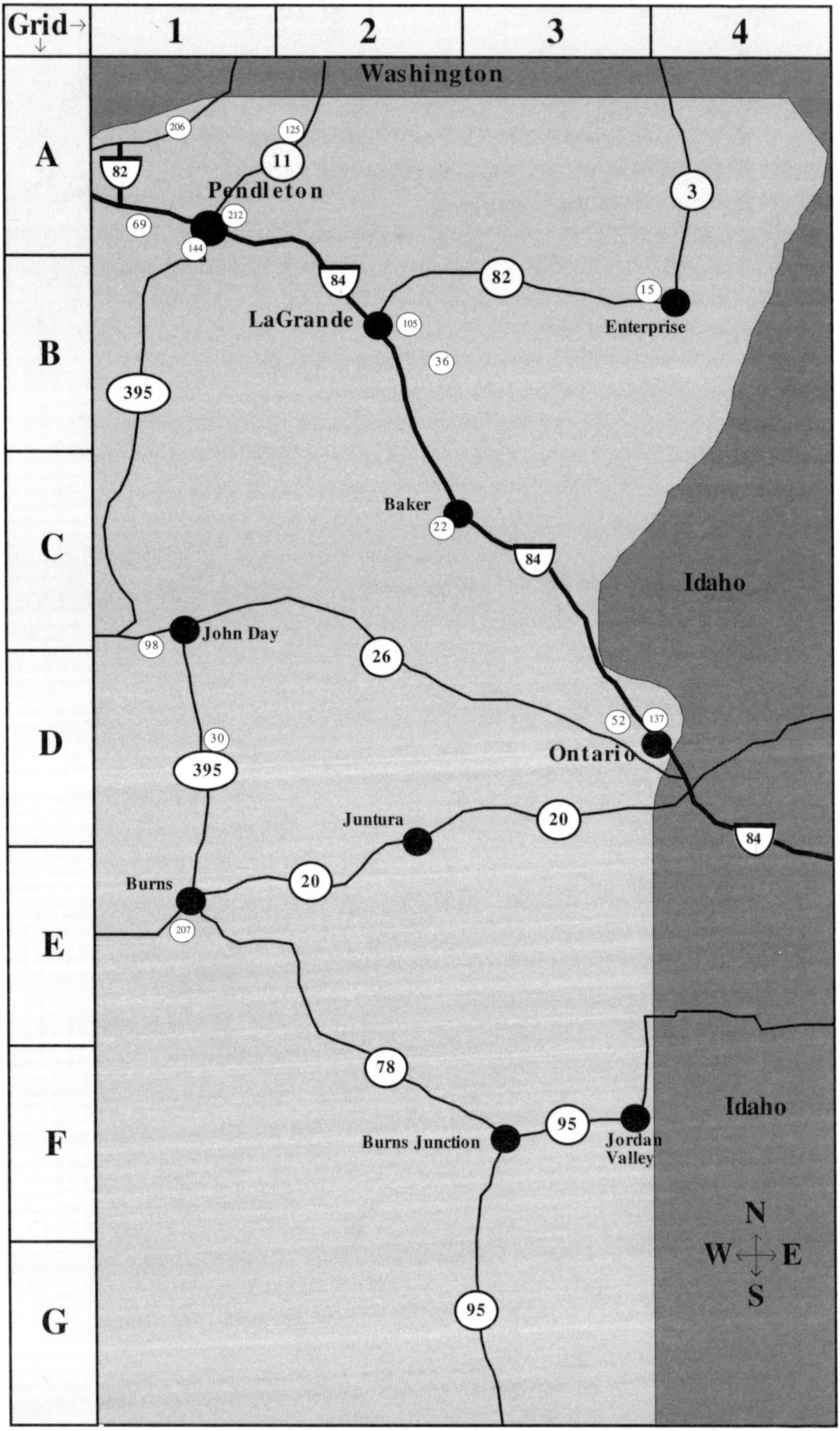

Agate Beach Golf Course (public, 9 hole course)

4100 North Coast Highway; Newport, OR 97365
Phone: (541) 265-7331. Fax: (541) 265-9673. Web: agatebeachgolf.com
Pro: Terry R. Martin, PGA. Superintendent: Terry R. Martin.
Rating/Slope: M 66.0/107; W 69.4/109. **Course record:** 62.
Green fees: $30/$15 all week long; no special rates; M/C, VISA.
Power cart: $24/$12. **Pull cart:** $2. **Trail fee:** $3/$6 for personal carts.
Reservation policy: yes, please call up to 7 days in advance for tee-times.
Winter condition: the course is open all year long, very dry and drains well.
Terrain: flat, some slight hills. **Tees:** grass. **Spikes:** metal spikes permitted.
Services: club rentals, lessons, restaurant, beer, wine, pro shop, driving range.
Comments: Well maintained course with medium sized greens that are fronted by few hazards. Fairways are fairly wide with large landing areas. This track has excellent drainage for winter and off season play. This easy to walk, picturesque golf course is a favorite for weekenders and vacationers on the Oregon Coast. Be sure to call ahead for tee times during the summer.

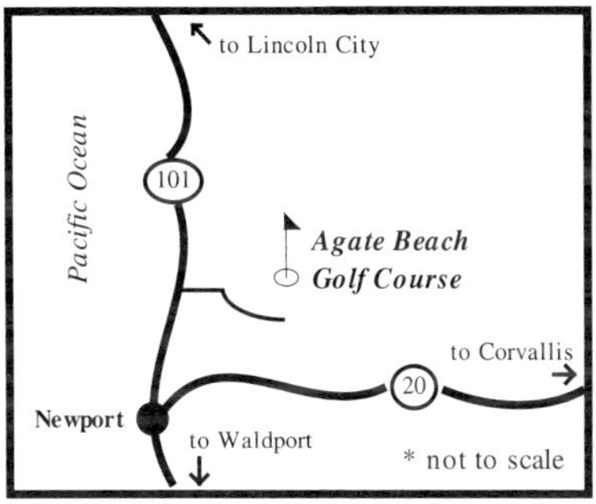

Directions: the golf course is located at the north end of Newport Oregon on the east side of Hwy 101, one mile north of the Fred Meyer shopping center. Look for signs marking the way to the course.

Course Yardage & Par:
M-2905 yards, par 36. W-2669 yards, par 38.

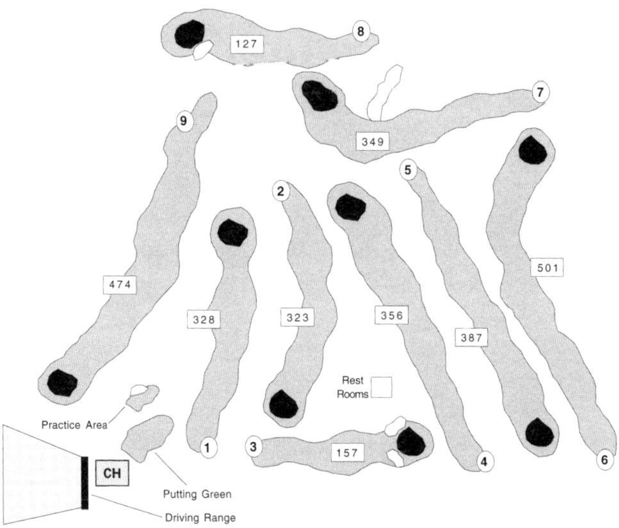

Alderbrook Golf Course (public, 18 hole course)

7300 Alderbrook Road; Tillamook, OR 97141
Phone: (503) 842-6413. Fax: (503) 842-4596. Web: none.
Owner: Neil Abrahamson. Manager: Jenean Hildebrand.
Rating/Slope: M 66.0/107; W 69.1/113. **Course record:** 62.
Green fees: $27/$15 all week long; Jr. rates $13/$7; M/C, VISA.
Power cart: $26/14. **Pull cart:** $2. **Trail fee:** $10 per day.
Reservation policy: call ahead for weekend tee times. May thru October only.
Winter condition: golf course is open all year long, weather permitting.
Terrain: flat, some hills. **Tees:** grass. **Spikes:** soft spikes only.
Services: club rentals, restaurant, beer, wine, pro shop, putting green.
Comments: mature trees line the fairways of this excellent par 69 layout. A creek comes into play on several holes throughout the course and is a major factor off the tee or on your approach shots. Greens are forgiving with few hazards fronting them. Excellent golf course to play while visiting the coast.

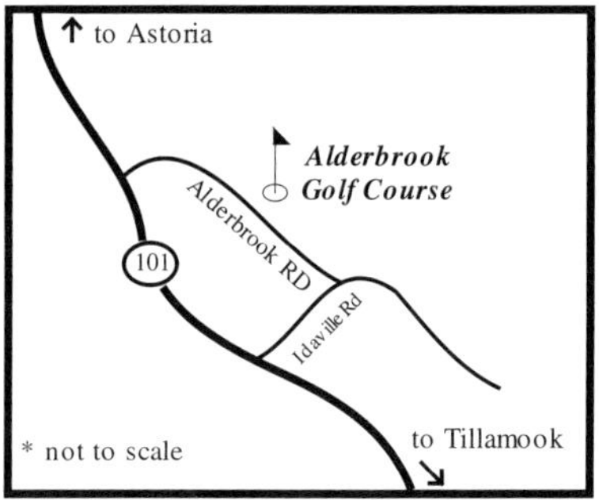

Directions: the golf course is located 4 miles north of Tillamook off of Hwy 101. Proceed 4 miles north on Hwy 101 and go east on Alderbrook Road (just north of the cheese factory). When you come to a fork in the road stay left. The golf course will be on your right, 1.9 miles ahead. Look for a sign marking your way to the golf course.

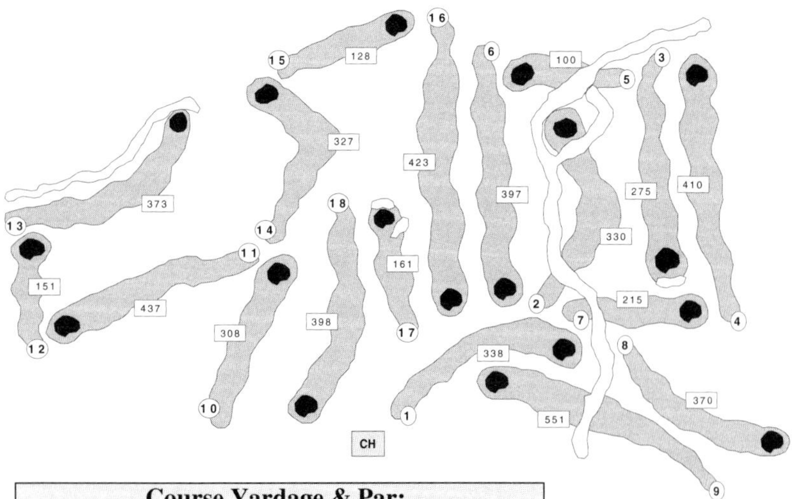

Course Yardage & Par:
M-5692 yards, par 69; W-5272 yards, par 71.

Alpine Meadows Golf Course (public, 9 hole course)

66098 Golf Course Road; Enterprise, OR 97828
Phone: (541) 426-3246. Fax: (541) 426-3246. Web: none.
Managers: Ken & Sue Storm. Superintendent: Jim Eldred.
Rating/Slope: M 68.6/114; W 69.3/117. **Course record:** 63.
Green fees: $22/$15 all week long; no special rates; M/C, VISA.
Power cart: $20/$10. **Pull cart:** $4/$2 **Trail fee:** $7 for personal carts.
Reservation policy: advance reservations are not needed or required.
Winter condition: the course is closed from November 1st to March 31st.
Terrain: flat, some hills. **Tees:** all grass. **Spikes:** soft spikes only.
Services: club rentals, lessons, snack bar, lounge, beer, wine, liquor, pro shop, putting/chipping greens, driving range. **Comments:** Beautiful setting in the Wallowa Mountains. Greens are challenging and kept in good condition throughout the season. Dual tee's are available for those wanting to play a full 18.

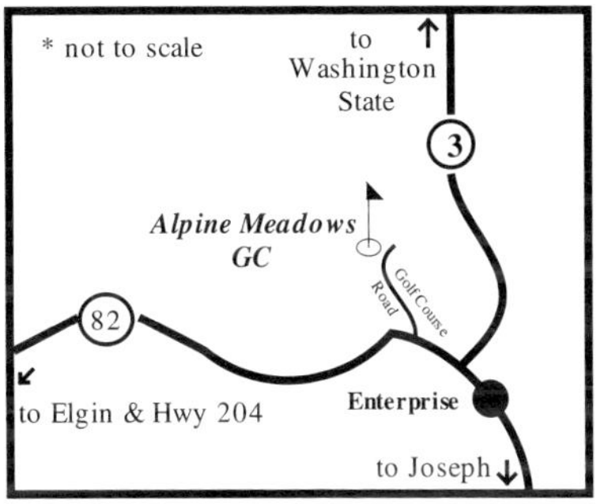

Directions: from Hwy 82 turn north on Golf Course Road (the road between the Safeway store). Proceed to the golf course, which will be on your left hand side. The golf course is located on the west end of the city. Look for signs marking your turn to the golf course.

Course Yardage & Par:
M-3067 yards, par 36.
W-2588 yards, par 36.
Dual tees for 18 holes:
M-6135 yards, par 72.
W-5125 yards, par 72.

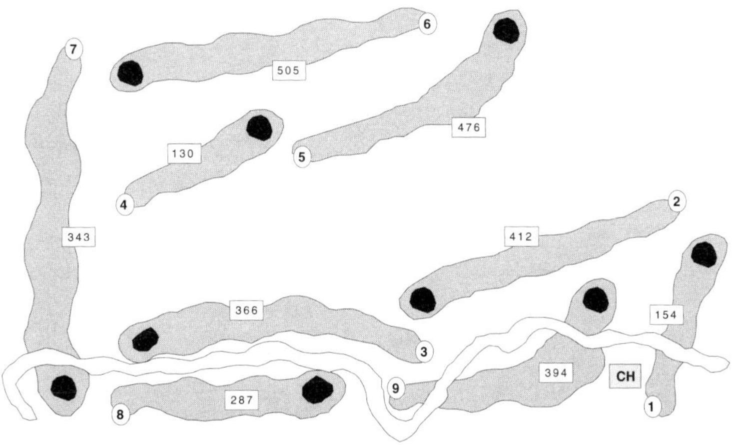

Applegate Golf (public, 9 hole course)

7350 New Hope Road; Grants Pass, OR 97527
Phone: (541) 955-0480. Fax: (541) 955-8156. Web: none.
Managers: John Briggs & Nancy Swinney.
Rating/Slope: M 65.2/115; W 65.2/107. **Course record:** 32.
Green fees: $16/$11 summer rate; winter rate $12; Jr. & Sr. rates; M/C, VISA.
Power cart: not available. **Pull cart:** $2. **Trail fee:** not allowed.
Reservation policy: you may call in advance for tee-times.
Winter condition: the golf course is open all year round. Dry conditions.
Terrain: flat, some hills. **Tees:** all grass. **Spikes:** soft spikes only.
Services: club rentals, snack bar, lounge, beer, wine, driving range.
Comments: newer golf course that opened in mid 1994 that features fairly flat terrain and tree lined fairways. Water is a major factor coming into play on over half the the holes at Applegate. Fairways are medium wide giving the golfer plenty of room off the tee. Greens are moderate with few slopes to them. The course has a very friendly atmosphere and feel. Great tournament location.

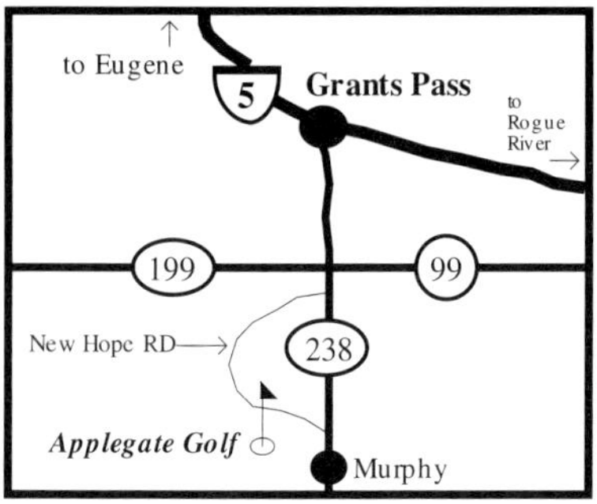

Directions: from I-5 N&S exit at Grants Pass to Highway 238 and head southbound to Murphy, Oregon. When you reach New Hope Road turn westbound and proceed 1.2 miles to the golf course. Your turn is 6.8 miles from Grants Pass. Look for signs.

Course Yardage & Par:
M-2612 yards, par 36. **W-2446 yards, par 36.**

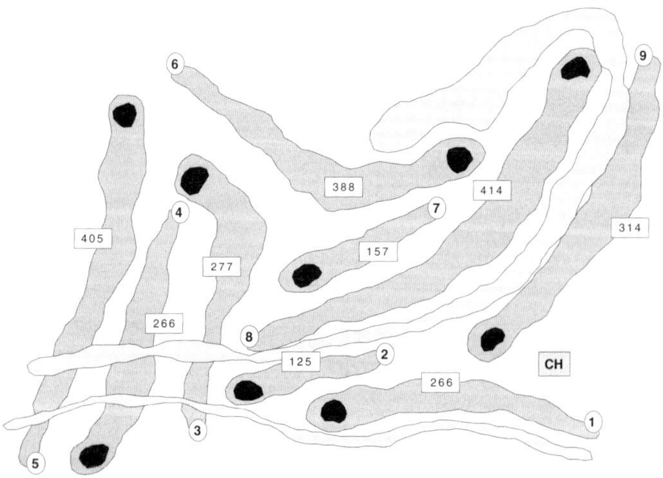

Arrowhead Golf Club (private, 18 hole course)

28301 South Highway 213; Molalla, OR 97038

Phone: (503) 829-8080. Fax: (503) 829-8367. Web: golfarrowhead.com

Dir. of Golf: Joe Clarizio. Pro: Rob Gibbons, PGA. Supt.: J.D. Clarizio.

Rating/Slope: C 69.8/125; M 68.4/123; W 69.3/120. **Course record:** 67.
Green fees: private club, members & guests of members only; reciprocates.
Power cart: private club. **Pull cart:** private club. **Trail fee:** private club.
Reservation policy: call up to one week in advance for members only.
Winter condition: the golf course is open all year long weather permitting.
Terrain: flat, easy walking. **Tees:** grass. **Spikes:** soft spikes only.
Services: club rentals, lessons, snack bar, restaurant, lounge, beer, liquor, pro shop, lockers, driving range, putting & chipping greens, practice bunker.
Comments: Situated along the banks of the Molalla River. A peaceful country club atmosphere. The driving range is open to the public for your practice needs. Good private facility with large, well conditioned greens and fairways.

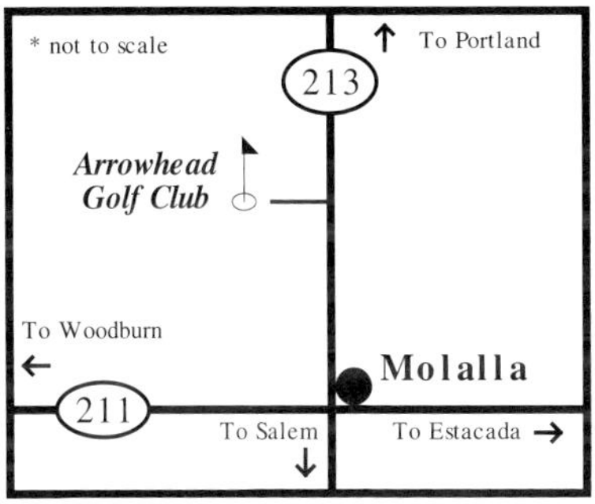

Directions: from I-205 N&S take exit #10 (Hwy 213) to Molalla, Oregon. From here proceed southbound on Hwy 213 for 14 miles. The golf course will be located on your right hand side when traveling southbound on Highway 213. Look for a sign indicating your turn.

Course Yardage & Par:
C-6410 yards, par 71.
M-6101 yards, par 71.
W-5206 yards, par 73.

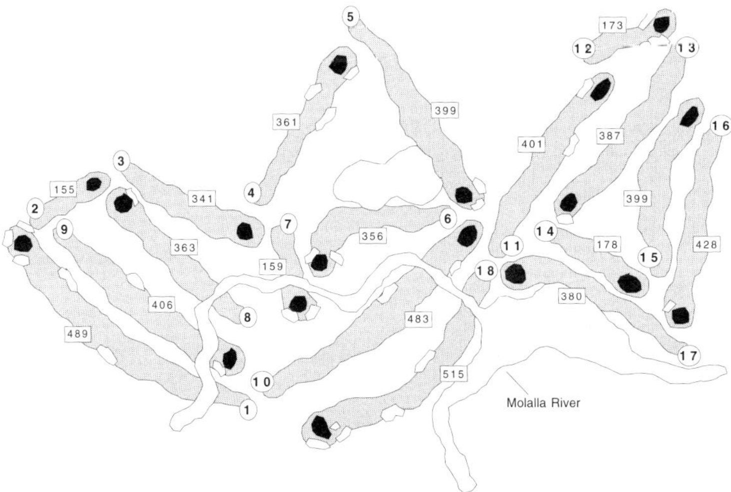

Aspen Lakes Golf Club (public, 27 hole course)

16900 Aspen Lakes Drive; P. O. Box 1600; Sisters, OR 97759
Phone: (541) 549-4653. Fax: (541) (541) 549-2050. Web: www.aspenlakes.com
Pro: Wayne Clark, PGA. Superintendent: Mark Shepherd.
Rating/Slope: C 73.8/132; M 71.4/127; W 74.6/133. **Course Record:** 68.
Green fees: $55/$29 all week long (peak season); $35/$25 spring and fall rates; twilight rates & early bird rates $40/$20; Jr. rates; M/C, VISA, AMEX.
Power cart: $28/$16. **Pull cart:** $5/$3. **Trail fee:** personal carts not allowed.
Reservation policy: please call up to 2 weeks in advance for tee times.
Winter condition: the golf course is closed during the winter months.
Terrain: flat, some rolling hills. **Tees:** all grass. **Spikes:** soft spikes only.
Services: club rentals, lessons, putting green, pro shop, driving range.
Comments: Excellent golf course that was named one of the "Top Ten Affordable Public Golf Courses" by *Golf Digest* magazine in 2001. The "Charity" 9 is now under construction and should be completed in 2003 or early in 2004. Towering pines line almost all the fairways and are a major factor in your course management. Greens are large and are guarded by water and sand. Great course.

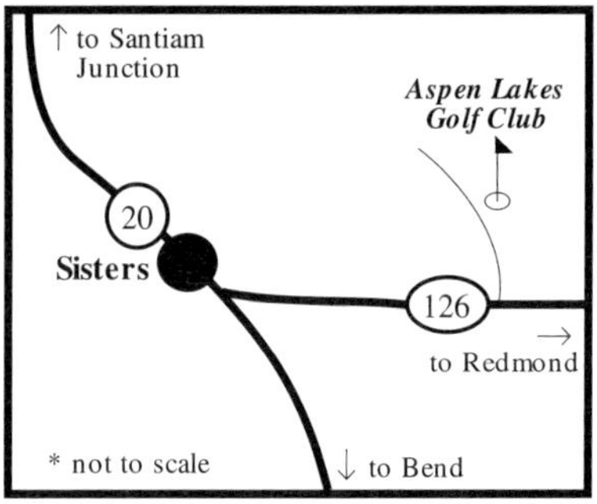

Directions: from Hwy 20 east and west turn eastbound on Hwy 126 heading towards Redmond Oregon. The course is located approximately 3.7 miles ahead on your left hand side.

Course Yardage & Par:

C-7302 yards, par 72.
M-6789 yards, par 72.
W-5497 yards, par 72.

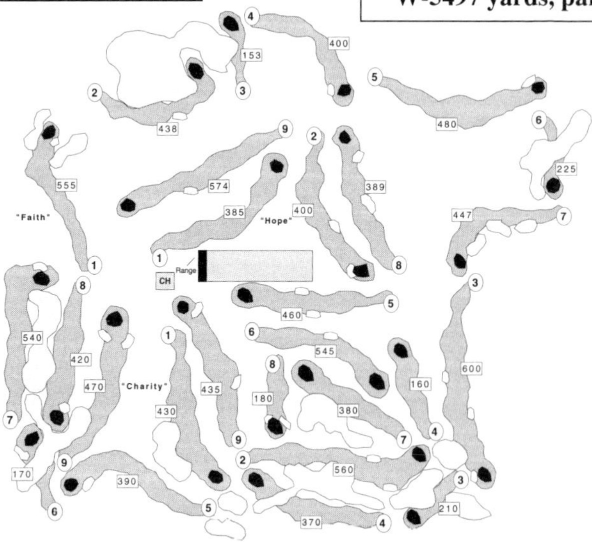

Astoria Golf & Country Club (private, 18 hole course)

33445 Sunset Beach Lane; Warrenton, OR 97146

Phone: (503) 861-2545. Fax: (503) 738-8359. Web: astoriagolf.com

Pro: John Kawasoe, PGA. Superintendent: John Whisler.

Rating/Slope: C 71.3/126; M 70.5/126; W 73.2/128. **Course record:** 64.

Green fees: private club, members and guests of members only, reciprocates.

Power cart: private club, members & guests of members only.

Pull cart: private club, members only. **Trail fee:** not allowed.

Reservation policy: please call ahead for golf course availablity.

Winter condition: the golf course is open all year long, weather permitting.

Terrain: relatively hilly. **Tees:** all grass. **Spikes:** soft spikes preferred.

Services: club rentals, lessons, restaurant, lounge, beer, wine, liquor, pro shop, lockers, showers, driving range, putting & chipping greens, club memberships.

Comments: Beautiful older course that was built in 1923. The track is situated on the stunning Oregon Coast. Greens are small with few undulations. Fairways are wide & rolling giving the golfer large landing areas. Good private course.

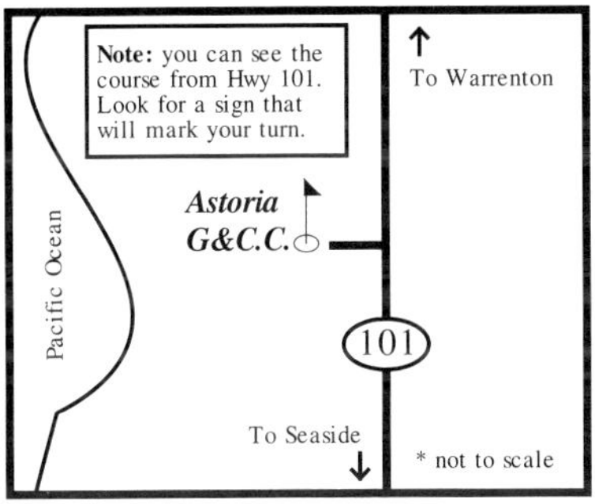

Directions: from Hwy 101 the course is located at the south end of Warrenton Oregon. From Hwy 101 turn west on Sunset Beach Lane. The clubhouse will be on your right. **Note:** the golf course can be seen from Hwy 101.

Course Yardage & Par:
C-6484 yards, par 72.
M-6281 yards, par 72.
W-5687 yards, par 74.

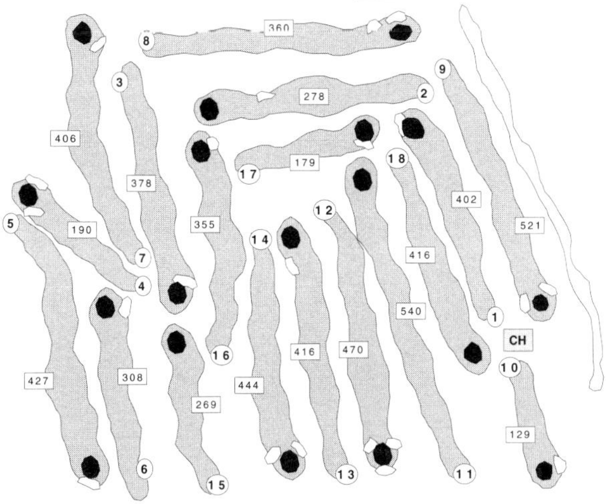

Auburn Center Golf Club (public, 9 hole course)

5220 Center Street NE; Salem, OR 97301
Phone: (503) 363-4404. Fax: none. Web: none.
Managers: Gregg & Cindy Smith.

Rating/Slope: the golf course is not rated. **Course record:** 27.
Green fees: \$11/\$6.50 all week long; Jr. and Sr. rates; no credit cards.
Power cart: no power carts are available for use. **Pull cart:** \$1.50.
Trail fee: personal carts are not allowed on the golf course at anytime.
Reservation policy: advance reservations are not needed or required.
Winter condition: wet conditions. The golf course is open all year long.
Terrain: flat, easy walking. **Tees:** grass. **Spikes:** metal spikes permitted.
Services: club rentals, snack bar, beverages, miniature golf, putting green.
Comments: Flat golf course, that is very easy to walk. Course is excellent for the beginner and senior golfer.

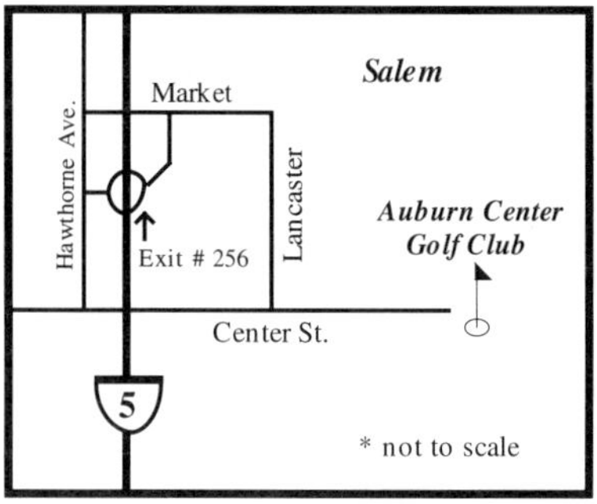

<u>**Directions:**</u> from I-5 S, take Market St. exit #256 and go east to Lancaster Dr. Go south (right) on Lancaster Dr. to Center St. and turn left. The course is located 1.1 miles ahead on Center St. The course will be on your right side. I-5N take Mission St exit #253 and go east on Mission St. (N Santiam Hwy) to Lancaster Dr. and go north on Lancaster Dr. to Center St. Turn right on Center St. and follow to course.

Course Yardage & Par:
M-1338 yards, par 29; W-1338 yards, par 29. **M-2708 yards, par 59; W-2708 yards, par 59.**

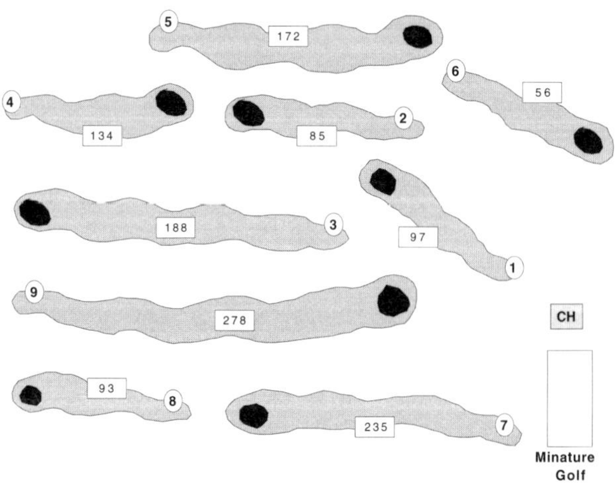

Awbrey Glen Golf Club (private, 18 hole course)

2500 N.W. Awbrey Glen Drive; Bend, OR 97701

Phone: (541) 388-8526. Fax: (541) 385-6011. Web: www.awbreyglen.com

Pro: JD Mowlds, PGA. Director of Golf: Mark Amberson, PGA.

Rating/Slope: T 72.3/129; C 70.5/125; M 68.6/121; W 70.3/128.

Green fees: private club, limited non-member play is available; M/C, VISA.

Power cart: available. **Pull cart:** available. **Trail fee:** private club.

Reservation policy: private club, members and guests only. Some outside play.

Winter condition: the golf course is closed during the winter months.

Terrain: rolling hills to hilly. **Tees:** all grass. **Spikes:** soft spikes only.

Services: lessons, snack bar, beer, wine, lockers, pro shop, restaurant, lounge, driving range, chipping green, 5 hole par 3, golf schools, private instruction.

Comments: This unique layout features five par 5's and five par 3's and the learning center is the best you'll find in the Northwest. Awbrey Glen Golf Club is a definite must play while in Bend. Please call ahead to inquire about outside play.

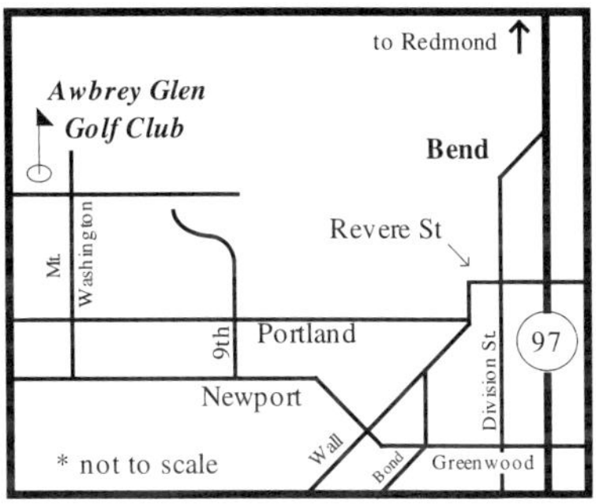

Directions: from Hwy 97 (3rd St.), turn west on Greenwood (turns to Newport), continue on Shevlin Park Road. Proceed to Mt. Washington Drive and turn right. Proceed to Awbrey Glen Drive and turn left. Proceed to the golf course.

Course Yardage & Par:
"Awbrey Loop" 598 yards, par 15.

Course Yardage & Par:
Tour: 7029 yards, par 72.
Championship: 6557 yards, par 72.
Members: 6179 yards, par 72.
Challenge: 5396 yards, par 72.

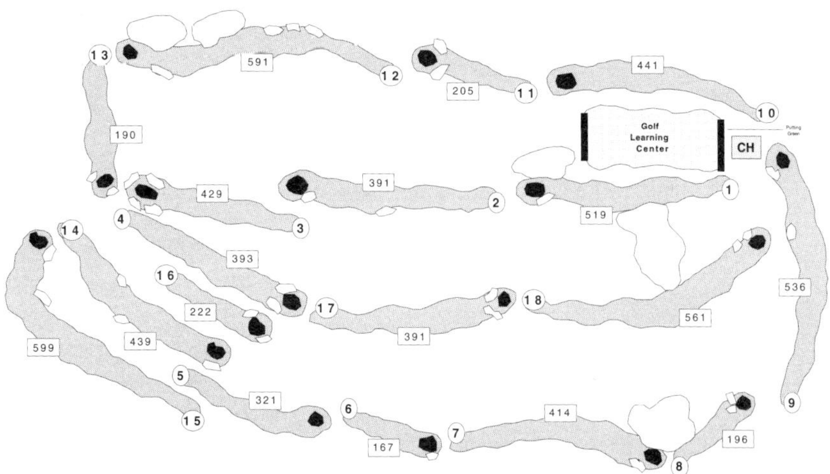

Baker Golf Club (public, 18 hole course)

2801 Indiana Avenue; Baker City, OR 97814
Phone: (541) 523-2358. Fax: (541) 523-2358.
Web-site: www.bakercity.com/golf_course
Pro: Ron Blankenship. Superintendent: Eric Moen.
Rating/Slope: C M 67.5/117; M 66.2/112; W 67.9/117. **Course record:** 62.
Green fees: W/D $22/$14; W/E $24/$15; Jr. rates; M/C, VISA.
Power cart: $20/$12. **Pull cart:** $4/$2. **Trail fee:** $5 for personal carts.
Reservation policy: please call 7 days in advance for your tee times.
Winter condition: the golf course is closed from November 15th to March 1st.
Terrain: flat, some hills. **Tees:** all grass. **Spikes:** metal spikes permitted.
Services: club rentals, lessons, lounge, beer, wine, liquor, beverages, pro shop.
Comments: the golf course is relatively short with wide open fairways, small greens and rolling terrain. Picturesque setting with mountain views from many of the teeing areas. Great public golf course for the money.

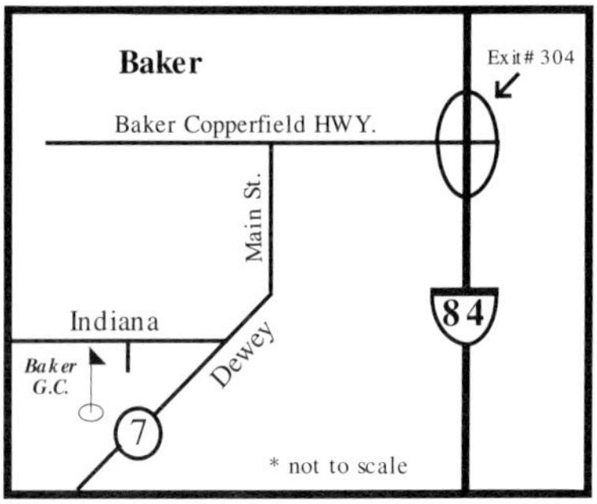

Directions: off of I-84 exit at City Center (Elm Street) #304. Follow Hwy 7 towards Sumpter. Turn right on Indiana Avenue, (look for a sign that is posted). The course is located at the top of the hill on your left hand side.

Course Yardage & Par:

C-5975 yards, par 70.
M-5697 yards, par 70.
W-5035 yards, par 72.

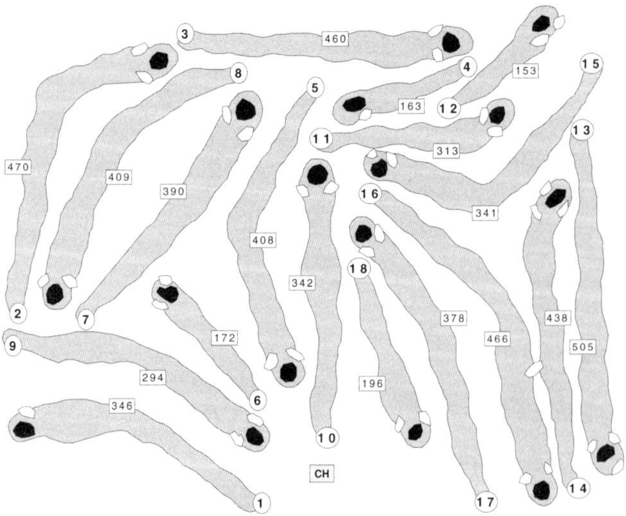

Bandon Dunes, The Bandon Dunes Course (resort, 18 hole course)

57744 Bandon Dunes Drive; Bandon, OR 97411
Phone: (541) 347-4380. Toll Free number: 1-888-345-6008
Fax: (541) 347-8161. Web: www.bandondunesgolf.com
GM: Hank Hickox. Superintendent: Troy Russell. Pro: Tim Hval, PGA.
Rating/Slope: T 76.8/150; C 74.6/145; M 72.1/141; W 72.1/128. **Record:** 67.
Green fees: $175 all week long; $140 hotel guests; M/C, VISA, AMEX, DIS.
Power cart: none. **Caddies:** $35. **Trail fee:** not allowed.
Reservation policy: please call in advance for all your tee times.
Winter condition: the golf course is open all year long. Dry conditions.
Terrain: flat, some hills. **Tees:** all grass. **Spikes:** no metal spikes permitted.
Services: club rentals, lounge, restaurant, snack bar, beer, wine, liquor, showers, lockers, pro shop, driving range, putting green, lodging accommodations.
Comments: voted the #1 new golf course in Amercia by *Golf Digest* in 1999. Bandon Dunes was voted #3 course where the public can play behind only Pebble Beach and Pinehurst. The course features rolling terrain, large greens and ocean views from nearly every vantage point on the course. Simply, spectacular.

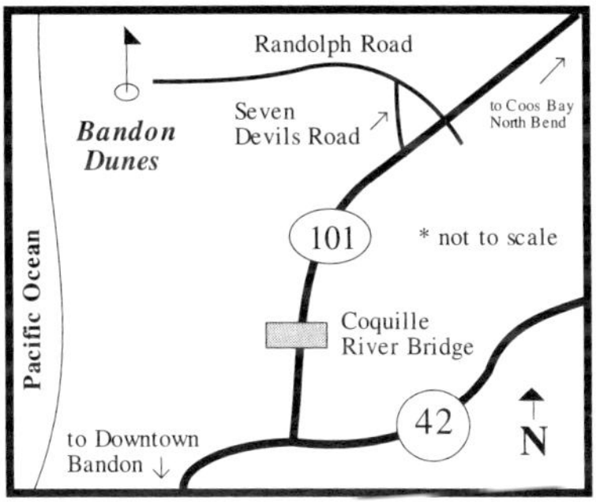

Directions: the golf resort is located 3 miles north of Bandon, Oregon on the west side of highway 101. Look for signs that are posted on highway 101 indicating your turn to the resort.

Course Yardage & Par:

T-6557 yards, par 72.
C-6174 yards, par 72.
M-5799 yards, par 72.
W-5107 yards, par 72.

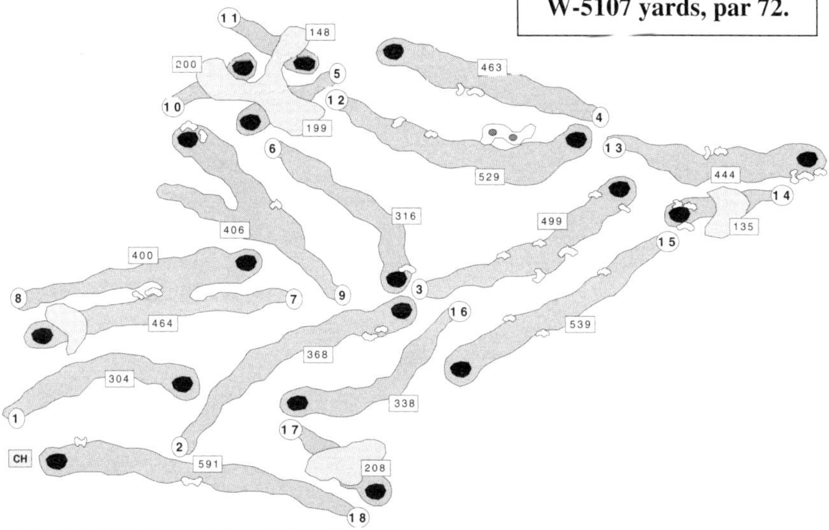

Bandon Dunes, The Pacific Dunes Course (resort, 18 hole course)

57744 Bandon Dunes Drive; Bandon, OR 97411
Phone: (541) 347-4380. Toll Free number: 1-888-345-6008
Fax: (541) 347-8161. Web: www.bandondunesgolf.com
GM: Hank Hickox. Supt.: Troy Russell. Pro: Jim Wakeman, PGA.
Rating/Slope: T 72.9/133; C 70.9/131; M 69.3/125; W 71.1/131. **Record:** 68.
Green fees: $175 all week long; $140 hotel guests; M/C, VISA, AMEX, DIS.
Power cart: none. **Caddies:** $35. **Trail fee:** personal carts not allowed.
Reservation policy: please call in advance for all your tee times.
Winter condition: the golf course is open all year long. Dry conditions.
Terrain: flat, some hills. **Tees:** all grass. **Spikes:** no metal spikes permitted.
Services: club rentals, lounge, restaurant, snack bar, beer, wine, liquor, showers, lockers, pro shop, driving range, putting green, lodging accommodations.
Comments: The second course to open at Bandon Dunes is the Pacific Dunes course designed by Tom Doak which opened for play in July 2001. The sand dunes and surrounding vegetation have been left untouched, creating a distinctly natural feel. Greens and fairways are large and immpecable. Worth the trip!

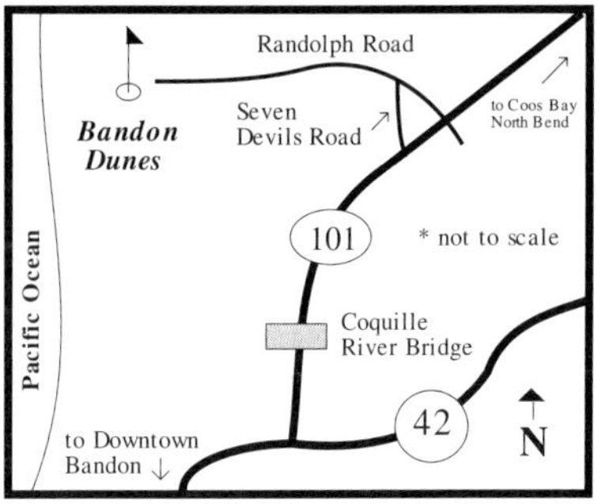

Directions: the golf resort is located 3 miles north of Bandon, Oregon on the west side of highway 101. Look for signs that are posted on highway 101 indicating your turn to the resort.

Course Yardage & Par:

T-7326 yards, par 72.
C-6844 yards, par 72.
M-6112 yards, par 72.
W-5178 yards, par 72.

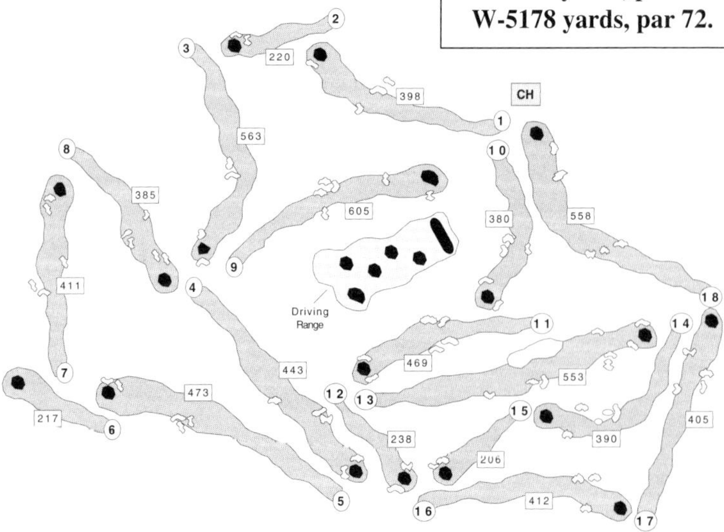

Bandon Face Rock Golf Course (public, 9 hole course)

3235 Beach Loop Drive; Bandon, OR 97411
Phone: (541) 347-3818. Fax: (541) 347-4781. Web: www.bandonbythesea.com
Manager: Margaret Miller. Superintendent: Jerry Brown.
Rating/Slope: M 61.6/106; W 62.1/99. **Course record:** 26.
Green fees: W/D $22/$12 all week long; no special rates; VISA, M/C.
Power cart: $22/$12. **Pull cart:** $2. **Trail fee:** $5 for personal carts.
Reservation policy: advance reservations are not needed or required for times.
Winter condition: the golf course is open all year long. Dry conditions.
Terrain: flat, easy walking course. **Tees:** grass. **Spikes:** metal spikes permitted.
Services: club rentals, lessons, snack bar, pop, small pro shop, putting area.
Comments: this 9 hole course winds along the scenic Johnson Creek. The golf course is located next to the ocean in a valley protected from the wind. Excellent walking golf course for the senior or first time golfer. Good public golf course.

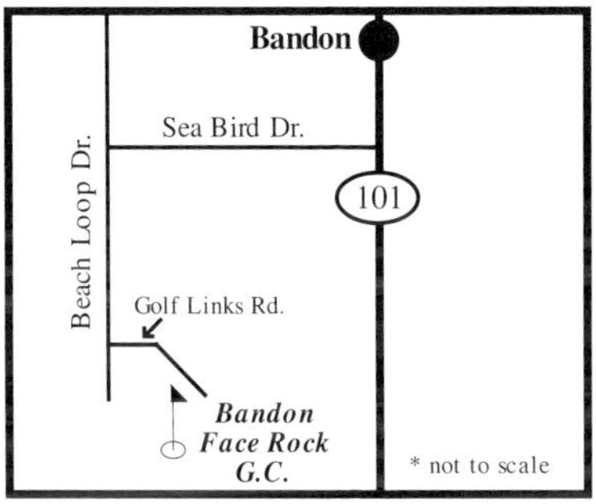

Directions: Course located in the south end of Bandon. From Hwy 101, go west on Sea Bird Drive to Beach Loop Road. At Beach Loop Drive turn left and travel .2 miles to the golf course which will be on your left. The golf course is located behind the Inn at Face Rock Motel. Look for signs the way is well marked.

Course Yardage & Par:

M-2096 yards, par 32.
W-1915 yards, par 32.
Dual tees for 18 holes:
M-4308 yards, par 64.
W-4011 yards, par 64.

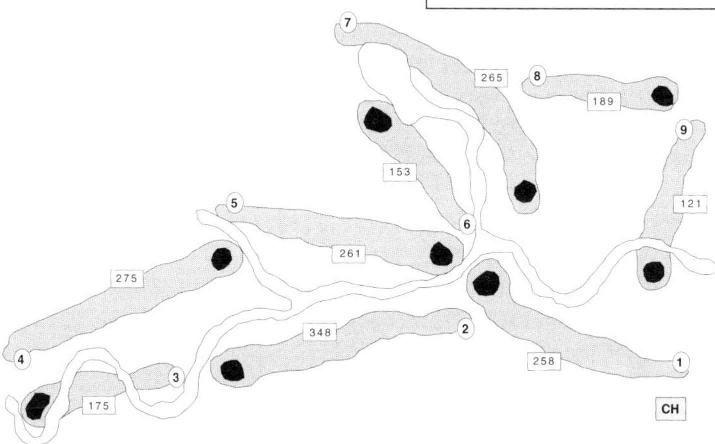

Battle Creek Golf Course (public, 18 hole course)

6161 Commercial Street SE; Salem, OR 97306
Phone: (503) 585-1402. Fax: (503) 365-3955. Web: none.
Pro: Dana Londin, PGA. Superintendent: Mike McAllister.
Rating/Slope: C 68.1/110; M 65.2/110; W 68.2/116. **Course record:** 64.
Green fees: W/D $25/$15; W/E $26/$16; Sr. rates $22/$11 (Wed.); M/C, VISA.
Power cart: $22/$11. **Pull cart:** $3/$2. **Trail fee:** $10 for personal carts.
Reservation policy: yes, please call 7 days in advance for your tee-times.
Winter condition: the golf course is open all year long, weather permitting.
Terrain: very flat. **Tees:** all grass tees. **Spikes:** metal spikes permitted.
Services: club rentals, lessons, caddy shack, restaurant, lounge, beer, wine, liquor, beverages, large pro shop, putting & chipping greens, driving range.
Comments: Challenging course with small, well bunkered elevated greens. Good drainage makes this golf course very playable in the winter months. Excellent course that can play much more difficult than the yardage indicates.

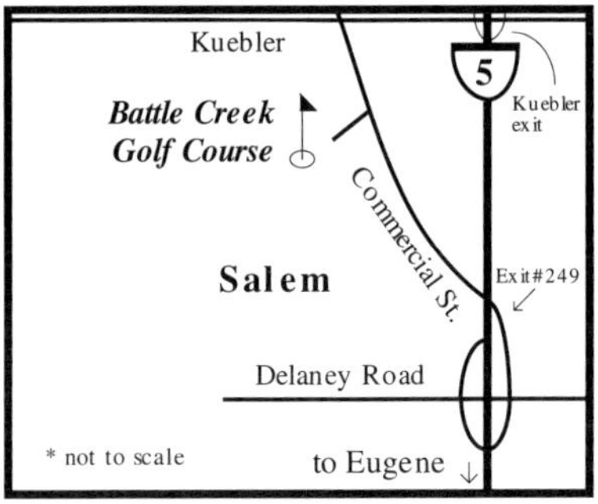

__Directions:__ I-5S. Take Kuebler exit. Keep right to Commercial St. Take a left on Commercial follow for 1 mile to the course on your right. I-5N take Salem exit #249. Follow road for approximately 1 mile. The golf course will be located on your left hand side. Course is located at the south end of Salem. Look for signs that are posted at your turns.

Course Yardage & Par:

C-6015 yards, par 72.
M-5395 yards, par 72.
W-4945 yards, par 72.

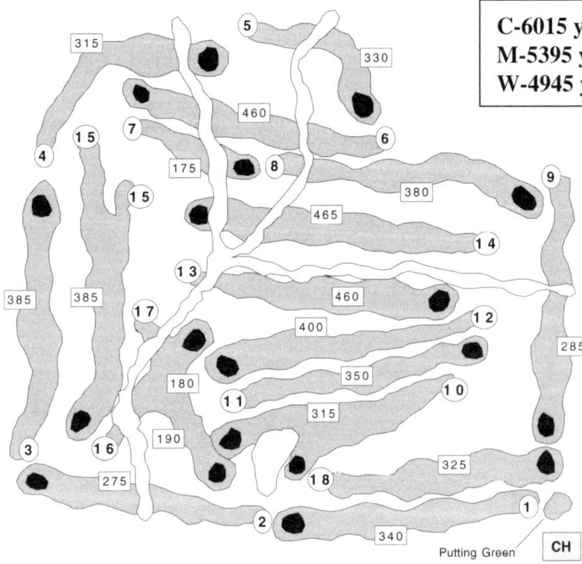

Bay Breeze Golf & Driving Range (public, 9 hole par 3)

2325 Latimer Road; Tillamook, OR 97141
Phone: (503) 842-1166. Fax: (503) 377-2746. Web: none.
Instructor: Mike Lehman. Superintendent: none.
Rating/Slope: the golf course is not rated. **Course record:** 24.
Green fees: $9 all week long; credit cards are accepted.
Power cart: power carts are not available. **Pull cart:** $1.
Reservation policy: reservations are not required or needed for play.
Winter condition: the course is closed from November 1st to February 15th.
Terrain: very flat. **Tees:** all grass. **Spikes:** metal spikes permitted.
Services: club rentals, pro shop, deli, covered driving range, putting green.
Comments: this short par 3 golf course features two lake holes and large bent grass greens with generous landing areas. The facility feature a covered driving range and putting course for those weekenders visiting the Oregon Coast.

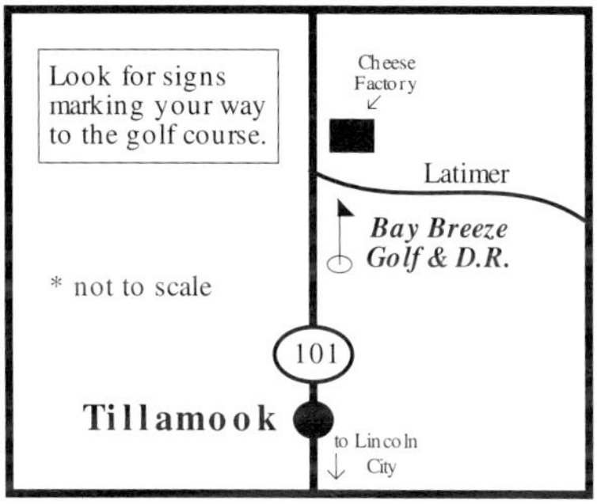

Directions: the golf course is located on Highway 101 directly across from the Tillamook Cheese factory on the east side of the Highway. Look for signs marking your turn to the parking lot.

Course Yardage & Par:

M-1061 yards, par 27.
W-853 yards, par 27.

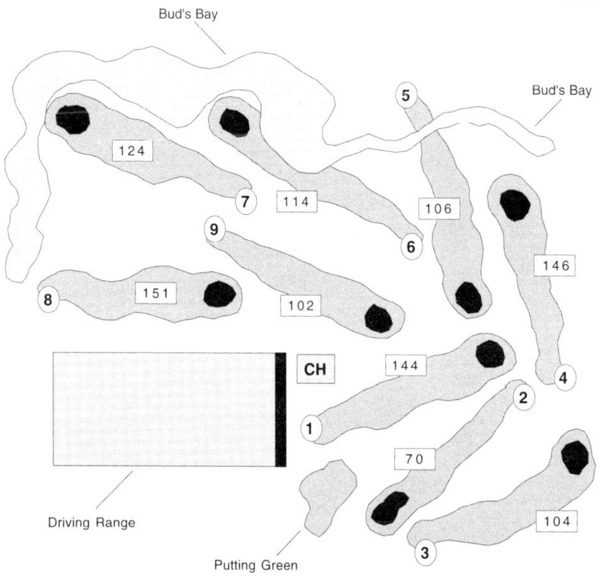

Bayou Golf Club (public, 9 hole course & 9 hole par 3 course)

9301 SW Bayou Drive; McMinnville, OR 97128
Phone: (503) 472-4651. Fax: (503) 472-4651. Web: none.
Pro: Don Schaefer. Superintendent: Kit Johnson.
Rating/Slope: C 71.4/130; M 70.2/125; W 69.9/123. **Course record:** 64.
Green fees: W/D $22/$13; W/E $24/$15; Jr. and Sr. rates, M/C, VISA.
Green fees for the Short 9: $12/$7 all week long; Jr./Sr. rates; M/C, VISA.
Power cart: $20/$12. **Pull cart:** $5/$3. **Trail fee:** $10/$6 for personal carts.
Reservation policy: yes, call ahead for tee-times. Suggested in summer.
Winter condition: The golf course is open all year long, weather permitting.
Terrain: gentle rolling hills. **Tees:** all grass. **Spikes:** soft spikes only.
Services: club rentals, lessons, snack bar, beer, wine, pro shop, driving range, putting & chipping greens. **Comments:** Course was built in 1964. Riverside setting with water hazards coming into play on all 9 holes. Good test of golf.

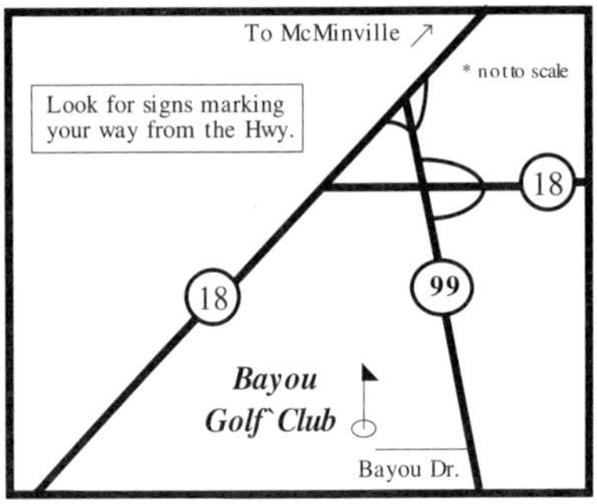

Directions: the golf course is located 1.25 miles southwest of McMinnville Oregon on Hwy 99W. Look for a large sign on the Hwy. If on Hwy 18 watch for signs for Hwy 99W southbound and follow to the golf course which will be on your right hand side.

Course Yardage & Par:

C-3221 yards, par 36.
M-3103 yards, par 36.
W-2610 yards, par 36.

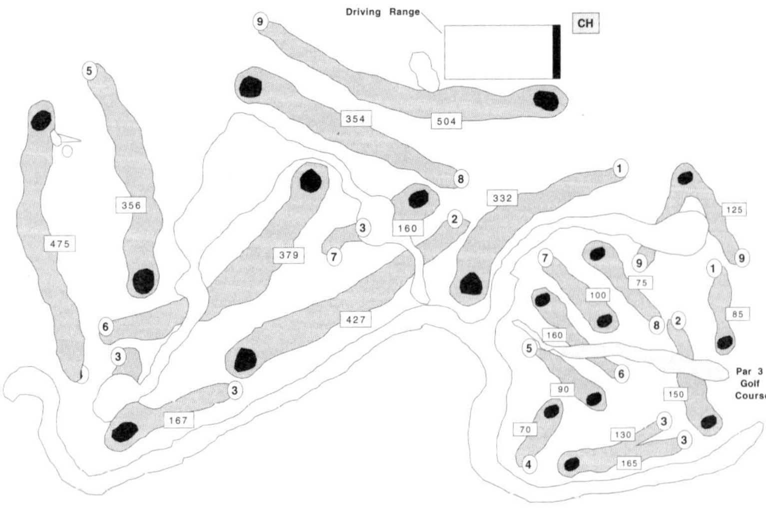

Bear Creek Golf Course (public, 9 hole course)

2355 South Pacific Highway; Medford, OR 97501
Phone: (541) 773-1822. Fax: (541) 773-8945. Web: golfbearcreek.com
Owner: Marla Corbin. Superintendent: Jeff Rosales.
Rating/Slope: M 56.6/85; W 56.6/86. **Course record:** 25.
Green fees: W/D $14/$8; W/E $16/$10; Play all day on Thursday for $9;
Jr. rates W/D $11/$6 W/E $13/$8; Sr. rates (M-F) $7; M/C, VISA, DISCOVER.
Power cart: not available. **Pull cart:** $1.75. **Trail fee:** not allowed.
Reservation policy: advance tee-time reservations are not needed or required.
Winter condition: the golf course is open all year long, weather permitting.
Terrain: flat, some hills. **Tees:** grass. **Spikes:** metal spikes permitted.
Services: club rentals, lessons, snack bar, beer, wine, beverages, pro shop, covered driving range, putting green & chipping area, 18 hole miniature course.
Comments: Very popular golf complex. Facility is kept in excellent shape during the peak season. Great golf course to take the family or first time golfer to. Water is a major factor on half the holes so be sure to bring plenty of balls.

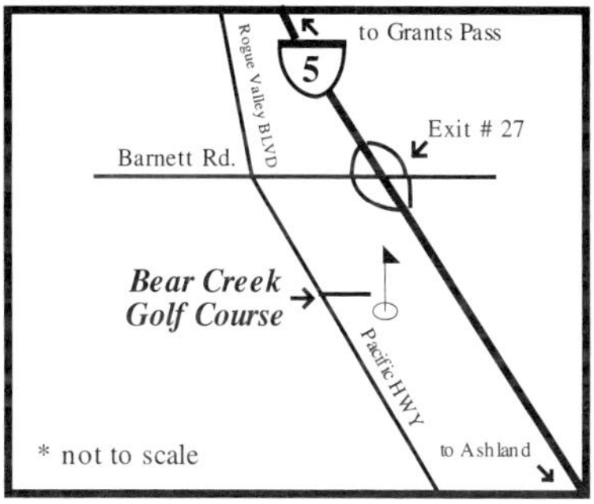

Directions: from I-5 northbound & southbound use exit #27 to Barnett Road Proceed to Highway 99 (Pacific Hwy). Turn southbound on Pacific Highway and proceed for 3/4 of a mile to the golf course. The golf course will be located on your left hand side. The course has great freeway access. Look for signs marking your way.

Course Yardage & Par:
M-1501 yards, par 29/30.   **W-1501 yards, par 30.**

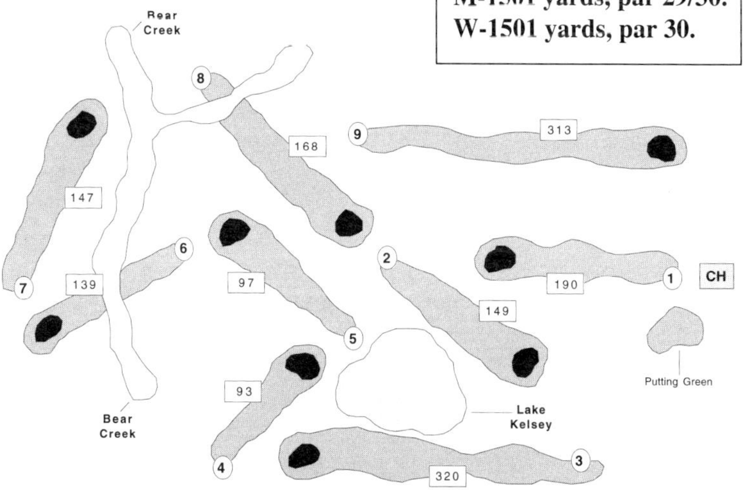

Bear Valley Meadows Golf Club (public, 9 hole course)

12 Valley Way; Seneca, OR 97873
Phone: (541) 542-9309. Fax: none. Web: none.
Manager: Sam Hornbeck. Superintendent: Lee Brune.
Rating/Slope: M 66.0/103; W 70.0/120. **Course record:** 62.
Green fees: $12/$7 all week long; no special rates; no credit cards.
Power cart: none available. **Pull cart:** $2. **Trail fee:** not allowed.
Reservation policy: tee times are on first come first served basis.
Winter condition: course closed from November from15th to March 1st.
Terrain: flat, some hills. **Tees:** all grass. **Spikes:** metal spikes permitted.
Services: club rentals, beverages, limited services.
Comments: newer golf course that is owned and maintained by the City of Seneca. The greens are on the small side and can be hard to hold during the summer months. The sports few hazards and the fairways are wide open.

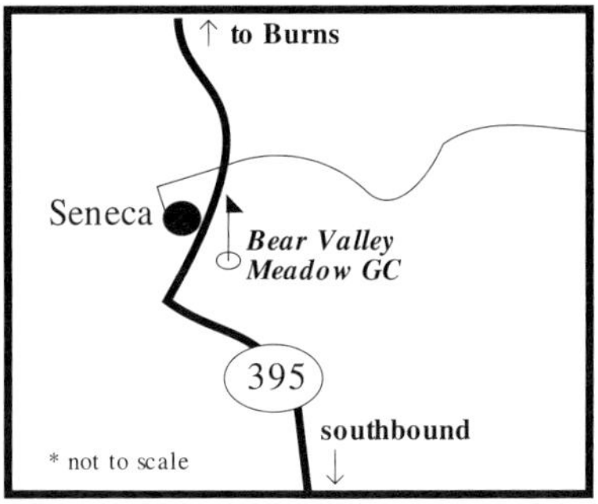

Directions: from Burns, Oregon turn southbound on Hwy 395 toward Seneca. Proceed for 34 miles to Seneca. The course is located on the left hand side of Hwy 395 right after the railroad tracks.

Course Yardage & Par:
M-2976 yards, par 33.
W-2791 yards, par 36.

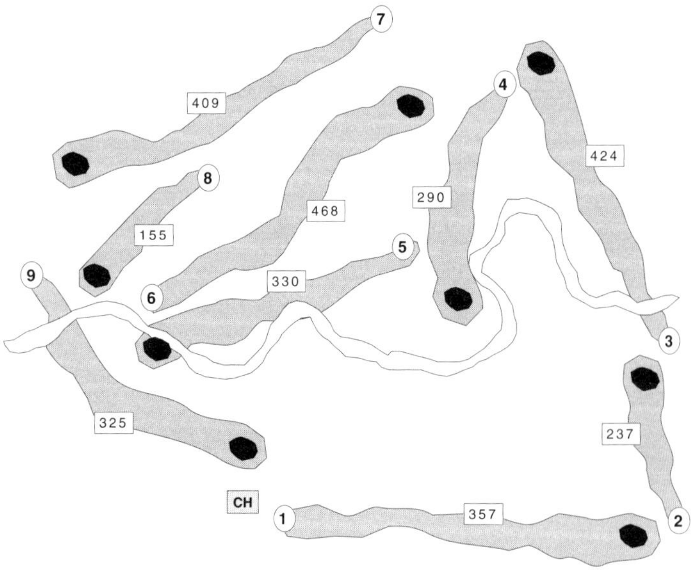

Bend Golf & Country Club (private, 18 hole course)

61045 Country Club Drive; Bend, OR 97702
Phone: (541) 382-7437. Fax: (541) 382-4603. Web: www.bendgolfclub.com
Pro: Erik Nielsen, PGA. Superintendent: Tom Baty.
Rating/Slope: C 73.1/133; M 71.0/130; W 71.1/126. **Course record:** 68.
Green fees: private club, members & guests only, reciprocates ; M/C, VISA.
Power cart: private club. **Pull cart:** private club. **Trail fee:** not allowed.
Reservation policy: private golf club members & guests of members only.
Winter condition: the golf course is open in winter, weather permitting.
Terrain: flat, some hills. **Tees:** all grass. **Spikes:** soft spikes only.
Services: lessons, snack bar, lounge, beer, wine, liquor, pro shop, lockers, showers, driving range, putting & chipping greens, club memberships.
Comments: Established in 1925, this is Bend's original private country club. The course features a traditional layout, in Ponderosa framed fairways. Whether walking or riding, you'll enjoy the par-like setting free from homesites. This is a true shot makers course that will challenge all levels of golfers. Great course!

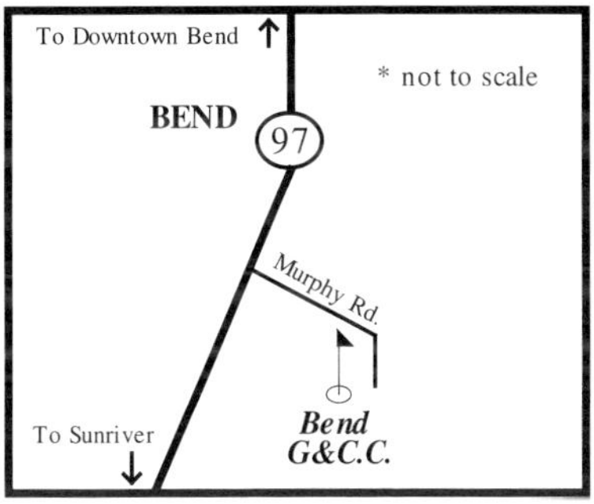

Directions: from Highway 97 turn on Murphy Rd. and proceed eastbound. Follow Murphy Rd. for 3/4 of a mile to Country Club Dr. The golf course will be just ahead on your right hand side.

Course Yardage & Par:

C-7026 yards, par 72.
M-6556 yards, par 72.
W-5857 yards, par 72.

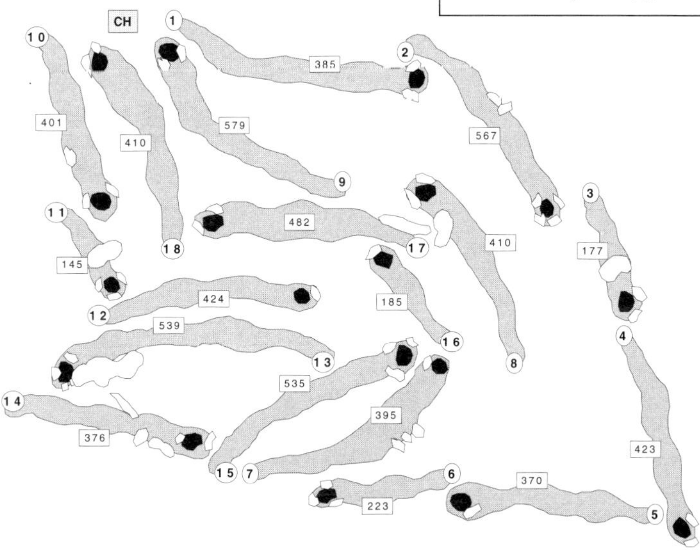

Black Butte Ranch (resort) Big Meadow (18 hole course)

P.O. Box 8000; Highway 20; Black Butte Ranch, OR 97759
Phone: (541) 595-1500, 1-800-399-2322. Fax: (541) 595-1293.
Pro: Greg Hanway, PGA. Supt.: Gus Johnson. Web: blackbutteranch.com
Rating/Slope: C 71.3/125; M 69.6/123; W 70.4/124. **Course record:** 65.
Green fees: Mon.- Thursday $55/$30; Friday-Sunday & Holidays $65/$30; off season rates are available; Jr. rates available; M/C, VISA, AMEX, DIS.
Power cart: $30. **Pull cart:** $4/$2. **Trail fee:** personal carts not allowed.
Reservation policy: *General public*: you may call up tp 30 days in advance for tee-times. *Ranch Guests*: you may call up to 45 days in advance for tee-times.
Winter condition: the golf course is closed from late October to mid March.
Terrain: flat, some hills. **Tees:** grass tees. **Spikes:** soft spikes only.
Services: club rentals, lessons, snack bar, beer, wine, pro shop, driving range.
Comments: excellent facility that is worth a special trip. Big Meadow course is of traditional design featuring tree-lined fairways, well bunkered greens and varied terrain. Great views of the Cascade Mountain Range and forests abound from nearly every hole on the course. This course is a must play for any golfer.

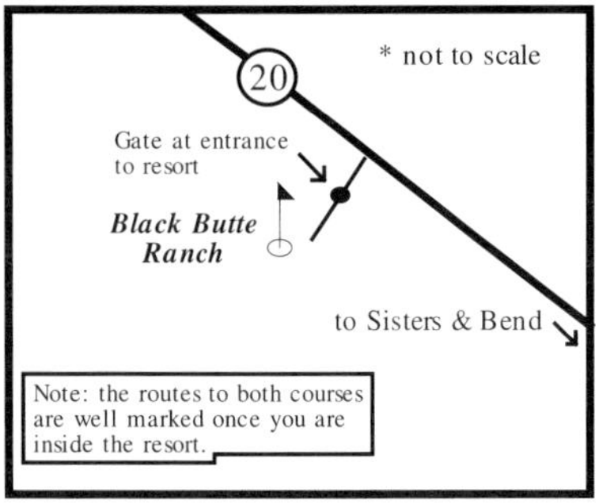

Directions: the golf course is located 8 miles west of Sisters Oregon on Hwy 20. The turn for the Black Butte Ranch is well marked. Once inside the complex the route to the golf course has plenty of signs to mark your way. Look for "Hawks Beard" signs as this runs around the entire complex.

Black Butte Ranch (resort) Glaze Meadow (18 hole course)

P.O. Box 8000; Highway 20; Black Butte, OR 97759
Phone: (541) 595-1500, 1-800-399-2322. Fax: (541) 595-1293.
Pro: Greg Hanway, PGA. Supt.: Gus Johnson. Web: blackbutteranch.com
Rating/Slope: C 70.7/122; M 69.5/119; W 70.8/126. **Course record:** 62.
Green fees: Mon.- Thursday $55/$30; Friday-Sunday & Holidays $65/$30; off season rates are available; Jr. rates available; M/C, VISA, AMEX, DIS.
Power cart: $30. **Pull cart:** $4/$2. **Trail fee:** personal carts not allowed.
Reservation policy: *General public*: you may call up tp 30 days in advance for tee-times. *Ranch Guests*: you may call up to 45 days in advance for tee-times.
Winter condition: the golf course is closed from late October to mid March.
Terrain: flat, some hills. **Tees:** grass tees. **Spikes:** soft spikes only.
Services: club rentals, lessons, snack bar, beer, wine, pro shop, driving range.
Comments: The fairways are narrow in spots leaving the golfer many lay up shots from the tee. Greens are large and well bunkered on nearly every hole. This is one of my most favorite golf courses in the state. Great golf.

Big Meadow Golf Course

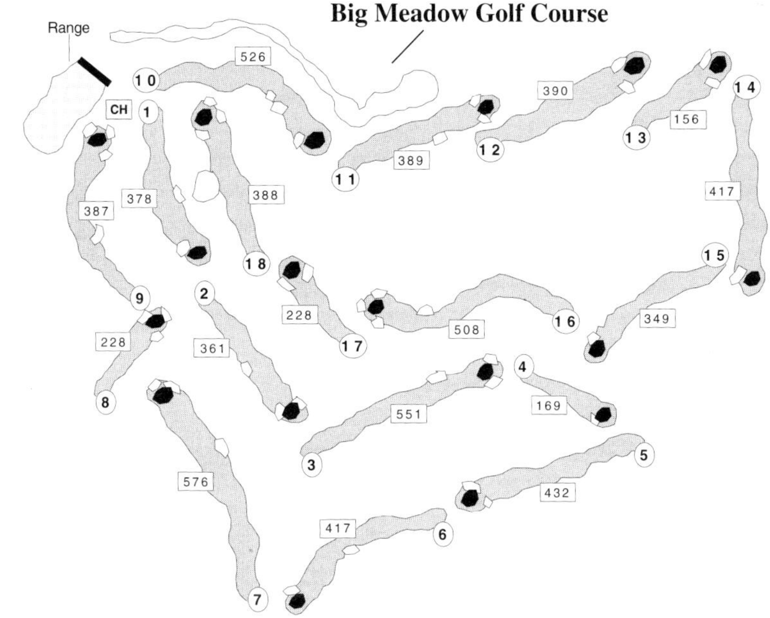

Course Yardage & Par:

C-6850 yards, par 72.
M-6456 yards, par 72.
W-5678 yards, par 72.
Big Meadow

Glaze Meadow Golf Course

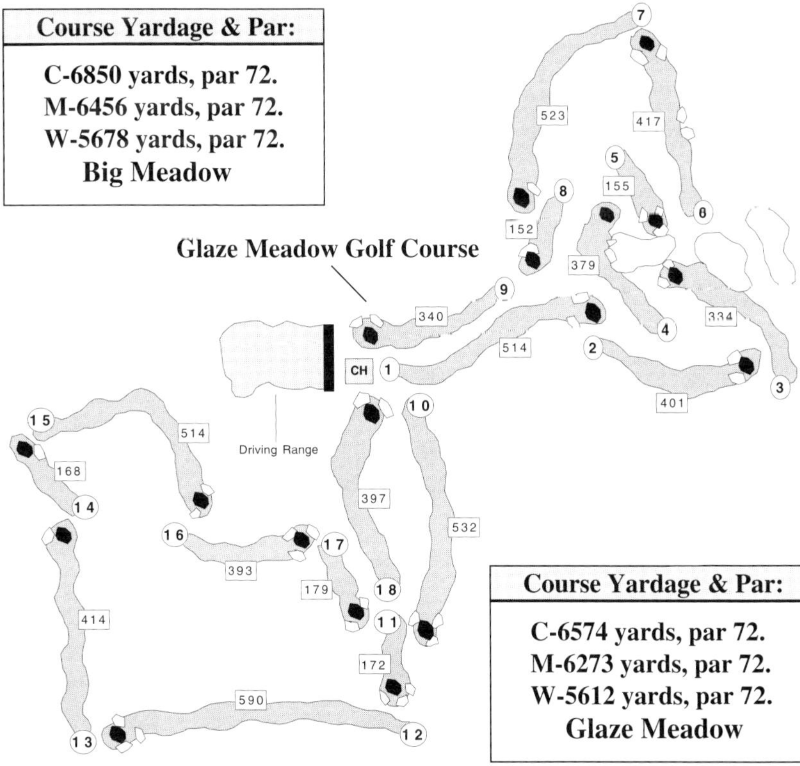

Course Yardage & Par:

C-6574 yards, par 72.
M-6273 yards, par 72.
W-5612 yards, par 72.
Glaze Meadow

Broadmoor Golf Course (public, 18 hole course)

3509 NE Columbia Boulevard; Portland, OR 97211
Phone: (503) 281-1337. Fax: (503) 288-9578. Web: none.
Pro: Scott Krieger, PGA. Superintendent: Joe Goodling.
Rating/Slope: C 70.2/121; M 68.2/113; W 69.5/111. **Course record:** 63.
Green fees: W/D $22/$11; W/E $24/$12; M/C, VISA for merchandise only.
Power cart: $22/$11. **Pull cart:** $2. **Trail fee:** personal carts are not allowed.
Reservation policy: yes, call Monday for the following week and weekend.
Winter condition: the golf course is open all year long, weather permitting.
Terrain: flat, some hills. **Tees:** all grass tees. **Spikes:** soft spikes only.
Services: club rentals, lessons, restaurant, beer, wine, beverages, pro shop, driving range, putting & chipping greens. **Comments:** Beautiful tree lined course with water and sand coming into play on several holes. One of Portland's most popular public golf courses that can get very busy during the peak season.

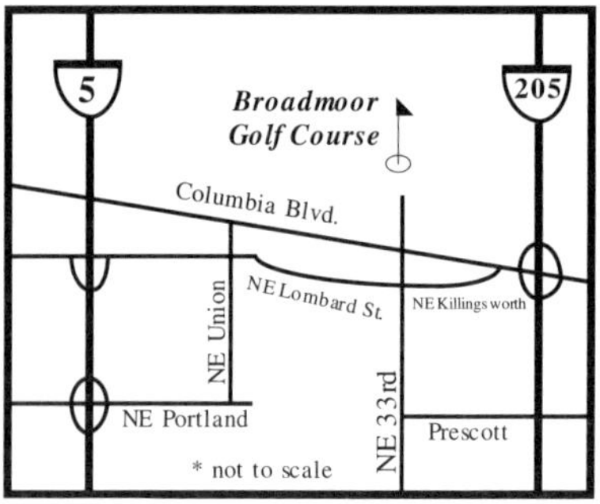

__Directions:__ from I-5 N&S take the Columbia Street exit and proceed eastbound for 1 mile to NE 33rd. Turn left to the golf course. From I-205 N&S take the Columbia Street exit and proceed westbound for 2 miles to the course on your left. Look for signs.

Course Yardage & Par:

C-6498 yards, par 72.
M-5966 yards, par 72.
W-5388 yards, par 74.

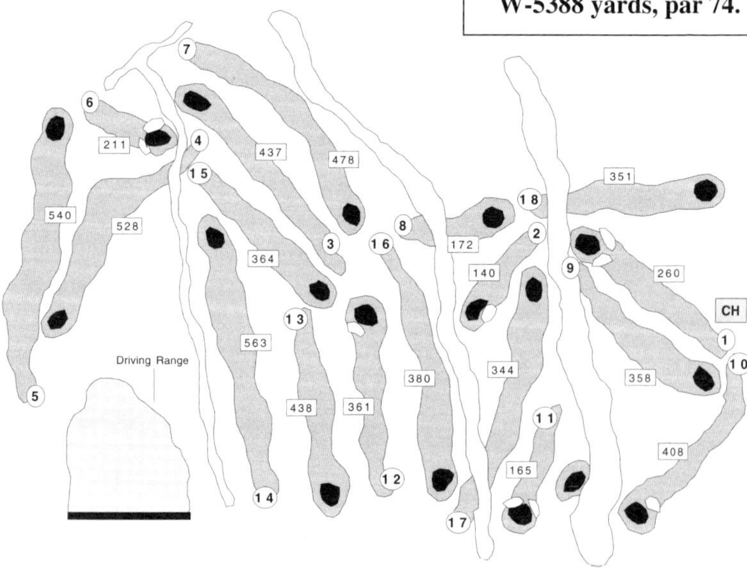

Broken Top Club (private, 18 hole course)

62000 Broken Top Drive; Bend OR 97702

Phone: (541) 383-0868. Fax: (541) 383-1963. Web: www.brokentop.com

Pro: Rick Wild, PGA. Superintendent: Trip Freeman.

Rating/Slope: C 73.4/136; M 70.7/128; F 67.6/118; W 70.5/127.

Green fees: private club, members only; pro reciprocation on a limited basis.

Power cart: available. **Pull cart:** yes. **Trail fee:** personal carts not allowed.

Reservation policy: private club, members and guests of members only.

Winter condition: as dictated by weather. Closed generally during the winter.

Terrain: flat, some hills. **Tees:** all bent grass. **Spikes:** soft spikes only.

Services: full service country club, driving range, putting & chipping greens.

Comments: this Tom Weiskopf, Jay Moorish designed golf course opened in July of 1993. The par 4, 364 yard, 11th is the course's signature hole. The course features classic championship design that plays over 7100 yards from the back.

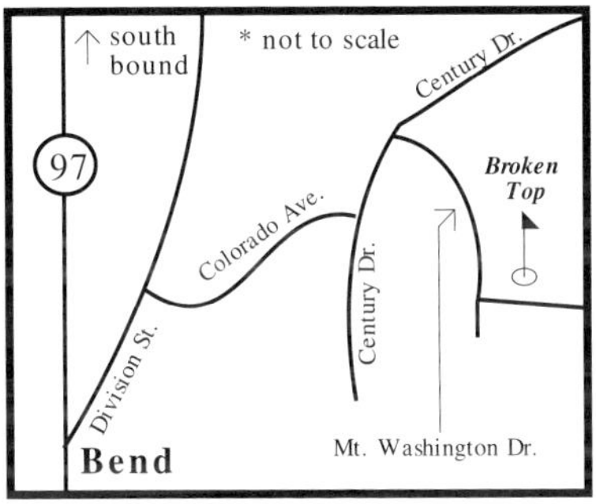

Directions: from Downtown Bend: Take US 97 South to Greenwood. Turn right at Greenwood (which eventually turns into Newport Ave.). Turn left on 14th Street. Continue straight at the 4-way stop at 14th and Galveston. Turn right on Simpson and continue to stop sign. Turn left at the stop sign on Mt. Washington Drive. Turn right on Broken Top Drive at the Club entrance.

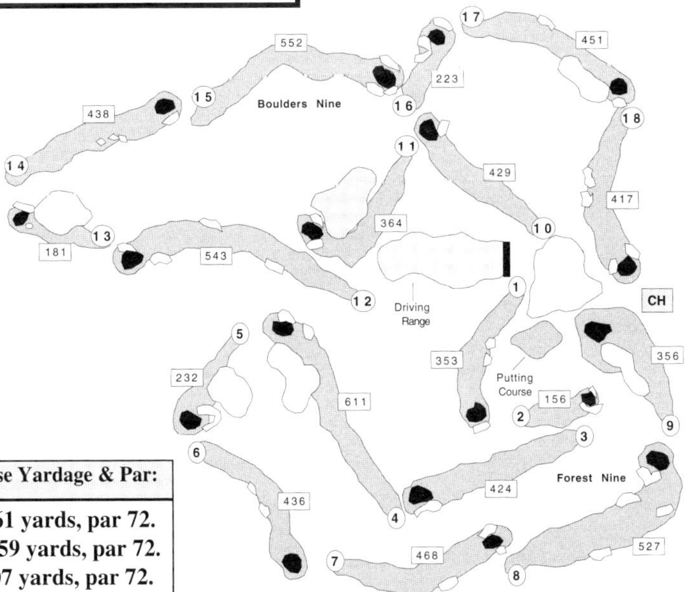

Course Yardage & Par:
C-7161 yards, par 72.
M-6559 yards, par 72.
F-5907 yards, par 72.
W-5281 yards, par 72.

Buffalo Peak Golf Club (public, 18 hole course)

1224 Fullton Street; SE of Union; Union, OR 97883
Phone: (541) 562-5527. Fax: none. Web: www.buffalopeakgolf.com
Manager: Ken Michrina. Superintendent: Rich Goodrick.
Rating/Slope: T 71.7/133; C 69.4/124; M 67.3/117; W 67.7/122. **Record:** 67.
Green fees: W/D $22/$13; W/E & Holidays $26/$15; M/C, VISA.
Power cart: $20/$12. **Pull cart:** $3/$2. **Trail fee:** $8/$5.
Reservation policy: yes, call up to 1 week in advance for tee times.
Winter condition: the golf course is open all year long, weather permitting.
Terrain: relatively hilly. **Tees:** all grass. **Spikes:** soft spikes required.
Services: club rentals, lessons, snack bar, lounge, beer, wine, liquor, pro shop, putting & chipping greens, driving range. **Comments:** newer golf course that features large, undulating greens that are firm and fast. This course captures the true spirit of links-style golf. Buffalo Peak is worth a special trip.

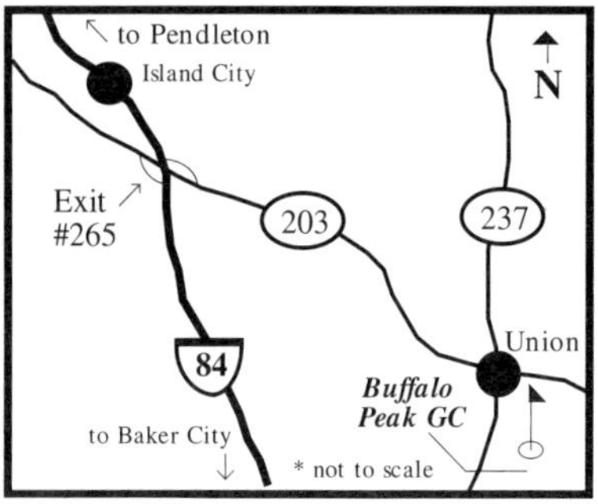

__Directions:__ from I-84W, take exit #285 at North Powder. Turn right onto Hwy 237 and travel through North Powder. Continue on the highway for 15 miles until you reach Union. Turn right on E Fulton St., proceed to course. From I-84E, take exit 265 at La Grande. Turn right onto Hwy 203 and follow it for 12 miles to Union. Travel through Union, turn left on E Fulton St. to the course.

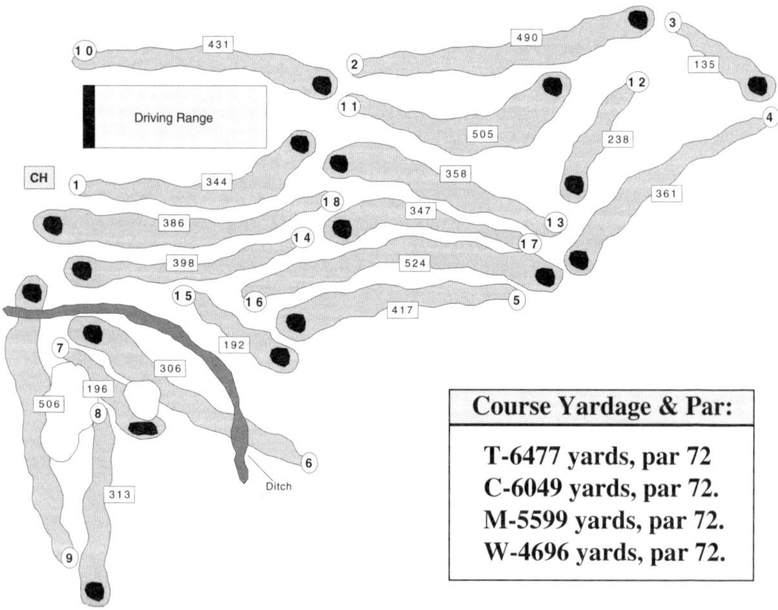

Course Yardage & Par:

T-6477 yards, par 72
C-6049 yards, par 72.
M-5599 yards, par 72.
W-4696 yards, par 72.

Cedar Bend Golf Club (public, 9 hole course)

34391 Squaw Valley Road; Gold Beach, OR 97444
Phone: (541) 247-6911. Fax: (541) 247-5608. Web: cedar-bend-golf.com
Manager: Kathy Boice. Superintendent: Alden Boice.
Rating/Slope: C 70.1/128; M 67.2/116; W 68.3/117. **Course record:** 67.
Green fees: $20/$15 all week long; Senior rates $18/$13 all week long; Junior rates $7/$5 all week long; twlight rates (M-T-W) $15/$10; M/C, VISA.
Power cart: $20/$15. **Pull cart:** $2/$1. **Trail fee:** $5 for personal carts.
Reservation policy: yes, call in advance for tee times. A must in the summer.
Winter condition: the golf course is open all year long, damp conditions.
Terrain: flat (easy walking). **Tees:** grass. **Spikes:** metal spikes permitted.
Services: club rentals, lessons, snack bar, lounge, beer, wine, liquor, pro shop, putting & chipping greens, driving range. **Comments:** Streams, lush fairways and well kept greens add to your game at this course. Good public course that is located in a great part of Oregon. The golf course is flat and very easy to walk.

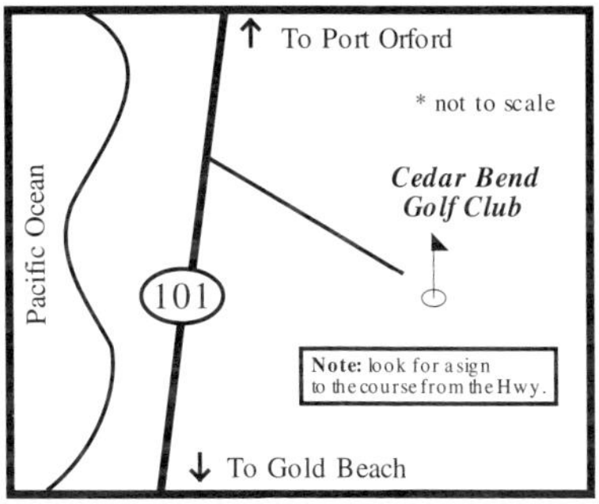

Directions: the golf course is located 12 miles north of Gold Beach and 14 miles south of Port Orford. **Note:** look for a sign on Hwy 101 for your turn to the golf course which is located 3 miles inland.

Course Yardage & Par:

C-3156 yards, par 36.
M-2872 yards, par 36.
W-2536 yards, par 37.
Dual tees for 18 holes:
C-6288 yards, par 72.
M-5892 yards, par 72.
W-5231 yards, par 74.

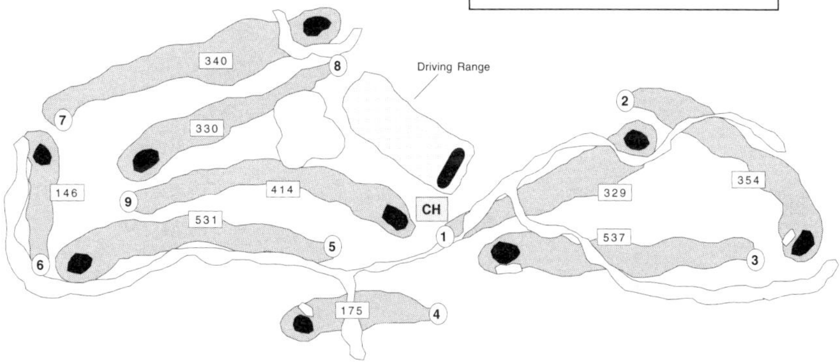

Cedar Links Golf Club (public, 18 hole course)

3155 Cedar Links Drive; Medford, OR 97504
Phone: (541) 773-4373. Fax: none. Web: www.cedarlinks.com
Pro: Scott Lusk, PGA. Superintendent: Travis Jantzer.
Rating/Slope: C 68.9/124; M 68.0/116; W 69.2/118. **Course record:** 61.
Green fees: W/D $24/$14; W/E $26/$16; M/C, VISA, DISCOVER.
Power cart: $20/$10. **Pull cart:** $3/$2. **Trail fee:** personal carts not allowed.
Reservation policy: yes, please call up to 7 days in advance for tee-times.
Winter condition: the course is open all year long weather permitting, dry.
Terrain: flat, some hills. **Tees:** all grass. **Spikes:** soft spikes preferred.
Services: club rentals, lessons, snack bar, restaurant, beer, wine, beverages, pro shop, putting & chipping greens, excellent driving range.
Comments: Family owned public golf course in the foothills of Medford. The golf course sports several water holes and well bunkered, tricky greens. Fairways have generous landing areas and are kept in excellent condition.

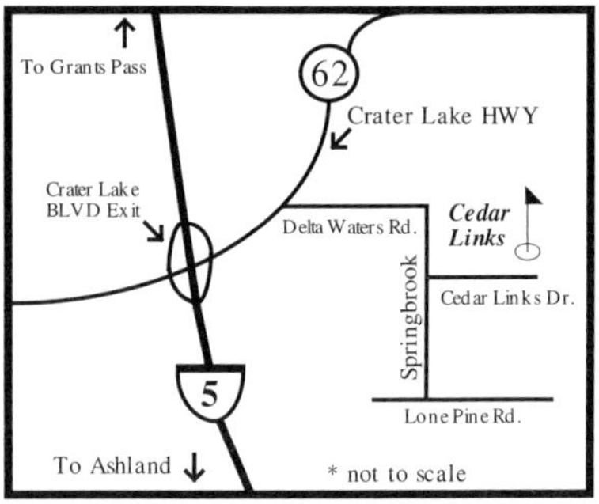

Directions: from I-5 N&S take Hwy 62 (Crater Lake Highway) exit #30 and go north. Turn right on Delta Waters Road. Proceed to Springbrook and turn right. At Cedar Links Drive, turn left to golf course which is located on your left hand side.

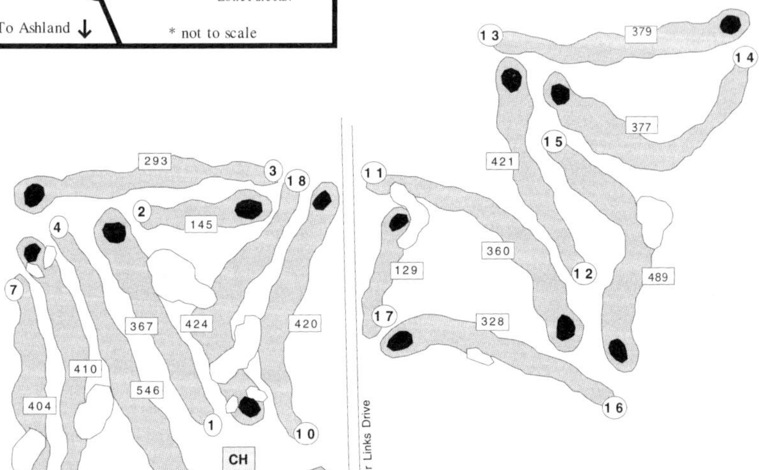

Course Yardage & Par:

C-6223 yards, par 70.
M-5903 yards, par 70.
W-5182 yards, par 71.

Charbonneau Golf & Country Club (public, 27 hole course)

32020 Charbonneau Drive; Wilsonville, OR 97070
Phone: (503) 694-1246. Fax: (503) 694-2323. Web: none.
Pro: Dennis Gavin, PGA. Superintendent: Mary Rock.
Rating/Slope: C 60.6/94; M 59.8/92; W 61.9/94. **Course record:** 54.
Green fees: W/D $26/$16; W/E $30/$18; winter rates; M/C, VISA.
Power cart: $22/$12. **Pull cart:** $3/$2. **Trail fee:** personal carts not allowed.
Reservation policy: yes, call 10 days in advance for tee-time reservations.
Winter condition: the golf course is open all year long with dry conditions.
Terrain: flat, some slight hills. **Tees:** grass. **Spikes:** soft spikes preferred.
Services: club rentals, lessons, restaurant, lounge, beer, wine, pro shop, putting & chipping greens, driving range. **Comments:** Beautiful executive course layout that gives all golfers a challenge. The golf course can always be found in great shape. Be sure to make Charonneau G. & C.C. part of any golf vacation.

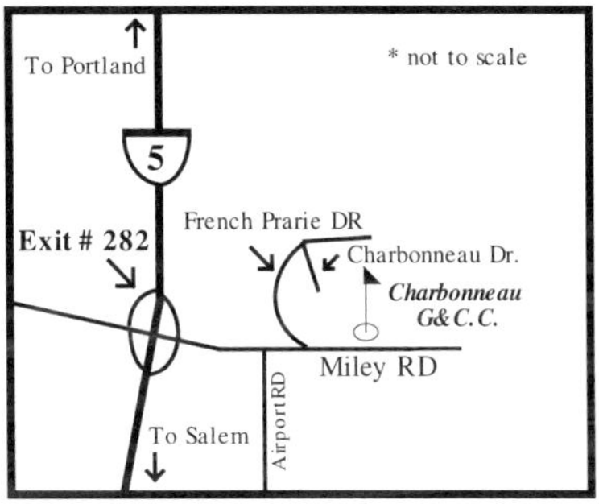

Directions: from I-5 North & South take the Charbonneau exit #282. Go east for approximately one mile to Charbonneau Village and proceed to the golf course. Look for signs along your route.

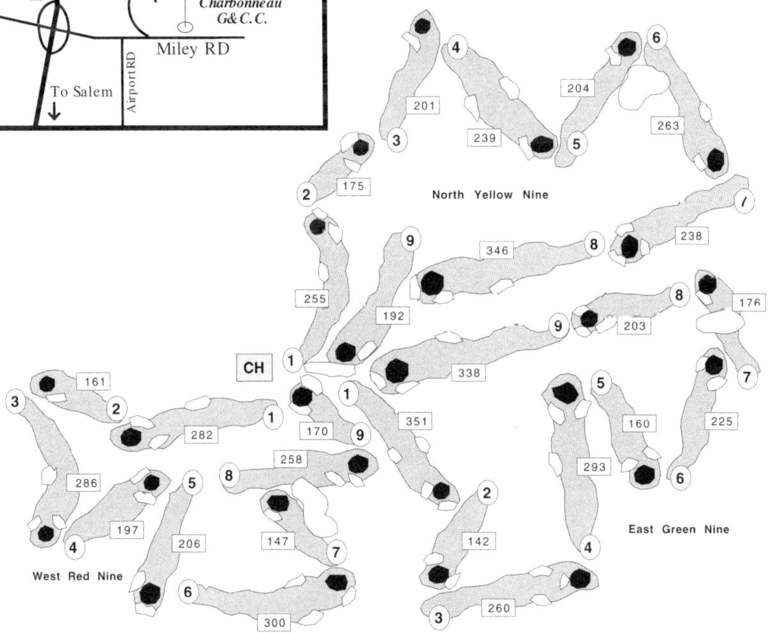

Course Yardage & Par:
North Yellow Nine: C-2172 yards, par 31; M-2026, par 31; W-1802, par 31.
East Green Nine: C-2180 yards, par 31; M-2111, par 31; W-1943, par 31.
West Red Nine: C-2047 yards, par 31; M-1936, par 31; W-1780, par 31.

Children's Course (public, 9 hole course)

19825 River Road; Gladstone, OR 97027
Phone: (503) 722-1530. Fax: (503) 722-1757. Web: none.
Pro/Superintendent: Phil Bostwick. Teaching Pro: Rianne Beiser.
Rating/Slope: the golf course is not rated. **Course record:** 25.
Green fees: Weekdays $9; Weekends $9; Sr. rates $6; Jr. rates $5.
Power cart: not available. **Pull cart:** $2. **Trail fee:** personal carts not allowed.
Reservation policy: please call in advance for your tee-times. No time limit.
Winter condition: the course is open all year long, weather permitting.
Terrain: flat (easy walking). **Tees:** all grass. **Spikes:** soft spikes preferred.
Services: club rentals, small pro shop, beverages, putting & chipping greens.
Comments: Short par 3 golf course that will challenge your short game. Excellent walking golf course. The golf course is located next to the Willamette River in a beautiful part of Oregon. Public tee times are available. This one of a kind course offers a full schedule of junior clinics, camps and tournaments.

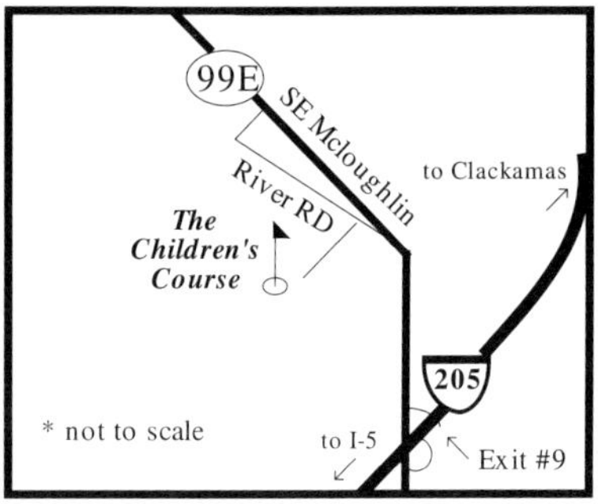

Directions: from I-205 N&S take exit #9 onto Hwy 99E to Gladstone. Proceed for .7 mi across bridge to light where you veer left onto River Road. Follow River Road to the entrance immediately on your left hand side. Look for signs marking your way to the golf course.

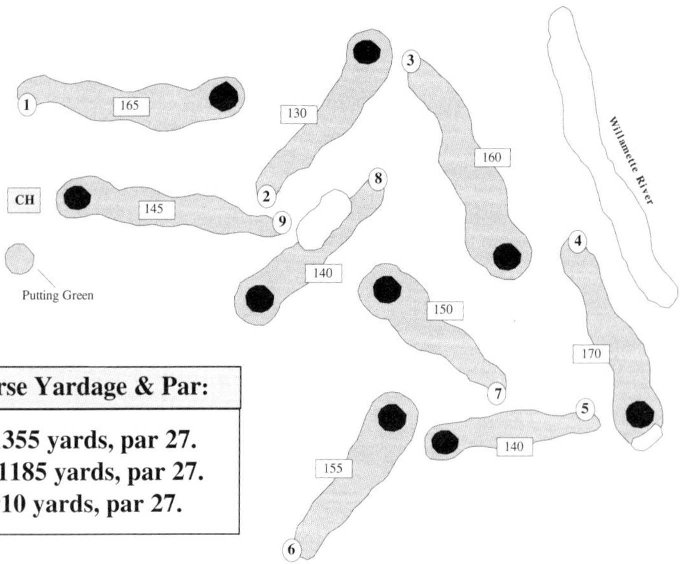

Course Yardage & Par:
B-1355 yards, par 27.
M-1185 yards, par 27.
F-910 yards, par 27.

Christmas Valley Golf Course (public, 9 hole course)

Physical address: #1 Christmas Tree Lane; Christmas Valley, OR 97641
Mailing address: P. O. Box 181; Christmas Valley, OR 97641
Phone: (541) 576-2216. Fax: (541) 576-2216. Web: none.
Rating/Slope: the golf course is not rated. **Course record:** 34.
Green fees: $15/$10 all week long; no special rates; no credit cards.
Power cart: none. **Pull cart:** none. **Trail fee:** personal carts are allowed.
Reservation policy: advance tee times are not needed. First come first served.
Winter condition: the golf course is open all year long weather permitting.
Terrain: flat (easy walking). **Tees:** all grass. **Spikes:** metal spikes permitted.
Services: club rentals, snack bar, restaurant, lounge, beer, wine, liquor, putting & chipping greens, lodge. **Comments:** this championship length golf course is challenging to players of all levels. Hazards such as sand and pot bunkers, water and sagebrush abound if you stray from the fairway. Fair public golf course.

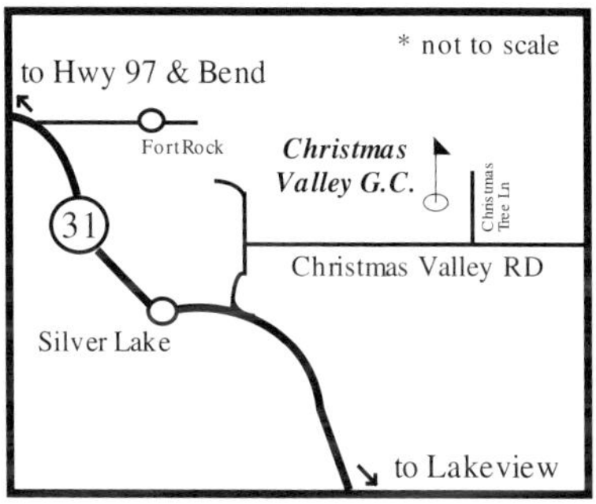

Directions: from Hwy 97 take Hwy 31 to Fort Rock/Christmas Valley exit. Take Co. Road 5-10 to Co. Road 5-14. 5-14 will become Christmas Valley Rd. at Christmas Valley. Follow this road to the golf course. **Note:** Look for signs marking your way to the golf course.

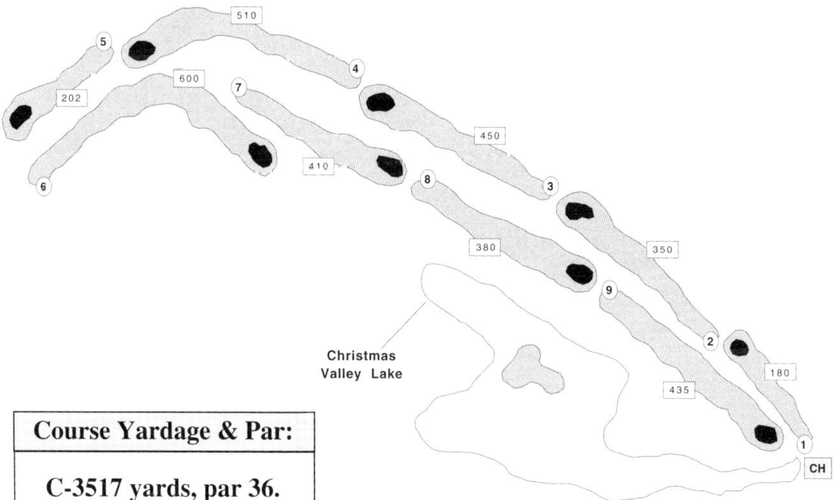

Course Yardage & Par:

C-3517 yards, par 36.
M-3393 yards, par 36.
W-3070 yards, par 38.

Circle Bar Golf Club (public, 9 hole course)

48447 West Oak Road; P. O. Box 214; Oakridge, OR 97463
Phone: (541) 782-3541. Fax: none. Web: none.
Pro Shop Manager: Carrol Slaven. Superintendent: Dave Daniels.
Rating/Slope: M 71.0/123; W 73.0/118. **Course record:** 33.
Green fees: W/D $15/$7; W/E $18/$9; no credit cards.
Power cart: $18/$12. **Pull cart:** $3/$2. **Trail fee:** $6 for personal carts.
Reservation policy: yes, a must in summer, please call ahead for tee-times.
Winter condition: open, wet, club house closed from November to March.
Terrain: relatively hilly. **Tees:** grass. **Spikes:** metal spikes permitted.
Services: club rentals, snack bar, beer, wine, pro shop, putting green, chipping green, banquet facilities. **Comments:** club memberships are available for those wanting to join the club. Water comes into play on over half the holes. Dual tees are available for those wanting to play a full 18. If you are looking for a course for a quick 9 holes that is off the beaten track, try Circle Bar Golf Club.

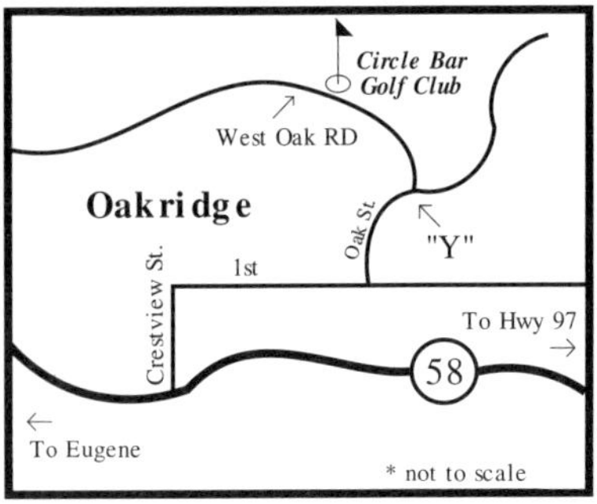

Directions: from Hwy 58 turn north on Crestview Street go across the train tracks to 1st. Turn right on 1st Street and proceed to Oak Street, turn left. Follow Oak Street to the "Y" in the road and turn left. This is West Oak Road. Follow this to the golf course. **Note:** Make sure you follow the signs marking your way.

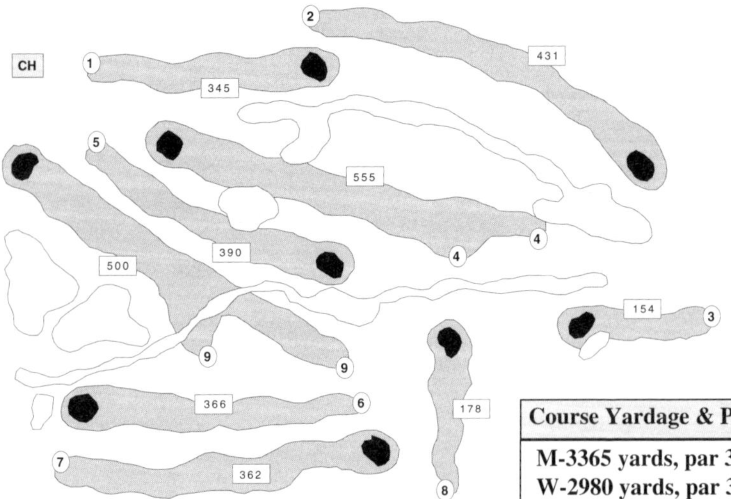

Course Yardage & Par:
M-3365 yards, par 36.
W-2980 yards, par 37.
Dual tees for 18 holes:
M-6648 yards, par 72.
W-5970 yards, par 73.

Claremont Golf Club (public, 9 hole course)

15800 NW Country Club Drive; Portland, OR 97229

Phone: (503) 690-4589. Fax: (503) 617-9433. Web: none.

Pro: Steve Morrison. Superintendent: Steve Bizon

Rating/Slope: C 68.4/124; M 67.6/122; W 70.0/122. **Record:** 31 (9 holes).
Green fees: W/D $23/$13; W/E $28/$14; Sr. rates (M-F $8); M/C, VISA.
Power cart: $13 (9 holes). **Pull cart:** $2. **Trail fee:** personal carts not allowed.
Reservation policy: yes, please call 1 week in advance for your tee times.
Winter condition: open all year long weather permitting, course drains well.
Terrain: flat (easy walking). **Tees:** all grass. **Spikes:** soft spikes preferred.
Services: club rentals, pro shop. **Comments:** excellent walking golf course. One of the finest 9 hole golf courses to emerge in the Portland area. Water comes into play on several holes and can make this course play difficult.

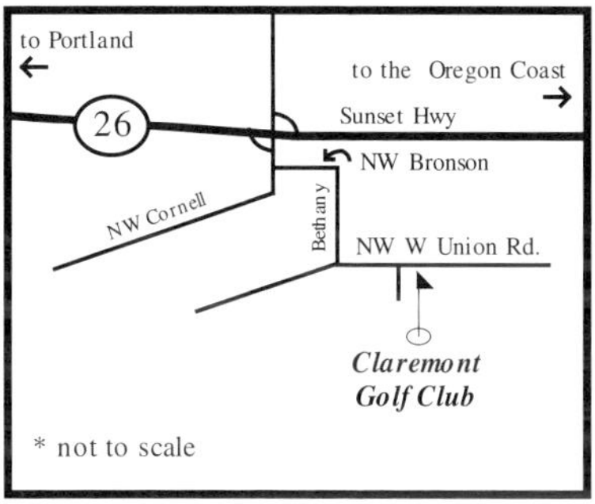

__Directions:__ from Highway 26 (Sunset Highway) take the Cornell/Bethany exit and turn right at the 2nd stoplight (Bethany Blvd.) Proceed to NW West Union Road and turn left. The golf course is located at the top of the hill on the right hand side.

Course Yardage & Par: Dual Tees 18 holes:	
C-3060 yards, par 36.	6120 yards, par 72.
M-2961 yards, par 36.	5922 yards, par 72.
W-2692 yards, par 36.	5384 yards, par 72.

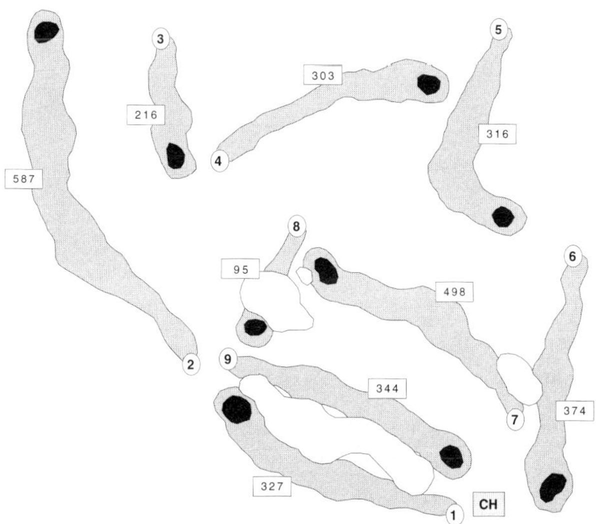

Colonial Valley Golf Course (public, 9 hole course)

75 Nelson Way; Grants Pass, OR 97526
Phone: (541) 479-5568. Fax: (541) 479-5568. Web: none.
Manager/Superintendent: Gerald Smith.
Rating/Slope: M 63.9/116; W 67.8/118. **Course record:** 28.
Green fees: $9 for nine holes, $6 for replay; no credit cards.
Power cart: none available. **Pull cart:** $1. **Trail fee:** $5 for personal carts.
Reservation policy: yes, groups of 12 or more please call 1 week in advance.
Winter condition: the golf course is open all year long, wet conditions.
Terrain: flat (easy walking). **Tees:** all grass. **Spikes:** metal spikes permitted.
Services: club rentals, lessons, snack bar, lounge, beer, wine, small pro shop.
Comments: the staff say that this course is the "Best kept secret in Southern Oregon". The track has wide fairways with medium to large sized well bunkered greens. If you are looking for a change of pace give Colonial Valley a try.

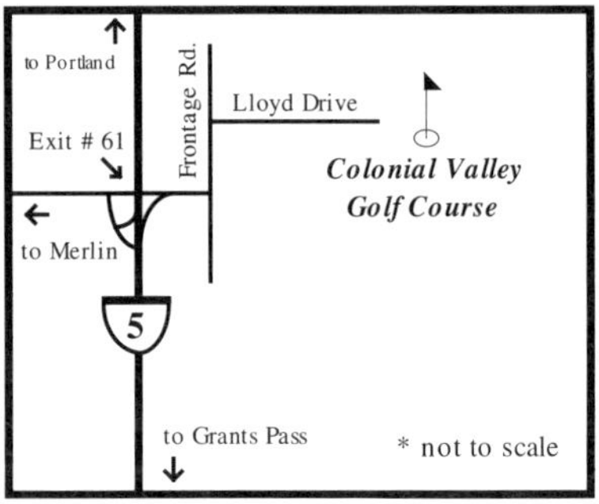

Directions: from I-5 N&S take Merlin exit #61, and go east to Frontage Road. Turn left and go north to Lloyd Drive andturn right on Lloyd Drive. Proceed 1/2 mile to the golf course on your right. **Note:** Look for signs marking your way to the golf course.

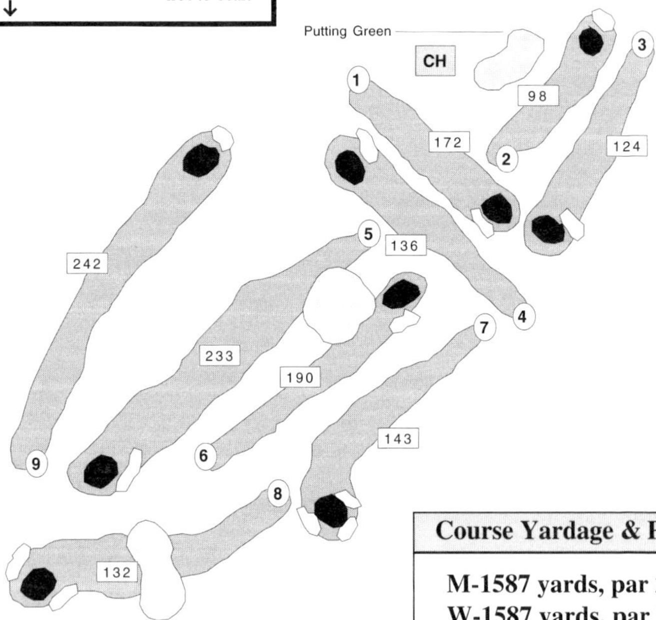

Course Yardage & Par:
M-1587 yards, par 29.
W-1587 yards, par 31.

Columbia Edgewater Country Club (private, 18 hole course)

2220 NE Marine Drive; Portland, OR 97211

Phone: (503) 285-8354. Fax: (503) 285-3977. Web: none.

Pro: Bryan Tunstill, PGA. Supt.: Gordon Kiyokawa. Course Record: 63.

Rating/Slope: T 72.1/131; C 70.3/129; M 69.9/126; W 72.9/129; W 70.8/124.

Green fees: private club, members and guests of members only; reciprocates.

Power cart: private club. **Pull cart:** private club. **Trail fee:** not allowed.

Reservation policy: private club members & guests only, 2 days in advance.

Winter condition: the golf course is open all year long, weather permitting.

Terrain: flat, some hills. **Tees:** grass. **Spikes:** no metal spikes in summer.

Services: lessons, snack bar, restaurant, lounge, pro shop, driving range.

Comments: old golf historic golf course built on rolling flood plains in 1925. Great private golf course that has large well bunkered greens. Fairways are tree-lined and in perfect condition all year long. Host club of a LPGA Tour event.

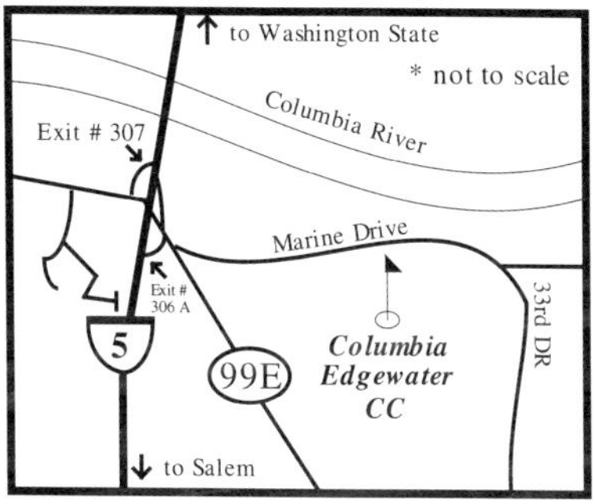

Directions: from I-5 S take Marine Drive exit #307 and proceed eastbound for .5 miles to the golf course. From I-5 N take exit #307 and proceed eastbound.Look for a sign to your turn to the course.

Course Yardage & Par:
T-6689 yards, par 71.
C-6331 yards, par 71.
M-6025 yards, par 71.
W-5750 yards, par 72.
W-5405 yards, par 72.

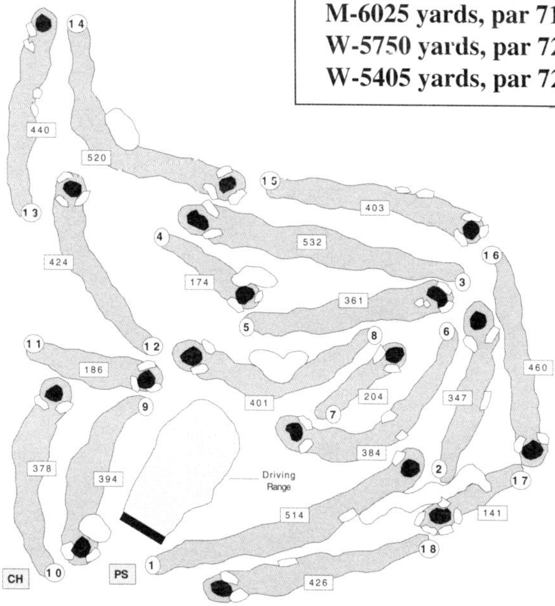

Colwood National Golf Club (public, 18 hole course)

7313 NE Columbia Boulevard; Portland, OR 97218
Phone: (503) 254-5515. Fax: (503) 254-9278. Web: none.
Pro: Toby Tommaso, PGA. Superintendent: Kendall Schaeffer.
Rating/Slope: C 68.5/114; M 66.8/108; W 69.1/110. **Course record:** 63.
Green fees: W/D $26/$14; W/E $28/$15; Jr. rates available; M/C, VISA.
Power cart: $22/$12. **Pull cart:** $3/$2. **Trail fee:** none.
Reservation policy: 1 week in advance for foursomes playing 18 holes only.
Winter condition: the golf course is open all year long with dry conditions.
Terrain: flat (easy walking). **Tees:** all grass. **Spikes:** soft spikes preferred.
Services: club rentals, lessons, restaurant, beer, wine, pop, lounge, pro shop, putting & chipping green. **Comments:** This public golf course built in 1932 is noted for it's excellent conditioned greens and well kept fairways. During the summer month's it becomes very busy with play from the greater Portland area.

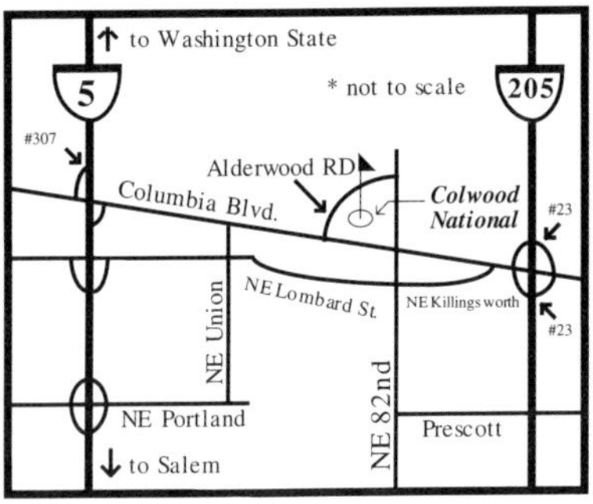

Directions: the golf course is located 1 mile east of Broadmoor off Columbia Boulevard. From I-5 northbound and southbound take NE Columbia Blvd. exit. Exit and go east for 6.7 miles. The golf course will be on your left hand side. From I-205 take exit 23B and stay on Columbia Blvd. for 1 mile. The golf course will be on the right hand side.

Course Yardage & Par:
C- 6158 yards, par 72.   **M-5794 yards, par 72.**   **W-5242 yards, par 75.**

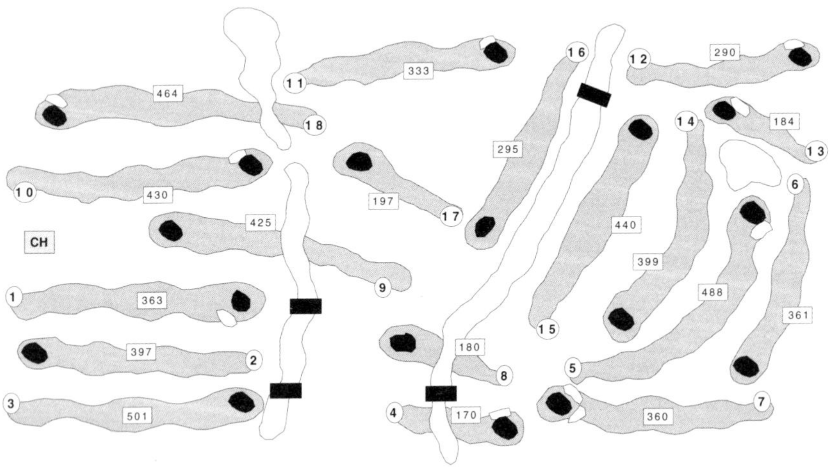

Condon Golf Course (public, 9 hole course)

North Lincoln Street; Condon, OR 97823
Phone: (541) 384-4266. Fax: none. Web: none.
Pro: none. Manager: none.
Rating/Slope: M 69.4/112; W 70.8/108. **Course record:** 70.
Green fees: $8/$6, look for rates on the current rate sheet; no credit cards.
Power cart: not available. **Pull cart:** not available. **Trail fee:** not available.
Reservation policy: prior reservations are not needed for play.
Winter condition: the golf course is always closed during the winter months.
Terrain: flat, some slight hills. **Tees:** grass. **Spikes:** metal spikes permitted.
Services: the golf course has very limited services, putting & chipping area's.
Comments: Green fees are often paid by the honor system. Golf course is very easy to walk with some rolling hills. Greens are on the small side and can be rough in spots. This rustic golf course lies on the NW edge of the city of Condon.

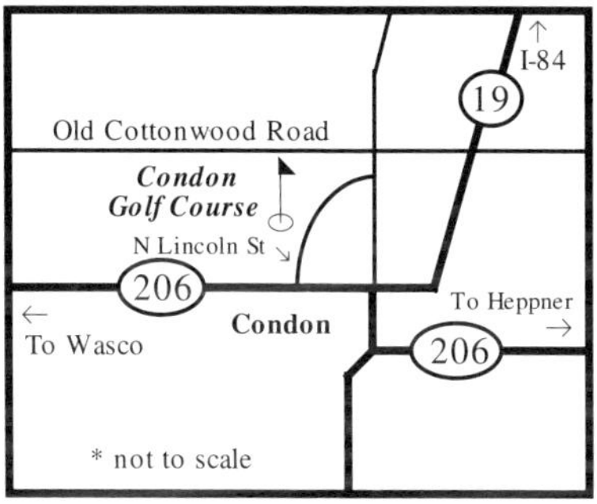

Directions: the golf course is located off of Highway 206 on North Lincoln Street in Condon. If coming from Highway 19 the golf course will be located at the north end of the city of Condon. **Note:** Be sure to look for a sign on the Highway marking the way to the golf course.

Course Yardage & Par:
M-3111 yards, par 36. **W-3111 yards, par 36.**

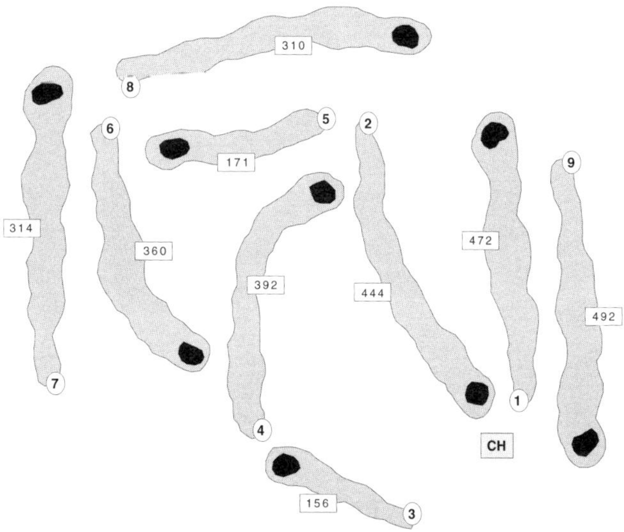

Coos Country Club (semi-private, 18 hole course)

999 Coos City-Sumner Road; Coos Bay, OR 97420
Phone: (541) 267-7257. Fax: (541) 269-0673. Web: www.scod.com/ccc
Pro: Jim Bartleson, PGA. Superintendent: Kent Kristensen.
Rating/Slope: C 70.0/137; M 67.8/128; W 65.2/117. **Course record:** 63.
Green fees: semi-private club call ahead for tee-times and prices; M/C, VISA.
Power cart: available. **Pull cart:** available. **Trail fee:** $10.
Reservation policy: please call in advance for all your tee times.
Winter condition: the golf course is open all year long with wet conditions.
Terrain: flat, some hills. **Tees:** all grass. **Spikes:** soft spikes preferred.
Services: club rentals, lessons, restaurant, beer, wine, liquor, beverages, pro shop, lockers, showers, driving range, putting green, chipping green.
Comments: The golf course is short, yet very demanding. Fairway's are narrow with water in play everywhere. Host of the Southwest Oregon Amateur every July 4th. Great course that is challenging. Don't let the lack of yardage fool you.

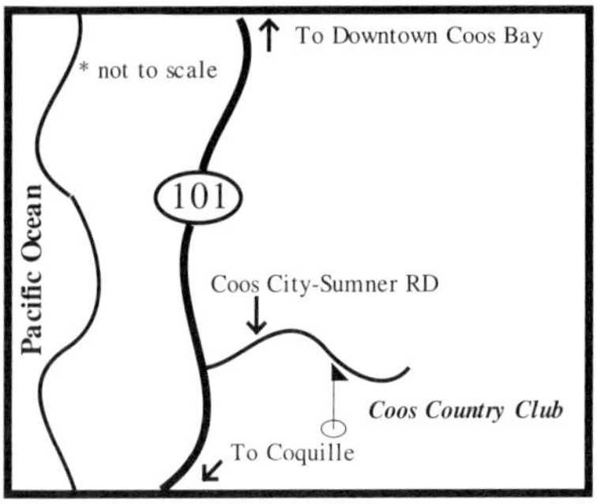

Directions: from Hwy 101 exit at Coos City-Sumner Road. Proceed on Coos City-Sumner Road for 1 mile to the golf course. The golf course is located approximately 5 miles south of the city.

Course Yardage & Par:
C-6052 yards, par 70.
M-5663 yards, par 70.
W-5180 yards, par 71.

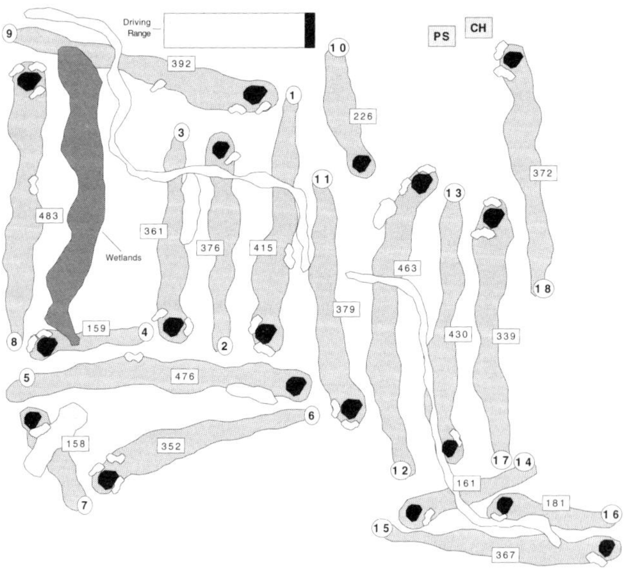

Coquille Valley Elks Golf Club (private, 9 hole course)

54942 Maple Heights Road, Coquille OR 97423
Phone: (541) 572-5367. Fax: (541) 572-7823. Web: none.
Manager: Don Mort. Superintendent: Cal napier.
Rating/Slope: C 62.8/103; M 62.4/102; W 66.4/118. **Course record:** 26.
Green fees: private club, members only; annual fees; non Elk guests $22.
Power cart: private club. **Pull cart:** private club. **Trail fee:** private club.
Reservation policy: private club, members only no public reservations.
Winter condition: the golf course is open all year long. Wet conditions.
Terrain: flat, some hills. **Tees:** grass. **Spikes:** soft spikes preferred.
Services: club rentals, restaurant, lounge, beer, pro shop, driving range.
Comments: course owned by the Coquille Valley Elks Lodge #1935. Home of the State Elks tournament over Labor Day weekend. Fairly good walking course with only one steep grade. Greens are large and flat and putt fairly well.

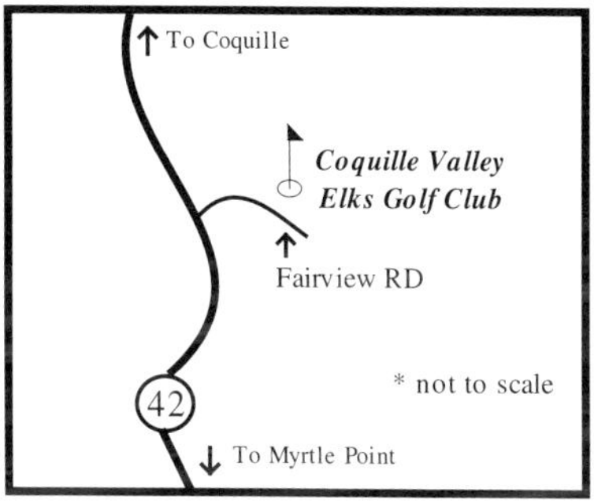

Directions: from I-5 N&S in Roseburg, Oregon take the Coos Bay/Winston exit. Proceed on Highway 42 for approximately 50 miles west to the golf course. The course is located half way between Myrtle Point and Coquille. Your turn to the golf course will be on Lee Valley Road. Look for signs indicating your way to the golf course.

Course Yardage & Par:
M-2216 yards, par 33; W-2165 yards, par 35.

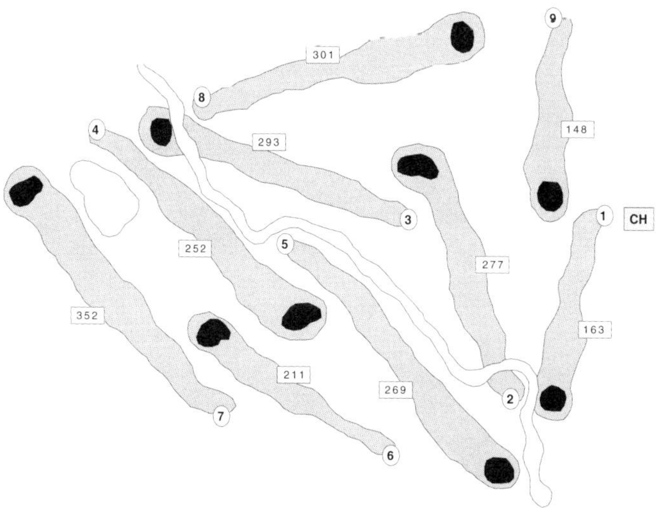

Corvallis Country Club (private, 18 hole course)

1850 SW Whiteside Drive; Corvallis, OR 97333
Phone: (541) 752-3484. Fax: (541) 752-5742. Web: none.
Pro: Mark Tunstill, PGA. Superintendent: Doug Hubert.
Rating/Slope: C 67.4/124; M 66.4/122; W 69.8/116. **Course record:** 64.
Green fees: private; reciprocates need a membership card $50.
Power cart: private club. **Pull cart:** private club. **Trail fee:** not allowed.
Reservation policy: yes, call 6 days in advance for members and guests only.
Winter condition: the golf course is open all year long, wet conditions.
Terrain: relatively hilly. **Tees:** all grass. **Spikes:** soft spikes only.
Services: club rentals, lessons, snack bar, restaurant, beer, wine, liquor, pro shop, driving range, putting/chipping greens, banquet room, club memberships.
Comments: The golf course is short, with small tricky greens. Most of the greens are well bunkered or have water nearby. You must play a position round of golf to score well as trees come into play from nearly every tee.

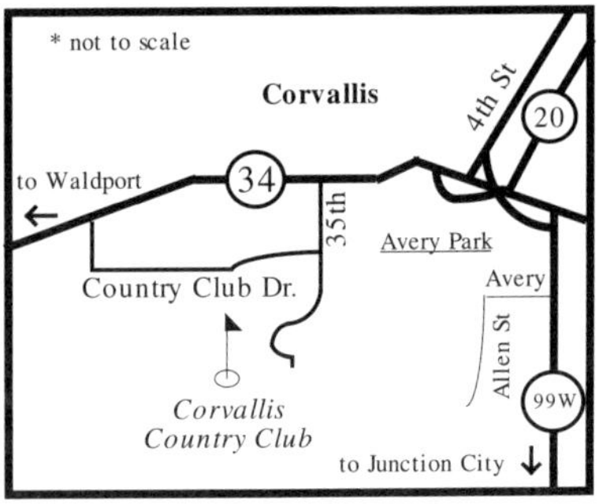

Directions: from I-5 N&S travel west on Hwy 34 to Philomath Hwy. Turn left, proceed to the 2nd light (35th St.), turn left and follow the road to the clubhouse.

Course Yardage & Par:
C-6045 yards, par 71. **M-5825 yards, par 71.** **W-5441 yards, par 74.**

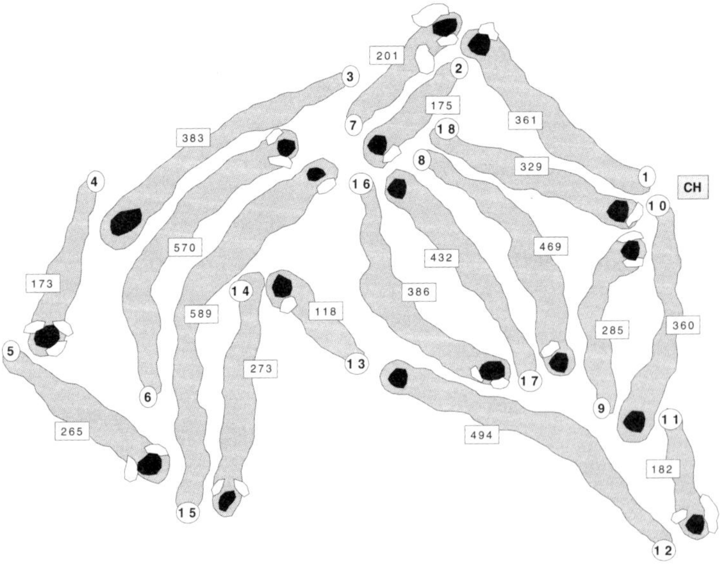

Cottonwood Lakes Golf Course & D.R. (public, 9 hole course)

3225 River Road South; Salem, OR 97302

Phone: (503) 364-3673. Fax: (503) 364-0730. Web: cottonwoodlakes.com

Pro: Scott Johnson. Superintendent: unavailable.

Rating/Slope: the golf course is not rated. **Course record:** 24.

Green fees: $14/$8.50 all week long; Jr. & Sr. rates $12/$7.50.

Green fees 18 hole putting course: $5 adults; $3 kids under 12 years old.

Power cart: none available. **Pull cart:** $2. **Trail fee:** not allowed.

Reservation policy: call up to 1 week in advance. Summer is a must.

Winter condition: the golf course is open all year long with damp conditions.

Terrain: flat (easy walking). **Tees:** all grass. **Spikes:** soft spikes only.

Services: club rentals, lessons, snack bar, pro shop, 50 tee covered range.

Comments: challenging par 3 golf course that will test almost every iron in your bag. The length of the holes vary from short to very long. Water comes in to play on three holes. Good course if you are looking for a change of pace.

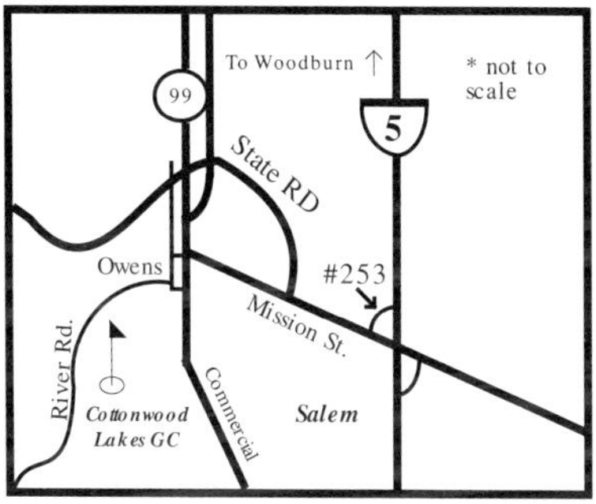

Directions: from I-5 north take Parkway exit #248 and go north on Commercial to Owens. Left on Owens to River Road. Left to the golf course. From I-5 south take exit #253 (Mission) and follow the above directions. Look for signs.

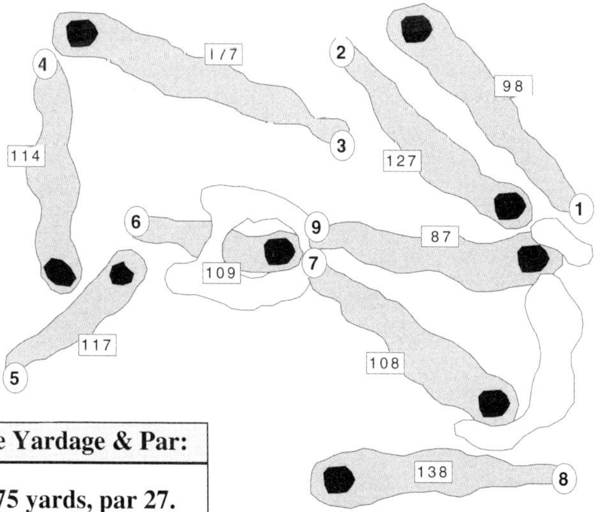

Course Yardage & Par:
M-1075 yards, par 27. **W-1075 yards, par 27.**

Country View (public, 9 hole course)

3780 Arabian Drive; Ontario, OR 97914
Phone: (541) 881-1171. Fax: (541) 881-1171. Web: none.
Manager: Scott McKinney. Superintendent: Scott McKinney.
Rating/Slope: C 66.2/103; M 64.1/96; W 66.6/110. **Course record:** 64.
Green fees: $16/$12 all week long; VISA, M/C.
Power cart: $18/$9. **Pull cart:** $2. **Trail fee:** $5 for personal carts.
Reservation policy: reservations are on a first come first served basis.
Winter condition: the golf course is closed from December to January.
Terrain: relatively hilly. **Tees:** all grass. **Spikes:** soft spikes only.
Services: club rentals, snack bar, driving range.
Comments: This 9 hole track offers great views of the surrounding countryside. The course is on the short side but do not let the yardage fool you, accuracy off the tee is crucial in scoring well. Both par 3's on this track are very challenging.

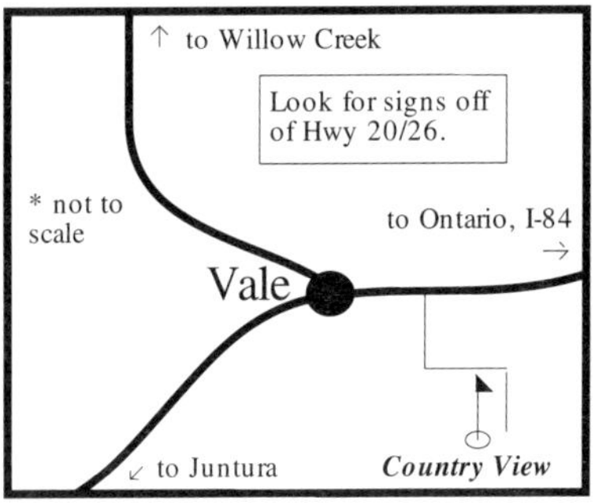

Directions: from I-84 E&W exit in Ontario, Hwy 20/26 to Vale Oregon. Proceed 6 miles heading westbound on Hwy 20/26. When you reach Butte Drive turn south. Proceed to Onion Ave. Proceed to Arabian Drive where you will turn southbound. Proceed straight up the hill to the golf course. The course is located halfway between Vale and Ontario. Look for signs from the Hwy.

Course Yardage & Par:
C-2991 yards, par 35; M-2689 yards, par 35; W-2410 yards, par 35.

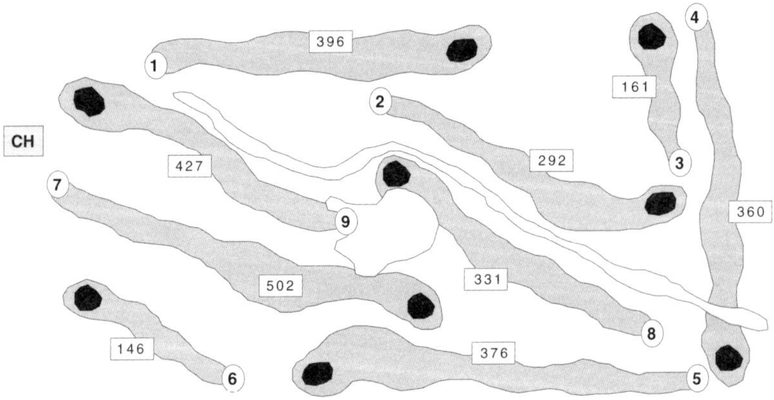

Creekside Golf Club (private, limited outside play 18 hole course)

6250 Clubhouse Drive South; Salem, OR 97306
Phone: (503) 363- 4653. Fax: (503) 581-9008. Web: none.
Pro: John McComish, PGA. Superintendent: Mark Wilson.
Rating/Slope: T 73.6/138; C 71.4/132; M 68.9/119; W 70.7/129. **Record:** 64.
Green fees: private club, outside play fees $40/$22; VISA, M/C, AMEX.
Power cart: $24/$12. **Pull cart:** $5/$3. **Trail fee:** private carts are not allowed.
Reservation policy: please call up to 5 days in advance starting at 6:30 am.
Winter condition: the golf course is open all year long. Drains well in winter.
Terrain: flat, some hills. **Tees:** all grass. **Spikes:** soft spikes preferred.
Services: club rentals, lessons, clubhouse, restaurant, pro shop, driving range.
Comments: Course designed by Peter Jacobsen and owned and operated by American Golf Corporation. Excellent layout that will challenge you at every turn. This is a very demanding golf course from tee to green. Greens are large and have swales that run through nearly every green. Shot placement from the tee and on approach shots is the key to scoring at Creekside. This newer track opened for play in 1994 and is spectacular. Great private golf course. The course offers outside play Monday thru Friday on a limited basis. Please call ahead.

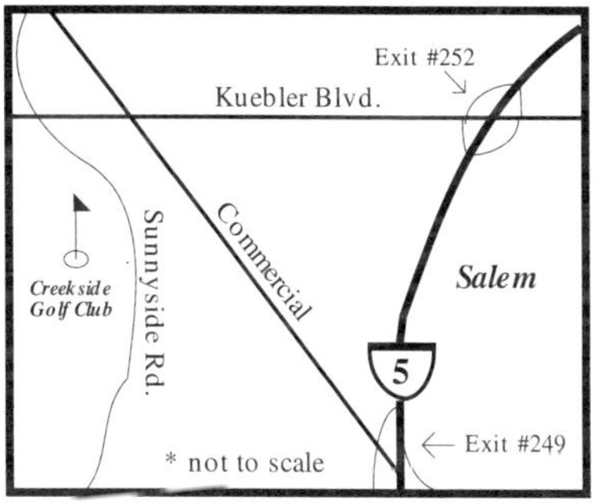

Directions: from I-5 N&S take the Kuebler exit in south Salem. Proceed westbound on Kuebler to Sunnyside Road. Turn south on Sunnyside Road for 1 mile to the golf course on the west side of the road. Look for signs.

Course Yardage & Par:

T-6887 yards, par 72.
C-6521 yards, par 72.
M-6009 yards, par 72.
W-5167 yards, par 72.

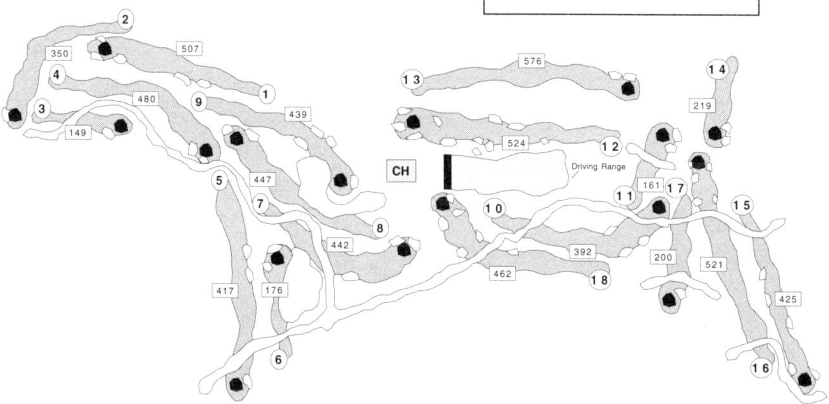

Crestview Hills Golf Course (public, 9 hole course)

1680 Crestline Drive; Waldport, OR 97394
Phone: (541) 563-3020. Fax: (541) 563-3849. Web: crestviewhillsgolf.com
Owners: Mark & Patricia Campbell. Superintendent: Ashland Glenn.
Rating/Slope: C 68.4/116; M 67.6/115; W 69.6/111. **Course record:** 32.
Green fees: $22/$14 all week long; no special rates; M/C, VISA.
Power cart: $20/$10. **Pull cart:** $2. **Trail fee:** $5 for personal carts.
Reservation policy: yes, taken 7 days in advance (suggested June to Sept.).
Winter condition: the golf course is open all year long, weather permitting.
Terrain: relatively hilly. **Tees:** all grass. **Spikes:** metal spikes permitted.
Services: club rentals, lessons, snack bar, beer, wine, pro shop, driving range.
Comments: Beautiful par 36 golf course that sits on top of a hill and is out of the coastal wind and fog. Rolling terrain will often result in some tricky lies from the fairway. Greens are on the small size and can be hard to hold in the summer. Family run course that play's much tougher than the yardage indicates.

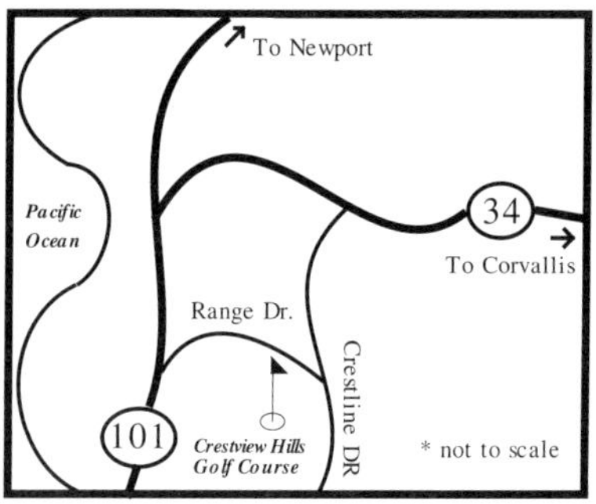

Directions: the course is located 1 mile south of Waldport Oregon. From Hwy 101 turn east on Range Drive (milepost 157) and proceed 1 mile to the course entrance on your right. Look for a sign marking your turn to the golf course. The way is well marked.

Course Yardage & Par:
C-3062 yards, par 36.
M-2881 yards, par 36.
W-2634 yards, par 36.

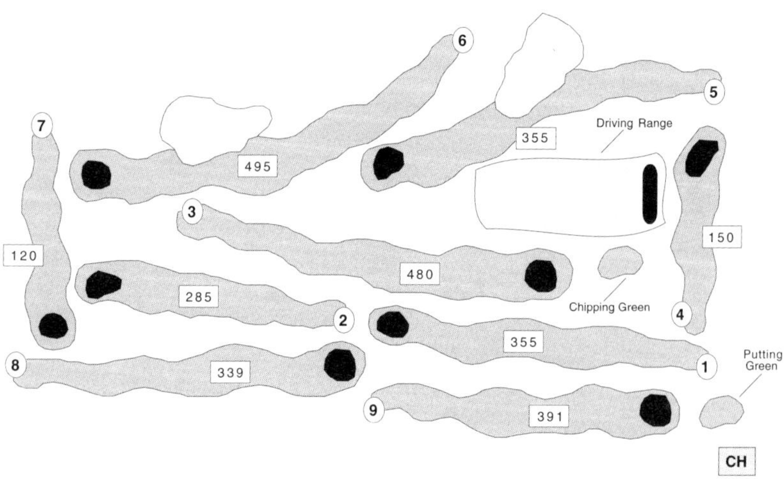

Crooked River Ranch Golf Course (semi-private, 18 hole course)

Mailing address: P.O. Box 1477; Crooked River Ranch, OR 97760
Physical address: 5195 Clubhouse Road; Crooked River Ranch, OR 97760
Phone: (541) 923-6343. Fax: (541) 548-0278.
Web-site: www.crookedriverranch.com/golf/body_golf
Pro: Scott Cravens, PGA. Superintendent: Richard Jensen.
Rating/Slope: C 65.9/105; M 64.6/103; W 67.1/117. **Course record:** 62.
Green fees: W/D $25/$15; W/E $30$17; winter, Jr. & Sr. rates; M/C, VISA.
Power cart: $25/$15. **Pull cart:** $3/$2. **Trail fee:** $7.50 for personal carts.
Reservation policy: call in advance for tee times. No waiting time.
Winter condition: the golf course is open weather permitting, dry conditions.
Terrain: flat, some hills. **Tees:** all grass. **Spikes:** soft spikes only.
Services: club rentals, lessons, snack bar, restaurant, lounge, beer, wine, liquor, pro shop, driving range, putting green. **Comments:** Golf is played here all year long when most all the other Central Oregon courses are snowed in. Scenic golf course that has many spectacular vistas from nearly every tee. Worth a trip.

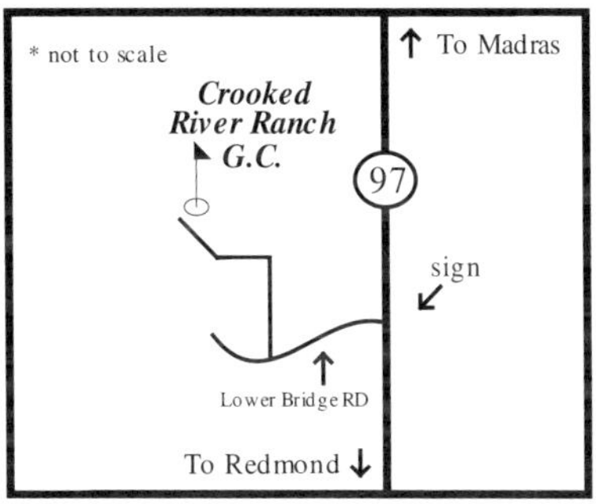

Directions: the course is located 7 miles from Highway 97. Turn off of Highway 97 at the Crooked River Ranch signs which are located on Highway 97 approximately 5 miles north of Redmond Oregon. Turn right (west) on 43rd St. and follow signs to the golf course.

Course Yardage & Par:
C-5749 yards, par 71.
M-5355 yards, par 71.
W-5000 yards, par 71.

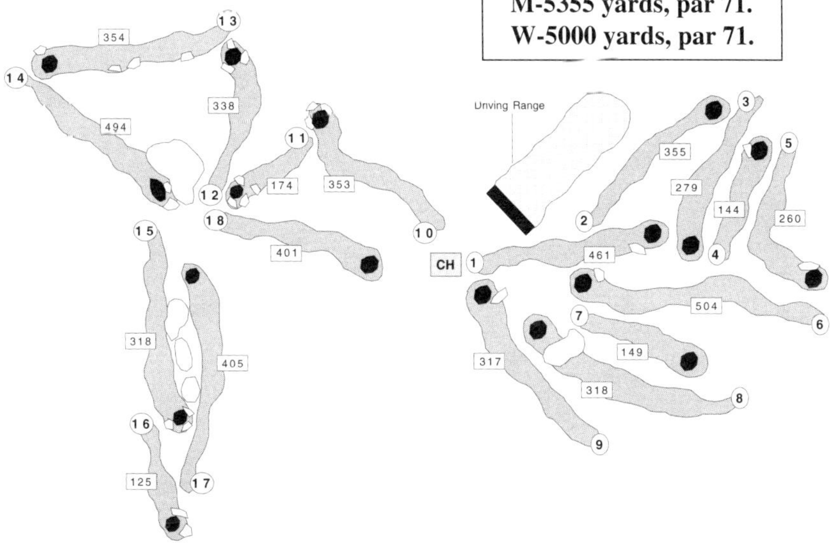

Cross Creek Golf Course (public, 9 hole course)

13935 Highway 22; Dallas, OR 97338
Phone: (503) 623-6666. Fax: none. Web: none.
Manager: Tim Tarpley. Superintendent: Jason Brewer.
Rating/Slope: C 72.6/124; M 70.0/123; M 67.2/112; W 66.6/106 **Record:** 67.
Green fees: W/D $23/$13; $28/$14; Jr. & Sr. rates; M/C, VISA.
Power cart: $22/$11. **Pull cart:** $2. **Trail fee:** $11 for personal carts.
Reservation policy: please call in advance for your tee-times. Recommended.
Winter condition: the golf course is open all year long. Drains very well.
Terrain: flat, some hills. **Tees:** all grass. **Spikes:** soft spikes only.
Services: club rentals, snack bar, beer, pro shop, driving range.
Comments: this 9 hole course is set in a beautiful setting of Oregon. The course features well drained soil, lots of mounding, plenty of creeks, lakes and sand bunkers. With the first 9 holes opening in spring of 1998 has fast become a local favorite. The 2nd 9 should be ready to go sometime in 2005.

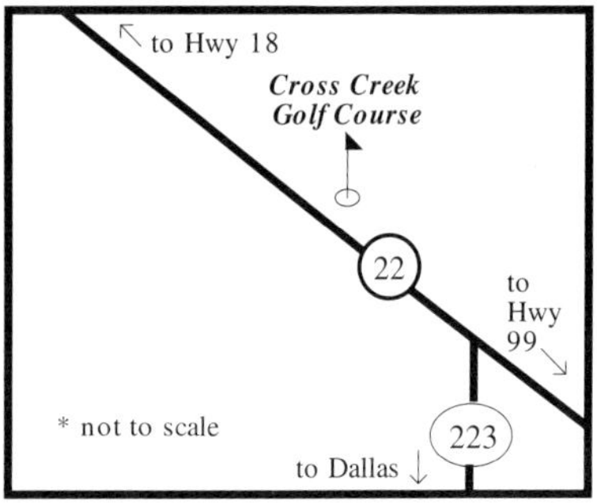

Directions: the course is located 5 miles west of Highway 99 on Highway 22.

Course Yardage & Par:
C-6818 yards, par 72.
M-6300 yards, par 72.
M-5678 yards, par 72.
W-4654 yards, par 72.
(2 times around)

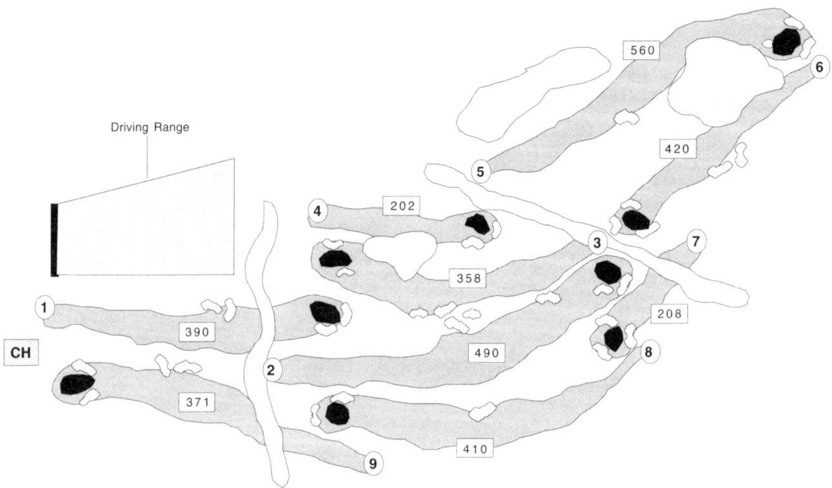

Crosswater (semi-private, 18 hole course)

Highway 97; P.O. Box 4818; Sunriver, OR 97707
Phone: (541) 593-6196. Fax: (541) 593-3449. Web: sunriver-resort.com
Pro: Dan Heater, PGA. Superintendent: Jim Ramey.

Rating/Slope: G 76.5/153; S 74.1/144; B 72.0/132; W 71.1/133. **Record:** 67.
Green fees: member only; reciprocates with Sunriver Lodge $145; M/C, VISA.
Power cart: private club. **Pull cart:** private club. **Trail fee:** not allowed.
Reservation policy: member's can call up to 10 days in advance for times.
Winter condition: the course is closed from November 1st to mid April.
Terrain: flat, some hills. **Tees:** all grass. **Spikes:** soft spikes only.
Services: the course offer's the golfer a full service clubhouse and golf facility, snack bar, club rentals, driving range, beverage service, putting/chipping greens.
Comments: this first rate facility that opened in 1995 and is nothing short of spectacular. The course is Heathland style having bentgrass throughout. If you ever get a chance to play Crosswater be sure to take it. It will not disappoint.

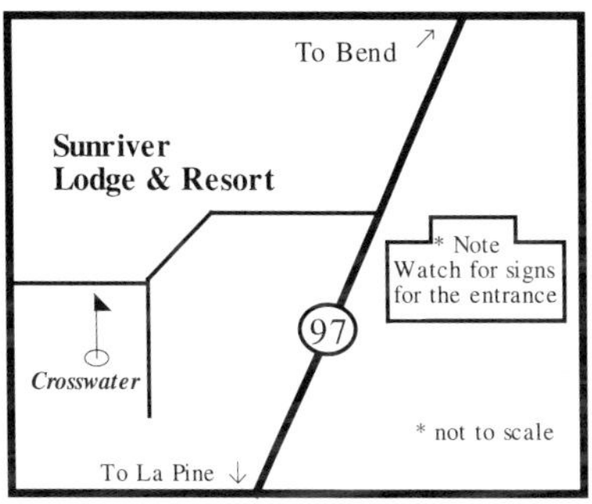

__Directions:__ the golf course is located approximately 15 miles south of Bend, Oregon off of Hwy 97 in Sunriver Oregon. The course is not located directly in the Sunriver complex but slightly south of it. You should, however, turn into the Sunriver complex to get to the course.

Course Yardage & Par:

Gold Tees: 7683 yards, par 72.
Silver Tees: 7273 yards, par 72.
Blue Tees: 6811 yards, par 72.
White Tees: 6185 yards, par 72.
Red Tees: 5359 yards, par 72.

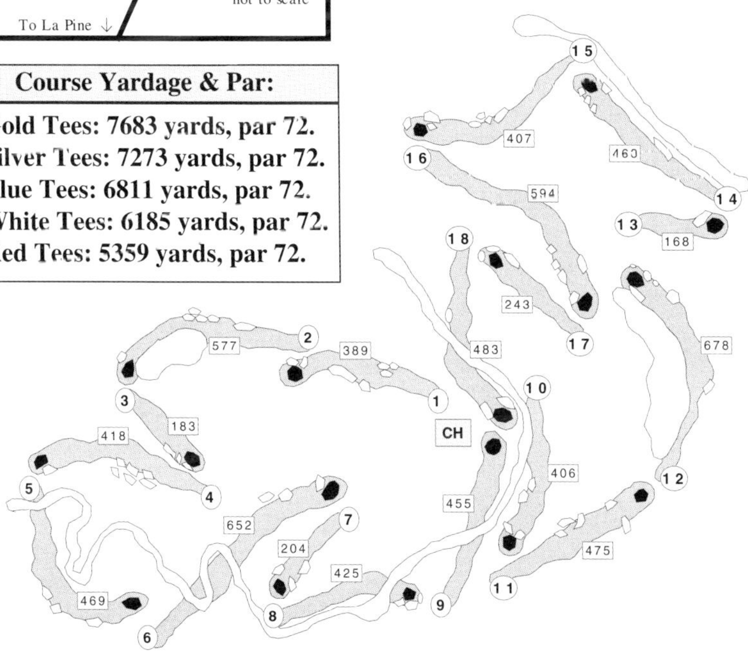

Dallas Golf Club (public, 9 hole course)

11875 Orr's Corner Road; Dallas, OR 97338
Phone: (503) 623-6832. Fax: none. Web: none.
Manager: Mike Tallon. Superintendent: Norm Thomas.
Rating/Slope: M 59.6/97; W 59.8/87. **Course record:** 55 18 holes/26 9 holes.
Green fees: $20/$11 all week long; Jr. & Sr. rates are available.
Power cart: $20/$10. **Pull cart:** $2. **Trail fee:** $14/$7 for personal carts.
Reservation policy: yes, please call ahead for your tee-times.
Winter condition: the golf course is open all year long. Dry, drains very well.
Terrain: flat, some hills. **Tees:** all grass tees. **Spikes:** soft spikes preferred.
Services: club rentals, lessons, pro shop, beverages, driving range, putting green.
Comments: Ponds and bunkers come into play on several of the holes. Excellent on course driving range to practice your game on. This course is well maintained and the greens are generally in excellent shape and putt very true. Good course to stop at if you are looking for a change of pace from the 6500+ yard track.

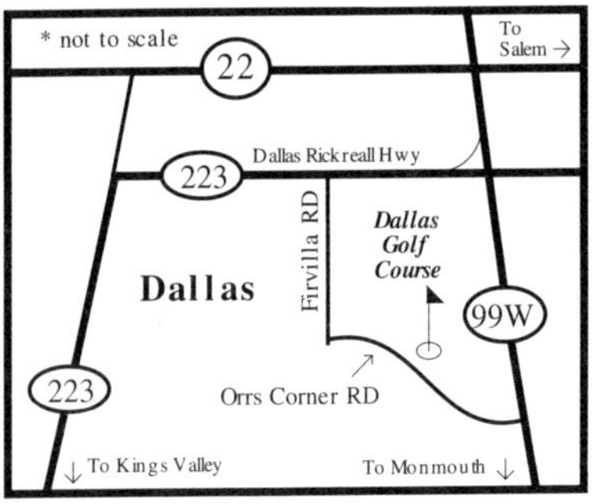

Directions: from Highway 22 exit southbound on Highway 99W for 1.7 miles to Orr's Corner Road. Turn westbound. The golf course is located 3 miles ahead on the right hand side of the road. Look for signs marking your way to the golf course. The route is well marked.

Course Yardage & Par:
M-1961 yards, par 31.   **W-1892 yards, par 31.**

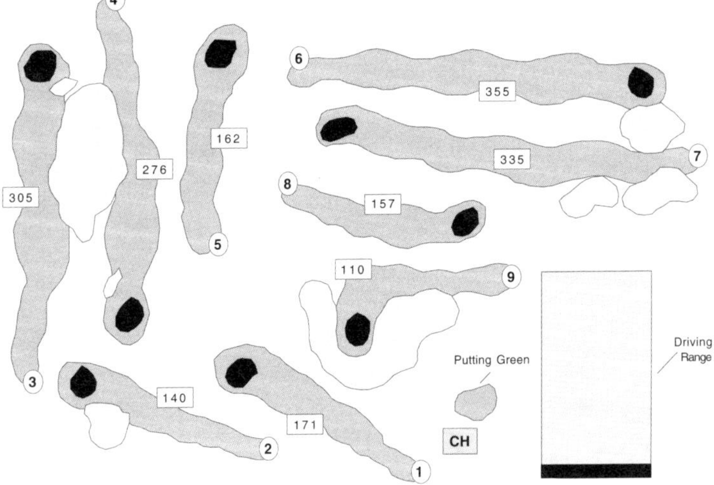

Dalles Country Club, The (private, 9 hole course)

4550 Highway 30 West; The Dalles, OR 97058

Phone: (541) 296-5252. Fax: (541) 298-5654. Web: none.

Pro: Bob Sproule, PGA. Superintendent: Ross Randolph.

Rating/Slope: M 69.8/120; W 73.9/130. **Course record:** 61.

Green fees: private club, members or guests of a members; reciprocates.

Power cart: private club. **Pull cart:** private club. **Trail fee:** not allowed.

Reservation policy: private club, members, guests and reciprocates only.

Winter condition: the golf course is open all year long weather permitting.

Terrain: flat, some hills. **Tees:** all grass. **Spikes:** soft spikes preferred.

Services: snack bar, restaurant, lounge, beer, wine, liquor, pop, pro shop, lockers, showers, putting & chipping greens, club memberships.

Comments: this course is ranked as one of the best nine hole golf courses in the state of Oregon by the National Golf Foundation. Good course that plays much longer than the yardage would indicate. Set in a great location of Oregon.

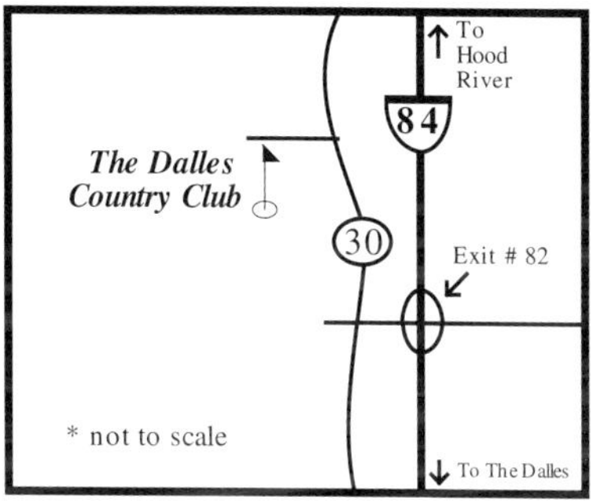

<u>**Directions:**</u> from I-84 east & west take exit #82 to Highway 30. Go westbound on Highway 30. The course is located just west of The Dalles off of Hwy 30.

Course Yardage & Par:
M-3070 yards, par 36.
W-2904 yards, par 36.
<u>**Dual tees for 18 holes:**</u>
M-6094 yards, par 71.
W-5831 yards, par 72.

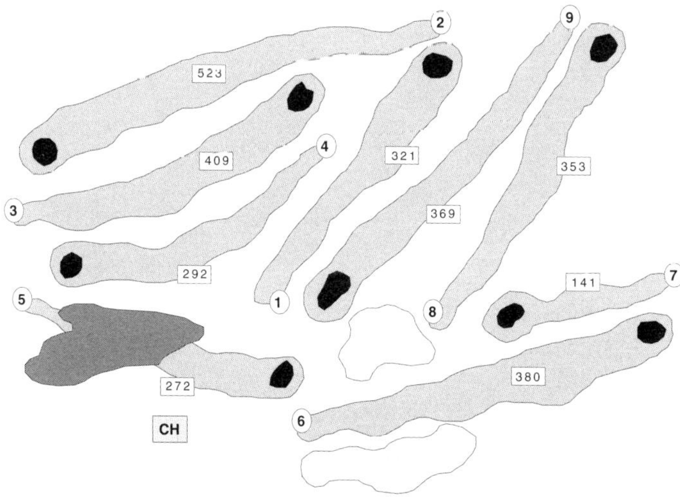

Diamond Woods Golf Course (public, 18 hole course)

96040 Territorial Road; Monroe, OR 97456 Web: diamondwoods.com
Phone: (541) 998-9707 or 800 559-GOLF. Fax:(541) 998-6824.
Managers: Jeff & Greg Doyle. Supt.: Greg Doyle. Pro: Steven Welker.
Rating/Slope: T 73.6/135; C 71.3/130; M 69.1/121; W 71.0/125.
Green fees: W/D 27/$16; W/E $35/$20; Jr. rates; play cards; M/C, VISA.
Power cart: $25/$13. **Pull cart:** $3. **Trail fee:** $10 per 9 holes.
Reservation policy: please call 7 days in advance for your tee-times.
Winter condition: the golf course is open all year long. Drains very well.
Terrain: flat, some hills. **Tees:** all grass. **Spikes:** soft spikes preferred.
Services: club rentals, snack bar, pro shop, driving range, beverage service.
Comments: The Willamette Valley's newest championship golf course promises to be a complete test of a golfer's game. The course spans over 168 acres of beautiful terrain that sports incredible views of the valley. It is a challenging array of golf holes requiring proficiency with all clubs. Worth a special trip.

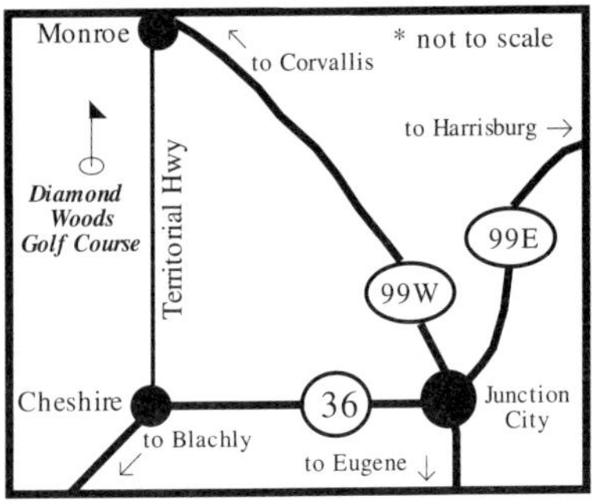

<u>Directions:</u> from *I-5S* take the Corvallis exit (Hwy 34), turn west for 10 miles. Turn south on Hwy 99, follow 99 17 miles to Monroe. At the "Y" in Monroe, go straight onto Territorial Rd. for 3 miles to the course. From *I-5N* exit at Beltline Rd. Take Beltline W to Hwy 99W. Go north on Hwy 99 for 14 miles, to the first signal in Junction City. Go left (west) 4 miles on Highpass Road to Territorial Rd. Turn north on Territorial Rd to the golf course.

Course Yardage & Par:

T-6927 yards, par 72.
C-6507 yards, par 72.
M-6081 yards, par 72.
W-5515 yards, par 72.

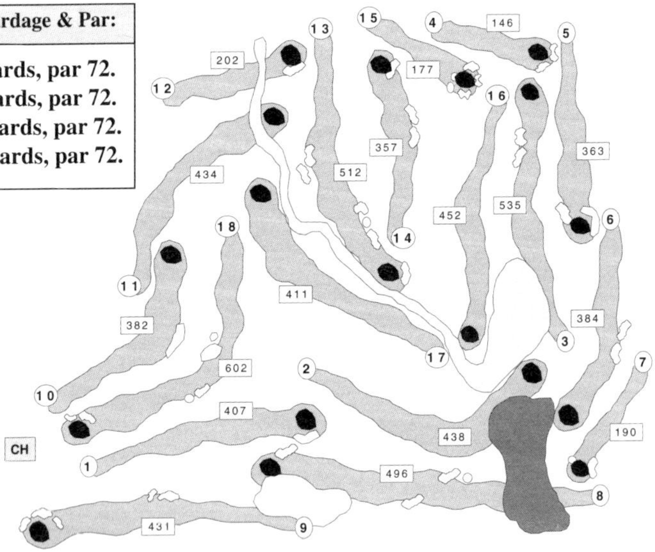

Dutcher Creek Golf Course (public, 18 hole course)

4611 Upper River Road; Grants Pass, OR 97526
Phone: (541) 474-2188. Fax: (541) 479-9609. Web: none.
Manager/Superintendent: Donovan Hauser. Course record: 30.
Rating/Slope: T 73.6/135; C 65.4/112; M 63.3/110; W 63.9/106.
Green fees: $24/$16 everyday of the week; M/C, VISA, DISCOVER.
Power cart: $22/$11. **Pull cart:** $1. **Trail fee:** $5 for personal carts.
Reservation policy: please call one week in advance for tee-times.
Winter condition: the golf course is open all year long. Good conditions.
Terrain: flat, some hills. **Tees:** all grass. **Spikes:** soft spikes preferred.
Services: club rentals, lessons, snack bar, beer, pro shop, practice green.
Comments: the golf course opened for play in July of 1994. An additional nine holes were opened in the summer of 2000. In the picturesque Rogue Valley lies Dutcher Creek Golf Course with mountain views and a year-round creek.

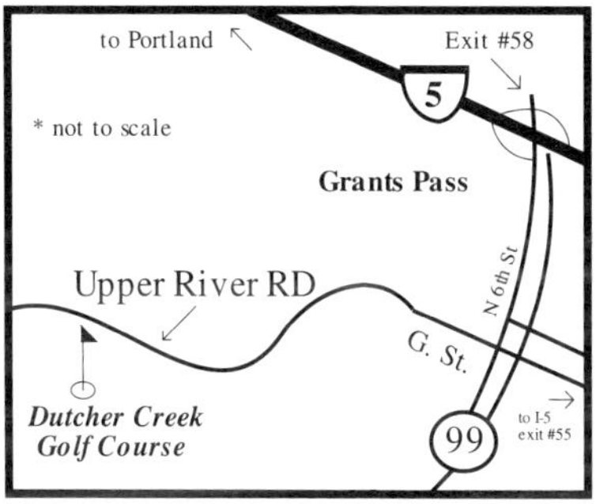

Directions: From I-5 N&S take exit #58 and travel toward downtown Grants Pass. Turn right on "G" street which turns into Upper River Road. Continue on Upper River Road to the course which will be on your left (4.1 miles from downtown Grants Pass).

Course Yardage & Par:

T-6927 yards, par 70.
C-5351 yards, par 70.
M-4980 yards, par 70.
W-4220 yards, par 70.

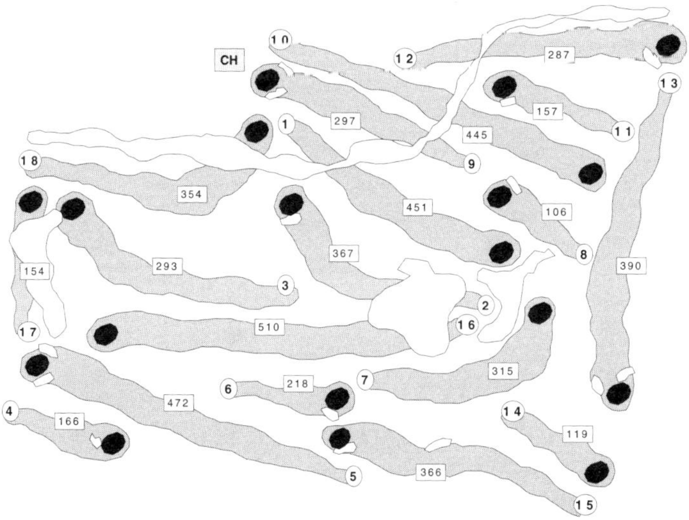

Eagle Creek Golf Course (public, 18 hole course)

25805 S.E. Dowty Road; Eagle Creek, OR 97022
Phone: (503) 630-4676. Fax: none. Web: none.
Manager: John Bastasch. Superintendent: John Bastasch.
Rating/Slope: C 70.1/125; M 66.7/110; W 67.8/121. **Course record:** 31.
Greens fee: W/D $7; W/E's & Holidays $9; no special rates; no credit cards.
Power cart: $8 for 9 holes. **Pull cart:** $3. **Trail fee:** no charge.
Reservation policy: yes, you may call anytime for advance reservations.
Winter condition: the golf course is open all year long weather permitting.
Terrain: flat (easy walking). **Tees:** all grass. **Spikes:** soft spikes preferred.
Services: construction is in progress on the clubhouse area so limited services are available at this time. **Comments:** Challenging golf course with hundreds of mature trees that line the fairways. Water comes into play on many holes and is a major factor. Greens are medium to small in size and can be hard to hold in the summer months. Fair conditioned golf course that can play tough.

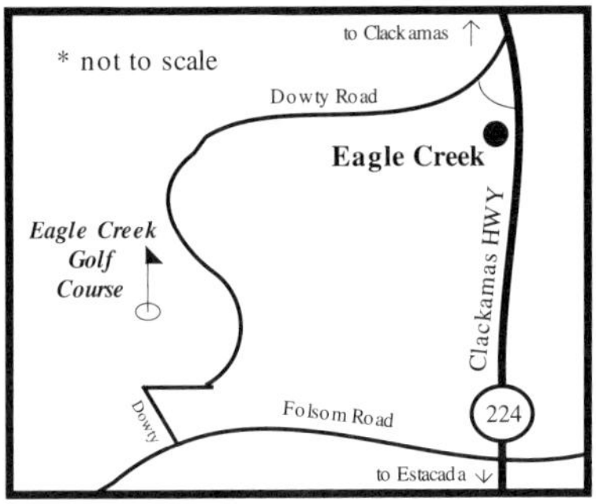

Directions: From Clackamas take Highway 224 to Eagle Creek, Oregon. Travel 1.75 miles to Folsom Road. Turn right and travel 1.1 miles to Dowty Road. Turn right. The golf course is located .6 miles ahead.

Course Yardage & Par:
C-6253 yards, par 70.
M-5590 yards, par 70.
W-4854 yards, par 70.

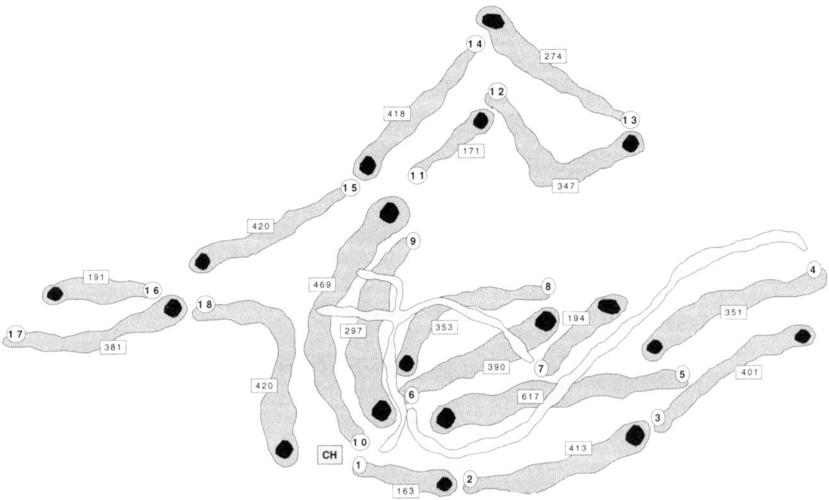

Eagle Crest Resort, Mid-Iron Course (public resort, 18 holes)

1522 Cline Falls Road; Redmond, OR 97756
Phone: (541) 923-5002. Fax: (541) 923-8822. Web: www.eagle-crest.com
Pro: Terry Anderson, PGA. Superintendent: John Thronson.
Rating/Slope: C 60.3/100; W 59.1/95; W 56.5/91. **Course record:** 55.
Green fees: $40, 18 hole loop course; M/C, VISA, AMEX, DIS.
please call 2 weeks in advance for tee-times (bankcard guarantee is required).
Power cart: $25/$16. **Pull cart:** $2/$1. **Trail fee:** personal carts not allowed.
Reservation policy: call 1 day in advance or call Thursday before weekend.
Winter condition: the course is open all year long. Rotates with Ridge course.
Terrain: flat, some hills & swails. **Tees:** all grass. **Spikes:** soft spikes required.
Services: club rentals, lessons, snack bar, restaurant, lounge, beer, wine, pro shop, driving range, putting green and chipping green, resort accomodations.
Comments: this new 4160 yard course sports a par of 63, 28 sand traps and 2 lakes. Very challenging course with a unique design. Proper ball placement off the tee is a must in order to score. Great course for the whole golfing family.

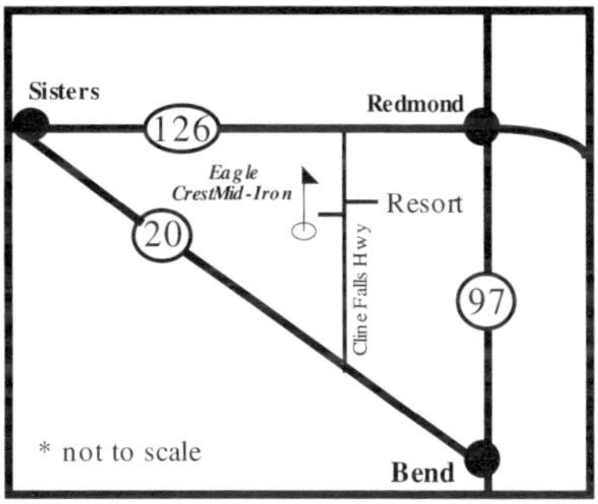

Directions: from Hwy 97 in Redmond Oregon, travel westbound on Hwy 126 towards Sisters, Oregon. Take the first left turn which will be Cline Falls Road, on the south side of the bridge crossing the Deschutes River. Travel 1/2 mile to the resort entrance. **Note:** look for signs.

Course Yardage & Par:
C-4175 yards, par 63. M-3693 yards, par 63. W-3008 yards, par 63.

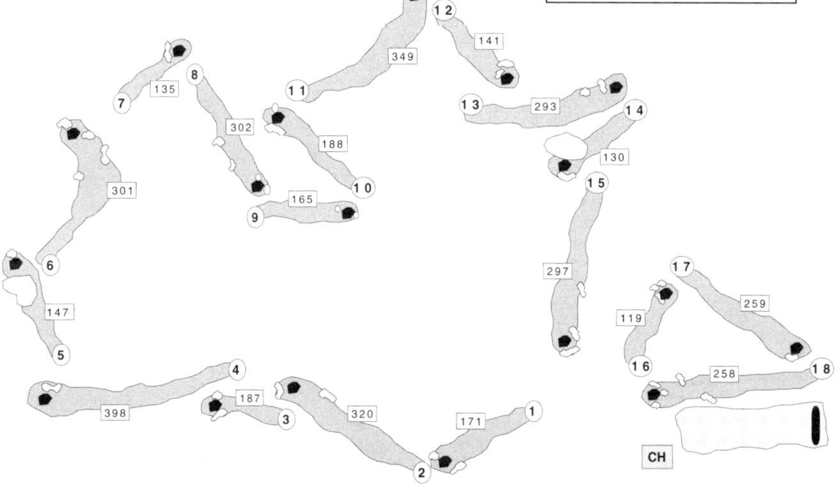

Eagle Crest Resort, Resort Course (public resort, 18 holes)

1522 Cline Falls Road; Redmond, OR 97756
Phone: (541) 923-4653. Fax: (541) 923-8822. Web: www.eagle-crest.com
Pro: Terry Anderson, PGA. Superintendent: John Thronson.
Rating/Slope: C 71.5/128; M 69.3/124; W 70.5/120. **Course record:** 65.
Green fees: $55/$36.75; winter rates are available; M/C, VISA, AMEX, DIS.
please call 2 weeks in advance for tee-times (bankcard guarantee is required).
Power cart: $25/$16. **Pull cart:** $2/$1. **Trail fee:** personal carts not allowed.
Reservation policy: call 1 day in advance or call Thursday before weekend.
Winter condition: the course is open all year long. Rotates with Ridge course.
Terrain: flat, some hills. **Tees:** all grass. **Spikes:** soft spikes required.
Services: club rentals, lessons, snack bar, restaurant, lounge, beer, wine, pro shop, driving range, putting green and chipping green, resort accomodations.
Comments: first rate facility that is kept in excellent condition. Greens are large and well bunkered. During the summer they are firm and fast. Plan to take a trip to central Oregon and play the Eagle Crest courses, they will not disappoint.

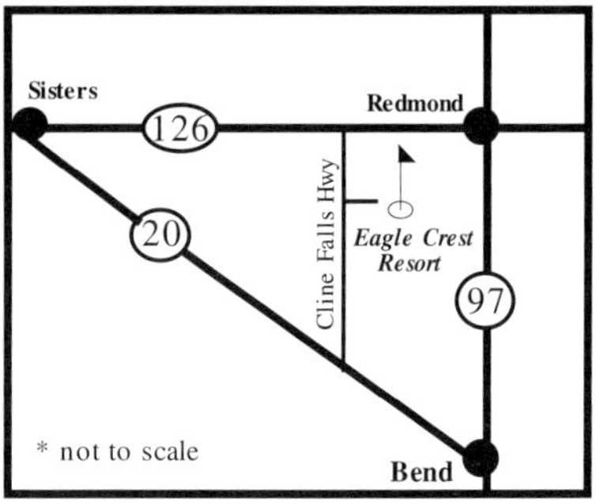

<u>**Directions:**</u> from Hwy 97 in Redmond Oregon, travel westbound on Hwy 126 towards Sisters, Oregon. Take the first left turn which will be Cline Falls Road, on the south side of the bridge crossing the Deschutes River. Travel 1/2 mile to the resort entrance. **Note:** look for signs.

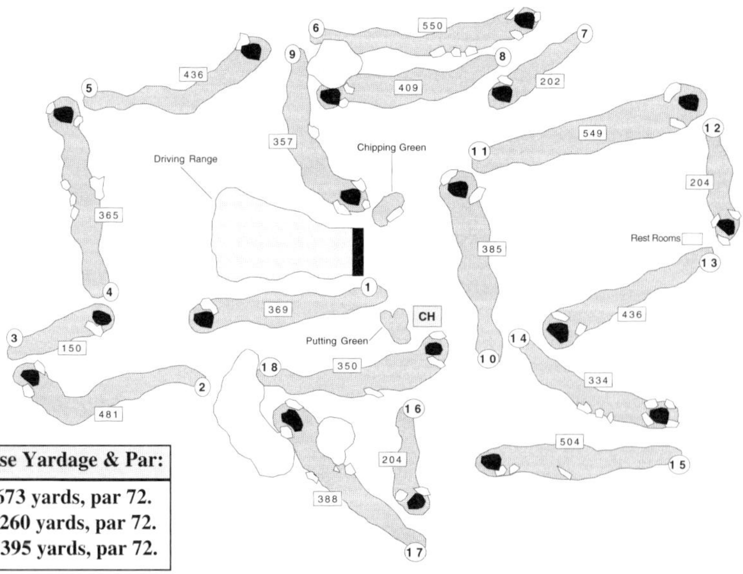

Course Yardage & Par:
C-6673 yards, par 72.
M-6260 yards, par 72.
W-5395 yards, par 72.

Eagle Crest Resort, Ridge Course (public resort, 18 holes)

1522 Cline Falls Road; Redmond, OR 97756
Phone: (541) 923-5002. Fax: (541) 923-8822. Web: www.eagle-crest.com
Pro: Terry Anderson, PGA. Superintendent: John Thronson.
Rating/Slope: T 73.0/131; C 70.7/125; M 68.6/120; W 66.1/115. **Record:** 65.
Green fees: $65/$43.50; winter rates are available; M/C, VISA, AMEX, DIS. please call 2 weeks in advance for tee-times (bankcard guarantee is required)
Power cart: $25/$16. **Pull cart:** $2/$1. **Trail fee:** personal carts not allowed.
Reservation policy: 1 day in advance or call Thursday before the weekend.
Winter condition: the course is open all year long. Rotates with Resort course.
Terrain: flat, some hills. **Tees:** all grass. **Spikes:** soft spikes preferred
Services: club rentals, lessons, snack bar, restaurant, lounge, beer, wine, pro shop, driving range, putting green and chipping green, resort accomodations.
Comments: course is cut out of old growth Juniper with gently rolling terrain. Greens are firm very fast and have some fairly dramatic slopes to them. Very challenging golf course with 69 traps and 4 lakes. New 18 hole putting course.

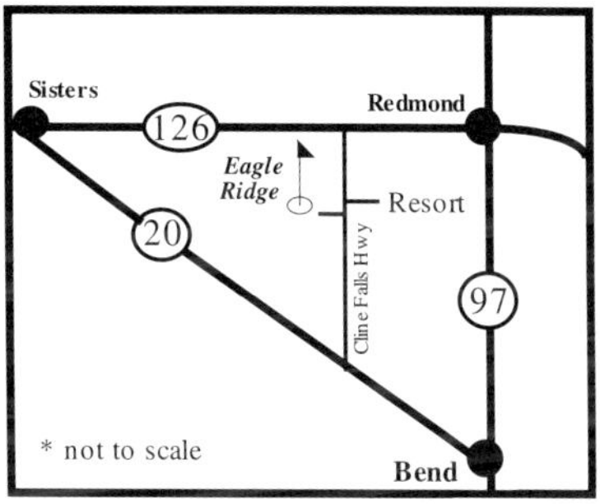

Directions: from Hwy 97 in Redmond Oregon, travel westbound on Hwy 126 towards Sisters, Oregon. Take the first left turn which will be Cline Falls Road, on the south side of the bridge crossing the Deschutes River. Travel 1/2 mile to the resort entrance. Look for signs to the golf course the way is well marked.

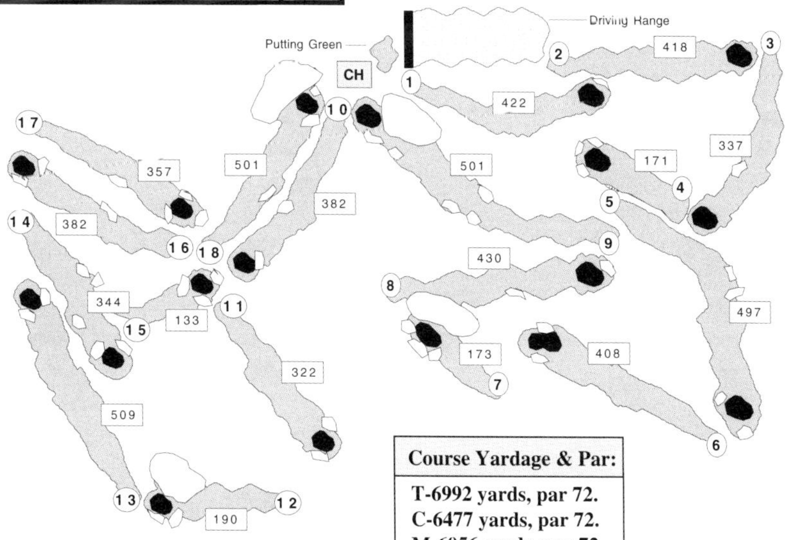

Course Yardage & Par:
T-6992 yards, par 72.
C-6477 yards, par 72.
M-6056 yards, par 72.
W-4773 yards, par 72.

Eagle Point Golf Course (public, 18 hole course)

100 Eagle Point Drive; Eagle Point, OR, 97524
Phone: (541) 826-8225. Fax: (541) 826-8170. Web: eaglepointgolf.com
Pro: Norm Homeier, PGA. Superintendent: Dave Stevens.
Rating/slope: T 74.3/135; C 71.7/128; M 69.5/118; W 69.7/119. **Record:** 66.
Green fees: High season $68; Low Season $20; M/C, VISA, AMEX.
Power cart: $10 per person. **Pull cart:** $5. **Trail fee:** yearly only.
Reservation policy: call in advance for your tee-times. Credit card required.
Winter condition: state-of-the-art drainage system allows year round play.
Terrain: gentle rolling hills. **Tees:** all grass. **Spikes:** soft spikes required.
Services: club rentals, lessons, lounge, snack bar, beer, pro shop, driving range.
Comments: ranked "3rd best new affordable public course in America for 1997" by *Golf Digest.* Designed by the renowned **Robert Trent Jones Jr.** this gem is exceptionally playable for the beginning golfer, with plenty of interest and challenge for the expert golfer. The best drainage system in Southern Oregon provides fantastic playing conditions all year long. Course is a must play for all.

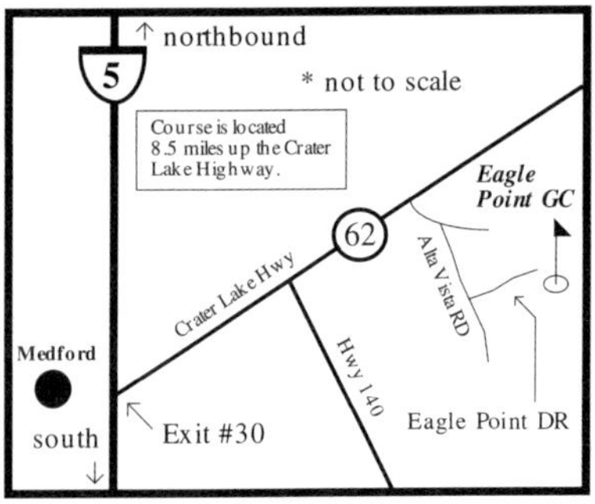

Directions: from I-5 (Medford area) take the Crater Lake Hwy 62 exit #30. Proceed 8.5 miles to Alta Vista Drive. Travel eastbound on Alta Vista for .5 miles to the course entrance which will be on your left hand side. Note: the course is located 10 minutes from the Medford International Airport. Look for signs that are posted.

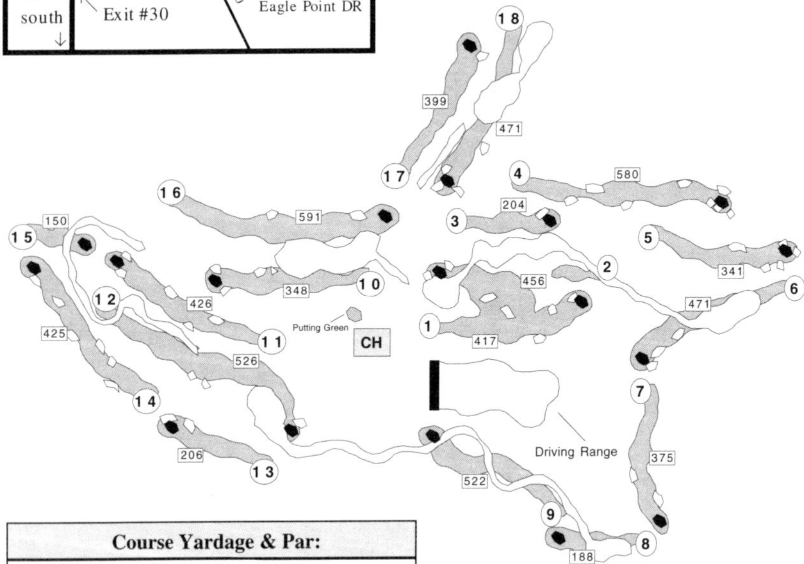

Course Yardage & Par:
T-7099 yards, par 72. C-6576 yards, par 72. M-6103 yards, par 72. W-5071 yards, par 72.

Eagles #275 Golf Course (private, 9 hole par 3 course)

1375 Irving Road; Eugene, OR 97404
Phone: (541) 688-9471. Fax: (541) 689-6371. Web: none.
Manager: The Trustees. Superintendent: none. Record: 23.
Rating/Slope: the golf course is not rated.
Green fees: private club, members and guests of members only.
Power cart: private club. **Pull cart:** private club. **Trail fee:** not allowed.
Reservation policy: private club members & guests only.
Winter condition: the golf course is open all year long, weather permitting.
Terrain: flat. **Tees:** all grass. **Spikes:** soft spikes required.
Services: full service lounge an dining, Eagle Lodge #275 on site.
Comments: this 9 hole par 3 track is owned and operated by the Fraternal Order of Eagles Lodge #275. The track itself is short in length. Do not let the lack of yardage fool you, this course can play tough. Evergreens line the fairways leaving the golfer little room off the tee. Greens are small and hard to hold.

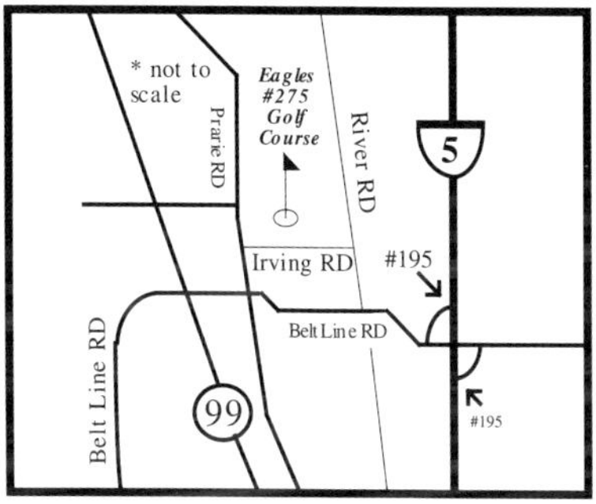

Directions: from I-5 N&S take the Beltline Road exit #195. Proceed westbound for 4.3 miles to NW Express Way where you will turn right. Proceed to Irving Road and turn right. The golf course is located on the right hand side of the street next to the Eagles Lodge.

Course Yardage & Par:
C-1295 yards, par 27.
M-1110 yards, par 27.
W-1110 yards, par 27.

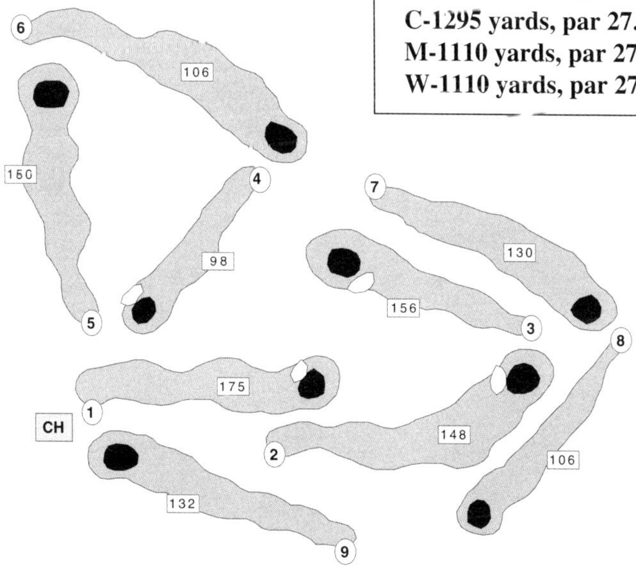

Eastmoreland Golf Course (public, 18 hole course)

2425 SE Bybee Boulevard; Portland, OR 97202
Phone: For Tee-Times: (503) 292-8570. Pro Shop: (503) 775-2900.
Fax: (503) 774-0482. Web-site: www.orgolf.org/eastmoreland
Pro: Clark Cumpston, PGA. Superintendent: Steve Hoiland.
Rating/Slope: C 72.2/127; M 69.8/120; W 72.5/119. **Course record:** 63.
Green fees: Monday-Thursday $25/$13; Friday-Sunday & Holidays $27/$14; Sr. rates $10 per 9 holes, Jr. rates $5 per 9 holes (more on the W/E); M/C, VISA.
Power cart: $26/$13. **Pull cart:** $3/$2. **Trail fee:** $4/$2 for personal carts.
Reservation policy: yes, please call 1 week in advance for tee-times.
Winter condition: the golf course is open all year long weather permitting.
Terrain: flat, some hills. **Tees:** all grass tees. **Spikes:** metal spikes permitted.
Services: club rentals, lessons, restaurant, beer, wine, pro shop, driving range.
Comments: scenic golf course rated in the top 25 public courses in *Golf Digest*. The U.S. National Amateur Public Links Championships was held here in 1990. The upgraded clubhouse and well managed pro shop are fantastic. If you are looking for a great public course try Eastmoreland G.C. it will not disappoint.

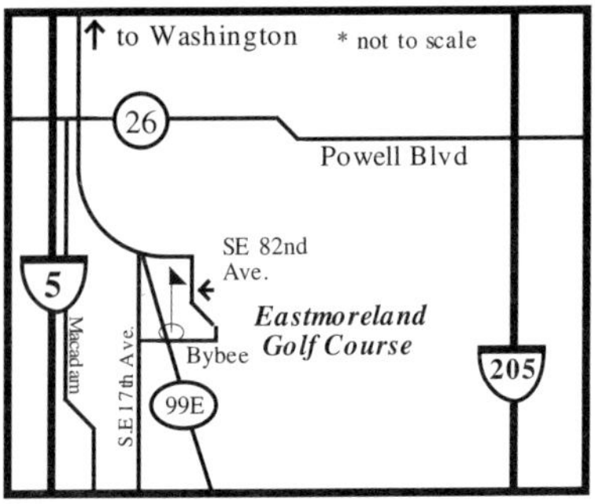

Directions: from I-5 N&S take the The Dalles/Oregon City exit. Follow signs to Oregon City onto Mcloughlin Blvd (99E) southbound. Take the Eastmoreland/Reed College exit. Turn right onto the overpass back over Mcloughlin. The clubhouse and parking lot are located left. Just across the overpass. Look for signs marking your way to the golf course.

Course Yardage & Par:

C-6655 yards, par 72; M-6106 yards, par 72; W-5646 yards, par 72.

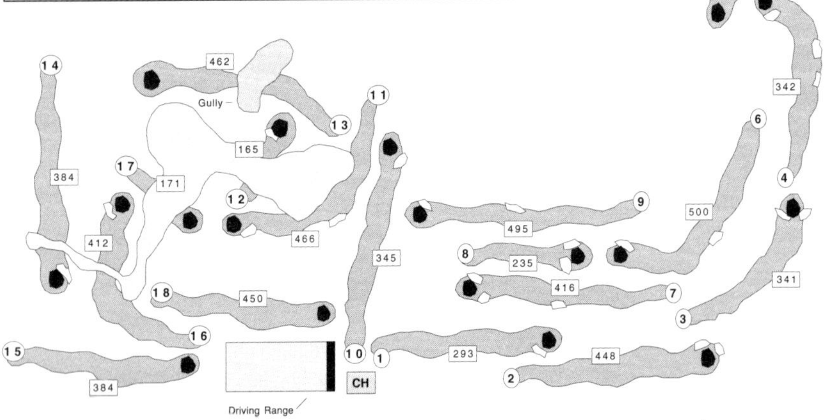

Echo Hills Golf Course (public, 9 hole course)

P.O. Box 187; 100 Golf Course Road; Echo, OR 97826
Phone: (541) 376-8244. Fax: (541) 376-8218. Web: none.
Manager: Randy Sperr. Superintendent: Randy Sperr.
Rating/Slope: M 67.4/112; W 68.7/111. **Course record:** 67.
Green fees: W/D $18/$9; W/E $22/$11; Jr. and winter rates; M/C, VISA.
Power cart: $20/$10. **Pull cart:** $3/$2. **Trail fee:** $7 for personal carts.
Reservation policy: advance reservations are required for weekend play.
Winter condition: the golf course is open all year long with dry conditions.
Terrain: very hilly. **Tees:** all grass. **Spikes:** metal spikes permitted.
Services: club rentals, snack bar, beer, wine, pro shop, beverages, driving range, putting & chipping greens. **Comments:** The course is well kept and very green during the peak golfing year. Hilly terrain makes this short course a challenge. The terrain will give the golfer a variety of different lies from the fairway.

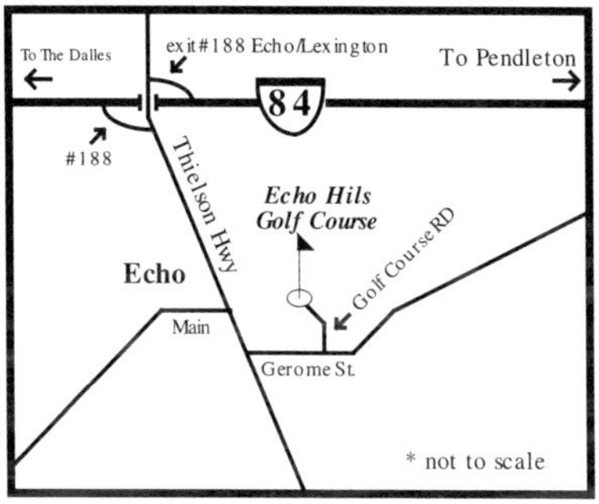

Directions: from I-84 E&W take the Echo/Lexington exit #188. Proceed for 1 mile to Gerome (Echo Schools). Golf course entrance will be ahead on your left hand side. **Note:** look for a sign marking your entrance to the course.

Course Yardage & Par:
M-2884 yards, par 36.
W-2531 yards, par 37.
Dual tees for 18 holes:
M-5867 yards, par 72.
W-5179 yards, par 74.

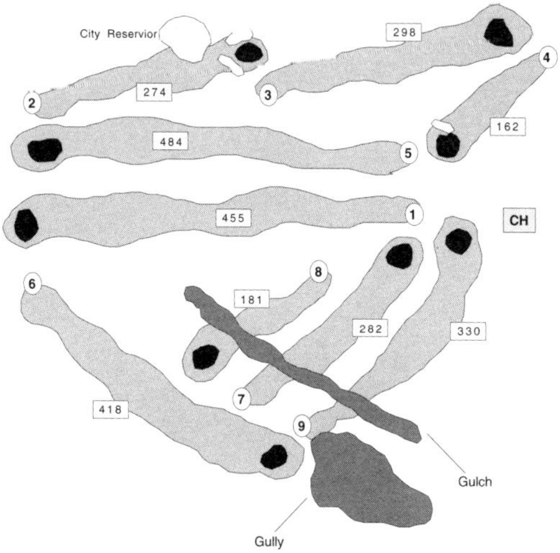

Elkhorn Valley Golf Course (public, 18 hole course)

32295 Little North Fork Road; Lyons, OR 97358
Phone: (503) 897-3368. Fax: (503) 897-4075. Web: elkhorngolf.com
Manager: Elizabeth Cutler. Superintendent: Bruce Cutler.
Rating/Slope: C 70.6/136; M 68.3/116; W 63.6/106; F 61.9/98. **Record:** 67.
Green fees: W/D $35/$20 after 2:00pm $25/$15; W/E $40/$22 after 2:00pm $30/$17; no other special rates; M/C, VISA, DISCOVER, AMEX.
Power cart: $22/$12. **Pull cart:** $3. **Trail fee:** no charge for personal carts.
Reservation policy: yes, please call anytime in advance for tee times.
Winter condition: the course is closed from November 1st to February 28th.
Terrain: flat (easy walking). **Tees:** all grass. **Spikes:** soft spikes preferred.
Services: club rentals, snack bar, beer, pro shop, putting & chipping greens.
Comments: rated by Sports Illistrated & Golf Digest as one of the top 10 nine hole courses in the nation, Elkhorn Valley is a must see and play. Situated in the mountains, Elkhorn is beautiful as well as challenging. After 23 years Elkhorn Valley opened the new back nine in June of 2000. Worth a special trip.

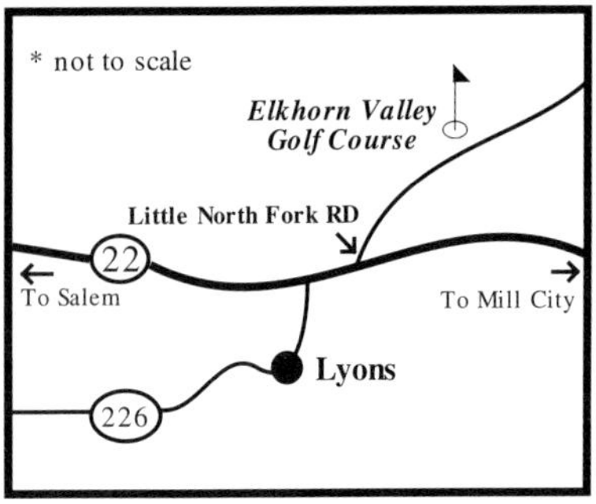

Directions: from Salem, take Hwy 22 east for 25 miles. Turn left at Swiss Village Restaurant /Little North Fork Road. Proceed for 11 miles to the golf course on your left.

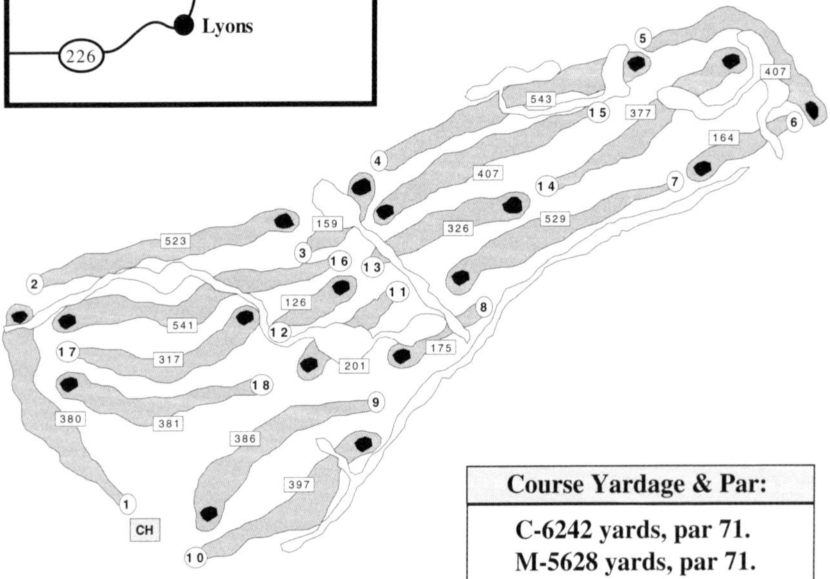

Course Yardage & Par:
C-6242 yards, par 71.
M-5628 yards, par 71.
W-4759 yards, par 71.
F-3774 yards, par 71.

Emerald Valley Golf Club (public, 18 hole course)

83301 Dale Kuni Road; Creswell, OR 97426
Phone: (541) 895-2174. Fax: (541) 895-2812. Web: none
Pro: Todd O'Neal, PGA. Superintendent: Scott Larsen.

Rating/Slope: C 73.0/126; M 70.8/122; W 74.7/129. **Course record:** 64.
Green fees: W/D $28/$18; W/E $32/$20; winter rates W/D $25/$16; W/E $30/$18; Jr. & Sr. rates; twlight rates after 2:00pm; M/C, VISA, AMEX.
Power cart: $25/$12.50. **Pull cart:** $3/$2. **Trail fee:** not allowed.
Reservation policy: yes, please call up to 1 week in advance for tee times.
Winter condition: the golf course is open all year long. Dry conditions.
Terrain: flat. **Tees:** all grass. **Spikes:** no metal spikes in summer.
Services: club rentals, lessons, snack bar, restaurant, lounge, beer, wine, liquor, beverages, pro shop, showers, driving range, putting and chipping greens.
Comments: Beautiful championship course which is in great condition all year round. Excellent greens that are well bunkered and fast during the peak golfing season. Fairways are large and have wide landing area's. Excellent course.

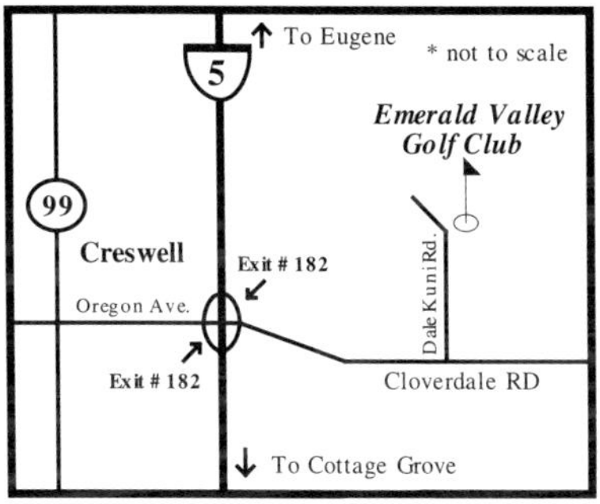

Directions: from I-5 N&S take the Creswell exit #182 and go east for .75 miles to Dale Kuni Road Turn north (left) on Dale Kuni Road and proceed for .5 miles to the golf course. Look for a sign on I-5 marking your exit.

Course Yardage & Par:

C-6873 yards, par 72.
M-6388 yards, par 72.
W-5803 yards, par 73.

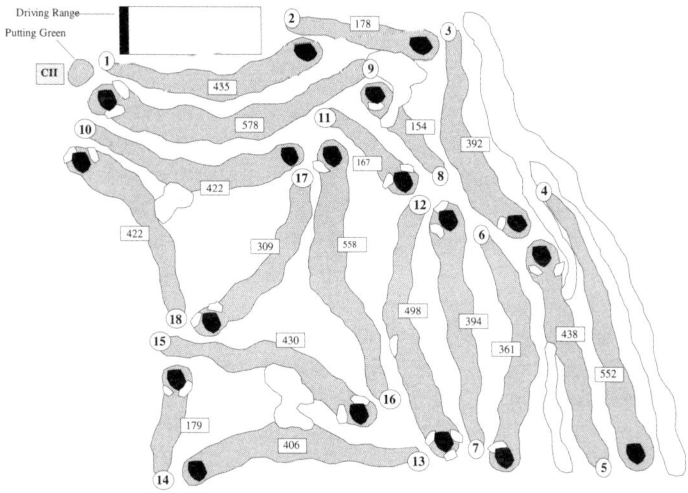

Eola Hills Golf Course (public, 18 hole course)

6335 Highway 22; Independence, OR 97351

Phone: (503) 378-0344. Fax: (503) 585-7944. Web: eolahillsgolf.com

Pro: Jason Brill, PGA. Superintendent: Pat Cook.

Rating/Slope: C 69.2/114; M 67.3/113; W 68.5/112. **Course record:** 63.
Green fees: $34/$20 all week long; Sr. rates $29/$15; VISA, M/C.
Power cart: $24/$14. **Pull cart:** $3. **Trail fee:** $10/$5 for personal carts.
Reservation policy: yes, please call in advance for your tee-times (a must).
Winter condition: the golf course is open all year long, damp conditions.
Terrain: flat (easy walking). **Tees:** grass. **Spikes:** soft spikes preferred.
Services: club rentals, lessons, restaurant, lounge, beer, wine, liquor, pro shop, putting green, driving range. **Comments:** one of the area's most popular golf courses. You will always find the greens and golf course in great condition. Excellent public course that can get very busy during the summer months.

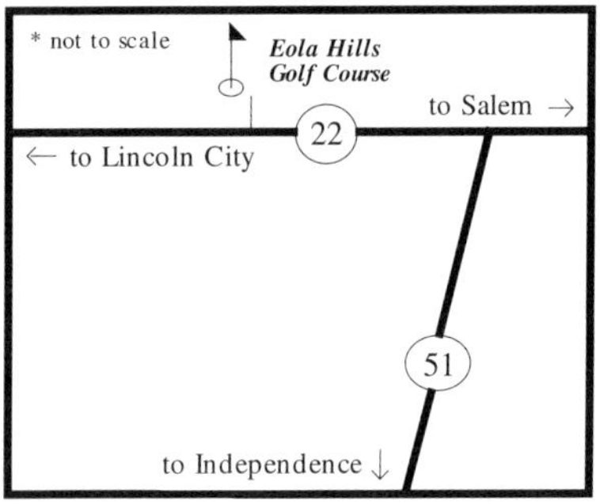

Directions: the golf course is located 6.1 miles west of Salem on the north side of Highway 22. Take exit #253 off of I-5 to Highway 22 in Salem, Oregon. Look for signs to Dallas, Ocean Beaches this will help direct you to the course which is right off Hwy 22.

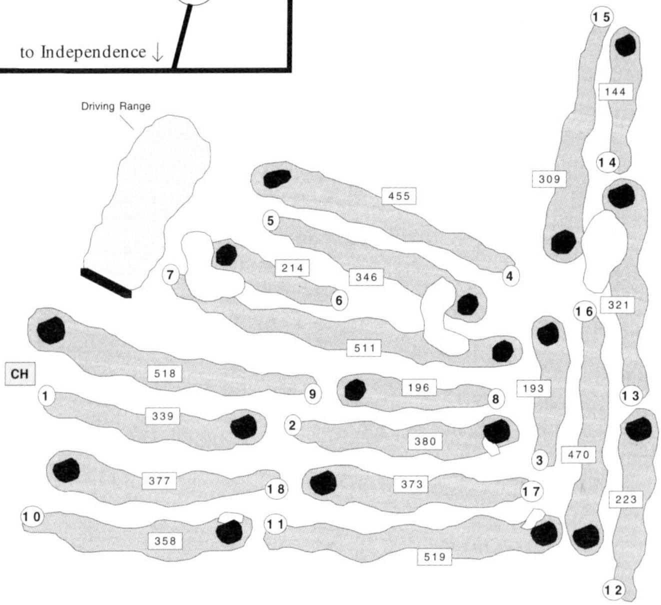

Course Yardage & Par:
C-6272 yards, par 72. M-5909 yards, par 72. W-5112 yards, par 72.

Eugene Country Club (private, 18 hole course)

255 Country Club Road; Eugene, OR 97401
Phone: (541) 344-5124. Fax: (541) 345-5365. Web: www.eugenecc.com
Pro: Ron Weber, PGA. Superintendent: Chris Gaughn.
Rating/Slope: T 73.7/139; C 71.5/134; M 68.9/126; W 72.6/129. **Record:** 66.
Green fees: private club, members & guests only; reciprocates; no credit cards.
Power cart: private club, members & guests of members only.
Pull cart: private club, complimentary. **Trail fee:** not allowed.
Reservation policy: private club members and guests of members only.
Winter condition: the golf course is open all year long weather permitting.
Terrain: relatively hilly. **Tees:** all grass. **Spikes:** no metal spikes permitted.
Services: full service private country club, driving range, putting green.
Comments: Eugene Country Club is one of the finest, best kept private golf facilities in the state of Oregon. Fairways are tree-lined and narrow in spots. Eugene is consistently voted in the top 100 golf courses in America.

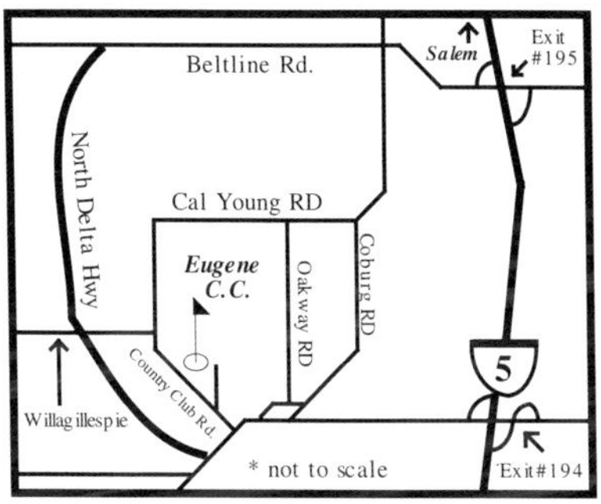

<u>**Directions:**</u> from I-5 N&S take exit #195 and head west on Beltline Road. From Beltline Road take the North Delta Hwy exit and go southbound. Proceed to Willagillespie and go east to Country Club Road and the golf course.

Course Yardage & Par:

T-6837 yards, par 72.
C-6421 yards, par 72.
M-5831 yards, par 72.
W-5587 yards, par 72.

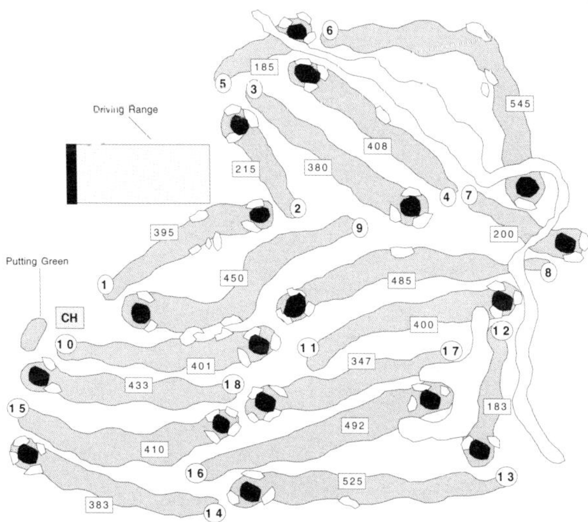

Evergreen Golf Club (public, 9 hole course)

11694 West Church Road NE; Mount Angel, OR 97362
Phone: (503) 845-9911. Fax: (503) 873-3598. Web: none.
Owners: Joe Druley & Maryann Mills. Superintendent: Joe Druley.
Rating/Slope: M 67.9/114; W 68.8/112. **Course record:** 66.
Green fees: W/D $23/$14; W/E $25/$15; M/C, VISA,
Monday thru Friday before 2:30pm, $99 for 10 rounds of 9 hole golf.
Power cart: $22/$11. **Pull cart:** $2/$1. **Trail fee:** $3 all day rate.
Reservation policy: yes, please call ahead for your weekend tee-times.
Winter condition: the golf course is open all year long, weather permitting.
Terrain: rolling hills. **Tees:** all grass. **Spikes:** soft spikes preferred.
Services: club rentals, lessons, restaurant, beer, wine, liquor, pro shop.
Comments: The golf course is very easy to walk with flat terrain on most of the holes. Water is a factor on two different holes. Greens are medium in size with few hazards. Beautiful views of Mt. Hood can be seen from several holes on the course. If you are looking for a course with a friendly feel try Evergreen.

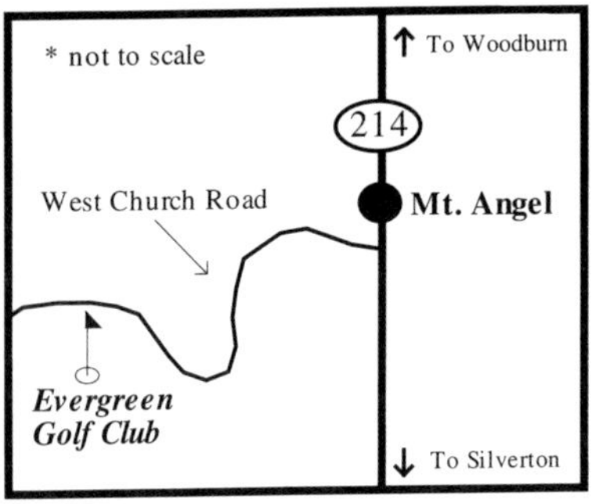

__Directions:__ from Hwy 214 go west on West Church Road. Follow West Church Road for 1.1 miles to the golf course entrance on your left.
Note: Look for the golf course sign on Hwy 214 that will indicate your turn.

Course Yardage & Par:
M-3021 yards, par 36. **W-2804 yards, par 37.**

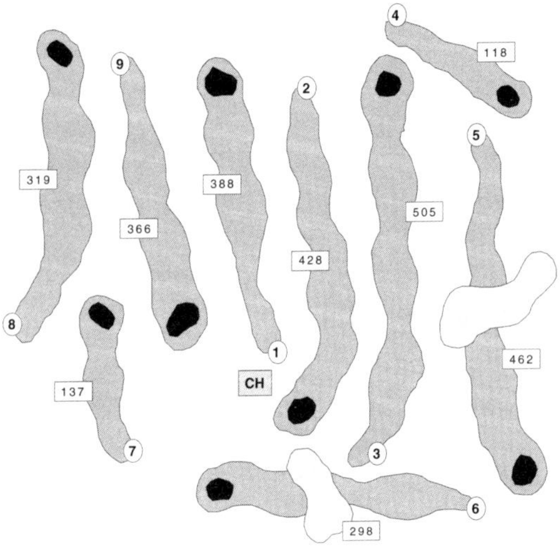

Fiddler's Green Golf Course & Driving Range (public, 18 holes)

91292 Highway 99 North; Eugene, OR 97402
Phones: (541) 689-8464 or call 1-800-548-5500. Fax: (541) 689-8387
Web-site: www.fiddlersgreen.com.
Owners: Alan, Tim, Matt Whalen. Superintendent: Kim R. Wenger.
Rating/Slope: no golf course ratings. **Course record:** 22, 9 holes/44, 18 holes.
Green fees: $12/$7 all week long; Jr. and Sr. rates; M/C, VISA, DIS.
Power cart: not available. **Pull cart:** $1.50. **Trail fee:** not allowed.
Reservation policy: no reservations are needed for advance tee-times.
Winter condition: the golf course is open. Wet from November to March.
Terrain: flat (easy walking). **Tees:** all grass. **Spikes:** metal spikes permitted.
Services: club rentals, lessons, snack bar, beer, wine, huge pro shop, lighted & covered driving range. **Comments:** facility has one of the largest on-course pro shops in the United States. Be sure to browse and shop after golf. Excellent facility to practice your entire game. Great course for beginners and families.

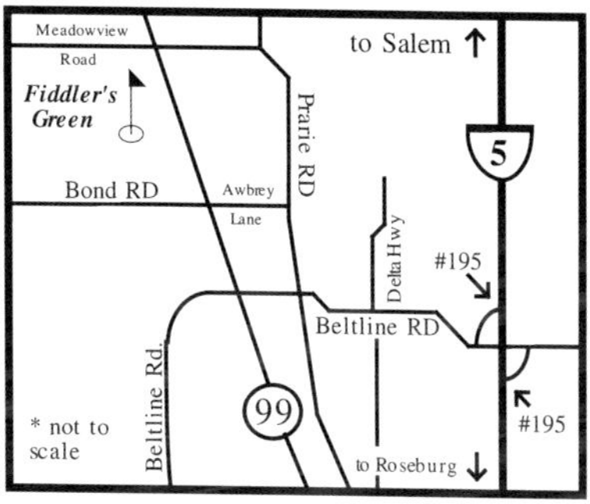

<u>**Directions:**</u> from I-5 take the Airport exit #195 (Beltline Rd.) to Hwy 99. You will travel on Beltline for approximately 5 miles. Go north on Hwy 99 as if going to the airport. Continue on Hwy 99 past the airport to the golf course on your left. If you are north of Eugene on I-5 you can also take the Halsey exit #216. Turn west to Halsey and proceed to the flashing stop light. Turn south on Hwy 99 through Halsey, Harrisburg and Junction City. Fiddlers Green is located 4 miles south of Junction City on the west side of the Hwy. Look for signs at your turn.

Course Yardage & Par:
M-2378 yards, par 54.
W-2378 yards, par 54.

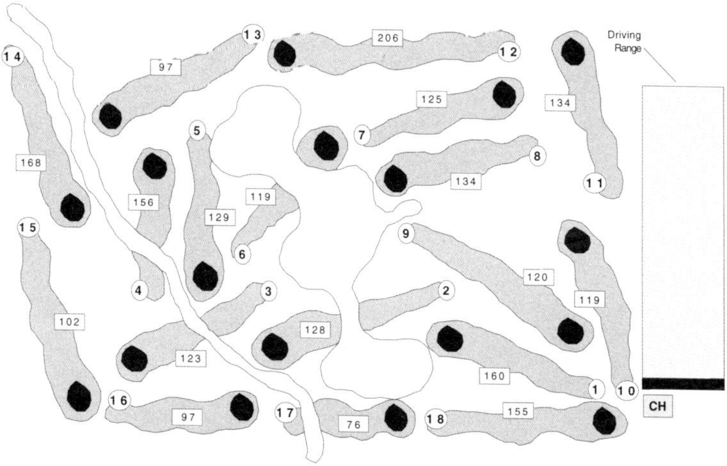

Forest Hills Country Club (semi-private, 9 hole course)

#1 Country Club Drive; Reedsport, OR 97467
Phone: (541) 271-2626. Fax: (541) 271-2626. Web: none.
Pro: Kevin Wheeler, PGA. Superintendent: Rick Miska.
Rating/Slope: M 69.1/123; W 70.6/122. **Course record:** 29 (9 holes).
Green fees: $25/$14 all week long; call for winter rates; M/C, VISA.
Power cart: $22/$12. **Pull cart:** $2. **Trail fee:** $10 for personal carts.
Reservation policy: yes, encouraged during summer months and on weekends.
Winter condition: the golf course is open all year long, with damp conditions.
Terrain: flat, some hills. **Tees:** all grass. **Spikes:** metal or soft spikes OK.
Services: club rentals, lessons, restaurant, lounge, beer, wine, liquor, pro shop, driving range, putting/chipping green. **Comments:** Relatively flat course that is easy to walk. Greens are large, undulating, and can be extremely tough to putt. Well taken care of facility that plays much longer than the yardage indicates.

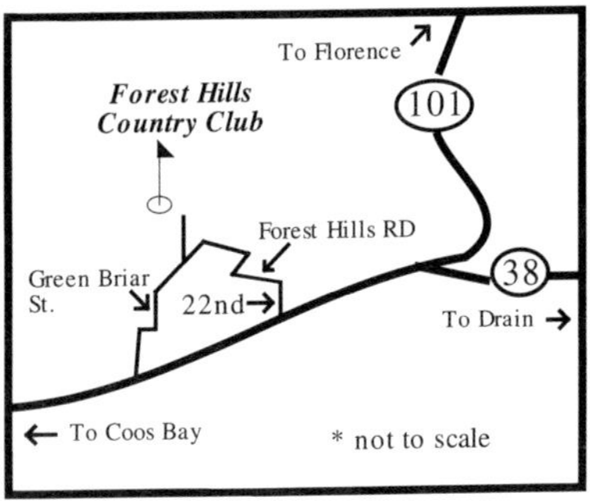

Directions: from Highway 101 turn westbound on 22nd Street. Turn right on Greenbriar. Turn right on Country Club Drive and proceed to the golf course. **Note:** Look for signs to the golf course marking your way.

Course Yardage & Par:

M-3108 yards, par 36.
W-2774 yards, par 37.
Dual tees for 18 holes:
M-6322 yards, par 72.
W-5548 yards, par 74.

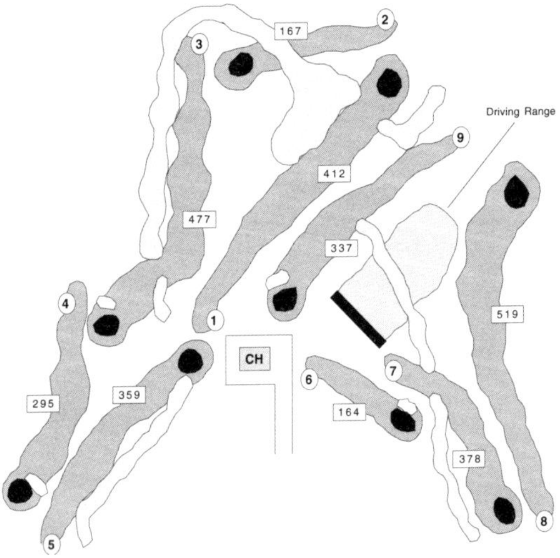

Forest Hills Golf Course (semi-private, 18 hole course)

36260 SW Tongue Lane; Cornelius, OR 97113
Phone: (503) 357-3347. Fax: (503) 359-0209. Web: golfforesthills.com
Pro: Andy Reehl, PGA. Manager: Dick Speros.
Rating/Slope: M 69.7/126; W 72.1/123. **Course record:** 64.
Green fees: W/D $34/$17; W/E $36/$18; Winter rates; M/C, VISA, AMEX.
Power cart: $24/$12. **Pull cart:** $2/$1. **Trail fee:** $10/$5.
Reservation policy: call 1 week in advance for tee times. A must in summer.
Winter condition: the golf course is open all year long. Damp conditions.
Terrain: flat, some hills. **Tees:** all grass. **Spikes:** soft spikes required.
Services: club rentals, lessons, snack bar, lounge, beer, wine, liquor, beverages, pro shop, driving range, putting & chipping greens. **Comments:** One of the most scenic courses in the state of Oregon. Greens are large and well bunkered. Fairways are wide with generous landing area's. Great public course.

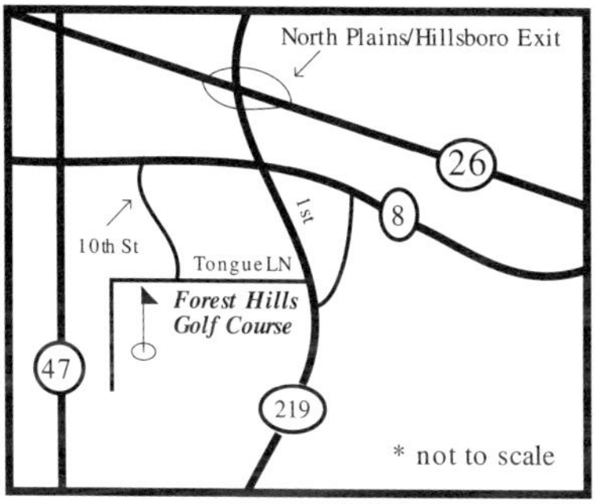

Directions: take Hwy 26 west to the Hillsboro-North Plains #57 exit. Go Back across the freeway and follow the road into Hillsboro. Proceed through Hillsboro until you are 3 miles south having made no turns. Turn right on Tongue Lane. Proceed to the golf course.

Course Yardage & Par:
M-6173 yards, par 72. **W-5673 yards, par 74.**

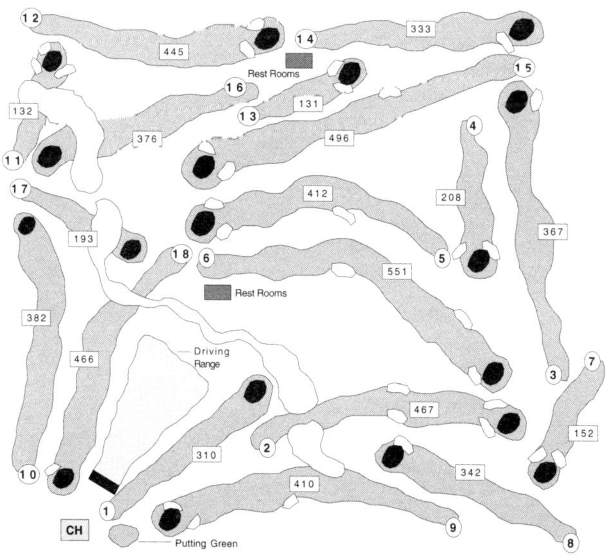

Frontier Golf Course (public, 9 hole par 3 course)

2965 North Holly Street; Canby, OR 97013
Phone: (503) 266-4435. Fax: (503) 266-4435. Web: none.
Owner: Joe Sisul. Superintendent: none.
Rating/Slope: the golf course is not rated. **Course record:** 24.
Green fees: $12/$7 all week long; Sr. rates.
Power cart: $6. **Pull cart:** $2. **Trail fee:** personal carts not allowed.
Reservation policy: advance reservations are not required for tee-times.
Winter condition: the golf course is closed from November to March.
Terrain: flat (easy walking). **Tees:** mats. **Spikes:** metal spikes permitted.
Services: club rentals, small pro shop, snacks, beverages, putting green.
Comments: economical course. Holes range in length from a 90 yard sand wedge to a 168 yard challenging par 3. Good track to bring the first time golfer.

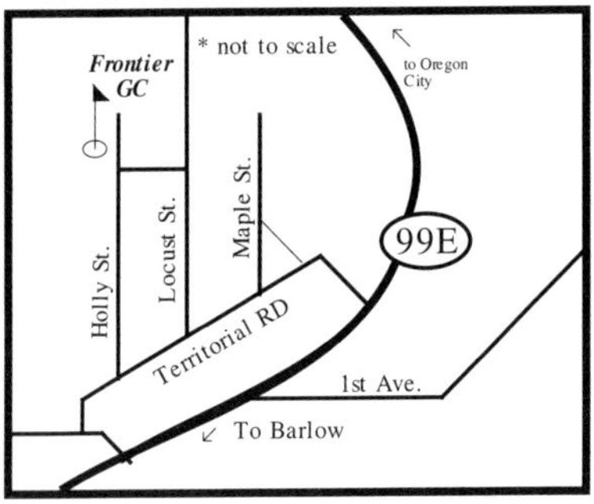

Directions: When in Canby on Highway 99E look for Ivy Street. Proceed 1 block west on Ivy Street. Proceed to Holly Street and turn westbound. The golf course will be located 1.8 miles ahead. Look for signs marking your turns.

Course Yardage & Par:

M-1063 yards, par 27.
W-1063 yards, par 27.

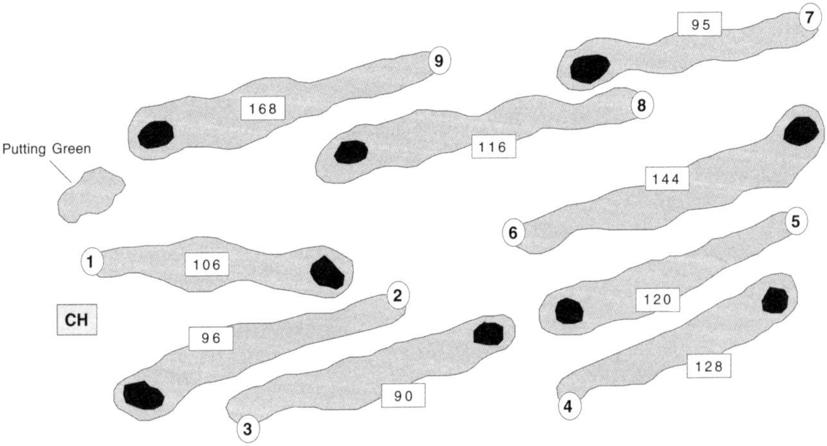

Gearhart Golf Links (public, 18 hole course)

1157 North Marion, P.O. Box 2758; Gearhart, OR 97138
Phone: (503) 738-3538. Fax: (503) 717-0265. Web: gearhartgolflinks.com
Pro: Jason Kunde, PGA. Superintendent: Jimmy Williams.
Rating/Slope: C 69.9/124; M 68.7/121; W 71.6/126. **Course record:** 63.
Green fees: (Monday thru Thursday) $35/$20; (Friday thru Sunday) $45/25; Senior rates (over 65); twilight rates; Jr. rates; military rates; M/C, VISA.
Power cart: $25/$15. **Pull cart:** $4/$2. **Trail fee:** $25/$15.
Reservation policy: requested. Please call in advance for all tee-times.
Winter condition: open all year long, drains well, good wet weather course.
Terrain: hilly. **Tees:** grass. **Spikes:** no metal spikes allowed.
Services: club rentals, lessons, snack bar, restaurant, lounge, beer, wine, liquor, beverages, pro shop, putting & chipping greens. **Comments:** Gearhart Golf Links is the oldest public golf course in Oregon or Washington. Established in 1892 as a 9 hole course, it was expanded to 18 holes in 1913. The course received a major renovation in 2000 including fairway irrigation, all new bunkering, all new tees, several new greens, mounding and reshaping in a Scottish Links redesign by golf architect William G. Robinson. The old course now offers a unique and challenging round of golf for all skill levels in the Scottish Links tradition of the game, in a picturesque coastal setting. Worth a trip.

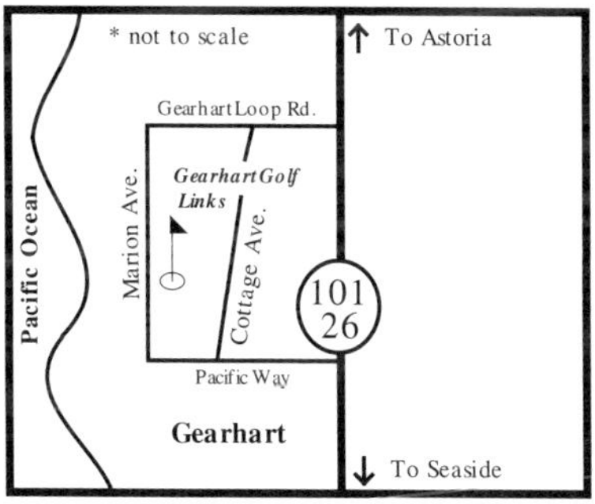

__Directions:__ the golf course is located 1/2 of a mile west of Hwy 101 on the Oregon coast in Gearhart Oregon. **Note:** Look for the sign to the resort and the golf course from Highway 101. The route to the golf course is well marked.

Course Yardage & Par:
C-6218 yards, par 72. **M-5922 yards, par 72.** **W-5353 yards, par 74.**

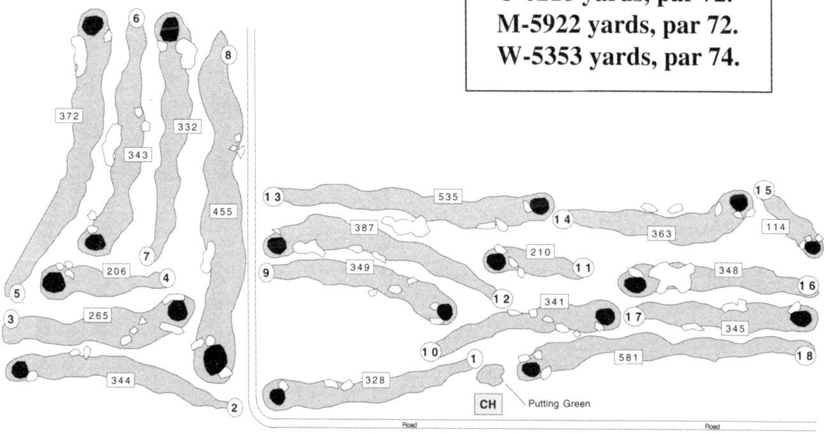

Glendoveer Golf Course (East Course) (public, 18 hole course)

14015 NE Glisan Street; Portland, OR 97230 Web-site: none.
Phone: (503) 253-7507, 292-8570, Tee-times. Fax: (503) 253-1772.
Director of Golf: Daran Dauble, PGA. Head Pro: Jim Chianello.
Rating/Slope: T 67.7/125; C 68.8/123; M 66.6/116; W 68.0/114. **Record:** 62.
Green fees: W/D $22/$11; W/E $24/$12; Senior rates (weekdays only $10). Junior rates (weekdays only $10); M/C, VISA.
Power cart: $24/$12. **Pull Cart:** $2. **Trail fee:** $7/$3.50 for personal carts.
Reservation policy: 7 days in advance in person, 6 days in advance by phone.
Winter condition: the golf course is open all year long. Dry conditions.
Terrain: undulating hills. **Tees:** all grass. **Spikes:** soft spikes preferred.
Services: club rentals, lessons, snack bar, restaurant, lounge, beer, wine, liquor, beverages, pro shop, lockers, showers, driving range, tennis, jogging trail, putting & chipping greens, practice area. **Comments:** this public golf course is kept in excellent condition and can be very busy during the peak season. The course plays fairly tight in spots with trees in play off the tee. Fair public track.

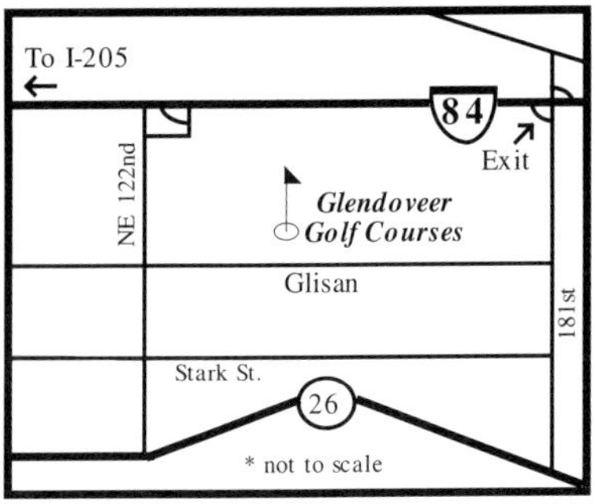

Directions: from I-84 east exit at 181st NE. Proceed southbound for 1.2 miles to Glisan Street. Turn westbound for .8 mile to the golf course. Look for signs marking your way to the golf course.

Glendoveer Golf Course (West Course) (public, 18 hole course)

14015 NE Glisan Street; Portland, OR 97230 Web-site: none.
Phone: (503) 253-7507, 292-8570, Tee-times. Fax: (503) 253-1772.
Director of Golf: Daran Dauble, PGA. Head Pro: Jim Chianello.
Rating/Slope: T 68.8/115; C 67.3/110; M 65.8/108; W 68.3/114. **Record:** 62.
Green fees: W/D $22/$11; W/E $24/$12; Senior rates (weekdays only $10). Junior rates (weekdays only $10); M/C, VISA.
Reservation policy: 7 days in advance in person, 6 days in advance by phone.
Winter condition: the golf course is open all year long. Dry conditions.
Terrain: flat, some hills. **Tees:** all grass. **Spikes:** soft spikes preferred.
Services: club rentals, lessons, snack bar, restaurant, lounge, beer, wine, liquor, beverages, pro shop, lockers, showers, driving range, tennis, putting & chipping greens, jogging trail. **Comments:** the golf course is in excellent condition all year long. Fairways are tree-lined and tight. Great driving range at the course location for those wanting to hit a bucket of balls. Good public golf course.

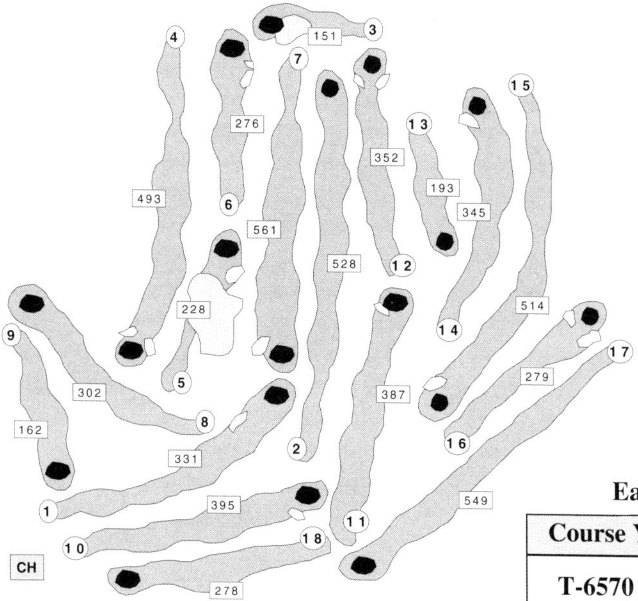

East Course

Course Yardage & Par:

T-6570 yards, par 73.
C-6135 yards, par 73.
M-5694 yards, par 73.
W-5100 yards, par 75.

West Course

Course Yardage & Par:

T-6086 yards, par 71.
C-5733 yards, par 71.
M-5427 yards, par 71.
W-5012 yards, par 75.

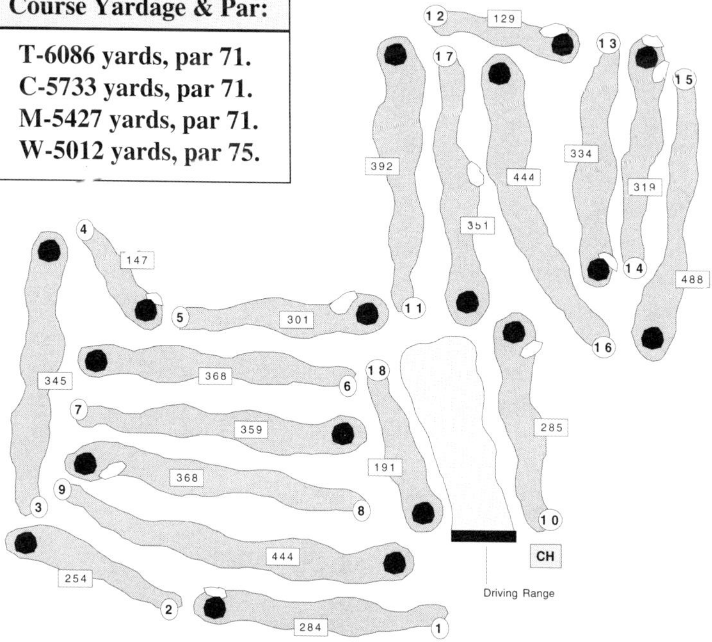

Golf City (public, 9 hole course)

2115 Highway 20; Corvallis, OR 97330
Phone: (541) 753-6213. Fax: (541) 753-6213. Web: none.
Pro: Jim Hays, PGA. Superintendent: none.
Rating/Slope: the golf course is not rated. **Course record:** 21.
Green fees: $7 all week long; no special rates.
Power cart: power carts are not available. **Pull cart:** $1. **Trail fee:** none.
Reservation policy: advance reservations are not required for starting times.
Winter condition: the golf course is open all year long, weather permitting.
Terrain: flat, some hills. **Tees:** grass/mats. **Spikes:** no metal spikes permitted.
Services: club rentals, lessons, snack bar, coffee shop, beer, wine, pro shop, putting green, miniature golf. **Comments:** this short par 3 course is home of the shortest par 4 on record. Greens are on the small size on can be hard to hold. If you are looking for a place to take the first time golfer to try "Golf City".

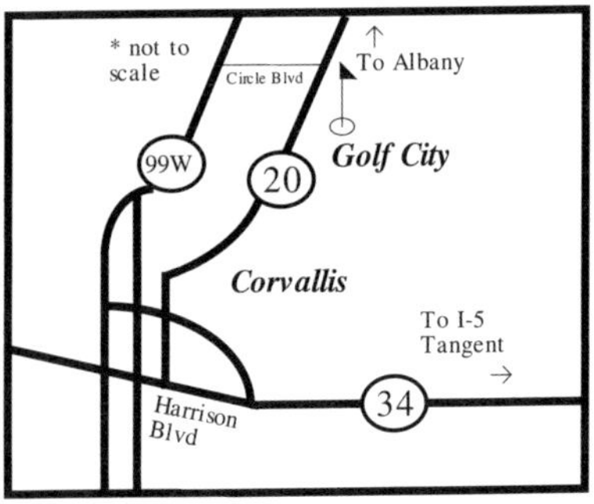

Directions: when entering Corvallis on Hwy 34. Proceed to Highway 20 and go eastbound (north to Albany). The course is located 2.1 miles ahead. Look for signs marking your turns to the golf course.

Course Yardage & Par:
M-801 yards, par 28.
W-801 yards, par 28.

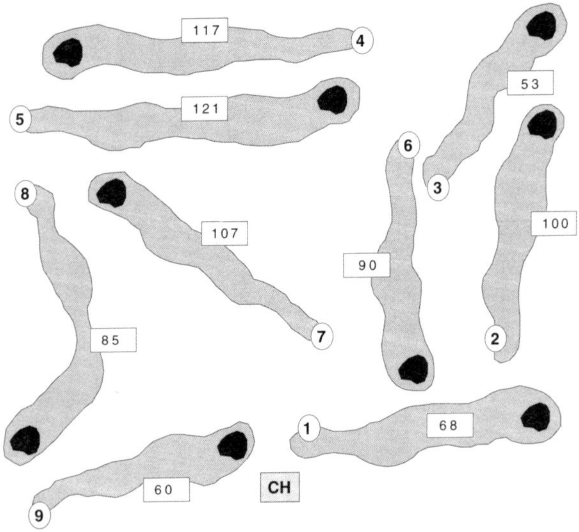

Golf Club of Oregon (public, 18 hole course)

905 NW Spring Hill Drive; Albany, OR 97321
Phone: (541) 928-8338. Fax: (541) 928-6519. Web: none.
Manager: Aaron O'Malley. Golf Director: Jerry Claussen.
Rating/Slope: C 67.5/110; M 66.8/108; W 68.1/110. **Course record:** 61.
Green fees: $25/$15; Jr. and Sr. rates (weekdays only); no credit cards.
Power cart: $20/$12. **Pull cart:** $3/$2. **Trail fee:** $10/$6 for personal carts.
Reservation policy: yes, call for weekend tee-times only, 7 days in advance.
Winter condition: the golf course is open all year long. Course drains fair.
Terrain: flat (easy walking). **Tees:** all grass. **Spikes:** metal spikes permitted.
Services: club rentals, lessons, snack bar, beer, wine, pro shop, lockers, putting green, driving range. **Comments:** The course is easy to walk and has a friendly atmosphere and staff. The course has good drainage and provides excellent play during the winter months. Fair test of golf for all levels. Good public golf course.

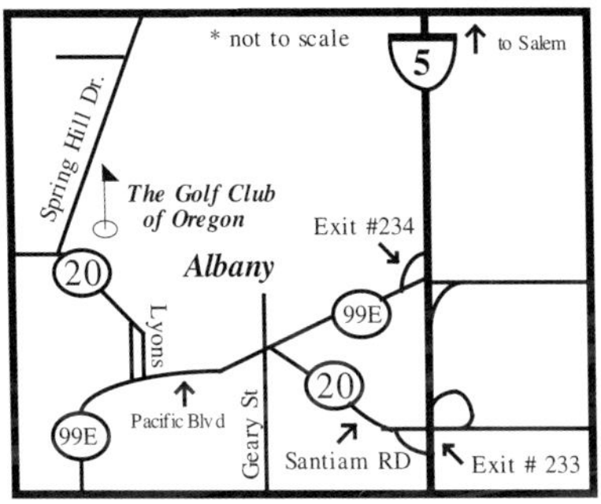

Directions: from I-5 N&S take exit #233 (Santiam Hwy 20) and go westbound to Main St. and turn right. Proceed to 1st Avenue and turn left (one way). Proceed to Lyons and turn right. Go over the bridge and take your first right on Spring Hill Drive. Proceed to the golf course on your right. Look for signs marking your way.

Course Yardage & Par:
C-5841 yards, par 70.
M-5584 yards par 70.
W-5103 yards, par 71.

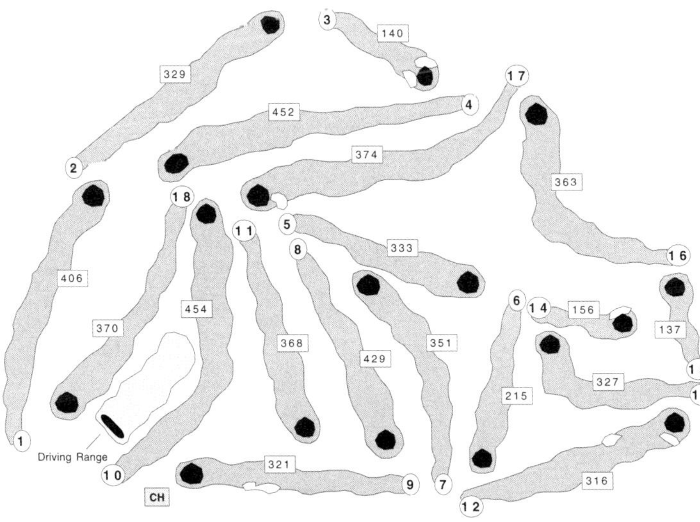

Grants Pass Golf Club (semi-private, 18 hole course)

230 Espey Road; Grants Pass, OR 97527
Phone: (541) 476-0849. Fax: (541) 476-2507. Web: none.
Pro: Ed Fisher, PGA. Superintendent: Scott Shillington.
Rating/Slope: C 70.6/131; M 69.2/121; W 72.6/123; F 70.1/115. **Record:** 63.
Green fees: $35/$21 all week long; M/C, VISA are honored.
Power cart: $24/$12. **Pull cart:** $2. **Trail fee:** personal carts are not allowed.
Reservation policy: yes, please call 2 days in advance for your tee-times.
Winter condition: the golf course is open all year long, weather permitting.
Terrain: relatively hilly. **Tees:** all grass. **Spikes:** metal spikes permitted.
Services: club rentals, lessons, snack bar, restaurant, lounge, beverages, beer, wine, liquor, pop, pro shop, lockers, showers, putting green, driving range.
Comments: beautiful layout that winds through trees and landscaped terrain. The greens are well bunkered and fairly large. Public play is available after members play on a daily basis, so call ahead to find out the availability of times.

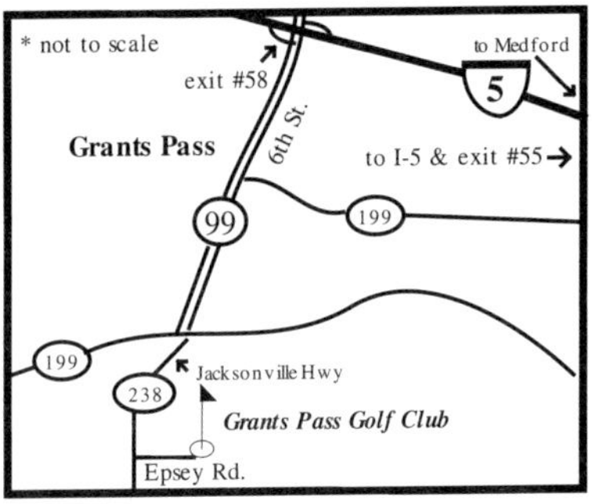

__Directions:__ from I-5 N&S take the Grants Pass exit #55 which will put you on 6th St. Follow across the river onto Hwy 238. Go south for 3 miles to Espey Road. Turn left to the golf course. The golf course is located approximately 6 miles from the freeway. Look for signs marking your way. The way to the golf course is well indicated.

Course Yardage & Par:
C-6438 yards, par 72. **M-6131 yards, par 72.** **W-5692 yards, par 73.** **F-5277 yards, par 73.**

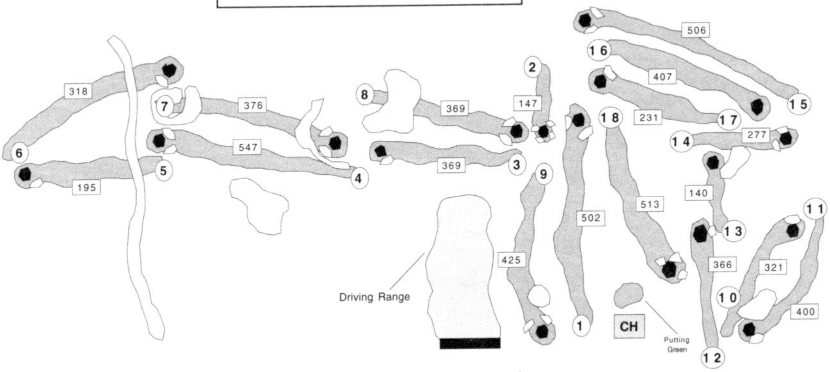

Greenlea Golf Course (public, 9 hole course)

26736 SE Kelso Road; Boring, OR 97009
Phone: (503) 663-3934. Fax: none. Web: www.greenleagolf.com
Owner: Muriel Markham. Superintendent: none.
Rating/Slope: the golf course is not rated. **Course record:** 26.
Green fees: W/D $10; W/E's & Holidays $12; no credit cards.
Power cart: power carts are not available. **Pull cart:** $2. **Trail fee:** no charge.
Reservation policy: Tee-times are on a first come first served basis.
Winter condition: closed from November 1st to March 1st.
Terrain: flat, some hills. **Tees:** all grass. **Spikes:** metal spikes permitted.
Services: club rentals, pro shop, vending machines, putting & chipping green.
Comments: two sets of tees are available for a full 18 hole round of golf. The golf course is easy to walk and has few hazards. Greens are small in size and have few hazards fronting them. Great course for a shorter game of golf.

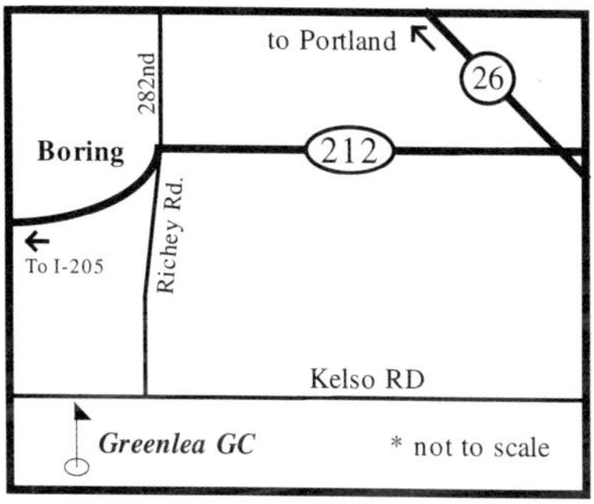

Directions: from Highway 212 turn right on Richey Road which will become SE Kelso Road. The golf course is located approximately 1.3 miles ahead on your left hand side. The golf course is located 1.5 miles south of Boring, Oregon. Look for signs marking your turn to the course.

Course Yardage & Par:
M-1510 yards, par 30. **W-1510 yards, par 30.**

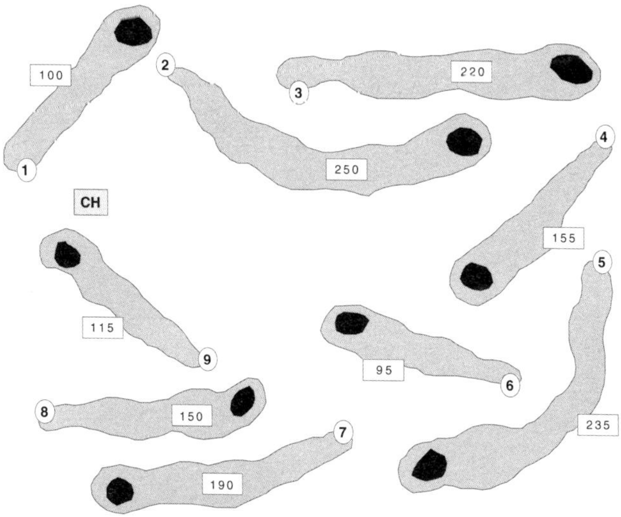

Greens at Redmond (public, 18 hole executive course)

2575 S.W. Greens Boulevard; Redmond, OR 97138
Phone: (541) 923-0694. Fax: (541) 923-1072. Web: none.
Pro: Dick Mason, PGA. Superintendent: Richard Seroup.
Rating/Slope: C 59.0/100; M 57.6/95; W 57.2/93. **Course record:** 25 (9 holes).
Green fees: $28/$16 all week long; winter rates; M/C, VISA.
Power cart: $16/$9. **Pull cart:** $2. **Trail fee:** $60 per year.
Reservation policy: please call up to 1 week in advance for tee-times.
Winter condition: the golf course is open all year long, weather permitting.
Terrain: flat, some hills. **Tees:** all grass. **Spikes:** no metal spikes permitted.
Services: club rentals, small pro shop, snack bar, lessons, beverages.
Comments: This challenging 18 hole executive course was designed by Robert Muir Graves and opened in spring of 1996. The course features a wide variety of holes that have water or native growth area's bordering the fairways. Holes range from 108 yards to over 300 in length. Great change of pace golf course.

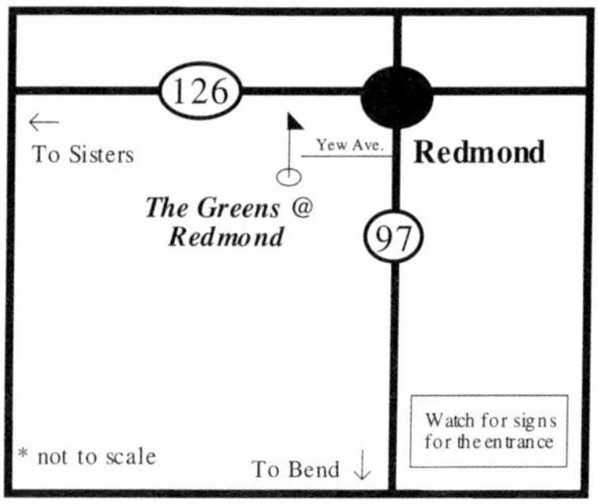

Directions: the course is located just off of Hwy 97 near the Wal-Mart store. The course is on the west side of Hwy 97. Turn on Yew Avenue. Signs are posted.

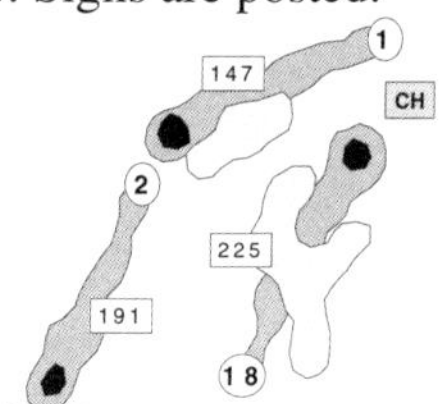
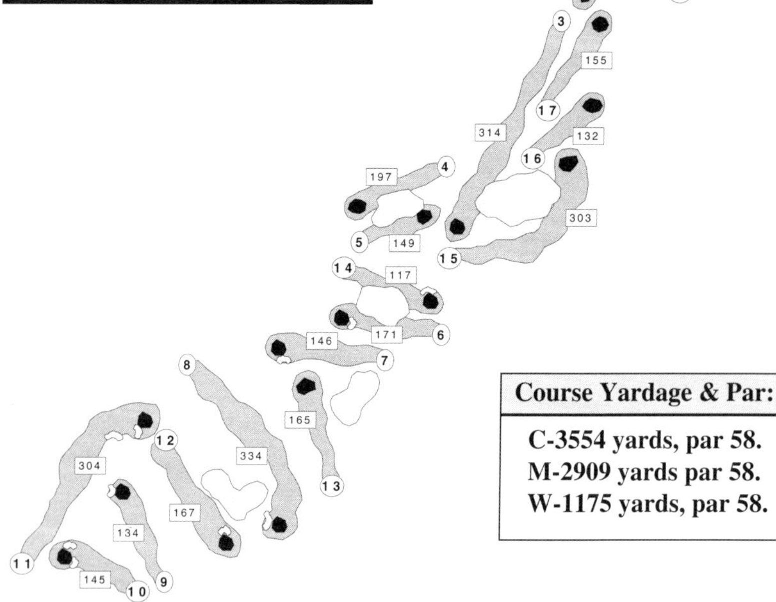

Course Yardage & Par:
C-3554 yards, par 58. M-2909 yards par 58. W-1175 yards, par 58.

Gresham Golf Course (semi-private, 18 hole course)

2155 NE Division; Gresham, OR 97030
Phone: (503) 665-3352. Fax: (503) 665-6402. Web: none.
Pro: Scott Sheilds, PGA. Superintendent: Chuck Wolsborn.
Rating/Slope: C 68.1/109; M 67.2/107; W 69.6/110. **Course record:** 62.
Green fees: W/D $22/$11; W/E $25/$15; Jr. rates (Mon.-Fri.) $7; M/C, VISA.
Power cart: $24/$14. **Pull cart:** $2. **Trail fee:** personal carts are not allowed.
Reservation policy: yes, call for tee-times (advised all year long).
Winter condition: the golf course is open all year long, weather permitting.
Terrain: flat, some hills. **Tees:** all grass. **Spikes:** no metal spikes permitted.
Services: club rentals, lessons, restaurant, lounge, beer, wine, liquor, pro shop, driving range, putting & chipping greens. **Comments:** The course is in excellent condition all year round. Fairways have wide landing area's with few hazards to contend with. The staff is friendly and helpful. Great walking course for seniors.

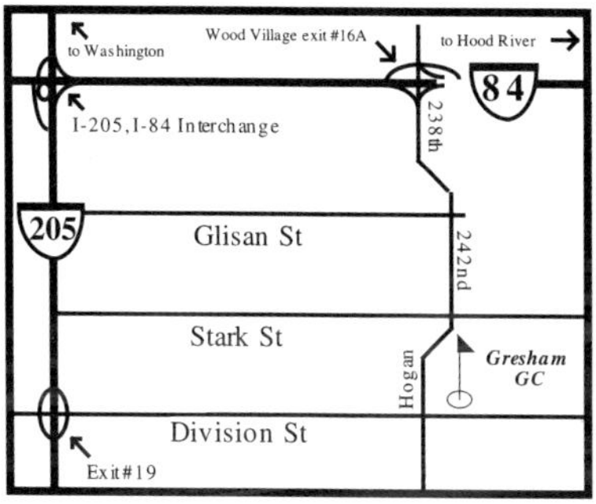

<u>**Directions:**</u> from I-205 take the Division Street exit. Proceed eastbound for 8 miles to the golf course. From I-84 take Wood Village exit and go southbound. Proceed to Division Street and turn left to the golf course. The golf course is located 1 block ahead on your left hand side.

Course Yardage & Par:
C-6028 yards, par 72. **M-5814 yards, par 72.** **W-5154 yards, par 72.**

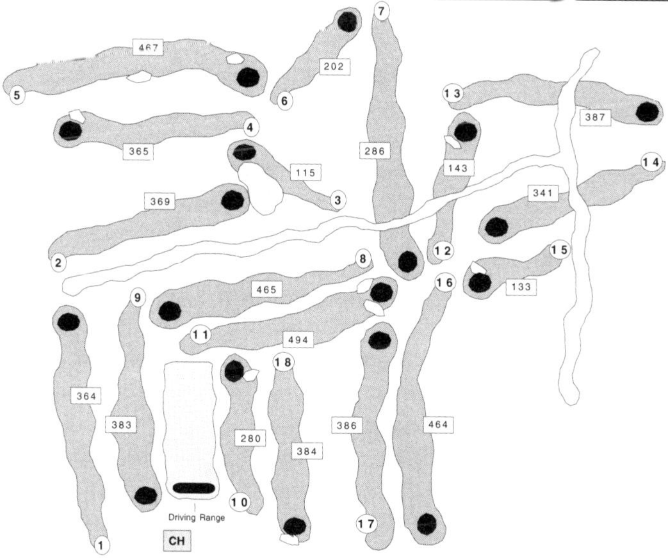

Harbor Links Golf Course (public, 18 hole course)

601 Harbor Isles Boulevard; Klamath Falls, OR 97601
Phone: (541) 882-0609. Fax: (541) 885-6833.
Web-site: www.harborlinksor.book4golf.com
Pro: Rocky Warner, PGA. Superintendent: James Skinner.
Rating/Slope: C 69.6/120; M 68.4/117; W 68.1/117. **Course record:** 63.
Green fees: $45/$25 all week long; winter rates; Jr. & Sr. rates; M/C, VISA.
Power cart: $22/$14. **Pull cart:** $3/$2. **Trail fee:** not allowed.
Reservation policy: yes, call 1 day ahead for all your tee-time reservations.
Winter condition: the course is open all year long, weather permitting, wet.
Terrain: flat (easy walking). **Tees:** all grass. **Spikes:** soft spikes only.
Services: club rentals, lessons, snack bar, restaurant, lounge, beer, wine, liquor, pro shop, putting & chipping greens, driving range. **Comments:** Located on Klamath Lake. A links type course with many water hazards. Good golf course that can play very tough during the peak golfing season. Fair public track.

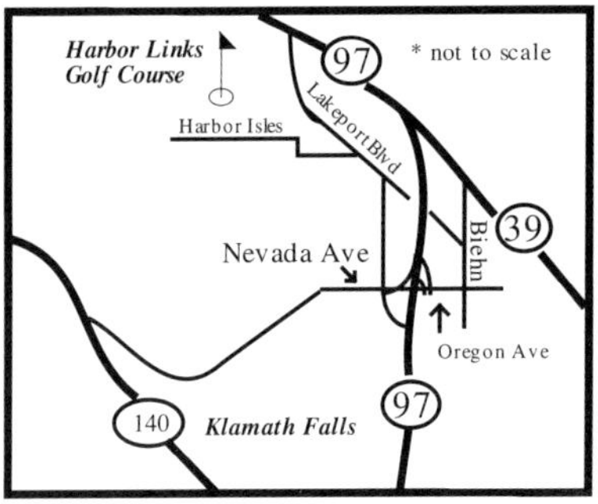

Directions: from Hwy 97 exit at Nevada Avenue and head westbound. Turn right at Montelus Street. Continue ahead to Lakeport Blvd. and turn left. Proceed to Harbor Isles Blvd. and the golf course. The course is located on Klamath Lake.

Course Yardage & Par:
C-6325 yards, par 72.
M-6090 yards, par 72.
W-4981 yards, par 72.

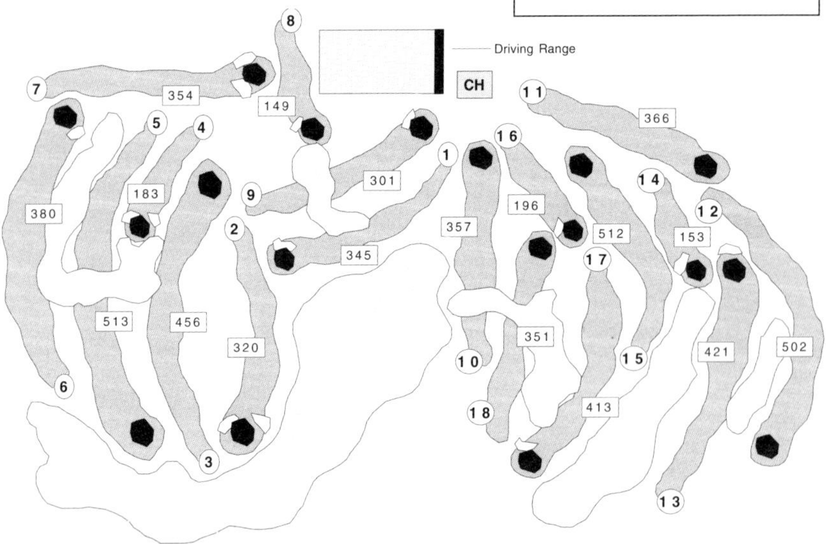

Hawk Creek Golf Course (public, 9 hole course)

48480 Hwy 101 S; P. O. Box 497; Neskowin, OR 97149
Phone: (503) 392-4120. Fax: (503) 392-4620. Web: none.
Owners: Darin & Judy Galle. Superintendent: none.
Rating/Slope: M 63.8/103; W 64.9/104. **Course record:** 29.
Green fees: $22/$12 all week long; no special rates; M/C, VISA.
Power cart: $22/$11. **Pull cart:** $2. **Trail fee:** $5 for personal carts.
Reservation policy: yes, reservations are taken for tee times in the summer.
Winter condition: the golf course is open all year, weather permitting.
Terrain: flat, some hills. **Tees:** all grass. **Spikes:** soft spikes preferred.
Services: club rentals, snack bar, very small pro shop, beer, wine, putting green.
Comments: the golf course is beautifully situated in a valley minutes from the scenic Oregon Coast. This track is short in length and can be rustic in certain area's of the course. Greens are small and have few hazards. Great golf course if you want to play a quick nine holes or if you want a low stress round of golf.

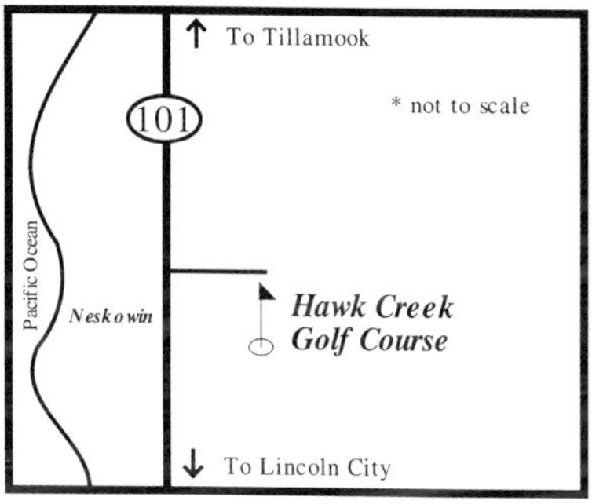

Directions: the golf course is located on the east side of Hwy 101 at Neskowin. Look for a black & white sign from Hwy 101 marking the entrance to the golf course. Your turn is well marked.

Course Yardage & Par:

M-2343 yards, par 34.
W-2343 yards, par 36.

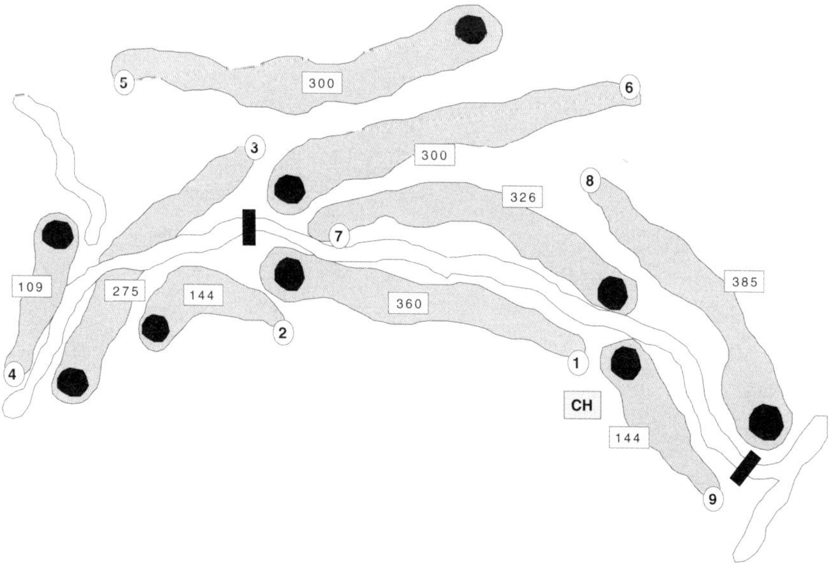

Heron Lakes Golf Club; Great Blue Course (public, 18 holes)

3500 North Victory Boulevard; Portland, OR 97217
Phone: (503) 289-1818. Fax: (503) 240-1925. Web: heronlakesgolf.com
Pro: Jack Young, PGA. Superintendent: J. Goodling.
Rating/Slope: T 73.3/135; C 71.3/130; M 69.4/124; W 70.1/120. **Record:** 67.
Green fees: $37/$19 Monday thru Thursday; $39/$20 Friday thru Sunday & Holidays; call for any other special rates; VISA, M/C, DISCOVER, AMEX.
Power cart: $26/$13. **Pull cart:** $5/$2.50. **Trail fee:** $4/$2.
Reservation policy: book on line at heronlakesgolf.com or call 6 days ahead by phone. You may obtain tee-times 7 days ahead when booking in person.
Winter condition: the golf course is open all year long, weather permitting.
Terrain: flat (easy walking). **Tees:** all grass. **Spikes:** soft spikes only.
Services: club rentals, lessons, snack bar, beer, well stocked pro shop, putting & chipping greens, driving range. **Comments:** Great Blue is one of the toughest public courses in the northwest. It is still a great buy at $39 for 18 holes of golf. The track has several bunkers fronting the large, undulating greens. Lakes come into play on almost every hole and are a major factor off the tee.

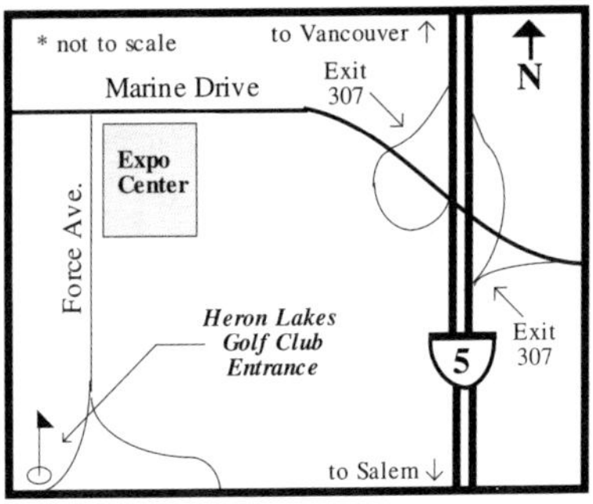

Directions: from *I-5N* take exit #307 stay in the left lane. Take Marine Dr. W. Loop under I-5 and take a right at the light (Marine Drive). Go to Force Ave. (first light) and take a left. Go on Force Ave. to the entrance. From *I-5S* take exit #307 get in the left lane. Take a left at the light (Marine Drive). Go on Marine Drive to Force Ave. (first light) and take a left. Go on Force Ave. to the course entrance.

Heron Lakes Golf Club; Greenback Course (public, 18 holes)

3500 North Victory Boulevard; Portland, OR 97217
Phone: (503) 289-1818. Fax: (503) 240-1925. Web: heronlakesgolf.com
Pro: Jack Young, PGA. Superintendent: J. Goodling.
Rating/Slope: C 71.6/123; M 68.7/118; W 69.4/113. **Course record:** 63.
Green fees: $25/$13 (M-Th); $27/$18 (Fri-Sun & Hol); VISA, M/C, DIS, AMEX.
Power cart: $26/$13. **Pull cart:** $5/$2.50. **Trail fee:** $4/$2.
Reservation policy: book on line at heronlakesgolf.com or call 6 days ahead by phone. You may obtain tee-times 7 days ahead when booking in person.
Winter condition: the golf course is open all year long, weather permitting.
Terrain: flat (easy walking). **Tees:** all grass. **Spikes:** soft spikes only.
Services: club rentals, lessons, snack bar, beer, large pro shop, driving range.
Comments: Course has some of the nicest greens in Oregon. You will find the course in excellent condition throughout the entire year. Fairways are large with wide landing area's. Greens are large with bunkers fronting them. The course has a driving range for those who want to practice before or after their round.

Greenback Course

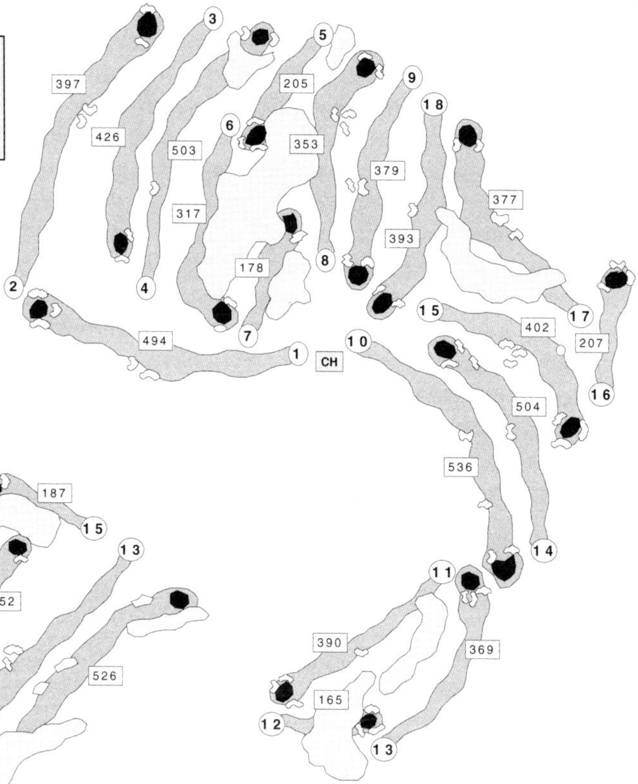

Course Yardage & Par:

(Greenback Course)
C-6595 yards, par 72.
M-5938 yards, par 72.
W-5224 yards, par 72.

Great Blue Course

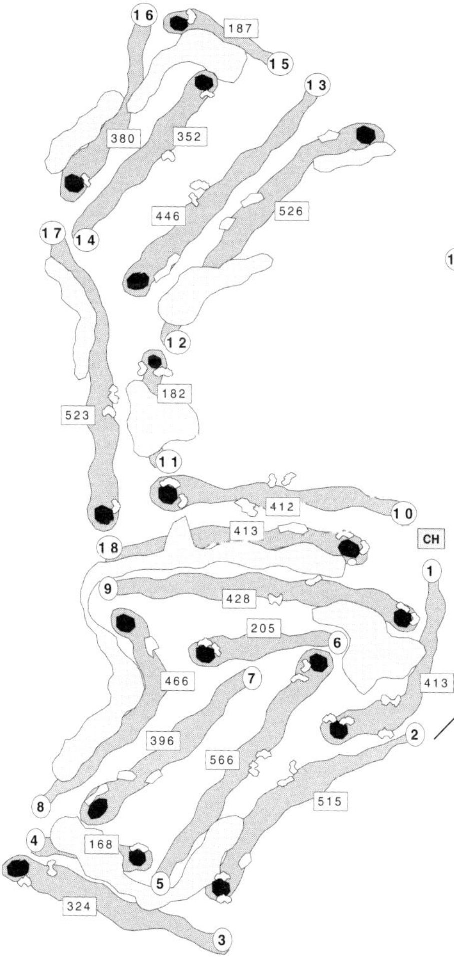

Course Yardage & Par:

(Great Blue Course)
T-6902 yards, par 72.
C-6491 yards, par 72.
M-6030 yards, par 72.
W-5258 yards, par 72.

Hidden Valley Golf Course (public, 9 hole course)

775 North River Road; Cottage Grove, OR 97424
Phone: (541) 942-3046. Fax: none. Web: none.
Owners: Joel & Karen Boede. Superintendent: Joel Boede.
Rating/Slope: M 65.1/117; W 66.0/114. **Course record:** 65 (18 holes).
Green fees: W/D $16/$9; W/E $18/$10; Sr. & Jr. rates (Mon.-Fri. $12/$7).
Power cart: $18/$11. **Pull cart:** $3/$2. **Trail fee:** $5/$3 for personal carts.
Reservation policy: yes, call 1 week in advance for weekend tee-times.
Winter condition: the golf course is open all year, wet, with good drainage.
Terrain: flat, some hills. **Tees:** all grass. **Spikes:** soft spikes preferred.
Services: club rentals, restaurant, lounge, beer, wine, liquor, pro shop, putting green, lockers. **Comments:** Large trees, narrow fairways and very small greens make shot placement extremely important on this course. Great golf course for a quick 9 holes. This track also has dual tees for 18 hole play.

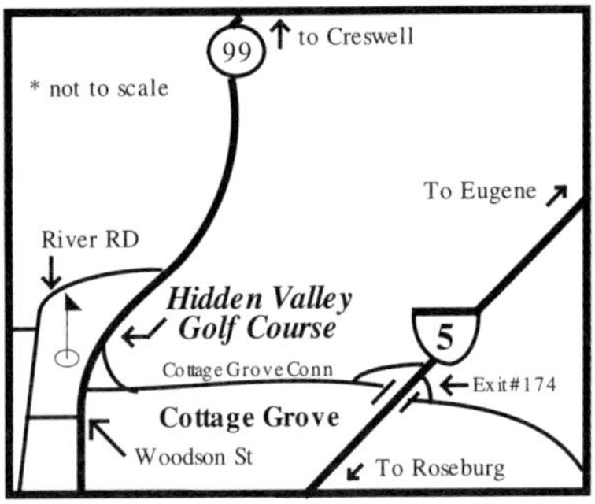

__Directions:__ from I-5 southbound take the first Cottage Grove exit (second exit if going northbound, #174) and proceed west for 1/2 mile. Veer left at Pacific Highway. Turn right on Woodson. Turn right to the golf course. Look for signs.

Course Yardage & Par:

M-2803 yards, par 35.
W-2375 yards, par 35.
__Dual tees for 18 holes:__
M-5471 yards, par 70.
W-4736 yards, par 70.

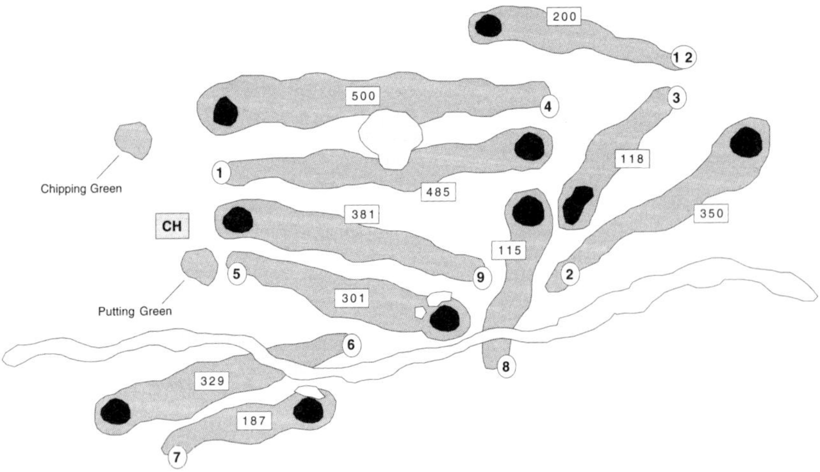

Highlands at Gearhart (public, 9 hole course)

#1 Highlands Road; Gearhart, OR 97138
Phone: (503) 738-5248. Fax: (503) 738-5865.
Web-site: www.discountdansgolf.com
Pro: Nick Maybry, PGA. Superintendent: Roger Frisinger.
Rating/Slope: M 59.0/94; W 59.0/94. **Course record:** 25.
Green fees: $22/$12 all week long; M/C, VISA.
Power cart: not available. **Pull cart:** $2. **Trail fee:** not allowed
Reservation policy: in summer only, call up to 7 days in advance for times.
Winter condition: the golf course is open all year long, weather permitting.
Terrain: flat, some hills. **Tees:** all grass. **Spikes:** metal spikes permitted.
Services: club rentals, pro shop with large inventory, snack bar, lessons.
Comments: This challenging 9 hole course is set in a beautiful ocean view setting. Hole #5 is the signature hole where a cliff comes into play. If you are looking for a change of pace try "Highlands" it is a great golf course. The pro shop has a huge golf club inventory for those looking for a new set of clubs.

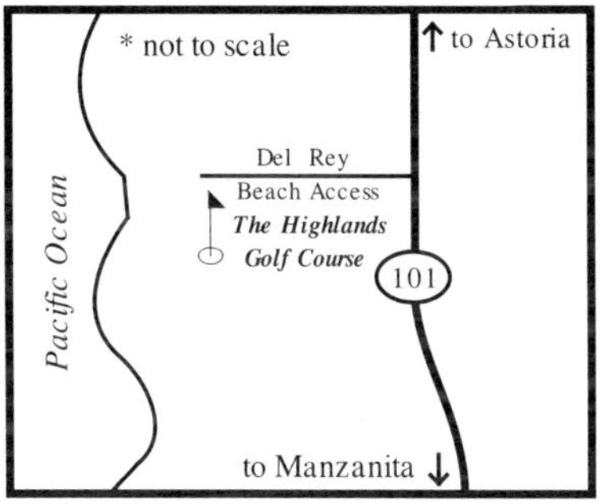

Directions: golf course is located 1 mile north of Gearhart, Oregon off of Highway 101. Take Del Rey Beach access off of Highway 101. Travel westbound for 1/4 mile to the golf course. Look for signs that are posted on the highway.

Course Yardage & Par:

Blue Nine:	**M-1761 yards, par 31.**
	W-1761 yards, par 30.
White Nine:	**M-1618 yards, par 30.**
	W-1618 yards, par 30.

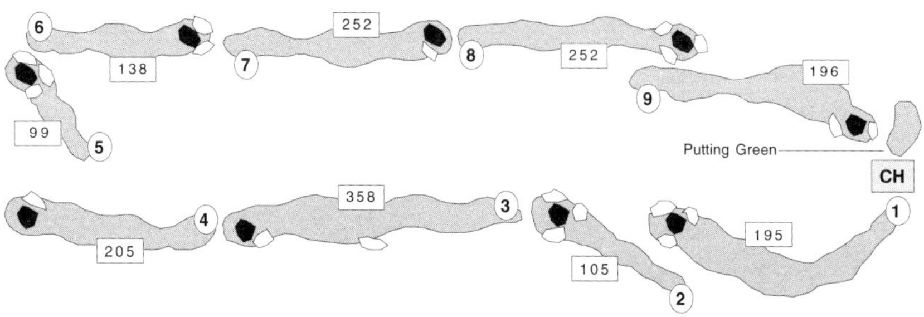

Hood River Golf & Country Club (public, 18 hole course)

1850 Country Club Road; Hood River, OR 97031
Phone: (541) 386-3009. Fax: (541) 386-1732. Web: none.
Pro: Dave Waller, PGA. Superintendent: Rick Schmidt.
Rating/Slope: C 68.4/112; M 67.6/111; W 68.4/110. **Course record:** 68.
Green fees: Mon.-Thu. $20/$12; Fri.-Sun. $24/$13; Jr. & Sr. rates; M/C, VISA.
Power cart: $24/$12. **Pull cart:** $2. **Trail fee:** $8 for personal carts.
Reservation policy: yes, call up to 1 week in advance for tee times.
Winter condition: the golf course is closed when snow covered only.
Terrain: relatively hilly. **Tees:** all grass. **Spikes:** metal spikes permitted.
Services: club rentals, lessons, snack bar, restaurant, lounge, beer, wine, liquor, pro shop, driving range, putting & chipping green. **Comments:** Beautiful setting with view's of Mt. Hood and Mt. Adams. The front 9 has wide fairways with medium sized greens. Water comes into play on three holes. Bunkers guard some greens on your approach shots. The new 9 features hilly terrain, narrow fairways and small greens. great golf course that has improved each and every year.

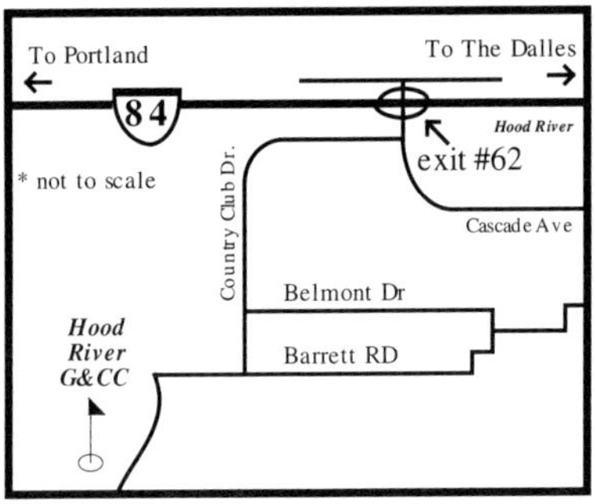

Directions: from I-84 E&W take exit #62. Go south and take Country Club Road for 2.2 miles. At stop, where road "T,s" turn right. The course is located 1.1 miles ahead on your right hand side.

Course Yardage & Par:

C-5918 yards, par 71.
M-5633 yards, par 71.
W-5279 yards, par 71.

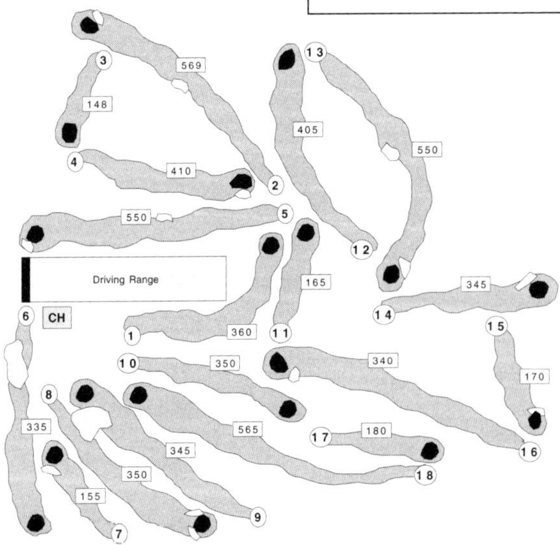

Illahe Hills Country Club (private, 18 hole course)

3376 Country Club Drive; Salem, OR 97302

Phone: (503) 581-3233. Fax: (503) 370-8068. Web: www.illahehills.com

Director of golf: Ron Rawls, PGA. Superintendent: Bill Swancutt.

Rating/Slope: C 72.4/130; M 70.8/128; W 72.7/126. **Course record:** 64.
Green fees: private club, members & guests of members only; no credit cards.
Power cart: private club. **Pull cart:** complimentary. **Trail fee:** not allowed.
Reservation policy: members only & guests only, 2 days in advance for times.
Winter condition: the golf course is open all year long, damp conditions.
Terrain: flat, some hills. **Tees:** all grass. **Spikes:** soft spikes May thru Sept.
Services: club rentals, lessons, snack bar, restaurant, lounge, beer, wine, liquor, beverages, pro shop, lockers, showers, putting & chipping greens driving range.
Comments: course has been host to several tournaments, including the 1981 U.S.G.A. Junior Girls National Championship. Great, tough golf course.

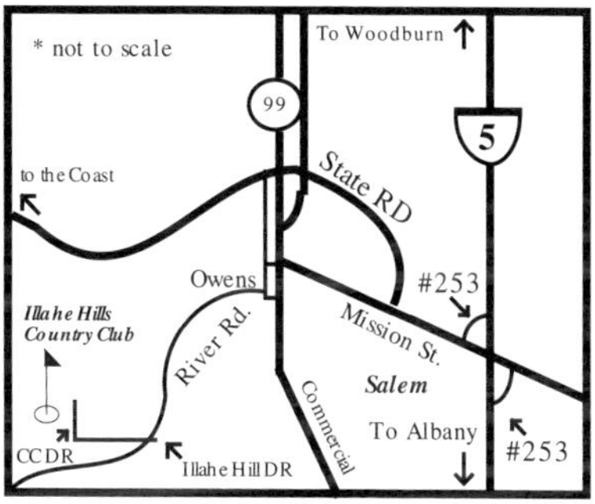

Directions: from I-5 N&S take the Mission exit and go westbound. Turn left on Commercial. At Owens, turn right. Follow Owens as it veers south and changes to River Road. Follow for 3.7 miles to the golf course. The golf course is located on the west side of the city.

Course Yardage & Par:
C-6735 yards, par 72.
M-6411 yards, par 72.
W-5621 yards, par 73.

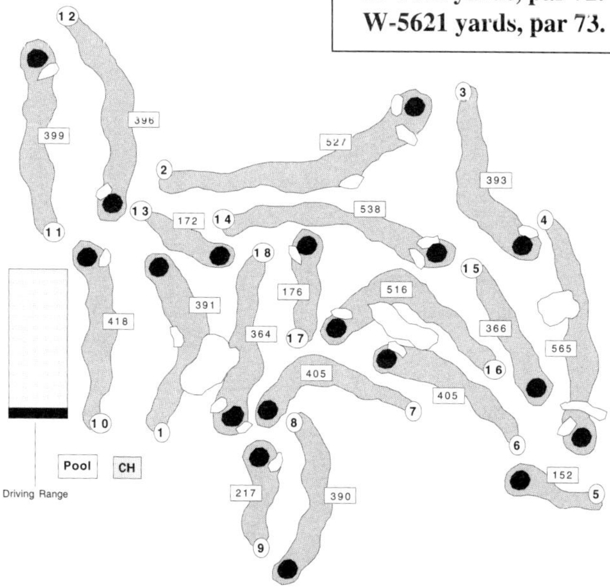

Illinois Valley Golf Club (public, 9 hole course)

Redwood Hwy 199, P.O. Box 924; Cave Junction, OR 97523
Phone: (541) 592-3151. Fax: (541) 592-3525. Web: none.
Pro: none. Superintendent: Jared Kinkade.
Rating/Slope: M 67.5/114; W 70.2/114. **Course Record:** 63.
Green fees: $18/$11 all week; Jr & Sr rates; winter special $10 all day.
Power cart: $20/$10. **Pull cart:** $2/$1. **Trail fee:** $7 all day rate.
Reservation policy: call 1 week in advance for weekends and holiday T-times.
Winter condition: course is open all year long. Dry conditions (drains well).
Terrain: flat (easy walking). **Tees:** all grass. **Spikes:** metal spikes permitted.
Services: club rentals, lessons, snack bar, beer, wine, pro shop, driving range, putting green. **Comments:** course has two sets of tees for those who want to play a full 18 holes. Excellent well kept golf course that plays over and through many water hazards. Greens are small in size and tend to be open in the front.

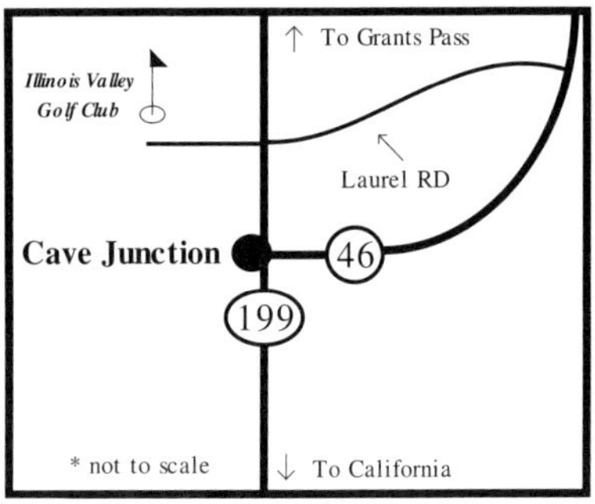

<u>Directions:</u> the golf course is located 1/2 mile north of the city of Cave Junction off of Highway 199. The golf course will be located on the west side of the Hwy. Look for signs at your turn to the course.

Course Yardage & Par:
M-3049 yards, par 36. **W-2727 yards, par 36.** **<u>Dual tees for 18 holes:</u>** **M-5985 yards, par 72.** **W-5348 yards, par 72.**

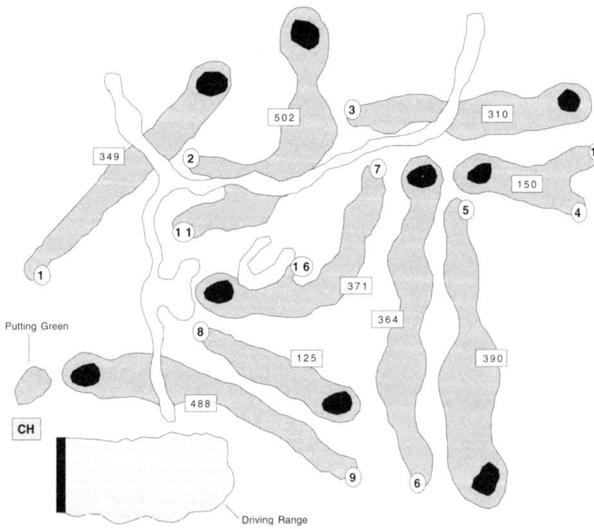

Indian Creek Golf Course (public, 18 hole course)

3605 Brookside Drive; Hood River, OR 97031

Phone: (541) 386-7770. Fax: (541) 386-7330. Web: www.indiancreekgolf.com

Pro: Harold Bluestein PGA. Superintendent: Tyson Jacobs.

Rating/Slope: C 71.2/129; M 68.5/112; W 68.4/115. **Course record:** 64.
Green fees: W/D $24/$13; W/E $32/$17; Sr/Jr rates $8, Sr rates M & W all day.
Power cart: $13.50/$7.50 per player. **Pull cart:** $3. **Trail fee:** $20.
Reservation policy: yes, taken up to 1 week in advance, tournaments anytime.
Winter condition: the golf course is open all year long, weather permitting.
Terrain: flat, rolling terrain. **Tees:** all grass. **Spikes:** soft spikes only.
Services: club rentals, lessons, pro shop, putting/chipping green, driving range, full service restaurant. **Comments:** the course provides excellent drainage for winter play. This track is fairly easy to walk with rolling hills. Great views of Mt. Hood and Mt. Adams. A 2001 *Golf Digest's* 4 star places to play award winner.

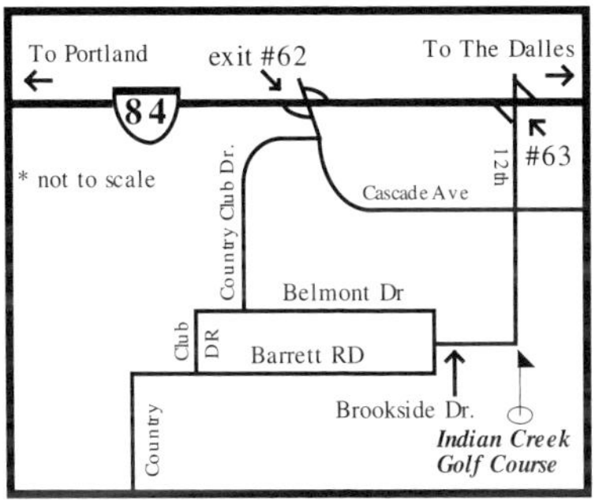

Directions: from I-84 E&W take exit #62. Turn Right and follow Cascade Street east to stoplight at 13th. Turn right on 13th and drive south approximately one mile to Brookside Drive. Turn right on Brookside Drive and drive for 8/10 of a mile to entrance.

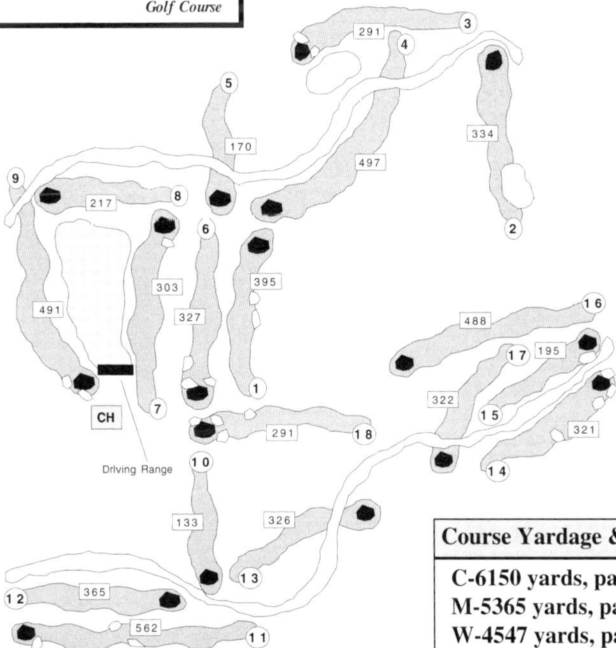

Course Yardage & Par:
C-6150 yards, par 72.
M-5365 yards, par 72.
W-4547 yards, par 72.

John Day Golf Club (semi-private, 9 hole course)

West Highway 26, P.O. Box 176; John Day, OR 97845
Phone: (541) 575-0170. Fax: none. Web: none.
Manager: Bev Pierson. Superintendent: Tom Moore.
Rating/Slope: M 66.9/116; W 69.9/122. **Course record:** 62.
Green fees: $20/$14 all week long; VISA; the clubhouse is private.
Power cart: $20/$10. **Pull cart:** $2/$1. **Trail fee:** $7 for personal carts.
Reservation policy: no advance reservations are needed. First come first served.
Winter condition: the golf course is closed on Mondays in winter months.
Terrain: flat, some hills. **Tees:** all grass. **Spikes:** metal spikes permitted.
Services: snack bar, beer, wine, liquor (in the clubhouse), beverages, pro shop, lockers, driving range, putting & chipping greens. **Comments:** course has two sets of tees to allow you to play a full 18 holes. Trees and water and narrow fairways are a major factor when playing this golf course. Fair golf course.

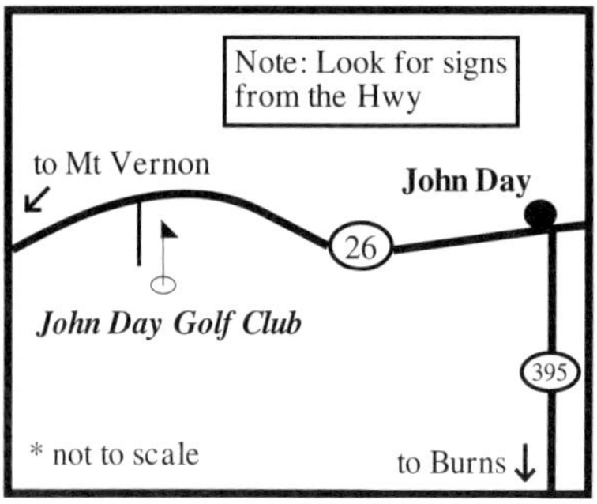

Directions: the golf course is located 3.1 miles west of the city of John Day Oregon on Highway 26. Make sure you look for a sign posted on the Highway to the golf course location.

Course Yardage & Par:

M-2955 yards, par 36.
W-2896 yards, par 38.
Dual tees for 18 holes:
M-5843 yards, par 71.
W-5334 yards, par 75.

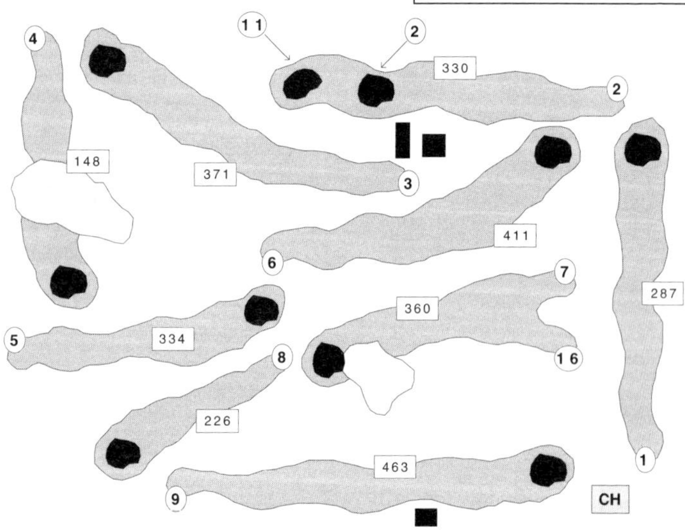

Juniper Golf Club (semi-private, 18 hole course)

139 SE Sisters Avenue; Redmond, OR 97756
Phone: (541) 548-3121. Fax: (541) 548-0808. Web: junipergolf.com
Pro: Bruce Wattenburger, PGA. Superintendent: Doug Voderberg.
Rating/Slope: C 70.0/125; M 68.6/121; W 70.4/123. **Course record:** 64.
Green fees: $35/$20 all week long; Jr. and winter rates; M/C, VISA.
Power cart: $25/$14. **Pull cart:** $2/$1. **Trail fee:** $7.50 daily rate.
Reservation policy: call up to 1 month in advance for starting times.
Winter condition: the golf course is open all year long, weather permitting.
Terrain: flat, some hills. **Tees:** all grass. **Spikes:** no metal spikes permitted.
Services: club rentals, lessons, snack bar, restaurant, beer, wine, beverages, liquor, pro shop, lockers, showers, putting & chipping greens, driving range.
Comments: This beautiful golf course wanders through Juniper trees and lava rock. Great golf course in the great spot of Central Oregon. Worth a trip.

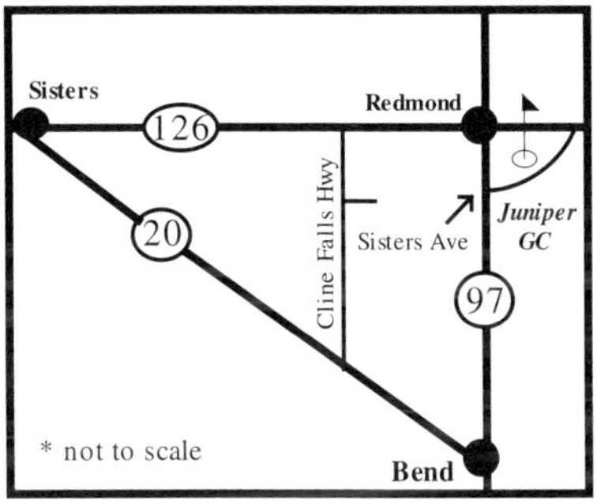

Directions: golf course located 1/4 mile off of Highway 97 at the south end of Redmond Oregon. Proceed east on Sisters Avenue for 1/4 mile to the golf course. Course located next to the City Airport. Look for signs that are posted along the route to the golf course.

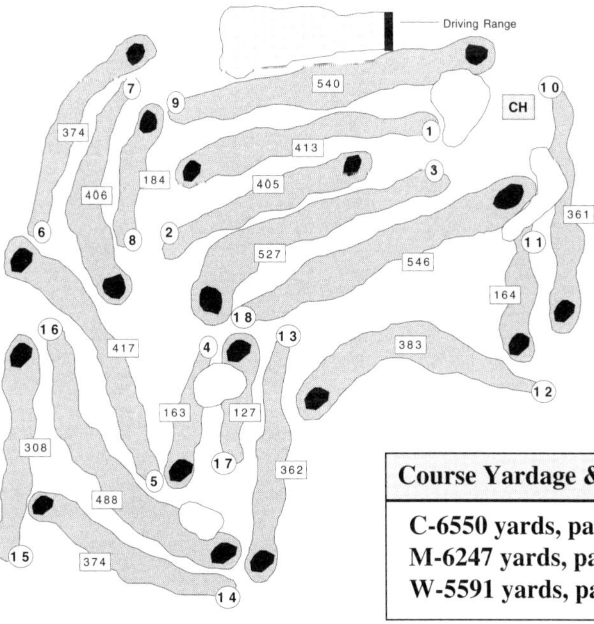

Course Yardage & Par:
C-6550 yards, par 72.
M-6247 yards, par 72.
W-5591 yards, par 72.

KAH-NEE-TA Resort (public, 18 hole course)

P.O. Box K; 100 Main Street; Warm Springs, OR 97761
Phone: (541) 553-1112, 1-800-831-0100. Fax: (541) 553-1071. Web: none.
Pro: Joe C. Rauschenburg, PGA. Superintendent: Troy Alderson.
Rating/Slope: C 70.7/124; M 68.0/119; W 70.2/119. **Course record:** 59.
Green fees: resort guest fees/public golfer fee $38/$22; Jr. rates $22; Sr. rates $30 (Mondays only); winter rates; M/C, VISA, DINERS, AMEX, DIS.
Power cart: $25/$13. **Pull cart:** $5. **Trail fee:** $10 for personal carts.
Reservation policy: yes, call up to 2 weeks in advance for tee-time reservations.
Winter condition: the golf course is open all year long. Dry course conditions.
Terrain: flat (easy walking). **Tees:** all grass. **Spikes:** soft spikes preferred.
Services: club rentals, lessons, snack bar, restaurant, lounge, beer, wine, liquor, beverages, pro shop, driving range, putting & chipping greens, practice bunker.
Comments: The pro states "this is where the birdies fly and eagles soar in over 300 days of sunshine a year". Excellent resort facility that features full service accomodations. Great vacation spot for the entire family. Worth a special trip.

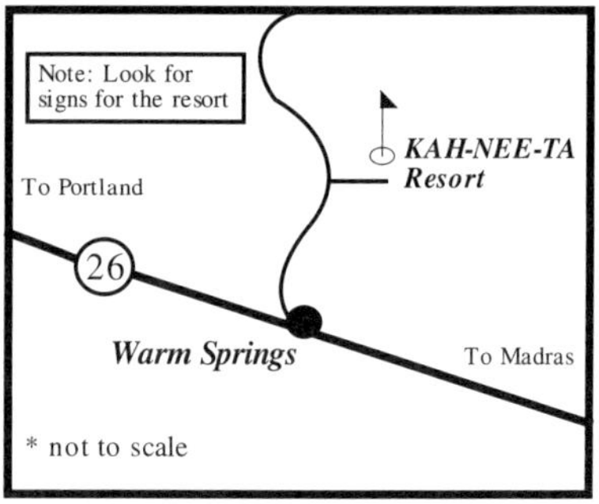

Directions: course is located 120 miles southeast of Portland on Hwy 26. Follow the signs to the resort. Golf course is located 11 miles north of Warm Springs Oregon. Follow the signs to the resort.

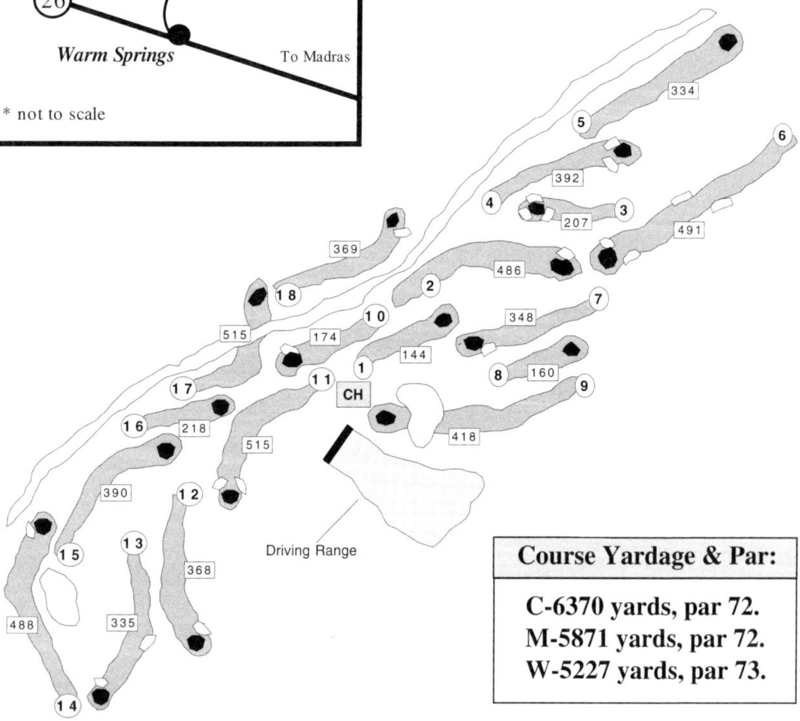

Course Yardage & Par:
C-6370 yards, par 72. **M-5871 yards, par 72.** **W-5227 yards, par 73.**

Kentuck Golf Course (public, 18 hole course)

680 Golf Course Lane; North Bend, OR 97459
Phone: (541) 756-4464. Fax: (541) 756-5722. Web: none.
Pro: none. Manager: none. Superintendent: Wally Culp.
Rating/Slope: M 64.6/101; W 64.1/100. **Course record:** 62.
Green fees: W/D $17/$10; W/E $19/$11; Jr. rates; M/C, VISA.
Power cart: $20/$10. **Pull cart:** $2. **Trail fee:** $5 for personal carts.
Reservation policy: yes, please call in advance for a tee time.
Winter condition: the golf course is open all year long. Wet conditions.
Terrain: flat (easy walking). **Tees:** all grass. **Spikes:** metal spikes permitted.
Services: club rentals, snack bar, pro shop, beer, wine, putting green.
Comments: the golf course is set in a beautiful area of Oregon and is challenging for any level of golfer. Creeks, ponds come into play on nearly every hole.

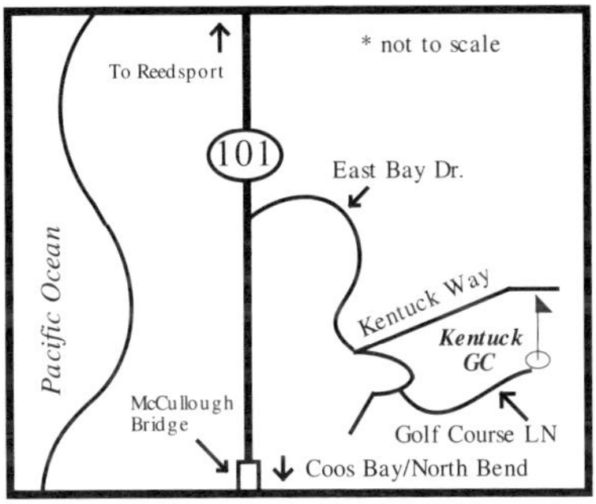

Directions: golf course located northeast of North Bend Oregon. Go eastbound on the East Bay Drive at the north end of the McCullough Bridge (where Highway 101 crosses the Coos Bay and Kentuck inlet). Follow the road to the southeast. Proceed for 3 miles to the golf course. Look for signs marking your way to the course.

Course Yardage & Par:
M-5372 yards, par 70.
W-4450 yards, par 70.

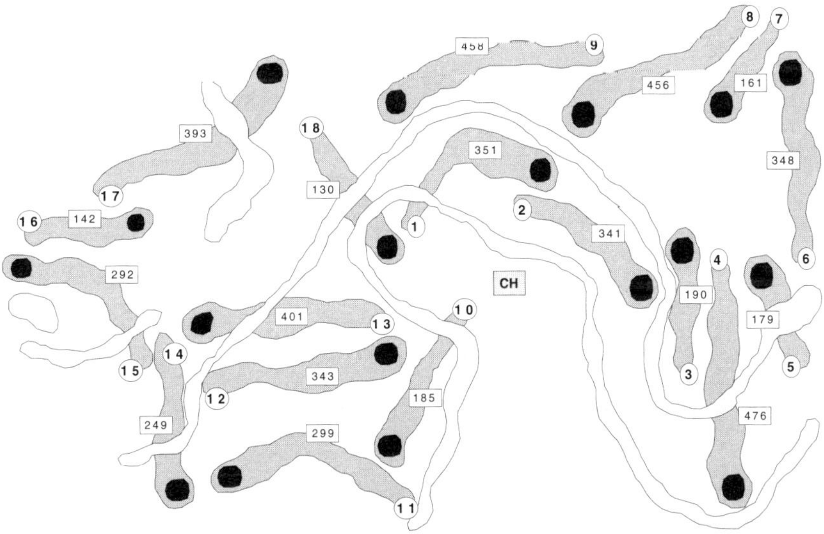

Killarney West Golf Club (public, 9 hole course)

1275 NW 334th; Hillsboro, OR 97124
Phone: (503) 648-7634. Fax: none. Web: none.
Owner: J. E. O'Meara. Superintendent: Jose Martinez-Ortega.
Rating/Slope: M 64.4/108; W 64.4/108. **Course record:** 32.
Green fees: W/D $16/$8; W/E $20/$10; accepts no credit cards.
Power cart: $18/9. **Pull cart:** $1. **Trail fee:** $9/$4.50 for personal carts.
Reservation policy: yes, taken for weekends and holidays. Call ahead 7 days.
Winter condition: the golf course is open all year. Dry conditions, drains well.
Terrain: flat, some hills. **Tees:** all grass. **Spikes:** metal spikes permitted.
Services: club rentals, snack bar, beer, small pro shop.
Comments: Course is very scenic with trees lining the fairways. Greens are medium in size and fairly flat. Water is a major factor on several holes throughout the course. The course plays much tougher than the yardage would indicate.

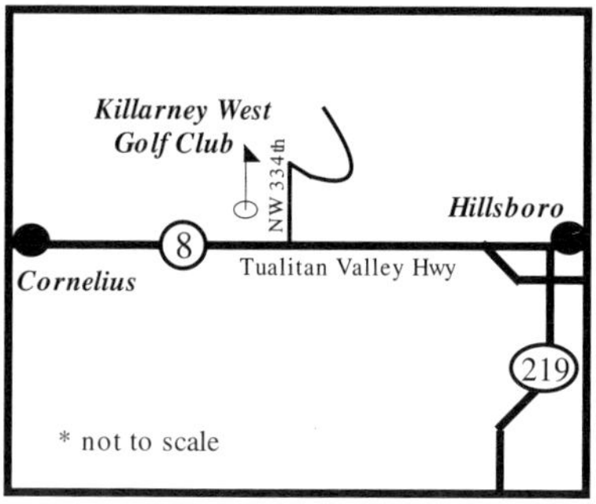

Directions: the golf course is located between Cornelius and Hillsboro Oregon off of Hwy 8. Proceed northbound on NW 334th for 1/2 mile to the golf course.

Course Yardage & Par:
M-2544 yards, par 36.
W-2544 yards, par 37.

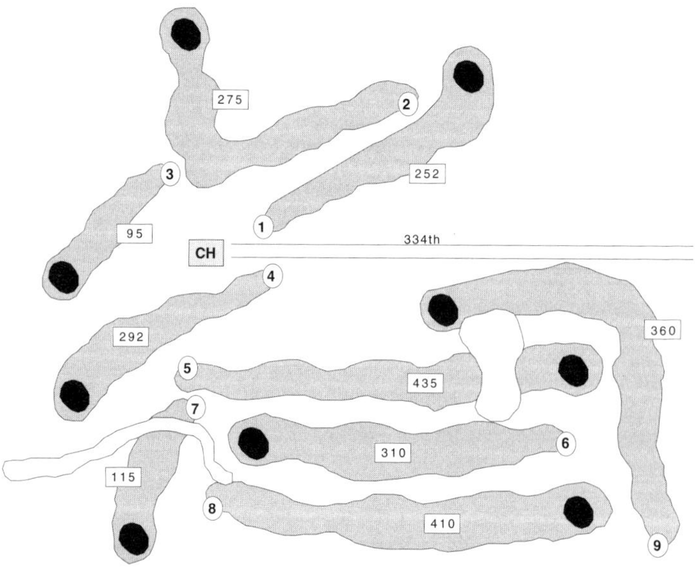

King City Golf Course (semi-private, 9 hole course)

15355 SW Royalty Parkway; King City, OR 97224
Phone: (503) 639-7986. Fax: none. Web: none.
Pro: Bob Gasper, PGA. Superintendent: Steve Fletchell.
Rating/Slope: M 62.4/100; W 64.2/103. **Course record:** 59.
Green fees: Monday thru Thursday $22/$11; Friday thru Sunday & Holidays $24/$12; call course for any other special rates; no credit cards.
Power cart: $20/$10. **Pull cart:** $2. **Trail fee:** personal carts are not allowed.
Reservation policy: yes, call for reservations during the summer, 7 days.
Winter condition: the golf course is open all year long with wet conditions.
Terrain: flat (easy walking). **Tees:** all grass. **Spikes:** metal spikes permitted.
Services: club rentals, pro shop, lockers, showers, putting & chipping greens.
Comments: the golf course is an excellent par 33 tract. The course is very easy to walk with very few hazards to contend with. Worth a trip if you are in the mood for something a little different than the 6400+ back-breaker golf course.

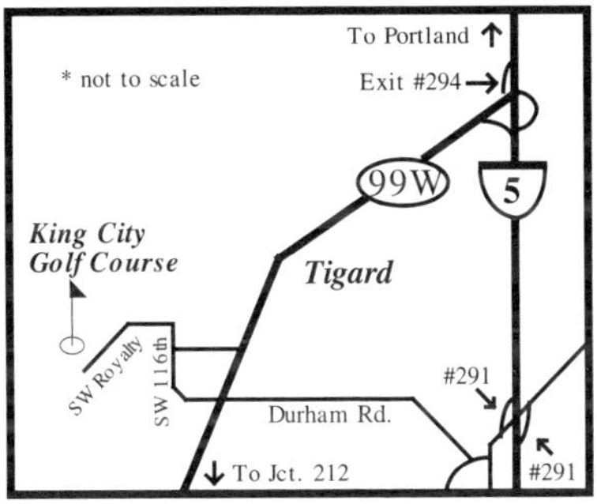

Directions: from I-5 N&S take exit for Hwy 99W #294 (West Pacific Highway). Travel south to King City. When in King City turn right on Durham Road. Proceed to SW 116th and go north then take the first left to SW Royalty and proceed ahead to the golf course. Look for signs that are posted along the way. The route is well marked.

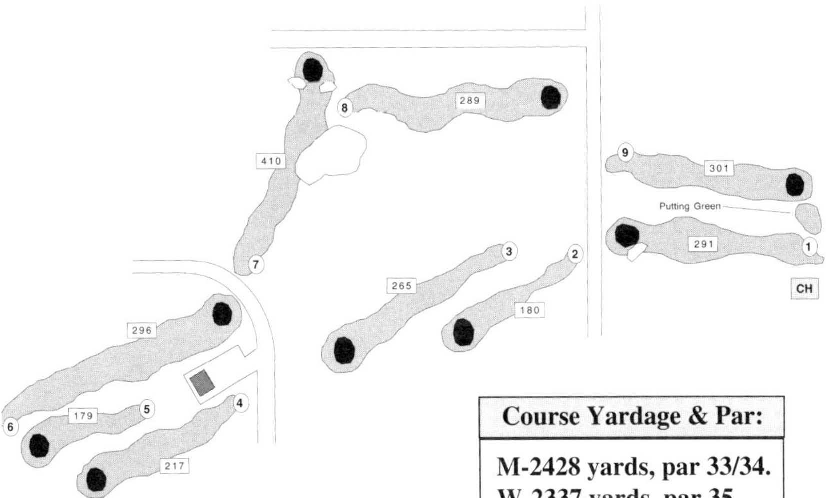

Course Yardage & Par:
M-2428 yards, par 33/34.
W-2337 yards, par 35.

Kinzua Hills Golf Club (semi-private, 6 hole course)

Off of Highway 19; Fossil, OR 97830
Phone: none. Fax: none. Web: none.
Manager: none. Pro: none.
Rating/Slope: M 60.8/99; W 61.0/95. **Course record:** 20.
Green fees: $8 all day rate; no credit cards.
Power cart: none available. **Pull cart:** none. **Trail fee:** not allowed.
Reservation policy: advance reservations are not taken. First come first served.
Winter condition: the golf course is open all year, weather permitting.
Terrain: flat, some hills. **Tees:** all grass. **Spikes:** metal spikes permitted.
Services: the golf course has very limited services, putting green.
Comments: The only 6 hole golf course in Oregon. Each hole has 3 sets of tees for 18 hole play. The greens and course are on the rough side but if you need a quick 9 holes give Kinzua Hills a try. Course is often on the honor system.

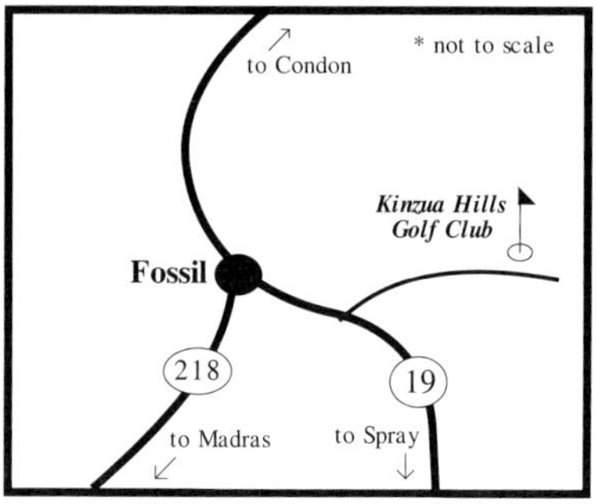

Directions: the golf course is located off Highway 19 in Fossil, Oregon. From Highway 19 go east toward Kinzua. While in Kinzua on Highway 19 travel northbound to the golf course. Look for signs.

Course Yardage & Par:
M-1463 yards, par 22. **W-1388 yards, par 24.** **(the par for 9 holes is 32).**

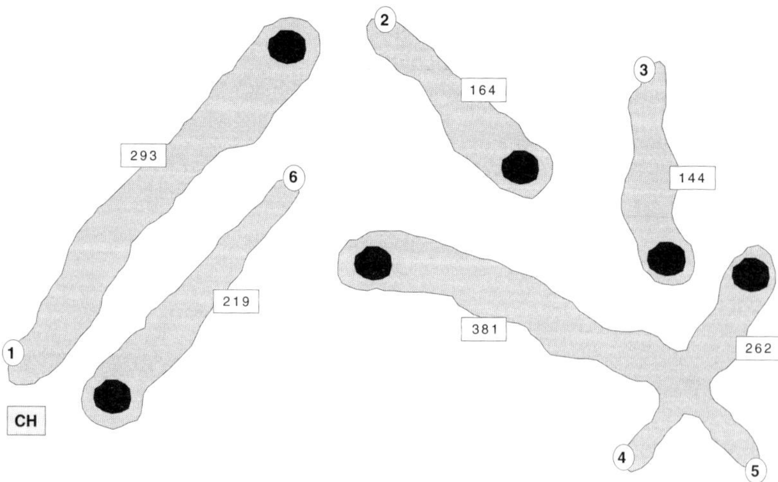

La Grande Country Club (private, 9 hole course)

10605 South McAlister Road, P.O. Box 836; Island City, OR 97850
Phone: (541) 963-4241. Fax: (541) 963-3891. Web: none.
Pro: Bill Rosholt, PGA. Superintendent: Steve Walker.
Rating/Slope: C 69.8/130; M 67.9/118; W 70.6/126. **Course record:** 63.
Green fees: some outside tee times are available, please call ahead; reciprocates.
Power cart: available. **Pull cart:** available. **Trail fee:** $7 for personal carts.
Reservation policy: private club members & guests of members only.
Winter condition: the golf course is open all year long, weather permitting.
Terrain: flat, some hills. **Tees:** all grass. **Spikes:** soft spikes required.
Services: club rentals, lessons, lounge, beer, wine, pro shop, driving range.
Comments: Long narrow course built amidst an apple orchard. Trees are in play off the tee as well as on your approach shots. Well bunkered postage stamp greens make this lush golf course a challenge for any level of golfer.

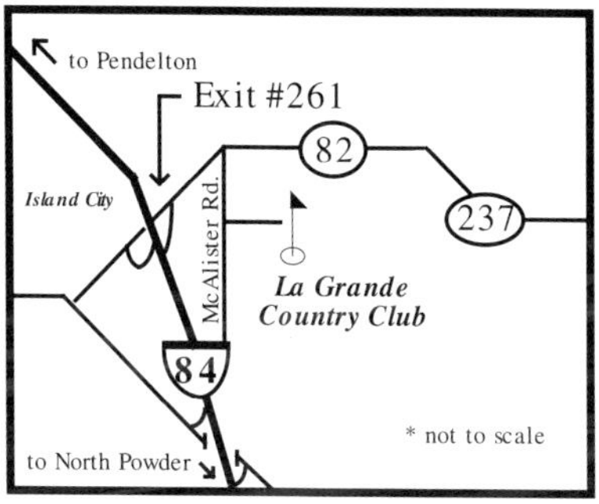

Directions: from I-84 E&W take the exit for Highway 82 exit in Island City, Ore. Proceed east for 2 miles then turn right on McAllister to the golf course which is 2 blocks ahead on your left hand side. Look for a sign marking your turn to the course.

Course Yardage & Par:

M-3267 yards, par 36.
W-2849 yards, par 38.
Dual tees for 18 holes:
M-6514 yards, par 72.
W-5653 yards, par 75.

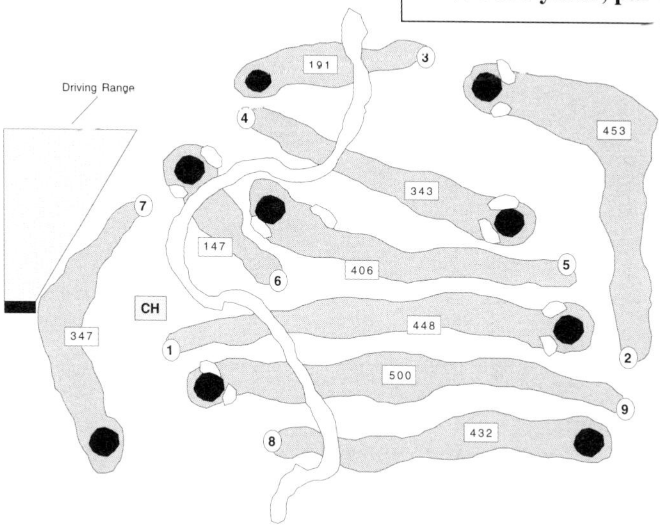

Lake Oswego Golf Course (public, 18 hole executive course)

17525 SW Stafford Road; Lake Oswego, OR 97034
Phone: (503) 636-8228. Fax: (503) 699-7465. Web: lakeoswegoparks.org
Manager/Director of Golf: Greg Carter, PGA.

Rating/Slope: the golf course is not rated. **Course Record:** 49.
Green fees: Monday thru Thursday $19/$11; Friday thru Sunday & Holidays $20/$12; Jr. & Sr. rates $13/$8 (Monday thru Friday). No credit cards.
Power cart: $6 handicapped only. **Pull cart:** $2. **Trail fee:** not allowed.
Reservation policy: make reservations by calling 7 days in advance for times.
Winter condition: the golf course is open all year long, damp conditions.
Terrain: flat, some hills. **Tees:** all grass. **Spikes:** metal spikes permitted.
Services: club rentals, lessons, snack bar, covered & lighted driving range.
Comments: golf course is great for seniors and those who want to practice their short game. The lighted and heated driving range is partially covered for use during inclement weather. For the beginner golfer Lake Oswego is sure to fit.

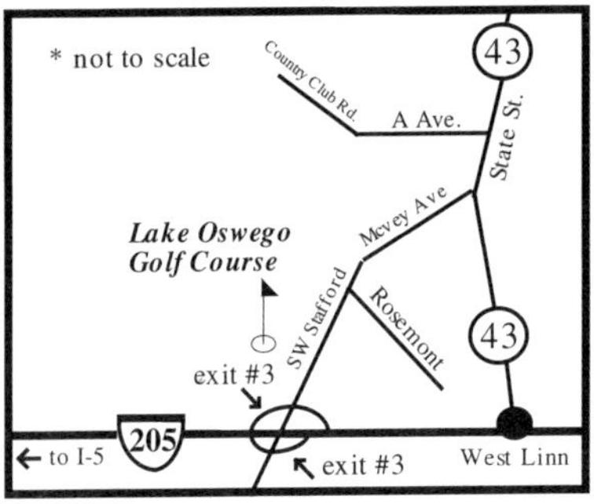

Directions: from I-205 exit (#3) at SW Stafford. Proceed for 2.5 miles northbound on SW Stafford. The course will be located on your left. You can also reach the course by taking Highway 43. Look for signs.

Course Yardage & Par:
M-2695 yards, par 54. **W-2695 yards, par 54.**

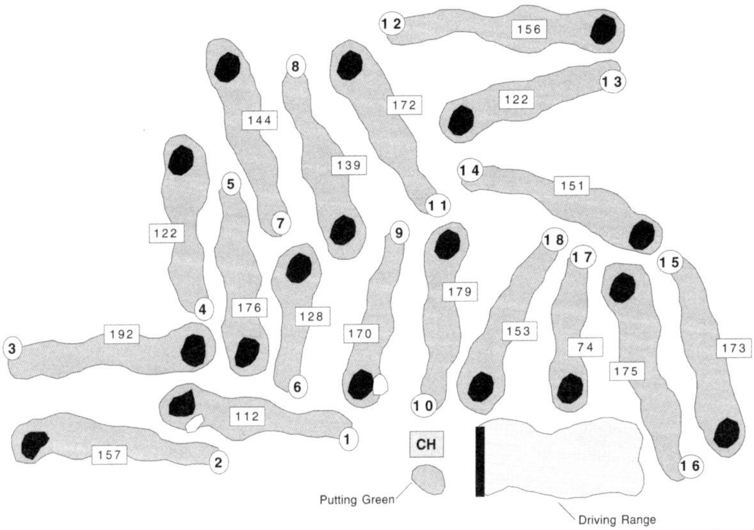

Lake Ridge Golf Course (public, 9 hole course)

Highway 140 West; HC 60, Box 199; Lakeview, OR 97630
Phone: (541) 947-3855. Fax: (541) 947-2653. Web: none.
Owners: Frank & Ann Zogan. Superintendent: Frank Zogan.
Rating/Slope: M 69.5/123; W 62.4/98. **Course record:** 65.
Green fees: $20/$10 all week long; Jr./Sr. rates; M/C, VISA.
Power cart: $15/$10. **Pull cart:** $3/$2. **Trail fee:** $8/$4 for personal carts.
Reservation policy: please call in advance for your tee times. No time limit.
Winter condition: the course is open all year long, weather permitting.
Terrain: flat (easy walking). **Tees:** all grass. **Spikes:** metal spikes permitted.
Services: club rentals, snack bar, beer, wine, pro shop, grass tee driving range.
Comments: This picturesque golf course is surrounded by the Warner Mountains and the Fremont National Forest. The golf course is in excellent condition during the summer months providing the golfer with lush fairways and firm greens. Worth a trip to the golf course if you are in the area.

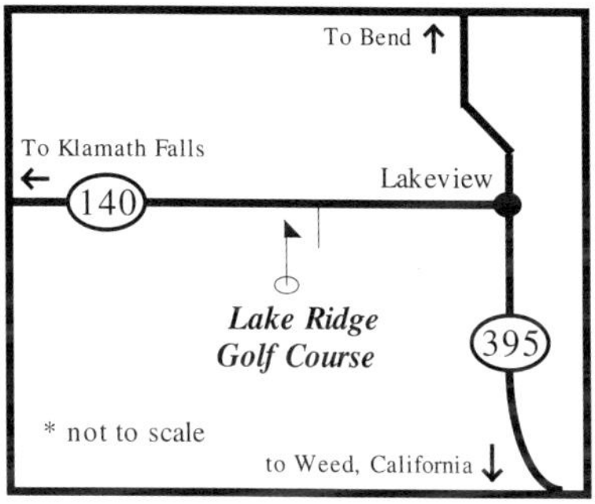

Directions: the golf course is located 3 miles west of Lakeview off Highway 140. From Klamath Falls travel 90 miles east on Highway 140 to the golf course. Look for signs marking your way to the course.

Course Yardage & Par:

M-3323 yards, par 36.
W-2965 yards, par 37.
Dual tees for 18 holes:
M-6647 yards, par 72.
W-5863 yards, par 74.

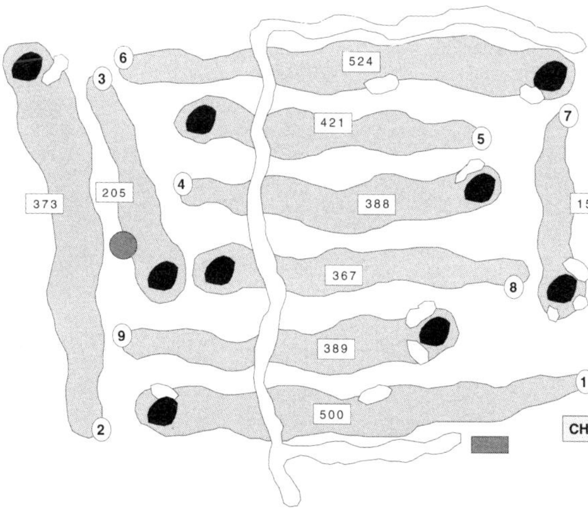

Lakeside Golf & Fitness Club (public, 18 hole course)

3245 NE 50th Street; Lincoln City, OR 97367
Phone: (541) 994-8442. Fax: (541) 994-2066. Web: www.lakeside-golf.com
PGA Director of Golf: Todd Young. Superintendent: Dr. Issam Dughi.
Rating/Slope: C 62.3/102; M 61.4/98; W 62.4/98. **Course record:** 60.
Green fees: $35/$20 Sunday thru Friday $40/$25 Saturdays; Jr. rates (17 and younger) $20/$12; Sr. rates 15% off the green fee; M/C, VISA.
Power cart: $25/$15. **Pull cart:** $3/$2. **Trail fee:** no personal carts allowed.
Reservation policy: yes, please call ahead for tee times (a must in the summer).
Winter condition: the golf course is open all year long, weather permitting.
Terrain: relatively hilly, walkable. **Tees:** grass. **Spikes:** metal spikes permitted.
Services: club rentals, lessons, snack bar, beer, wine, pop, pro shop, lockers, putting/chipping green, indoor range, racquet ball, tennis, health & fitness center.
Comments: good test golf with conditions improving yearly. Greens are medium in size well bunkered and tricky. Fairways are rolling and narrow in spots.

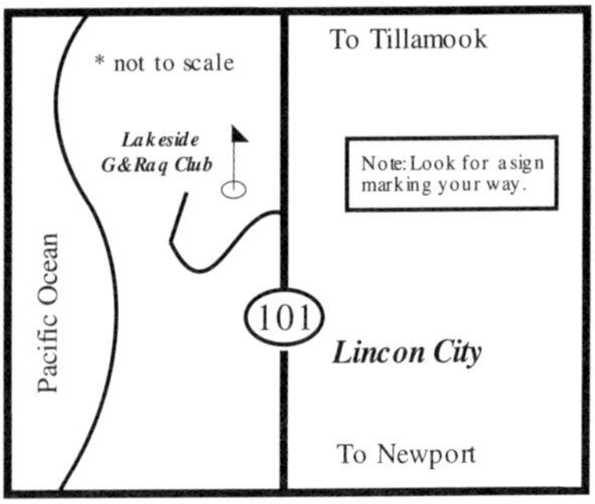

Directions: the golf course is located on the west side of Highway 101 at the very north end of Lincoln City. Turn off Highway 101 on N.E. Devils Lake Road. Follow N.E. Devils Lake Road to the golf course complex. Look for a sign marking the entrance to the course.

Course Yardage & Par:

C-4458 yards, par 65.
M-4256 yards, par 65.
W-3948 yards, par 69.

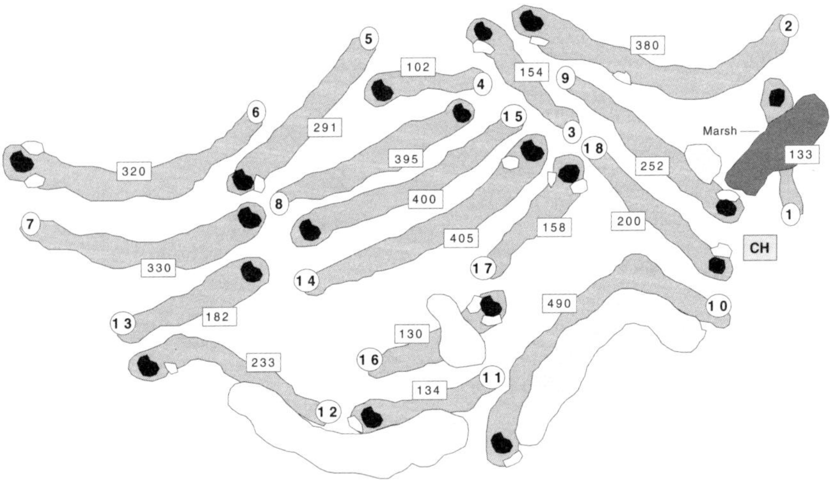

Langdon Farms Golf Club (public, 18 hole course)

24377 NE Airport Road; Aurora, OR 97002
Phone: (503) 678- 4653. Fax: (503) 678-3263. Web: www. langdonfarms.com
Pro: Terry Balinski, PGA. Superintendent: Phil Lagao.
Rating/Slope: P 73.5/128; C 71.7/125; R 69.0/118; PL 65.7/107. **Record:** 67.
Green fees: fluctuates, please call (cart included); M/C, VISA, DISCOVER.
Power cart: included in fee. **Pull cart:** available. **Trail fee:** not allowed.
Reservation policy: yes, please call up to 30 days in advance for tee times.
Winter condition: open year round, weather permitting. Very dry conditions.
Terrain: links style, depressed fairways. **Tees:** grass. **Spikes:** no metal spikes.
Services: club rentals, lessons, snack bar, lounge, restaurant, pro shop, practice range, putting greens, putting course (bentgrass), learning center, showers.
Comments: Designed by award winning architects John Fought & Robert Cupp. Depressed fairways give Langdon Farms a very unique look, one not found in the State of Oregon. Large Bentgrass greens highlighted with ground contours create chipping zones which truely makes Langdon Farms "one of a kind". A "state of the art" practice area boasts the largest grass teeing surface in the NW. Langdon Farms is truely one of the finest golf venues in the state of Oregon.

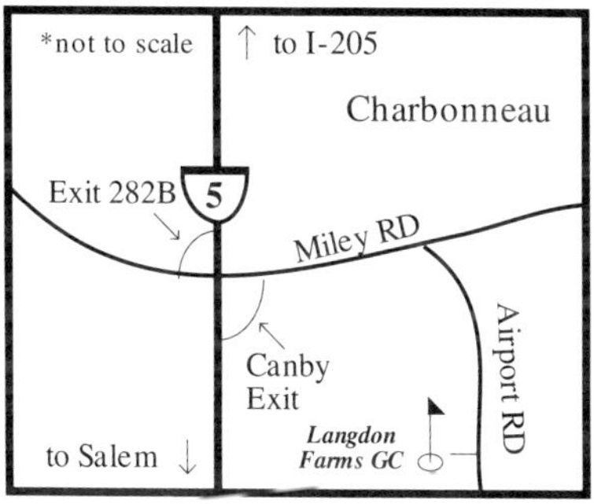

Directions: from I-5S take exit #282B. Travel eastbound then turn right on NE Airport Road. Travel 1 mile to the main entrance. From I-5N take the Canby exit turn right and then turn right on NE Airport Road. Follow to main entrance.

Course Yardage & Par:

Professional: 6931 yards, par 71.
Champion: 6522 yards, par 71.
Resort: 6052 yards, par 71.
Player: 5246 yards, par 71.

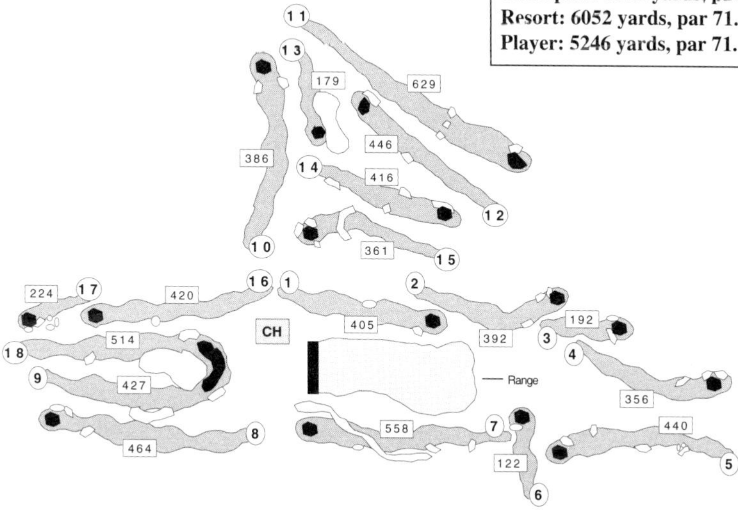

Laurel Hill Golf Course (public, 9 hole course)

9450 Old Stage Road; P.O. Box 167; Gold Hill, OR 97525
Phone: (541) 855-7965. Fax: none. Web: none.
Managers: Jan & Peter Fish. Superintendent: Dan Alexander.
Rating/Slope: M 63.0/92; W 61.6/88. **Course record:** 27.
Green fees: W/D $14/$8; W/E $16/$9; Jr. & Sr. rates; M/C, VISA.
Power cart: not available. **Pull cart:** $1. **Trail fee:** no charge for your cart.
Reservation policy: yes, call ahead of time, (recommended on the weekends).
Winter condition: the golf course is open all year long, damp to dry course.
Terrain: flat, some hills. **Tees:** grass & mats. **Spikes:** metal spikes permitted.
Services: club rentals, lessons, snack bar, beer, wine, beverages, pro shop, covered driving range, putting green, GHIN 9 hole handicapping service.
Comments: A challenging irons course of great scenic beauty, but not intimidating for beginners. Greens are on the small size and can be difficult to hold. Great golf course to bring the entire family to.

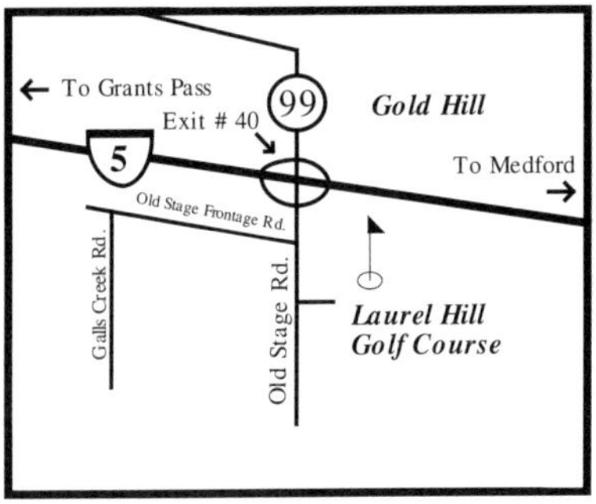

Directions: from I-5 N&S take exit #40 (Gold Hill/Jacksonville). Travel east for .25 miles on Old Stage Road to the golf course. The golf course will be located on your left hand side. Look for signs marking your turn to the parking lot.

Course Yardage & Par:
M-1915 yards, par 31. **W-1915 yards, par 31.**

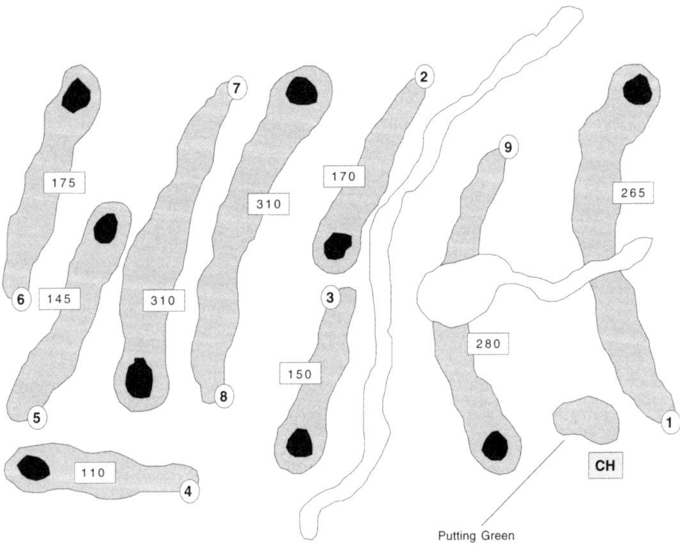

Laurelwood Golf Course (public, 9 hole course)

2700 Columbia Avenue; Eugene, OR 97403

Phone: (541) 484-4653. Fax: (541) 343-3012. Web: www.laurelwoodgolf.com

Pro: Kit Wilbur. Superintendent: James Matson.

Rating/Slope: C 70.0/121; M 67.3/112; W 69.2/115. **Course record:** 60.

Greens fee: $16/$10 all week long; Jr. & Sr. rates; M/C, VISA, AMEX.

Power cart: $18/$10. **Pull cart:** $3/$2. **Trail fee:** $5 (9 holes).

Reservation policy: yes, call 7 days ahead, especially in the summer months.

Winter condition: the course is open all year long, good conditions.

Terrain: relatively hilly. **Tees:** all grass. **Spikes:** metal or soft spikes allowed.

Services: club rentals, lessons, sandwiches, beer, juices, pro shop, covered driving range, putting & chipping greens, full club repair, wedding receptions.

Comments: this nine hole track was selected as the best course in Eugene in the October 2000 issue of "Eugene Weekly". Excellent course for a quick 9 holes.

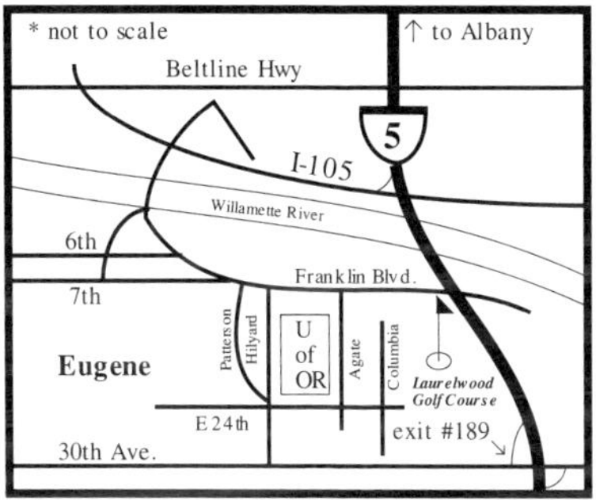

Directions: I-5 northbound take 30th Ave. exit to Hilyard. Turn right on Hilyard to E 24th turn right on E 24th. Proceed to Columbia and take a right. Proceed to the top of the hill. The pro shop is on the lower level. From I-5 southbound take the Eugene/University exit. Follow signs to the University of Oregon (Franklin Blvd to Agate St). Turn right on Agate St. to E 24th. Turn left on E 24th for 1 block. Turn right on Columbia St. to the course.

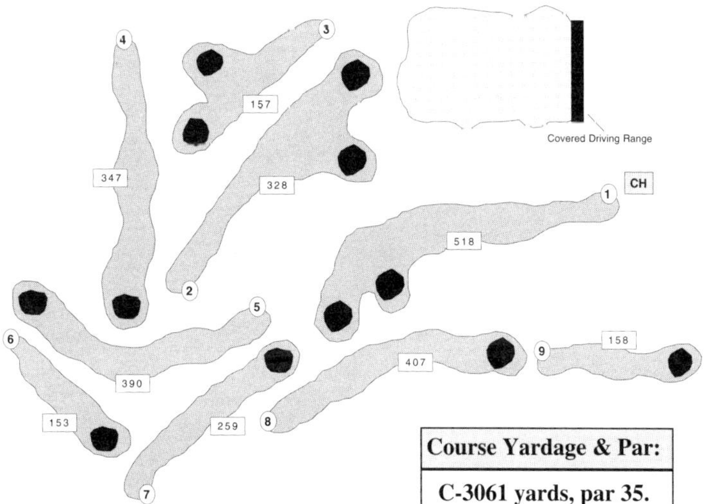

Course Yardage & Par:

C-3061 yards, par 35.
M-2735 yards, par 35.
W-2460 yards, par 36.

Lost Tracks Golf Club (public, 18 hole course)

60205 Sunset View Drive; Bend, OR 97702
Phone: (541) 385-1818. Fax: (541) 317-9589. Web: none.
Pro: Ian McLean, PGA. Superintendent: N/A.
Rating/slope: C 71.8/124; M 68.8/120; W 69.7/127. **Course record:** 68.
Green fees: $60/$35 all week long (walking) $75/$45 all week long (riding); Jr. & Sr. rates, off season rates and twilight rates available; M/C, VISA.
Power cart: included in green fee. **Pull cart:** $4/$2. **Trail fee:** not allowed.
Reservation policy: call up to 30 days in advance with a credit card guarantee.
Winter condition: dry, the golf course is closed during inclement weather.
Terrain: flat, rolling terrain. **Tees:** all grass. **Spikes:** soft spikes only.
Services: rentals, lessons, lounge, restaurant, snack bar, beer, pro shop, range.
Comments: the golf course is bordered by national forest land and carved out of a stand of Ponderosa and high desert pines. Lava rock outcroppings, sparkling lakes, and seaside sand filled bunkers are everywhere. Worth a special trip.

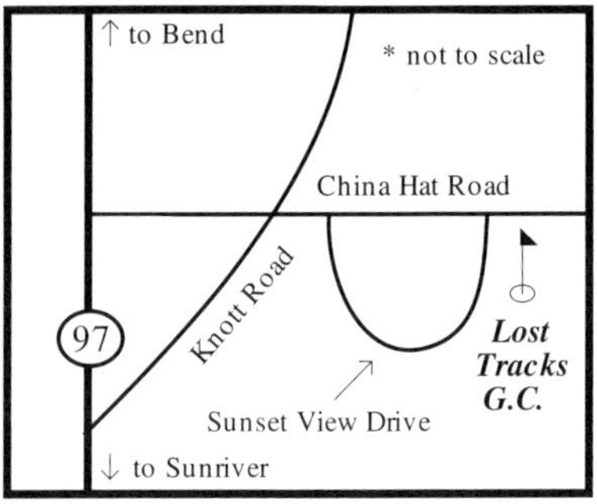

<u>**Directions:**</u> from Hwy 97 South turn east on China Hat Road. Proceed straight ahead, crossing Knott Road. Turn right on Sunset View Drive to the golf course.

Course Yardage & Par:
C-6875 yards, par 72.
M-6230 yards, par 72.
W-5282 yards, par 72.

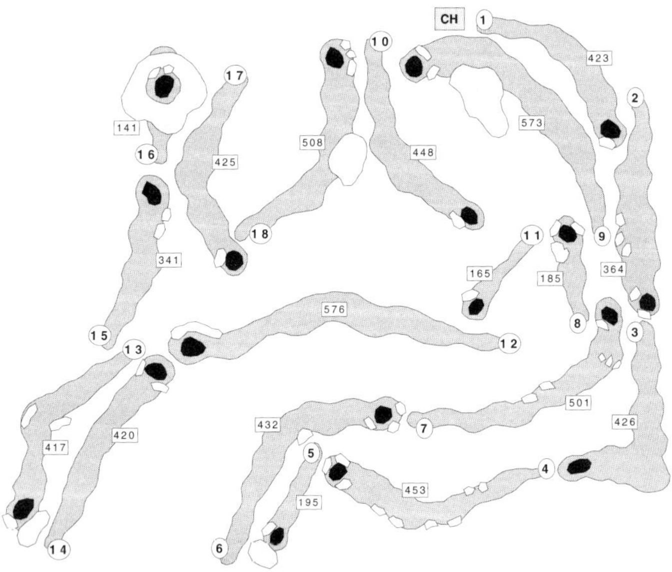

Mallard Creek Golf Course (public, 18 hole course)

31966 Bellinger Scale Road; P.O. Box 368; Lebanon, OR 97355
Phone: (541) 259-4653. Fax: (541) 259-2289. Web: mallardcreekgc.com
GM: Mark Tunstill, PGA. Superintendent: Ryan Jennings.

Rating/slope: T 73.6/140; C 72.2/135; M 69.7/125; W 71.1/136. **Record:** 65.
Green fees: W/D $40; W/E $45; Jr. & Sr. rates available; M/C, VISA.
Power cart: $24. **Pull cart:** $3/$2. **Trail fee:** personal carts not allowed.
Reservation policy: call up to 14 days in advance for all your tee-times.
Winter condition: dry conditions. The golf course is open all year long.
Terrain: flat, some hills. **Tees:** all grass. **Spikes:** soft spikes required.
Services: club rentals, lessons, lounge, restaurant, snack bar, beer, wine, liquor, pro shop, covered/ & lighted driving range, tennis courts, RV resort.
Comments: a challenging course from the back tees. Water comes into play on 6 holes and is a major factor on your club selection. Mature trees line most fairways coming into play for the big hitter. Several elevation changes provide dramatic holes giving the course true personality. Worth a special trip.

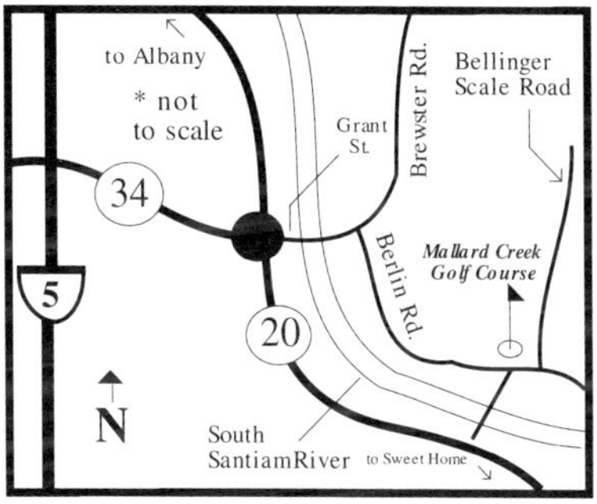

Directions: from I-5 N&S exit eastbound @ Hwy 34 exit Proceed east toward Lebanon. Proceed to Lebanon on Hwy 34 to Grant Street (which will become Brewster Rd.). Go straight on Grant until you reach Berlin Road. Turn right on Berlin Road (south). Proceed on Berlin Road until you come to Bellinger Scale Rd. turn left (north) to course on your left.

Course Yardage & Par:
T-6833 yards, par 72.
C-6730 yards, par 72.
M-6120 yards, par 72.
W-4860 yards, par 72.

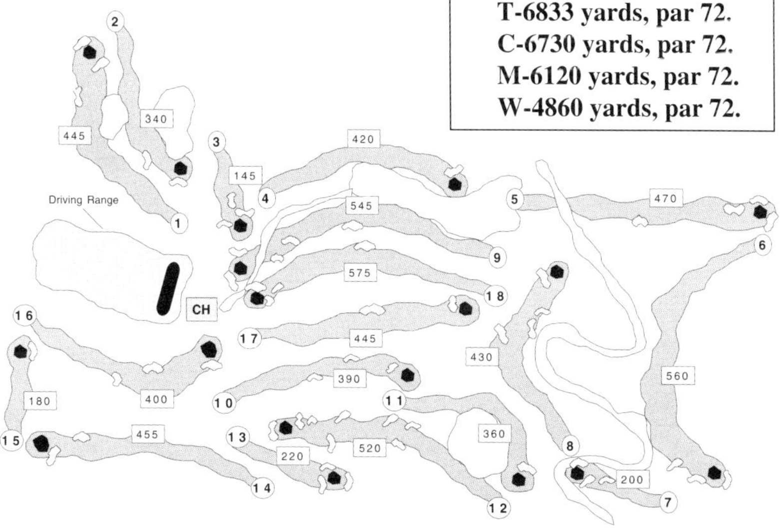

Manzanita Golf Course (public, 9 hole course)

P.O. Box 21; Lakeview Drive; Manzanita, OR 97130
Phone: (503) 368-5744. Fax: (503) 368-6744. Web: none.
Owners: Steve and Penny Erickson.
Rating/Slope: M 61.2/97; W 62.8/102. **Course record:** 29.
Green fees: $28/$15 all week long; M/C, VISA.
Power cart: none. **Pull cart:** $2 (per 9 holes). **Trail fee:** not allowed.
Reservation policy: yes, taken 7 days in advance and recommended in summer.
Winter condition: the golf course is open all year long, damp turf conditions.
Terrain: flat, some hills. **Tees:** all grass. **Spikes:** metal spikes permitted.
Services: club rentals, snack bar, pro shop, driving range, putting green.
Comments: Picturesque course located on the beautiful Oregon coast. Greens are medium in size and well bunkered. Fairways are narrow giving the golfer very tight landing area's. This golf course which is not a back-breaker is worth the trip if you are driving the Oregon coast and want to play a quick 9 holes.

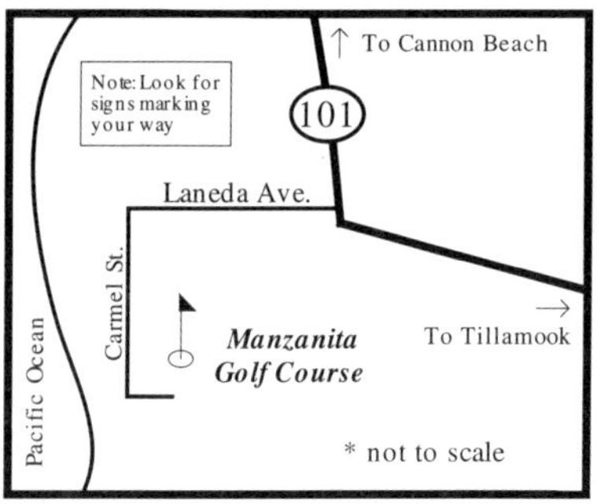

Directions: from Hwy 101 N&S take Manzanita Junction exit toward the beach. You will be on Laneda Avenue. Follow Laneda for .6 miles to S Carmel Avenue (there is a sign to the golf course) turn left. Go through residential area for .8 miles to the golf course on your left. The golf course is located at the intersection of Lakeview Drive and NeCarney Blvd.

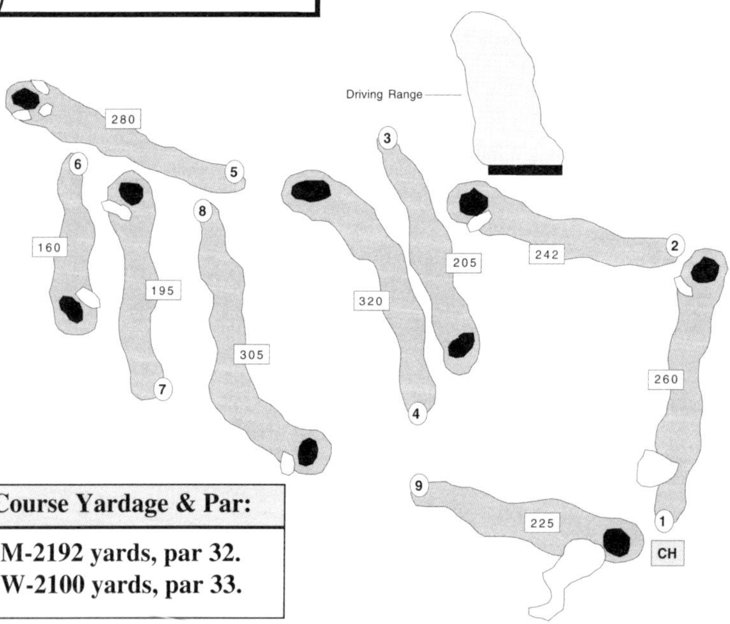

Course Yardage & Par:

M-2192 yards, par 32.
W-2100 yards, par 33.

Marysville Golf Course (public, 9 hole course)

2020 SW Allen Lane; P.O. Box 1203; Corvallis, OR 97339
Phone: (541) 753-3421. Fax: none. Web: none.
Owner: R. M. Hoselton & Sons. Superintendent: none.
Rating/Slope: M 68.4/110; W 69.2/104. **Course record:** 31.
Green fees: W/D $18/$12; W/E $22/$12; annual memberships; no credit cards.
Power cart: Sr.'s only $15. **Pull cart:** $3. **Trail fee:** no charge for your cart.
Reservation policy: call in advance to the golf course for the tee time policy.
Winter condition: the course is open all year long, weather permitting, dry.
Terrain: flat, walkable course. **Tees:** all grass. **Spikes:** metal spikes permitted.
Services: club rentals, beer, small pro shop, practice area, putting green.
Comments: Family owned course that is well kept and offers a great family golfing atmosphere. The golf course is fairly wide open with only a few hazards coming into play off the tee. The course plays much longer than the yardage.

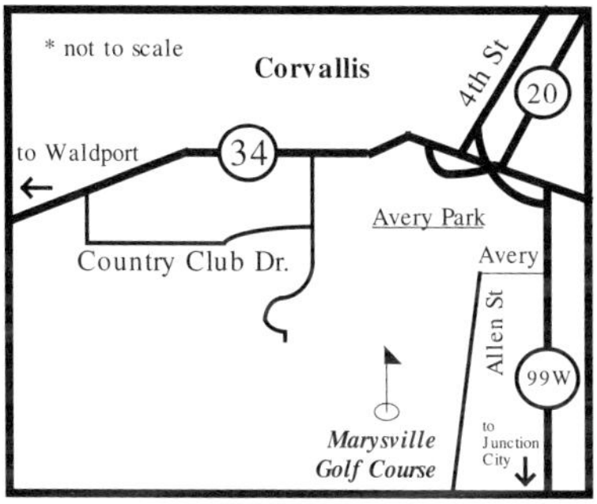

Directions: from Highway 20, take Avery Park exit. When entering the park, take left hand fork. Go to four way stop. Continue straight on S.W. Allen Lane to the golf course. From Hwy 99W south of Corvallis go to Avery Lane & turn west. Go to four way stop. Turn left on S.W. Allen Lane. Go straight on S.W. Allen Lane to the golf course.

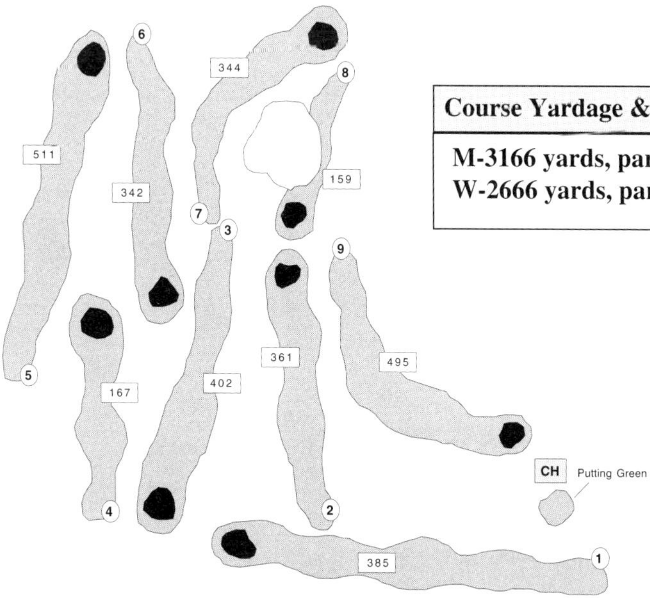

Course Yardage & Par:

M-3166 yards, par 36.
W-2666 yards, par 39.

McKay Creek Golf Course (public, 9 hole course)

1416 N.W. Jackson Street; Hillsboro, OR 97124
Phone: (503) 693-7612. Fax: none. Web: www.mckaycreekgolf.com
Pro: Craig Wilcox, PGA. Superintendent: Jason Reding.
Rating/Slope: C 64.8/103; M 63.0/93; W 66.8/106. **Course record:** 65.
Green fees: W/D $17/$9; W/E $21/$11; Jr. & Sr. rates $15/$8 (M-F).
Power cart: $19/$10. **Pull cart:** $2. **Trail fee:** $5 for personal carts.
Reservation policy: please call ahead for tee-time reservation policies.
Winter condition: the golf course is open all year long, weather permitting.
Terrain: flat, easy walking. **Tees:** all grass. **Spikes:** soft spikes required.
Services: club rentals, snack bar, lessons, beer, wine, pro shop, driving range.
Comments: this 9 hole track opened for play in 1996. The golf course features tree-lined fairways, medium sized greens and McKay Creek running through many holes. The course has a covered, 22 station lighted driving range.

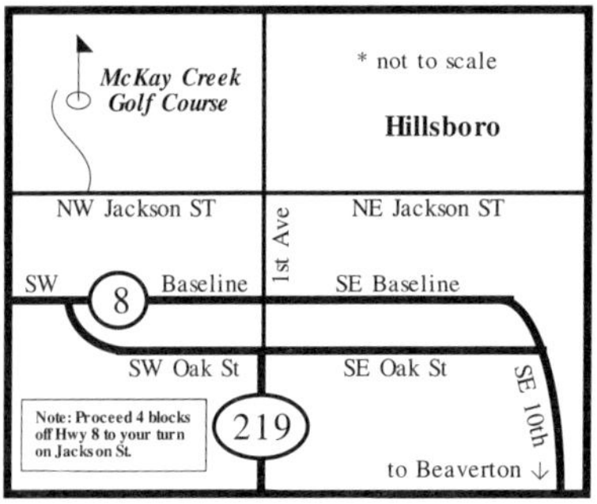

Directions: the golf course is located off of Hwy 8 in Hillsboro Oregon. Turn north on 1st Avenue. Follow 1st 4 blocks to Jackson Street. Turn left on Jackson. Proceed 9 blocks to the golf course which will be on your left hand side. Look for signs.

Course Yardage & Par:

C-2760 yards, par 36.
M-2445 yards, par 36.
W-2445 yards, par 36.

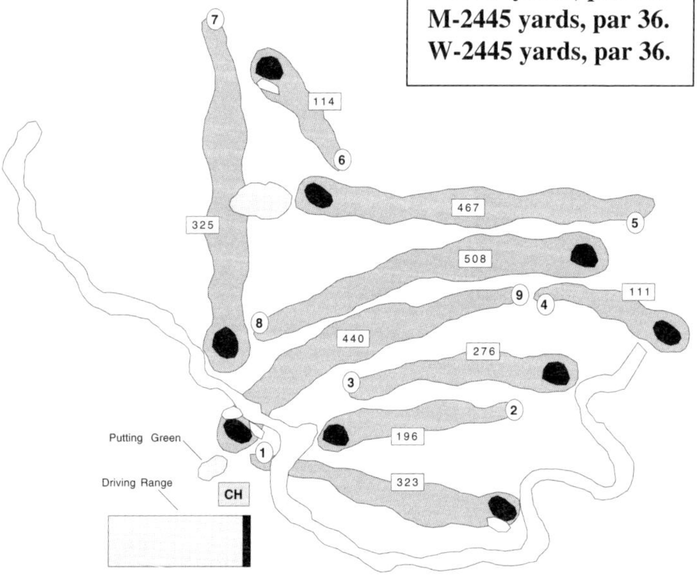

McKenzie River Golf Course (public, 9 hole course)

Mailing Address: P. O. Box 98; Walterville, OR 97489
Street Address: 41723 Madrone Street; Springfield OR 97478
Phone: (541) 896-3454. Fax: none. Web: none.
Owners: Rod Omlid. Superintendent: Rod Omlid.
Rating/Slope: M 65.9/104; W 65.5/103. **Course record:** 29.
Green fees: W/D $24/$16; W/E $26/$16; Jr. rates W/D only; no credit cards.
Power cart: $10 per nine holes. **Pull cart:** $2. **Trail fee:** none.
Reservation policy: yes, call 3 days in advance for your starting times.
Winter condition: the golf course is open all year long, dry (drains well).
Terrain: flat (easy walking). **Tees:** grass. **Spikes:** soft spikes preferred.
Services: club rentals, snack bar, beer, pro shop, putting & chipping green.
Comments: the golf course has a 10 hole punch card for your green fees at $98. Pride of ownership shows on this well kept manicured facility that is nestled in between the McKenzie River and surrounding mountains. The owners of the course invite you to see why they are the " Jewel on the river".

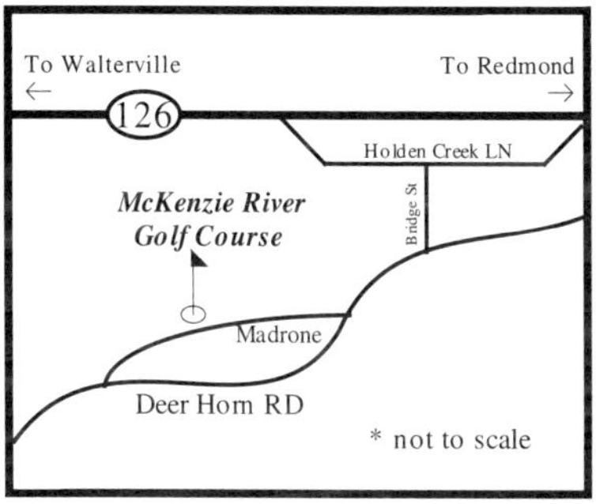

Directions: from Highway 126 exit at Holden Creek Lane. Follow the road past mile post 17 to Bridge Street which crosses the river. Turn right on Deerhorn Road then another right on Madrone Street which leads to the clubhouse.

Course Yardage & Par:

M-2783 yards, par 35.
W-2304 yards, par 35.
Dual tees for 18 holes:
M-5629 yards, par 70.
W-4746 yards, par 70.

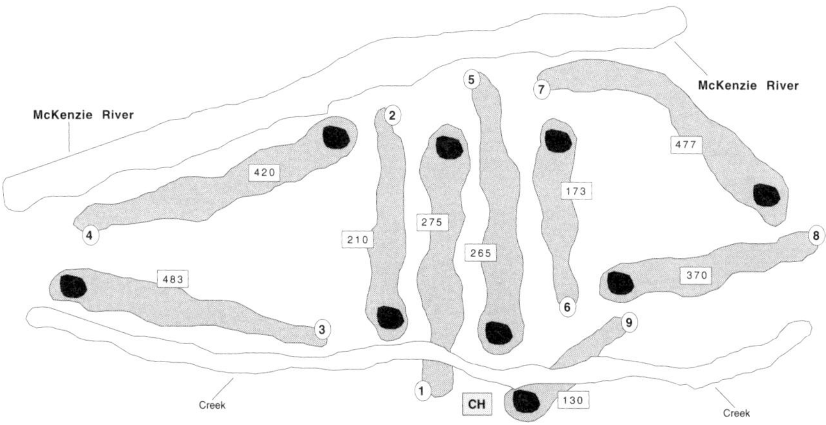

McMenamins Pub Course (public, 18 hole par 3 course)

2126 SW Halsey; Troutdale, OR 97060
Phone: (503) 669-8610. Fax: (503) 665-4209. Web: none.
Manager: Mike McMenamin. Superintendent: Curt Morgan
Rating/Slope: the golf course is not rated. **Course record:** 52.
Green fees: W/D $14/$7; W/E $16/$8; M/C, VISA.
Power cart: none. **Pull cart:** $2 (per 9 holes). **Trail fee:** not allowed.
Reservation policy: tee times 8am to dark call the front desk for reservations.
Winter condition: the golf course is open all year long, damp turf conditions.
Terrain: relatively hilly. **Tees:** all grass. **Spikes:** soft spikes only.
Services: club rentals, putting green, vending machines.
Comments: this par 3 layout that measures under 1200 yards for 18 holes is not your typical par 3. All holes are under 90 yards in length and play to postage stamp size greens. The terrain is on the hilly side giving the golfer a wide variation of shot making. Be sure to visit the on course pub after your round.

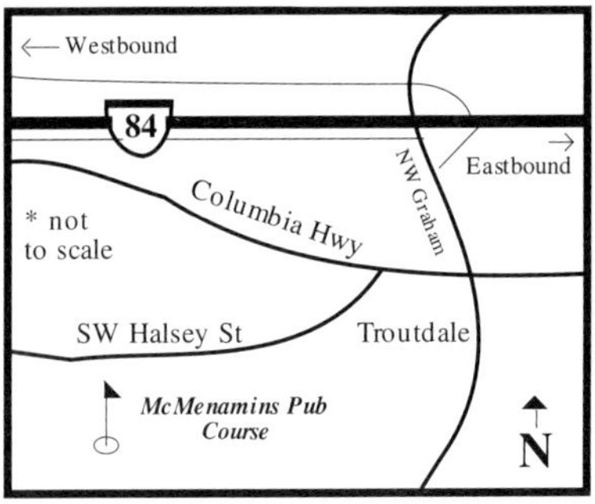

Directions: from I-84 E&W exit south at the Troutdale exit. Exit to NW Graham Road. Turn right on Graham Road to Columbia Hwy. Turn right on Columbia Hwy. Follow this to SW Halsey Street Turn left on Halsey Street and follow Halsey until you reach the golf course on your left hand side. The course is located in the McMenamin Edgefield Manor complex. Look for signs that are posted.

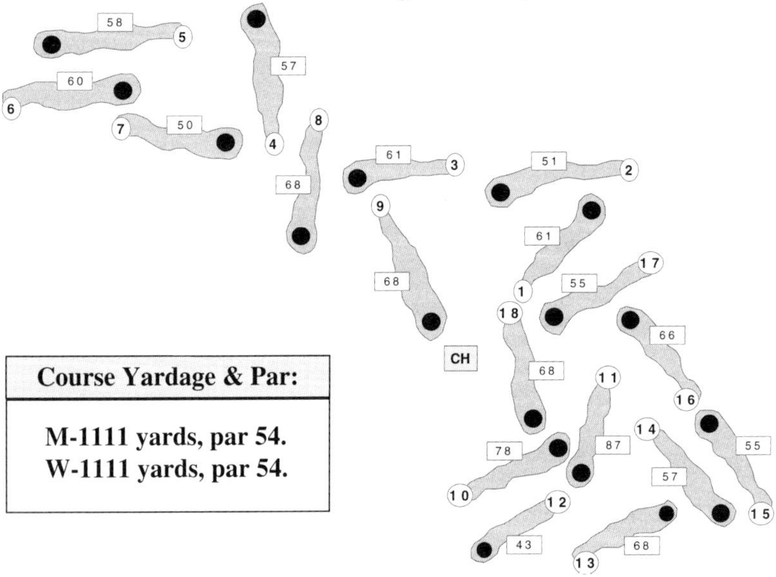

Course Yardage & Par:

M-1111 yards, par 54.
W-1111 yards, par 54.

McNary Golf Club (semi-private, 18 hole course)

155 McNary Estates Drive North; Keizer, OR 97303
Phone: (503) 393-4653. Fax: (503) 393-4881. Web: www.mcnarygolf.com
Pro: Rich Brown, PGA. Superintendent: David Bashaw.
Rating/Slope: C 69.2/121; M 67.9/119; W 70.4/117. **Course record:** 63.
Green fees: $40/$20 all week long; Sr. rates; M/C, VISA.
Power cart: $24/$14. **Pull cart:** $2. **Trail fee:** not allowed.
Reservation policy: yes, public can call up to 3 days in advance for tee-times.
Winter condition: the golf course is open all year long, damp conditions.
Terrain: flat, easy walking. **Tees:** grass. **Spikes:** soft spikes preferred.
Services: club rentals, lessons, snack bar, restaurant, lounge, beer, wine, liquor, pro shop, putting & chipping greens. **Comments:** this challenging course offers wide, open fairways with large well bunkered greens. The facility is well taken care of and offers the golfer a country club look and feel. Worth a trip.

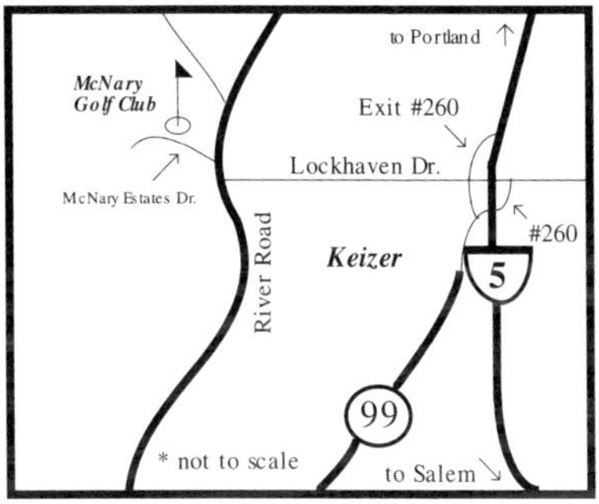

Directions: from I-5 N&S take exit #260 (Lockhaven) and go west on Lockhaven proceed for 1.3 miles to River Road, turn right and proceed to McNary Estates Dr. and turn left to the golf course. Look for signs marking your entrance to the course.

Course Yardage & Par:

C-6215 yards, par 71.
M-5960 yards, par 71.
W-5325 yards, par 71.

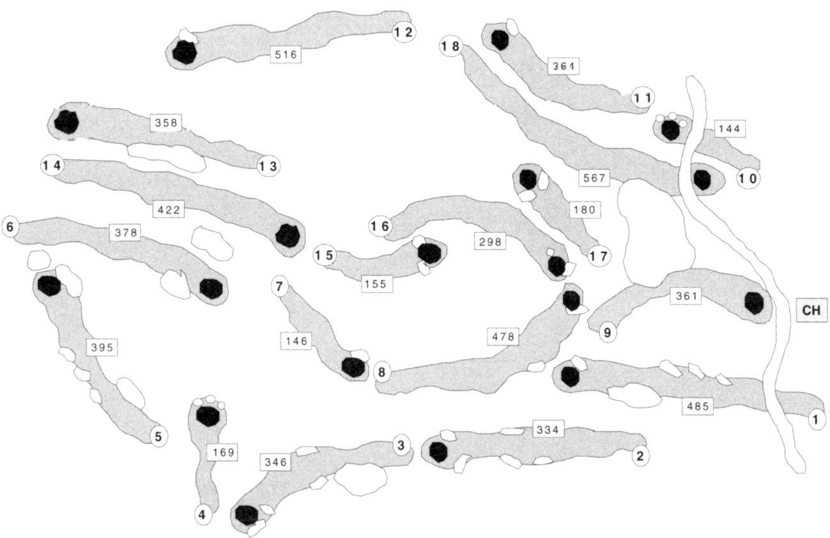

Meadow Lakes Golf Course (public, 18 hole course)

300 Meadow Lakes Drive; Prineville, OR 97754
Phone: (541) 447-7113. Fax: (541) 447-7831. Web: none.
Pro: Lee Roberts, PGA. Superintendent: Wayne Van Matre.
Rating/Slope: T 71.7/125; C 70.3/122; M 67.6/116; W 69.0/121. **Record:** 66.
Green fees: Monday to Sunday $34; winter rates $25 (all day).
Power cart: $24/$15. **Pull cart:** $3/$2. **Trail fee:** personal carts not allowed.
Reservation policy: call 7 days in advance for your tee times.
Winter condition: the golf course is open all year long, weather permitting.
Terrain: beautifully mounded. **Tees:** grass. **Spikes:** soft spikes required.
Services: fully stocked pro shop, club rentals, lessons, lounge, restaurant, snack bar, liquor, putting green, driving range. **Comments:** A beautiful newer course. Ten ponds, 16 surface acres of water, 2000 trees, and 66 bunkers will challenge you at every turn. *Golf Digest* "Environmental Leader in Golf" award winner. If you get the chance be sure to include Meadow Lakes on any golf trip to Oregon.

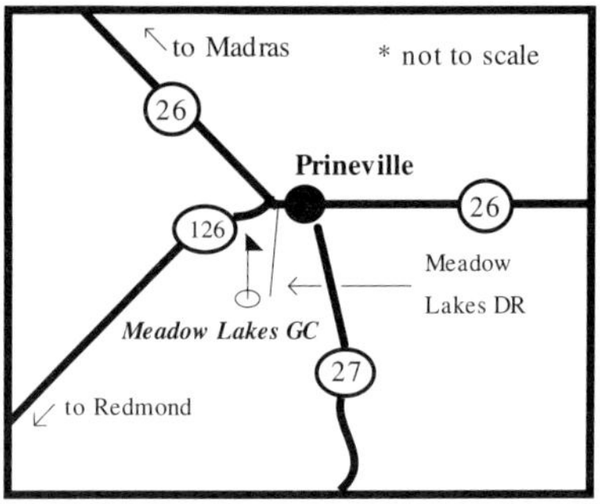

Directions: from Portland take Hwy 26 through Madras to Prineville. In Prineville the highway becomes 3rd street. Meadow Lakes Dr. will be on your right. There will be signs to mark your way to the course.

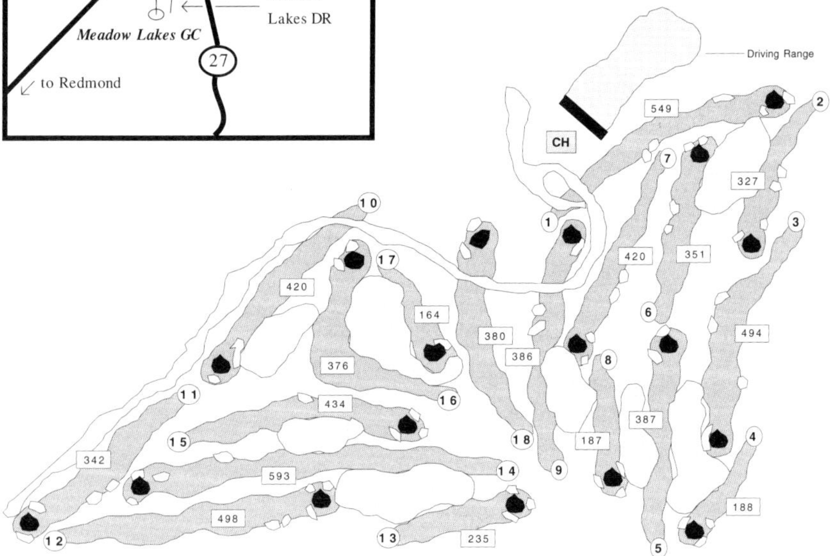

Course Yardage & Par:	
T-6731 yards, par 72.	M-5849 yards, par 72.
C-6398 yards, par 72	W-5155 yards, par 72.

Meadowlawn Golf Club (public, 9 hole course)

3898 Meadowlawn Loop SE; Salem, OR 97301
Phone: (503) 363-7391. Fax: none. Web: www.meadowlawngolf.com
Pro: Brain Weaver, PGA. Superintendent: Mark Turnquist.
Rating/Slope: M 59.6/95; W 61.0/95. **Course record:** 26.
Green fees: W/D $22/$13; W/E $25/$13; no special rates; M/C, VISA.
Power cart: $20/$10. **Pull cart:** $2. **Trail fee:** $12/$6 for personal carts.
Reservation policy: yes, call 1 day in advance for your starting times.
Winter condition: the golf course is open all year long. Wet during the winter.
Terrain: very flat. **Tees:** all grass. **Spikes:** metal spikes permitted.
Services: club rentals, lessons, beverages, snack bar, pro shop, putting green.
Comments: The course has rolling hills and is very easy to walk. The golf course plays very tight in places, putting an emphasis on shot placement. This Salem golf course is a senior and beginner/intemediate golfer favorite.

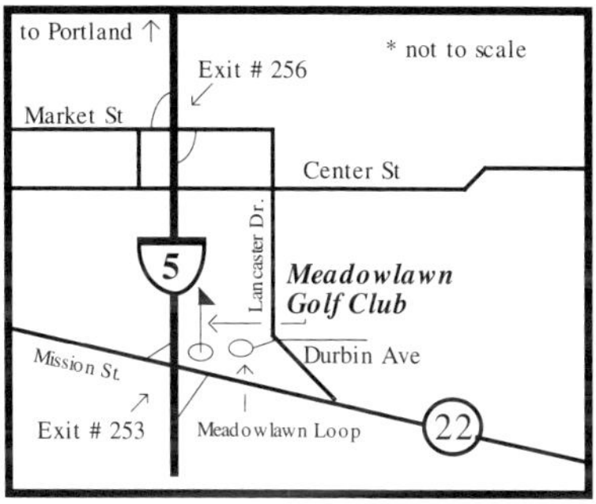

__Directions:__ from I-5 exit #256 (Market St-Silverton). Eastbound on Market St. for .6 mi to Lancaster Dr. Turn right on Lancaster Dr. Proceed for 1.9 mi to Durbin St. then take a right, then immediate right on Meadowlawn Loop SE which curves around to the course on your left. Or take exit #253 and go east on Mission to the first exit you come to. Turn left on Lancaster. Proceed to Durbin Street. Left on Durbin Street. Follow above directions.

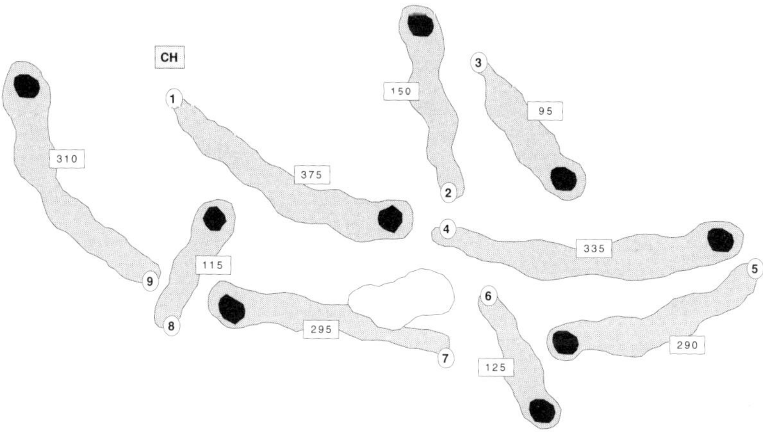

Course Yardage & Par:
M-2090 yards, par 32; W-2090 yards, par 34.

Meriwether National Golf Club (public, 27 hole, 9 hole exc.)

5200 SW Roodbridge Road; Hillsboro, OR 97123
Phone: (503) 648-4143. Fax: (541) 640-9757. Web: none.
Pro: Kevin Winston, PGA. Superintendent: Doug Sather.
Rating/Slope: North/West C 71.3/121; M 69.5/118; W 72.3/113. **Record:** 64.
Greens fee: W/D $26/$14; W/E $30/$16; Jr./Sr. rates; M/C, VISA.
Power cart: $20/$11. **Pull cart:** $2. **Trail fee:** no personal carts allowed.
Reservation policy: yes for weekends and holidays. A must in the summer.
Winter condition: the golf course is open all year long. Damp conditions.
Terrain: flat (easy walking). **Tees:** all grass. **Spikes:** soft spikes preferred.
Services: clubhouse with banquet facilities, club rentals, lessons, snack bar, pro shop, driving range. **Comments:** the golf course is very challenging, and includes one of the toughest par 4's in the state. Great public golf course that also has a covered driving range and a short 9 hole course measuring 1789 yards from the back tees. Meriwether is a must play for any northwest golfer.

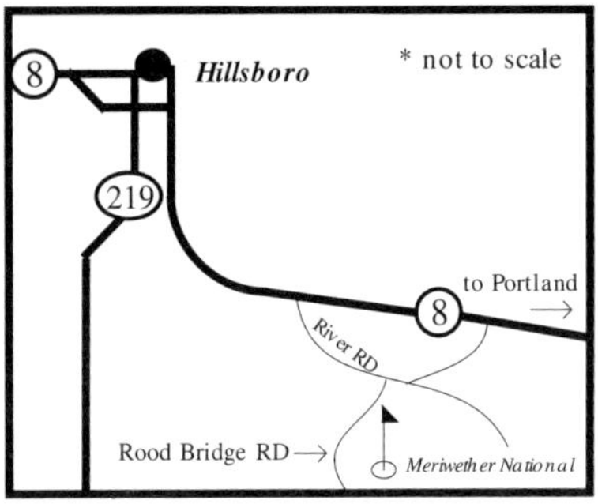

Directions: the course is located at the west edge of Hillsboro, OR. From Hwy 8, proceed east to River Rd. Turn south on River Rd. Turn right on Rood Bridge Rd and follow this to the golf course.

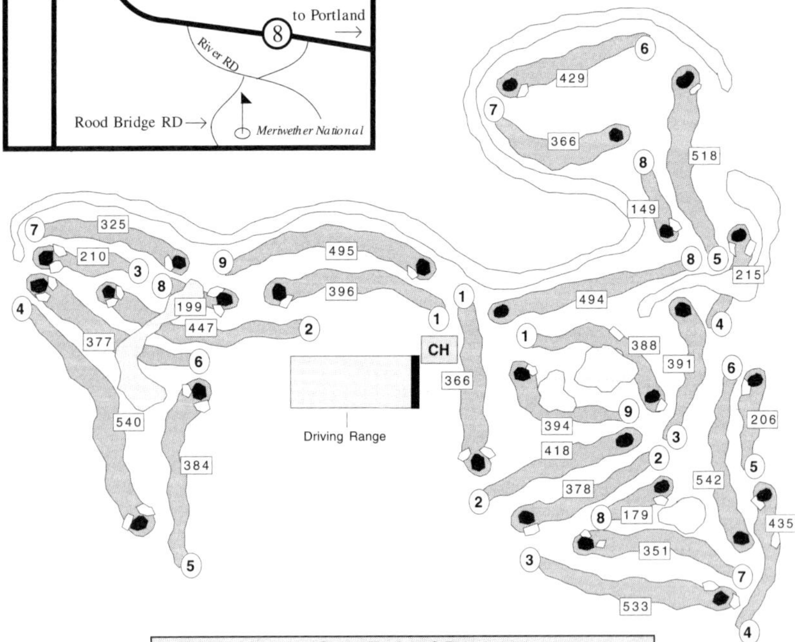

Course Yardage & Par:		
(South Course)	(West Course)	(North Course)
C-3406 yards, par 36.	C-3346 yards, par 36.	C-3373 yards, par 36.
M-3151 yards, par 36.	M-3178 yards, par 36.	M-3186 yards, par 36.
W-2813 yards, par 36.	W-2852 yards, par 36.	W-2914 yards, par 37.

Michelbook Country Club (private, 18 hole course)

1301 Michelbook Lane; McMinnville, OR 97128

Phone: (503) 472-8079. Fax: (503) 435-1334. Web: www.michelbook.com

Pro: Mel Chaufty, PGA. Superintendent: Bob Fluter.

Rating/Slope: C 71.5/127; M 70.1/128; W 71.1/128. **Course record:** 63.
Green fees: private club, members & guests only, reciprocates $45.
Power cart: private club. **Pull cart:** private club. **Trail fee:** private club.
Reservation policy: private club members & guests of members only.
Winter condition: the golf course is open all year long. Dry conditions.
Terrain: flat (easy walking). **Tees:** grass. **Spikes:** soft spikes only (summer).
Services: club rentals, lessons, snack bar, restaurant, beer, lounge, pro shop, driving range, putting & chipping greens. **Comments:** The golf course can be very tight in places. Lakes, bunkers and tree lined fairways put and emphasis on shot making. Greens are fast and can be hard to hold in summer. Great course.

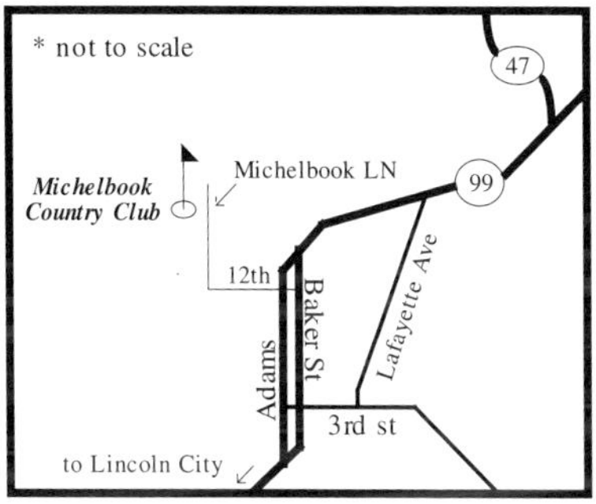

Directions: from Hwy 99 (Pacific Hwy W). Follow Hwy 99 into town and make a right turn onto 12th Avenue. Proceed to Michelbook Lane and the golf course. From Hwy 18 (River Hwy) come into town and go north on Baker St. and then take a left on 12th Ave. to the golf course.

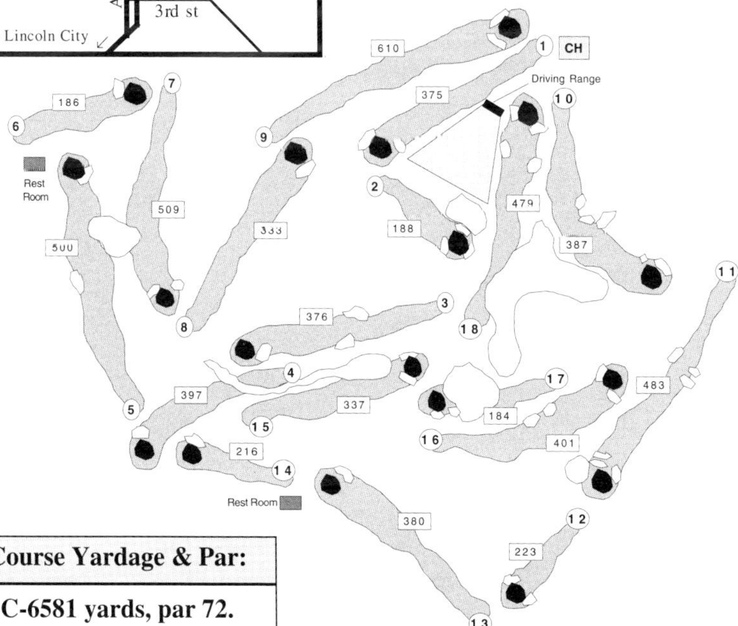

Course Yardage & Par:
C-6581 yards, par 72.
M-6212 yards, par 72.
W-5599 yards, par 72.

Middlefield Village G. C. & D. R. (public, 18 hole course)

91 Village Drive; Cottage Grove, OR 97424

Phone: (541) 942-8730. Fax: (541) 942-7745. Web: none.

Manager: Kimberly Coffey. Superintendent: Loren Erickson.

Rating/Slope: M 63.3/101; W 63.8/102. **Course record:** 64.

Green fees: W/D $20/$14; W/E $24/$16; Jr. & Sr., college rates W/D $16/$10.

Power cart: $18/$10. **Pull cart:** $2. **Trail fee:** $8/$4 for personal carts.

Reservation policy: please call 1 week in advance for tee times.

Winter condition: the golf course is open all year long. Drains well in winter.

Terrain: flat (easy walking). **Tees:** all grass. **Spikes:** soft spikes preferred.

Services: club rentals, snack bar, beer, wine, pro shop, driving range.

Comments: excellent easy to play golf course that is well kept. The gentle rolling fairways and the scenic setting along the Row River add to this Bunny Mason designed track. Be sure to stop by if you are in the area. Good course.

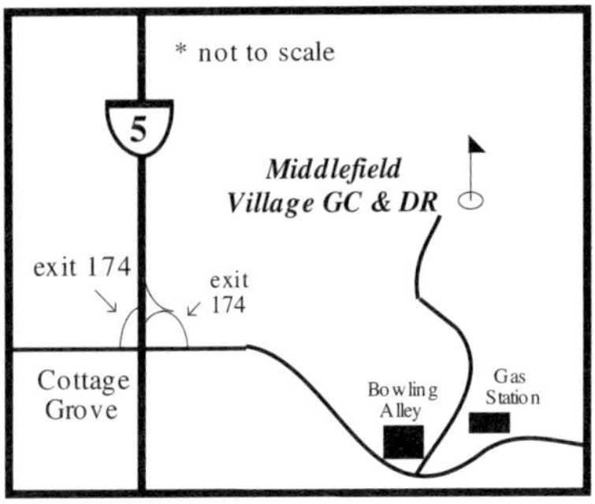

__Directions:__ from I-5 north and south in Cottage Grove take exit # 174. Proceed to Middlefield Village and the golf facility. Look for signs marking your turns to the golfing facility. The course is located 20 minutes south of Eugene, Oregon.

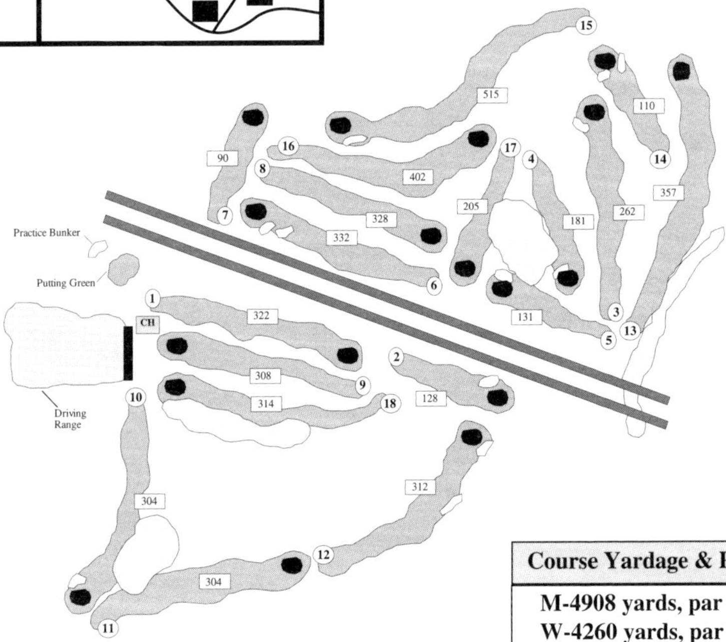

Course Yardage & Par:

M-4908 yards, par 68.
W-4260 yards, par 68.

Milton-Freewater Golf Course (public, 18 hole course)

W 301 Catherine Street; Milton-Freewater, OR 97862
Phone: (541) 938-7284. Fax: (541) 938-6411. Web: none.
Pro/Manager: G.R. Gillette. Superintendent: Tony Anfinson
Rating/Slope: M 57.6/83; W 58.0/85. **Course record:** 54.
Green fees: $15.75/$10.50; Jr. & Sr. rates $12.60/$8.40; VISA, M/C.
Power cart: $20/$14. **Pull cart:** $1. **Trail fee:** $6 for personal carts.
Reservation policy: yes, call 3 days in advance for weekends, holiday T-times.
Winter condition: the golf course is open all year long. Dry (drains well).
Terrain: flat, back 9 is hilly. **Tees:** grass. **Spikes:** soft spikes only.
Services: club rentals, lessons, restaurant, lounge, pro shop, putting green.
Comments: the golf course is tight in places and is perfect to help you improve your iron play. Water comes into play on several holes. Fair public course.

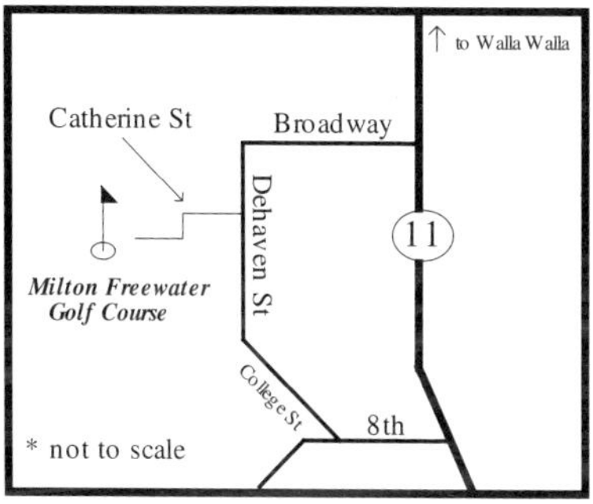

Directions: golf course located in Milton-Freewater behind the high school, west on Hwy 11. Look for sign on highway for the turn to the golf course. When in Milton-Freewater turn westbound on 2nd NW for .2 miles. Turn right on Dehaven Street. Proceed to Catherine Street and turn left.

Course Yardage & Par:
M-3346 yards, par 60.   **W-3314 yards, par 61.**

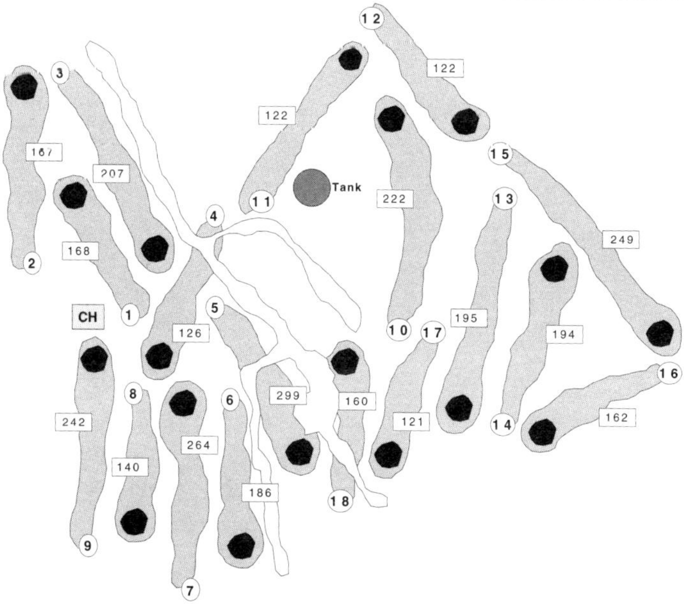

Mountain High Golf Course (public, 18 hole course)

20505 Murphy Road; Bend, OR 97702
Phone: (541) 382-1111. Fax: (541) 382-0364. Web: none.
Manager: Ed Cecil. Superintendent: Ron Loucks.
Rating/Slope: C 72.1/132; M 69.2/122; F 67.3/115; W 69.2/120. **Record:** 69.
Green fees: $48/$27, includes cart; spring rates; M/C, VISA.
Power cart: includued in fee. **Pull cart:** none. **Trail fee:** not allowed.
Reservation policy: yes, call 7 days in advance for all tee-times.
Winter condition: the golf course is closed from November 1st to mid-March.
Terrain: flat, rolling hills. **Tees:** all grass. **Spikes:** soft spikes preferred.
Services: club rentals, pro shop, snack bar, beer, wine, lessons, driving range.
Comments: Fantastic island green on hole #5. Water will come into play on over half the course. O.B. is everywhere and puts a real emphasis on accuracy. Fairways are lined with large Pondersa pines and are spectacular. Great course.

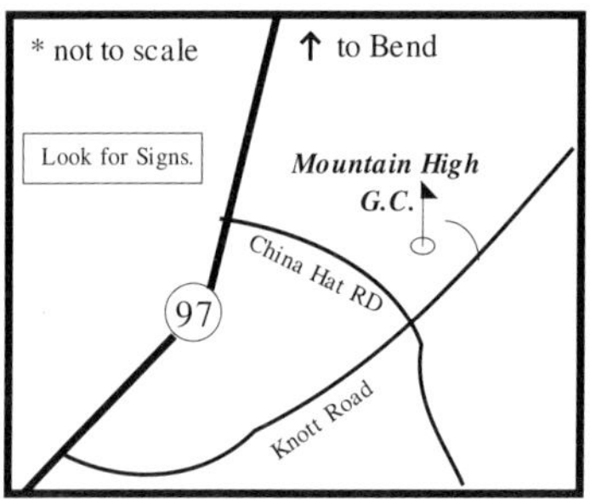

Directions: from Bend go south on Hwy 97. Take left on China Hat Road. Proceed approximately .25 miles to the entrance of the golf course. Look for signs from Hwy 97.

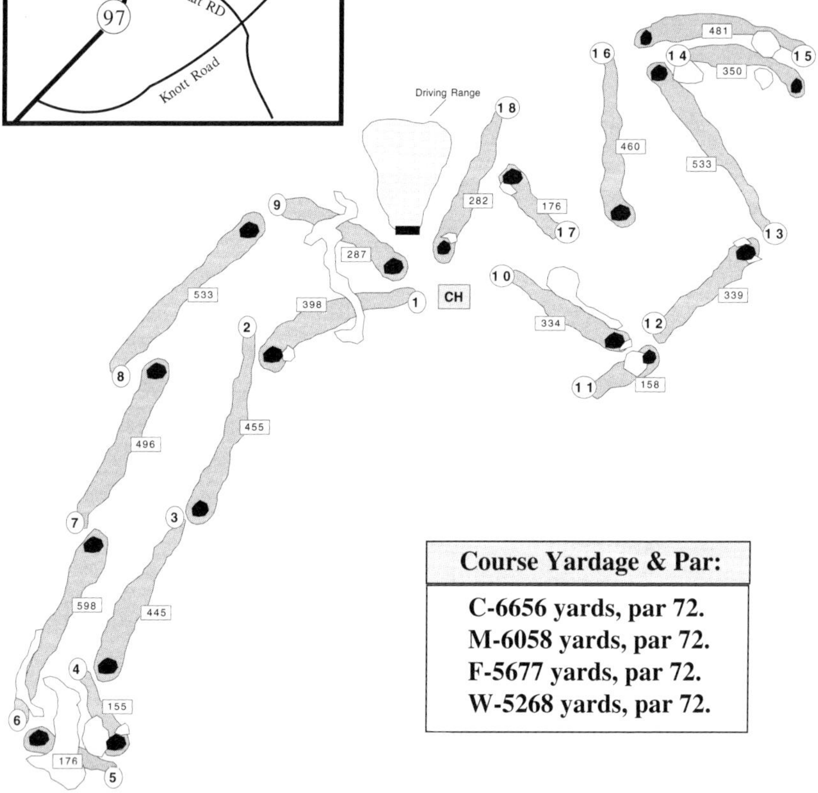

Course Yardage & Par:

C-6656 yards, par 72.
M-6058 yards, par 72.
F-5677 yards, par 72.
W-5268 yards, par 72.

Mountain View Golf Course (public, 18 hole course)

27195 SE Kelso Road; Boring, OR 97009
Phone: (503) 663-4869. Fax: (503) 663-4515. Web: none.
Pro: Toby Tommaso. Superintendent: not availble.
Rating/Slope: C 68.7/119; M 66.1/115; W 70.3/113; F 69.2/113. **Record:** 61.
Green fees: W/D $22/$11; W/E $25/$15; Jr. & Sr. rates; M/C, VISA.
Power cart: W/D $23/$14; W/E $25/$15. **Pull cart:** $3. **Trail fee:** $11/$6.
Reservation policy: yes, call 1 week in advance for your starting time.
Winter condition: the golf course open, weather permitting. Dry winter course.
Terrain: flat, some hills. **Tees:** all grass. **Spikes:** soft spikes preferred.
Services: club rentals, lessons, snack bar, restaurant, lounge, beer, wine, liquor, pro shop, putting & chipping greens, driving range. **Comments:** this golf course offers beautiful mountain views and some of the driest winter play in the area.

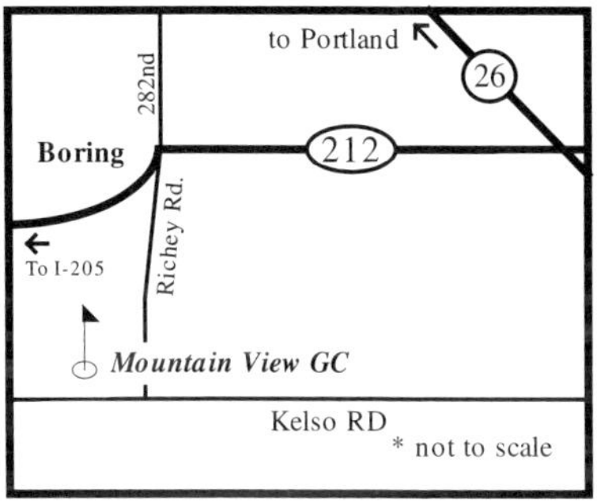

<u>**Directions**</u>**:** from Hwy 26 turn west at flashing yellow light in Boring, proceed 3 miles to the course on your right. You can also exit at Boring Rd (212) and go west to Richey Road. Turn left and proceed to Kelso Road and turn right to the course.

Course Yardage & Par:
C-6058 yards, par 71.
M-5934 yards, par 71.
W-5572 yards, par 71.
F-5140 yards, par 73.

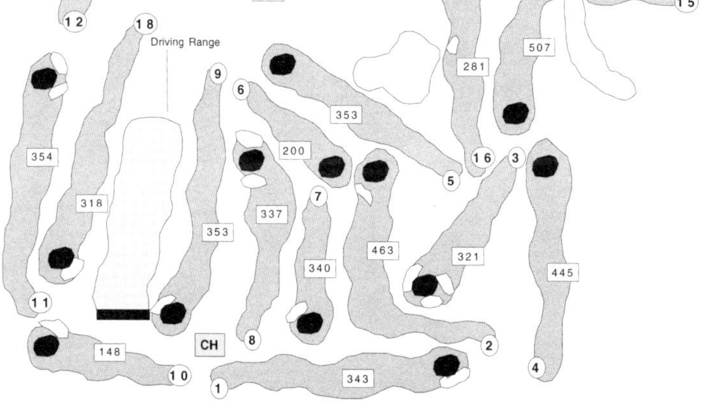

Myrtle Creek Golf Course (public, 18 hole course)

P.O. Box 6007; 1316 Fairway Drive; Myrtle Creek, OR 97457
Phone: (541) 863-4653. Fax: (541) 863-4768. Web: myrtlecreekgolf.com
Pro: Keith Johnson, PGA. Superintendent: Jerry Whiteaker.
Rating/Slope: T 72.7/139; C 71.2/134; M 69.0/127; W 69.7/122. **Record:** 65.
Green fees: W/D $35; W/E $39; winter rates; Jr. & Sr. rates.
Power cart: $22/$14. **Pull cart:** $4/$2.50. **Trail fee:** $7 for personal carts.
Reservation policy: please call up to 14 days in advance for tee times.
Winter condition: the golf course is open, weather permitting. Dry course.
Terrain: flat, some rolling hills. **Tees:** all grass. **Spikes:** soft spikes preferred.
Services: club rentals, lessons, snack bar, restaurant, pro shop, driving range.
Comments: this golf course offers beautiful views of the surrounding countryside. Opened in early summer of 1997 this Graham Cooke designed layout features large, well bunkered greens. Great highland course that is worth a trip.

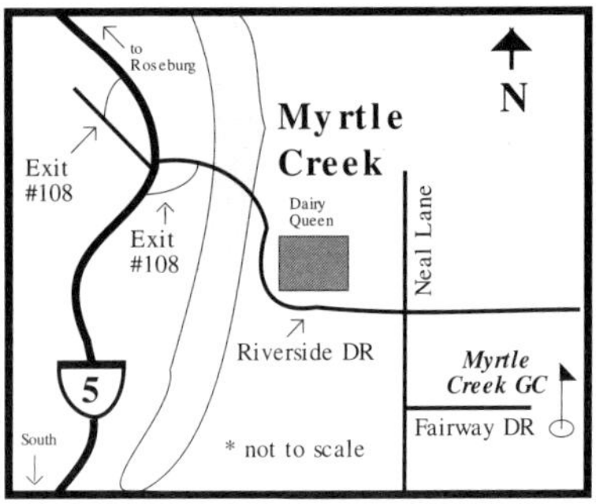

Directions: from I-5 N&S take the Myrtle Creek exit #108. Proceed eastbound and head through the downtown Myrtle Creek. Proceed through the traffic light, cross the bridge and make a hard left onto Riverside Drive. Take a right off Riverside at Neal Lane, then turn left at Fairway Drive to the course.

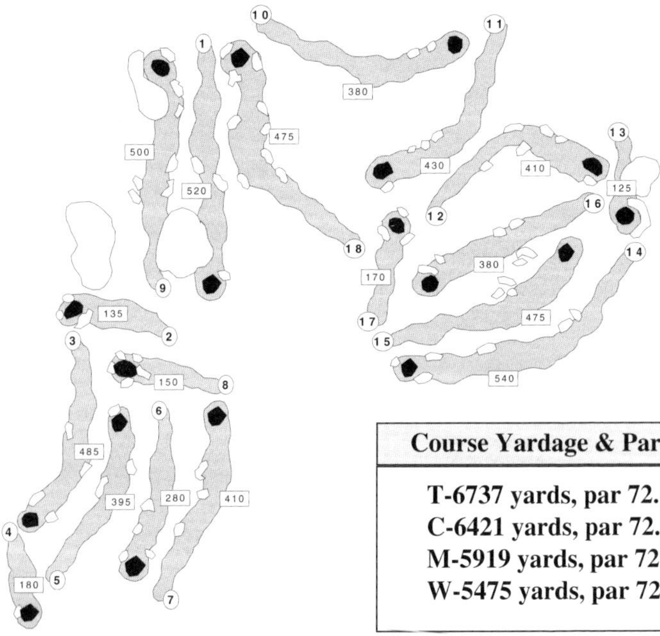

Course Yardage & Par:

T-6737 yards, par 72.
C-6421 yards, par 72.
M-5919 yards, par 72.
W-5475 yards, par 72.

Neskowin Beach Golf Course (public, 9 hole course)

48405 Hawk Avenue; P.O. Box 855; Neskowin, OR 97149
Phone: (503) 392-3377. Fax: none. Web: none.
Pro: Tom Clark, PGA. Superintendent: Linda Eversole.
Rating/Slope: M 65.4/104; W 68.8/122. **Course record:** 28.
Green fees: $22/$12 all week long; M/C, VISA.
Power cart: $20/$10. **Pull cart:** $2. **Trail fee:** not allowed.
Reservation policy: yes, recommended but not required (a must in summer).
Winter condition: the course is closed from November 1st to March 15th.
Terrain: flat (easy walking). **Tees:** grass/mats. **Spikes:** metal spikes permitted.
Services: club rentals, lessons, snack bar, beverages, pro shop, putting green.
Comments: this course has fabulous, well kept turf which is seems to always be green no matter the weather conditions or the time of year. Small flat greens and creeks that wander through the track make this golf course a real challenge. The track is tucked away from the wind even though the course is located on the scenic Oregon Coast. Tee-times are a must during the peak summer season.

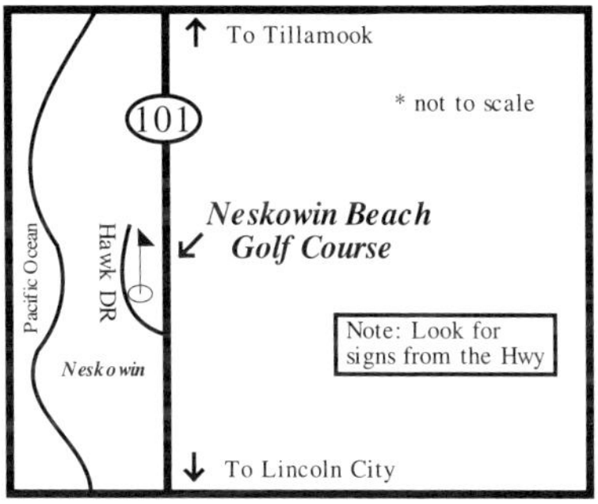

Directions: from Highway 101, turn north on Hawk Avenue. The golf course is located 1/4 mile ahead on your right hand side. Look for a sign on Highway 101 marking your turn to the golf course.

Course Yardage & Par:
M-2519 yards, par 35.
W-2448 yards, par 35.

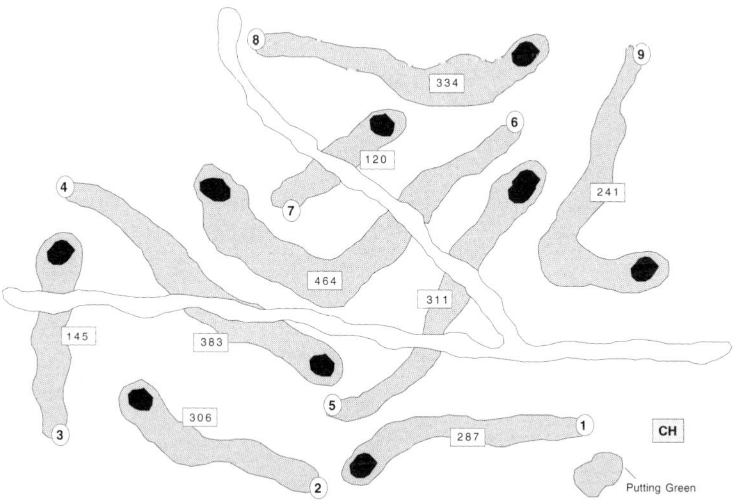

Nine Peaks Golf Course (public, 18 hole course)

1152 NW Golf Course Road; Madras, OR 97741
Phone: (541) 475-3511. Fax: (541) 475-7301. Web: none.
Owners: Kevin & Deirdre O'Meara. Superintendent: none.
Rating/Slope: M 73.4/116; W 69.2/112. **Course record:** 61.
Green fees: $22/$12 all week long; M/C, VISA, DISCOVER, NOVUS.
Power cart: $20/$12. **Pull cart:** $2. **Trail fee:** $6/$3 for personal carts.
Reservation policy: please call ahead for tee-times policies.
Winter condition: open all year, however closed periodically due to snow.
Terrain: flat (easy walking). **Tees:** grass. **Spikes:** soft spikes preferred.
Services: club rentals, lessons, snack bar, beer, wine, pro shop, putting green.
Comments: the course is very flat and is easy to walk. The new nine has several challenging greens guarded by bunkers and water. Great views of the Cascade Mountain Range. This golf course is worth a special trip if in Central Oregon.

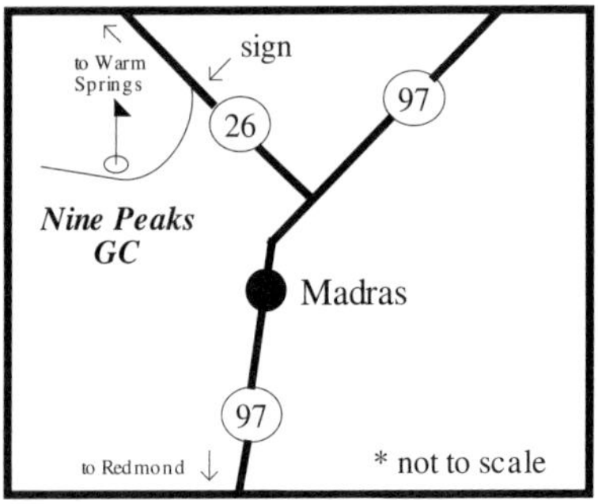

Directions: the golf course is located off of Highway 26, 1.25 miles west of Madras, Oregon. Look for the signs on Highway 26 marking your turn to the golf course. The location of your turn to the golf course is well marked.

Course Yardage & Par:
C-6582 yards, par 72. **M-6280 yards, par 72.** **W-5745 yards, par 72.**

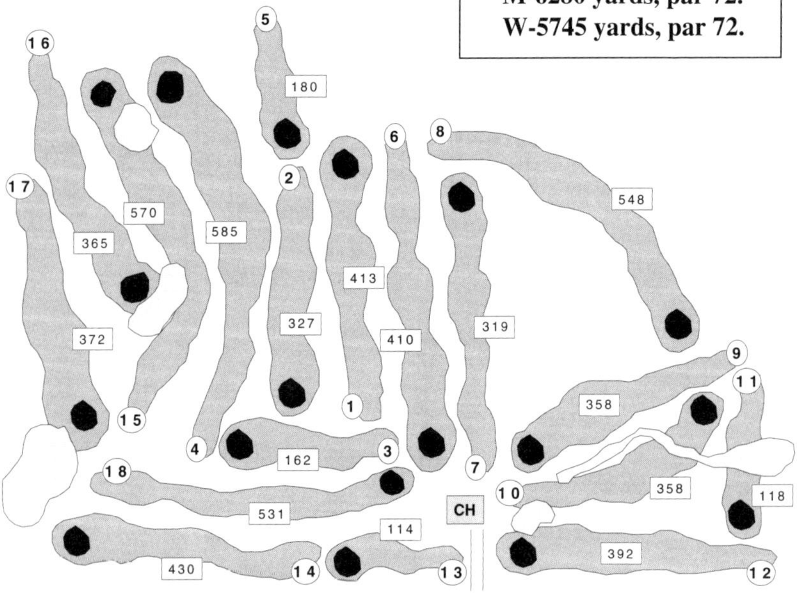

Northwest Aluminum Golf Club (private 9 hole par 3)

3313 West 2nd Street; The Dalles, OR 97058
Phone: (541) 296-6161. Fax: none. Web: none.
Pro: none. Superintendent: none.
Rating/Slope: the golf course is not rated. **Course record:** 23.
Green fees: private golf course for members and employees only.
Power cart: private course. **Pull cart:** private course. **Trail fee:** private course.
Reservation policy: private golf course for employees and guests only.
Winter condition: the golf course is closed November 1st to February 28th.
Terrain: flat, easy walking course. **Tees:** all grass. **Spikes:** soft spikes only.
Services: very limited services. putting green.
Comments: this company owned and operated golf course was built in 1957 and is exclusively reserved for company employees and their guests. There are some trees that come into play on this short "pitch and putt" course. Greens are small and very hard to hold in the summer.

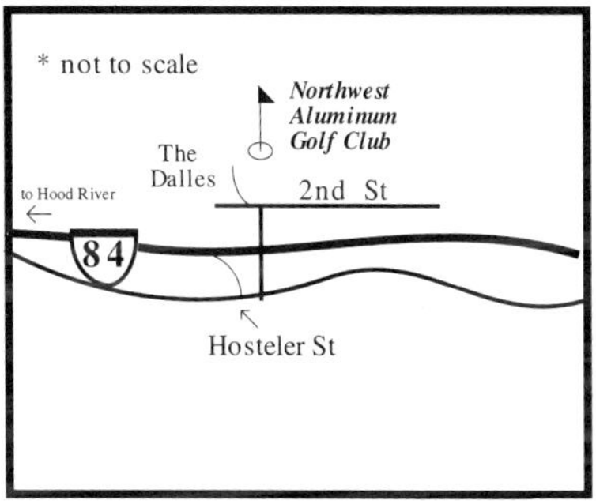

<u>**Directions:**</u> from I-84 going East and West, take exit #82 and make a left turn onto 6th Street E, when you come to Hostletler Road turn left. Proceed to the golf course on West 2nd Street.

Course Yardage & Par:
M-1103 yards, par 27.
W-1103 yards, par 27.

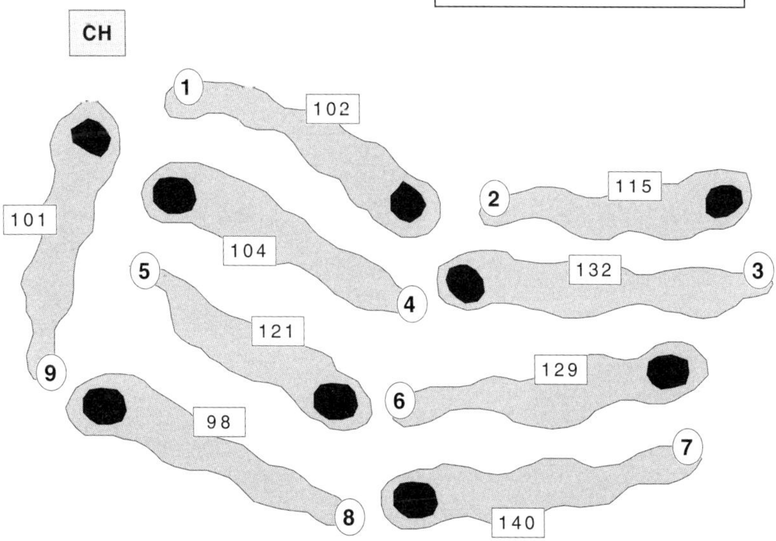

Oak Hills Golf Club (public, 18 hole course)

1919 Recreation Lane; Sutherlin, OR 97479
Phone: (541) 459-4422. Fax: (541) 459-2788. Web: www.golfoakhills.com
Pro: Jeff Bright, PGA. Superintendent: Scott Zielinski.
Rating/Slope: T 73.1/133; C 71.2/128; M 69.2/121; W 70.6/120. **Record:** 63.
Green fees: W/D $22/$16; W/E $29/$18; winter & Sr. rates; M/C, VISA.
Power cart: $22/$12. **Pull cart:** $3. **Trail fee:** $10 for personal carts.
Reservation policy: yes, call 1 week in advance for your tee-time reservation.
Winter condition: the golf course is open all year long, weather permitting.
Terrain: flat, rolling hills. **Tees:** grass. **Spikes:** soft spikes preferred.
Services: club rentals, lessons, snack bar, restaurant, lounge, beer, wine, pro shop, driving range, putting & chipping green. **Comments:** the course has been completely remodeled to provide an outstanding golfing experience. Tree-lined fairways alternates with open links style design. New RV park is now open with 41 full hook up spaces. Special rates for RV golfers on a daily, weekly basis.

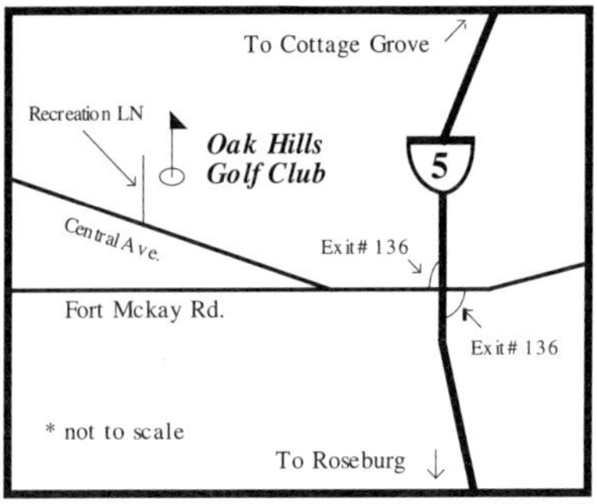

__Directions:__ from I-5 N&S take exit #136 (Sutherlin). Upon exiting the freeway go west approximately .75 miles down the road. When you come to the sign take a right and follow to the golf course. The golf course is located near the freeway.

Course Yardage & Par:
T-6937 yards, par 72.
C-6458 yards, par 72.
M-6065 yards, par 72.
W-5519 yards, par 72.

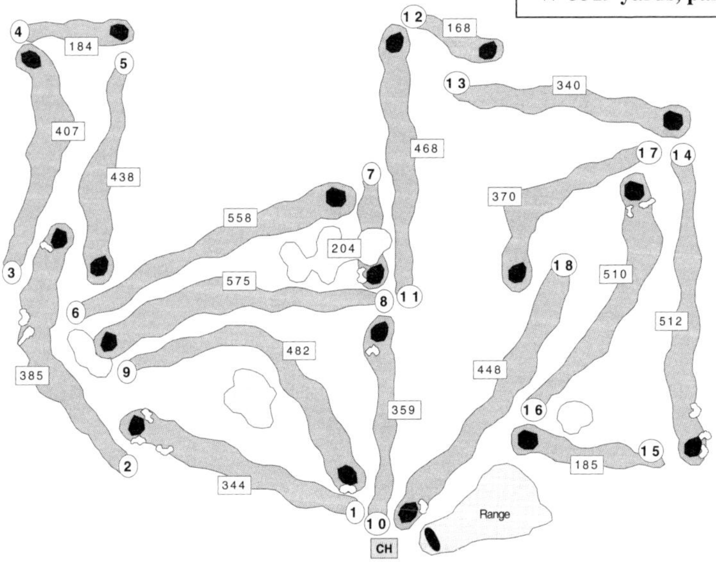

Oak Knoll Public Golf Course (public, 9 hole course)

3070 Highway 66; Ashland, OR 97520
Phone: (541) 482-4311. Fax: (541) 482-4311. Web: none.
Pro: Bob Haney. Superintendent: Bob Ford.
Rating/Slope: M 68.8/118; W 70.2/108. **Course record:** 62.
Green fees: October-April $15/$10; May-September $20/$14; M/C, VISA. Monday thru Friday Green fee cart combo (summer) $25/$18, lower in winter.
Power cart: $20/$12. **Pull cart:** $3/$2. **Trail fee:** personal carts not allowed.
Reservation policy: yes, please call ahead for tee-times. 7 days maximum.
Winter condition: the golf course is open all year long. Very dry winter course.
Terrain: flat, some hills. **Tees:** all grass. **Spikes:** metal spikes permitted.
Services: club rentals, lessons, restaurant, beer, wine, driving range, pro shop.
Comments: course has 2 sets of tees for those people wanting to play a full 18 holes. Fairways are narrow in spots putting emphasis on driving accuracy. Creeks are factors on other holes. Your company tournaments are welcome.

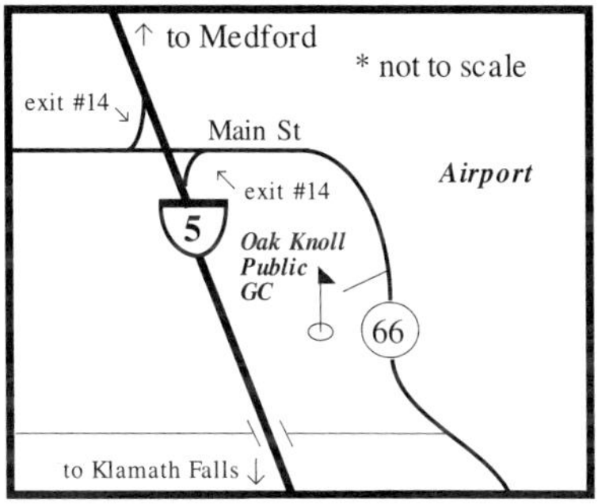

<u>**Directions:**</u> from I-5 take exit #14 (Southern Oregon State College). Head east on Hwy 66. The golf course will be located .75 miles on your right hand side. **Note:** The golf course is located across from the Ashland City Airport. Look for signs marking your way.

Course Yardage & Par:
M-3020 yards, par 36. **W-2656 yards, par 38.** <u>**Dual tees for 18 holes:**</u> **M-6035 yards, par 71.** **W-5229 yards, par 74.**

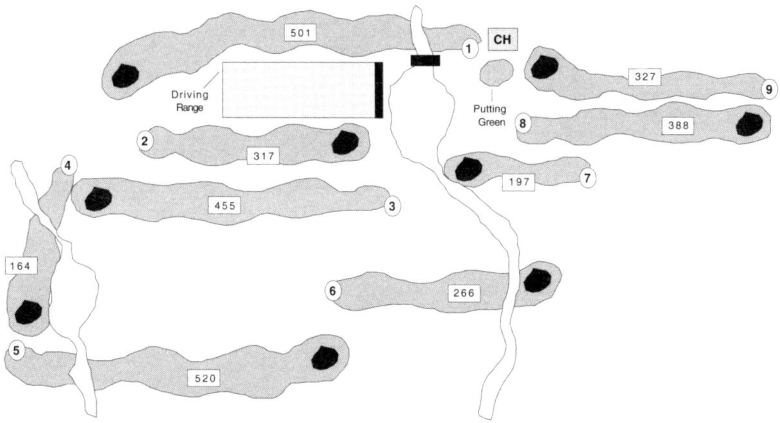

Oakway Golf Course (public, 18 hole course)

2000 Cal Young Road; Eugene, OR 97401
Phone: (541) 484-1927. Fax: none. Web: none.
Manager: Kimberly Coffey. Superintendent: Loren Erickson.
Rating/Slope: M 58.6/91; W 59.0/92. **Course record:** 54.
Green fees: W/D $20/$12; W/E $22/$14; Sr. rates $16/$10 (M-F); M/C, VISA.
Power cart: $18/$10. **Pull cart:** $2. **Trail fee:** personal carts are not allowed.
Reservation policy: none needed. Course is run on a 1st come 1st served basis.
Winter condition: the golf course is open all year long. Wet conditions.
Terrain: flat, some hills. **Tees:** all grass. **Spikes:** soft spikes preferred.
Services: club rentals, restaurant, beer, wine, pro shop, putting/chipping greens.
Comments: One of the nicest short courses in the state of Oregon. The course is easy to walk. Excellent course for seniors who want to play a highly competive course but do not want the length. Fairways can play very tight on certain holes.

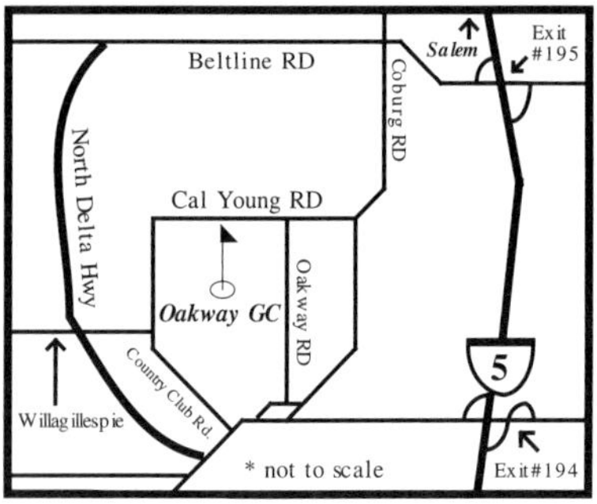

Directions: from I-5 take exit #195. Head west on Beltline Road. Take the Coburg Road exit and go south. At Cal Young Road turn right. The golf course will be 1/4 mile ahead on your left hand side.

Course Yardage & Par:
M-3576 yards, par 61.
W-3249 yards, par 61.

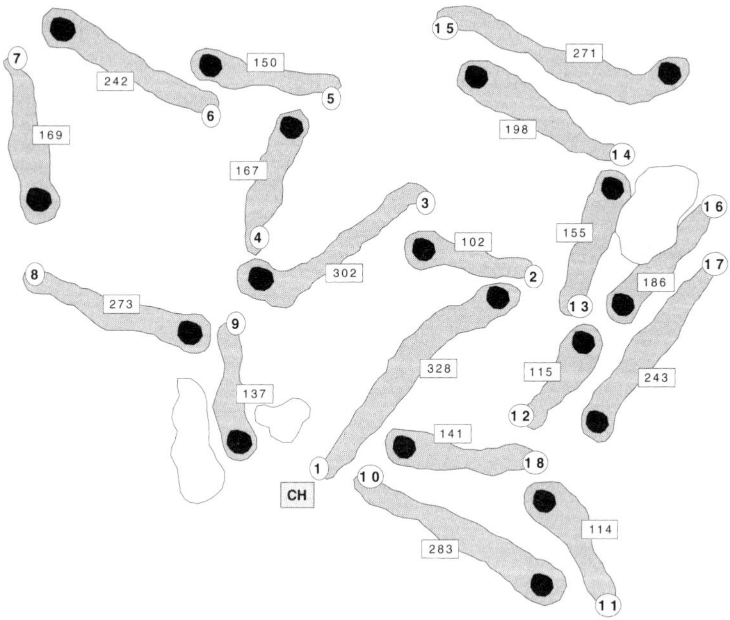

Ocean Dunes Golf Links (public, 18 hole course)

3345 Munsel Lake Road; Florence, OR 97439
Phone: (541) 997-3232; 1-800-468-4833. Fax: (541) 997-3232.
Web-site: www.oceandunesgolf.com
Pro: Vern Smith, PGA. Superintendent: Richard Weight.
Rating/Slope: C 70.0/124; M 68.0/119; W 70.6/121. **Course record:** 68.
Green fees: $38/$20; Sr. rates; $30/$16; winter rates lower; M/C, VISA.
Power cart: $26. **Pull cart:** $3/$2. **Trail fee:** $10 for personal carts.
Reservation policy: yes, please call ahead for weekend reservations (a must).
Winter condition: the golf course is open all year long. Very dry conditions.
Terrain: flat, rolling some hills. **Tees:** grass. **Spikes:** soft spikes preferred.
Services: club rentals, lessons, banquet facilities, beer, wine, pro shop, indoor driving range, putting and chipping greens, group and tournament facilities.
Comments: This course is built on sand dunes which keeps it dry during the winter. The course plays like a real links course that you would find in Scotland. Greens are large and rolling and can be a good test for even the best putter. Fairways give the golfer a wide variety of lies. Worth a special trip.

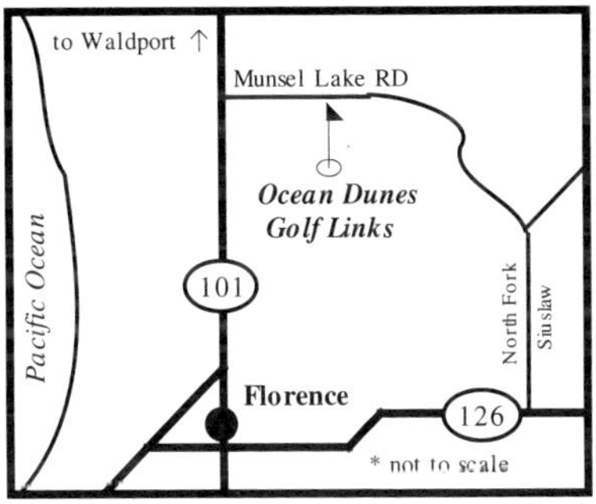

Directions: from Highway 101 turn eastbound on Munsel Lake Road and proceed to the golf course. From Hwy 126 (Florence Hwy) go north on North Fork Siuslaw. When you reach Munsel Lake Road turn left to the golf course. The golf course will be located on your left hand side. Look for signs marking your turn to the golf course.

Course Yardage & Par:

C-6055 yards, par 71.
M-5613 yards, par 71.
W-5068 yards, par 73.

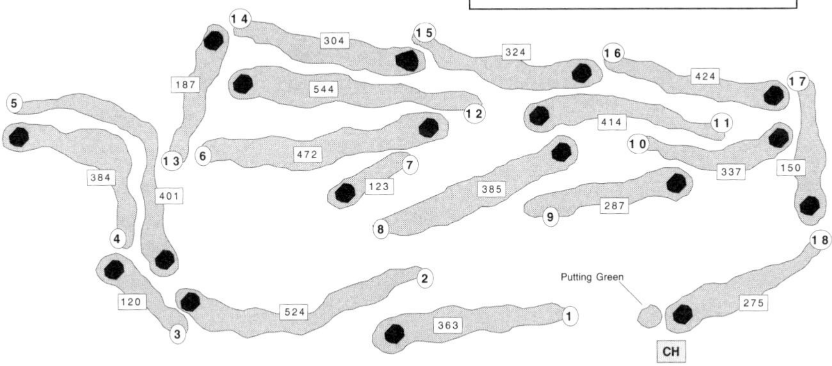

Olalla Valley Golf Course (public, 9 hole course)

1022 Olalla Road; Toledo, OR 97391
Phone: (541) 336-2121. Fax: (541) 336-4024. Web: none.
Owner: Chip Abarno. Superintendent: Mike Abarno.
Rating/Slope: M 69.9/123; W 73.5/123. **Course record:** 63.
Green fees: $24/$12 all week long; M/C, VISA.
Power cart: $20/$10. **Pull cart:** $2. **Trail fee:** $3.
Reservation policy: yes, required for weekend tee times. Call 7 days ahead.
Winter condition: the golf course is open all year long, course drains very well.
Terrain: course is very hilly. **Tees:** all grass. **Spikes:** metal spikes permitted.
Services: club rentals, restaurant, beer, wine, beverages, pro shop, putting green.
Comments: Excellent winter course. Nine hole golf course that has 2 sets of tees for 18 hole play. Water comes into play on nearly every hole. The course can be very demanding in spots so concentration is a must for a good score.

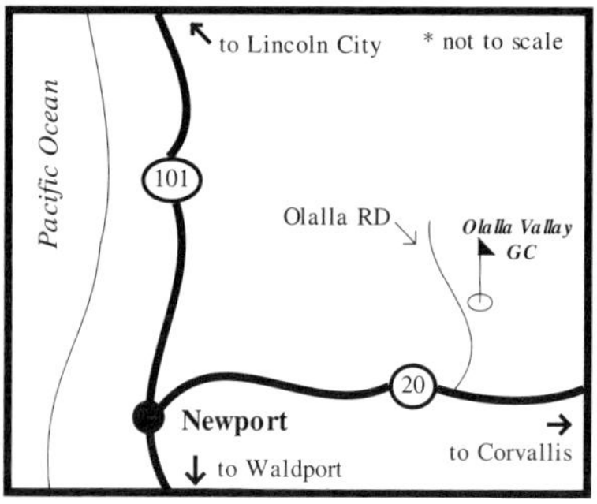

Directions: on Highway 101 the golf course is located 6 miles east of Newport. From Highway 20 (from Corvallis) go west 45 minutes to the golf course. Exit on to Olalla Road from Highway 20. There are signs from each direction you can follow to the golf course.

Course Yardage & Par:
M-2949 yards, par 36.
W-2587 yards, par 37.
Dual tees for 18 holes:
M-6027 yards, par 72.
W-5507 yards, par 74.

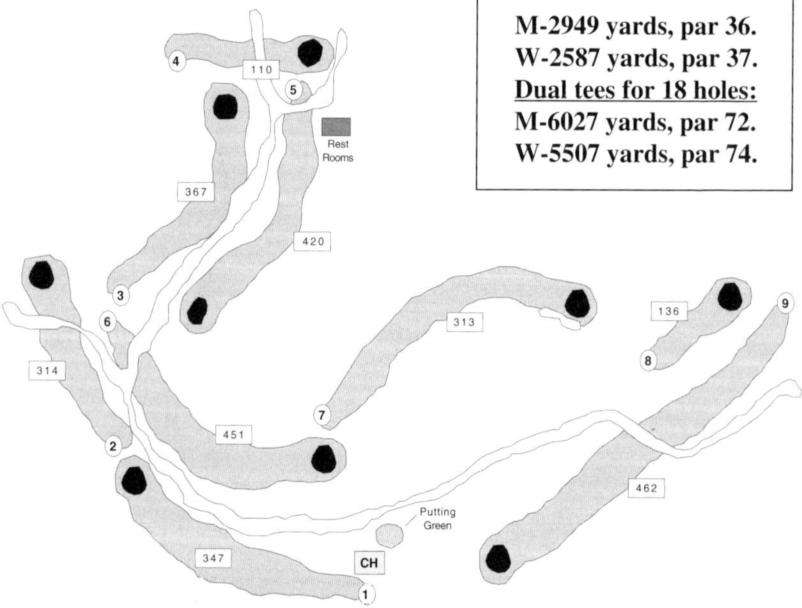

Ontario Golf Club (public, 18 hole course)

1345 Golf Course Road; Ontario, OR 97914

Phone: (541) 889-9022. Fax: (541) 889-9397. Web: none.

Pro/Manager: Dave Parker, PGA. Superintendent: Jerry Troy.

Rating/Slope: C 69.4/113; M 68.1/111; W 69.5/115. **Course record:** 64.

Green fees: $18/$12 all week long; Jr. & Sr. rates available; M/C, VISA.

Power cart: $18/$9. **Pull cart:** $3/$2. **Trail fee:** $6 for personal carts.

Reservation policy: yes, required for weekend tee times. Call 7 days ahead.

Winter condition: the course is closed from November 15th to February 15th.

Terrain: flat, some hills. **Tees:** all grass. **Spikes:** metal spikes permitted.

Services: club rentals, lessons, snack bar, lounge, beer, wine, liquor, pro shop, lockers, putting & chipping greens, driving range, club memberships.

Comments: The greens are large and have bunkers fronting them on nearly every hole. Easy walking course that is challengeing to every level of golfer.

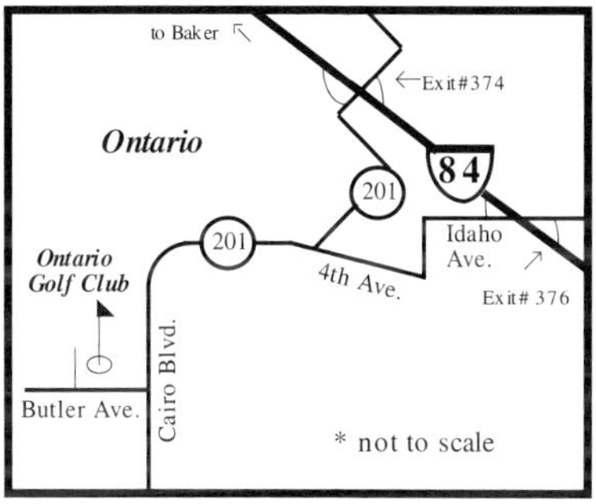

Directions: from I-84 take exit #376 and proceed westbound on Idaho. Turn left on 9th and proceed to 4th Avenue. At 4th Avenue turn right to Cairo Boulevard. Turn left on Cairo Boulevard. Proceed to Butler Blvd. and turn right on Butler Blvd. Follow to Golf Course Road and turn right to the golf course. The golf course is located next to the airport on the southwest edge of the city.

Course Yardage & Par:

C-6632 yards, par 72.
M-6080 yards, par 72.
W-5790 yards, par 74.

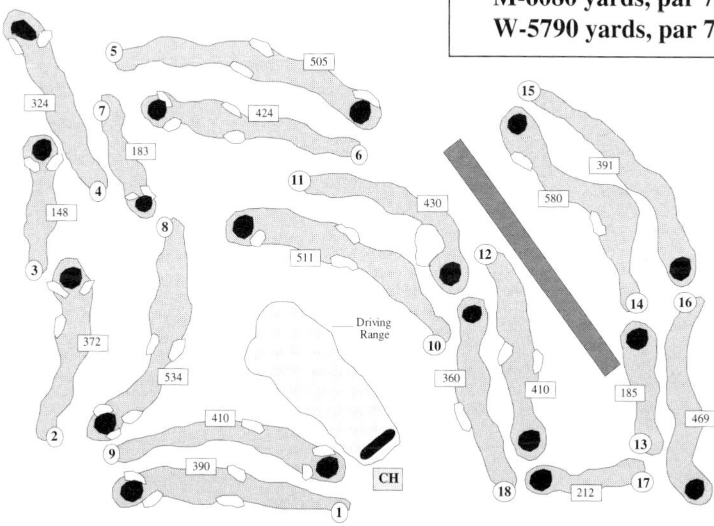

Oregon City Golf Club (public, 18 hole course)

20124 South Beavercreek Road; Oregon City, OR 97045
Phone: (503) 656-2846. Fax: (503) 656-0290. Web: none.
Pro: Bill Hagedon. Owner: John Herberger.
Rating/Slope: C 67.8/112; M 66.0/108; W 68.4/119. **Course record:** 62.
Green fees: W/D $26/$13; W/E's & Holidays $34/$17; Winter rates available; Jr. & Sr. rates (Monday thru Friday) $20/$10 for Sr.'s /$9 for Jr.'s; M/C, VISA.
Power cart: $25/$15. **Pull cart:** $3. **Trail fee:** $5 for personal carts.
Reservation policy: yes, you can call 2 weeks in advance for your tee-times.
Winter condition: the golf course is open all year long, dry (drains well).
Terrain: gentle, rolling hills. **Tees:** grass. **Spikes:** soft spikes only.
Services: club rentals, lessons, snack bar, beer, pop, pro shop, putting green, banquet room (seats up to 130 persons). **Comments:** This is the 3rd oldest golf course in the state of Oregon still in operation. Excellent drainage and a good maintenance schedule provide very dry course conditions even in winter. Very friendly public course that has been a joy to play every time I have visited.

<u>**Directions:**</u> from I-205 N&S take exit # 10 (Park Place). Head southbound on Highway 213. At the 3rd light go left (eastbound) on Beavercreek Road. The golf course is located 1.5 miles ahead on your left. Look for signs along the way.

Course Yardage & Par:
C-5872 yards, par 71.
M-5516 yards, par 71.
W-5198 yards, par 75.

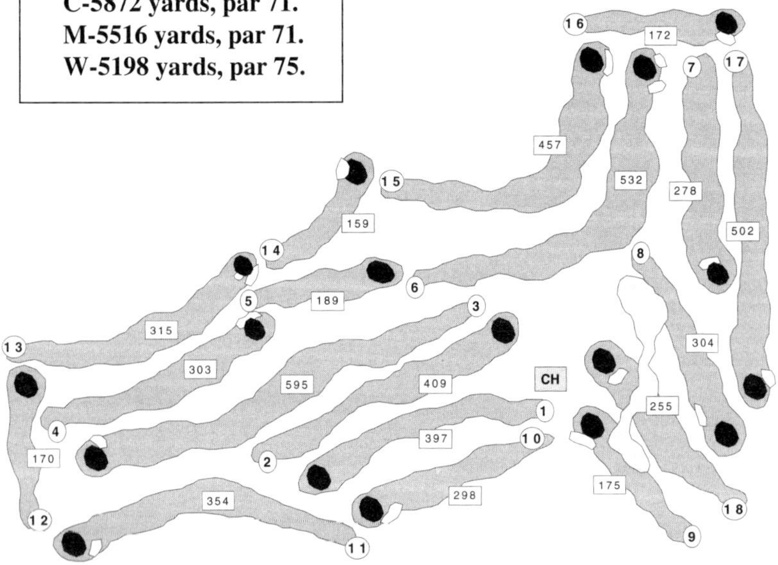

O.G.A. Members Course (public, 18 holes)

2850 Hazelnut Drive; Woodburn, OR 97071

Phone: (503) 981-6105. Fax: (503) 981-5662. Web: www.orgolf.org

Pro: Chuck Siver, PGA. Superintendent: Kirk Kundrick.

Rating/Slope: T 71.7/131; C 70.4/125; M 68.7/118; W 71.8/128. **Record:** 61.
Green fees: W/D $48/$39; W/E $53/$31; special rates for OGA members.
Power cart: $25/$13. **Pull cart:** $2. **Trail fee:** personal carts are not allowed.
Reservation policy: call up to 5 days in advance for all your tee-times.
Winter condition: the course is open, weather permitting. Drains very well.
Terrain: rolling hills. **Tees:** all grass. **Spikes:** soft spikes only please.
Services: club rentals, lessons, snack bar, beer, wine, pro shop, driving range, full service restaurant and lounge in the clubhouse, putting & chipping greens.
Comments: This course has a unique double green on holes 9 and 18. Water comes into play on several holes, some holes offer a peek-a-boo view of Mount Hood. This course is worth a trip anytime. Lower rates for all OGA members.

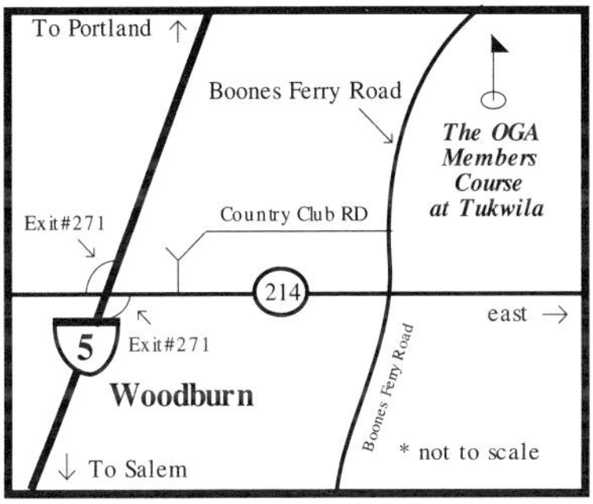

__Directions:__ From I-5 N&S take exit #271, Woodburn. Head eastbound for approximately 1.5 miles to Boones Ferry Road and turn left. The golf course is ahead on the right hand side of the road. Look for signs marking your way to the golf course.

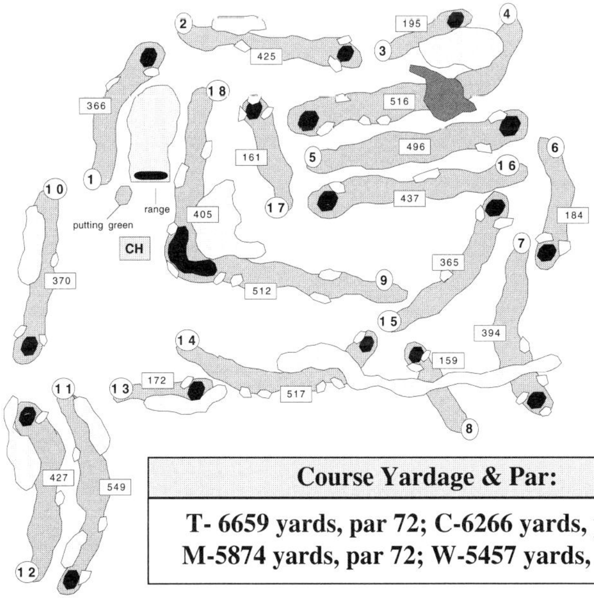

Course Yardage & Par:
T- 6659 yards, par 72; C-6266 yards, par 72. M-5874 yards, par 72; W-5457 yards, par 72.

Oregon Golf Club (private, 18 hole course)

25700-A SW Pete's Mountain Road; West Linn, OR 97068
Phone: (503) 650-7805. Fax: (503) 650-7580. Web: www.oregongolfclub.com
Pro: Scott Leritz, PGA. Superintendent: Russell Vandehey.
Rating/Slope: J 74.4/135; C 72.1/132; M 69.8/123; W 71.1/125. **Record:** 63.
Green fees: private club, members & guests only; limited reciprocation.
Power cart: yes. **Pull cart:** yes. **Trail fee:** personal carts not allowed.
Reservation policy: private club, members & guests only. No public play.
Winter condition: the golf course is open all year long. Dry conditions.
Terrain: very hilly. **Tees:** all grass. **Spikes:** no metal spikes in summer.
Services: full service private facility, driving range, putting & chipping greens.
Comments: the golf course was co-designed by PGA Tour player Peter Jacobsen. Layout is of championship caliber with bunkers on nearly every hole. Host of 2003 Oregon Open & the 2004 Oregon Amateur. Excellent golf course.

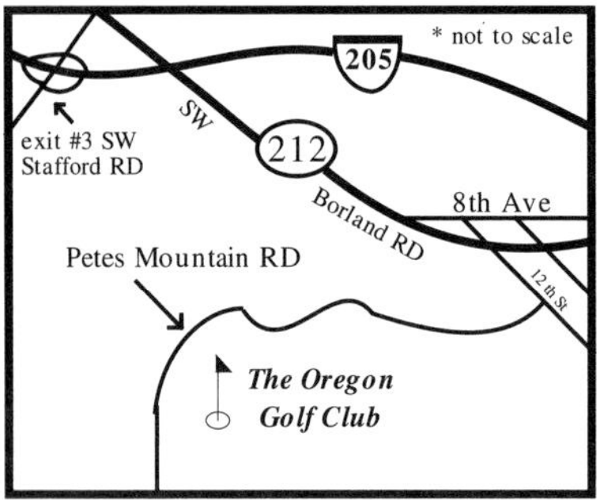

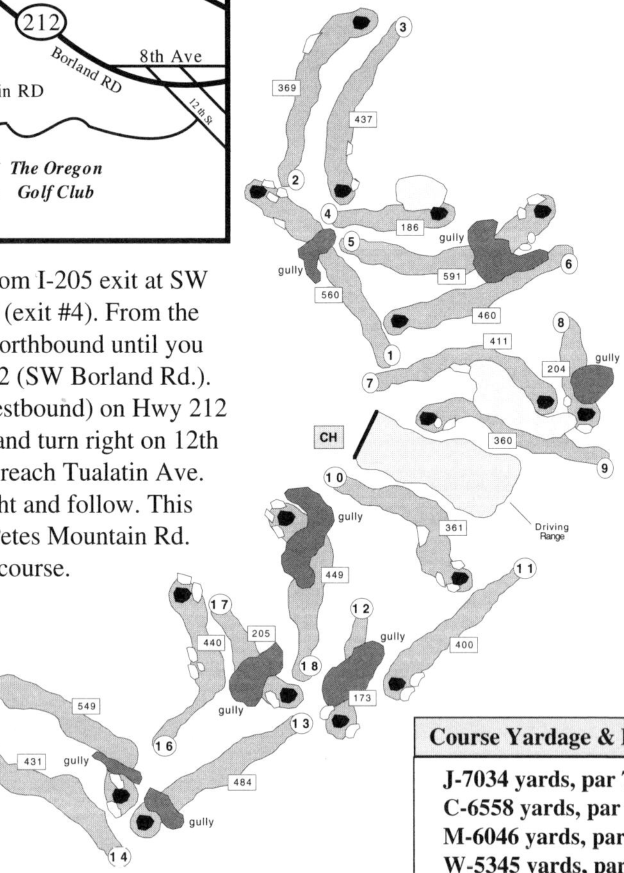

Directions: from I-205 exit at SW Stafford Road (exit #4). From the exit proceed northbound until you reach Hwy 212 (SW Borland Rd.). Turn right (westbound) on Hwy 212 to West Linn and turn right on 12th St. When you reach Tualatin Ave. veer to the right and follow. This will become Petes Mountain Rd. Follow to the course.

Course Yardage & Par:

J-7034 yards, par 72.
C-6558 yards, par 72.
M-6046 yards, par 72.
W-5345 yards, par 72.

Orenco Woods Golf Club (public, 9 hole course)

22200 NW Birch; P.O. Box 25; Hillsboro, OR 97123
Phone: (503) 648-1836. Fax: (503) 644-8874. Web: none.
Manager: Brandon Sassaman. Superintendent: Tim Hamel.
Rating/Slope: M 65.8/114; W 68.2/116. **Course record:** 63.
Green fees: $22/$12 all week long; Jr. & Sr. rates; M/C, VISA.
Power cart: $24/$12. **Pull cart:** $2. **Trail fee:** $12/$6 for personal carts.
Reservation policy: yes, call 7 days in advance for times (a must for weekends).
Winter condition: the golf course is open all year long, damp conditions.
Terrain: very hilly. **Tees:** all grass. **Spikes:** metal spikes permitted.
Services: club rentals, lessons, snack bar, beer, wine, pro shop, driving range.
Comments: course is hilly and presents a good challenge. The greens are small which puts a premium on shot making. A creek is in play on nearly every hole.

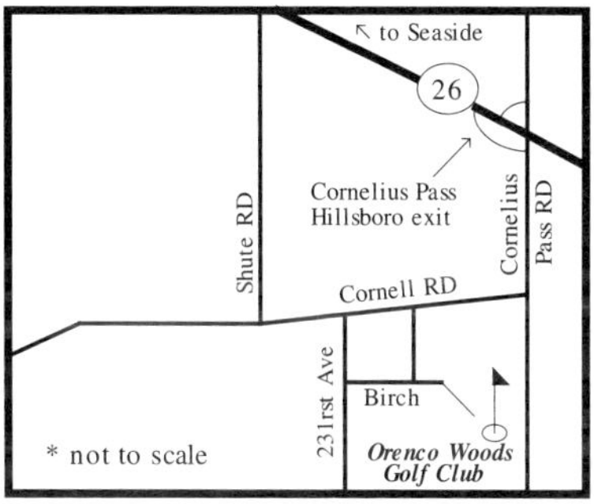

Directions: take Hwy 26 out of Portland going west. Take Cornelius Pass/Hillsboro exit. Proceed south on Cornelius Pass Rd. to NW Cornell Rd. and turn right. Proceed to NW 231st Ave. and turn left to NW Birch. Proceed and turn left to the course.

Course Yardage & Par:
M-2626 yards, par 35.
W-2454 yards, par 36.
Dual tees for 18 holes:
W-5080 yards, par 72.
M-5376 yards, par 71.

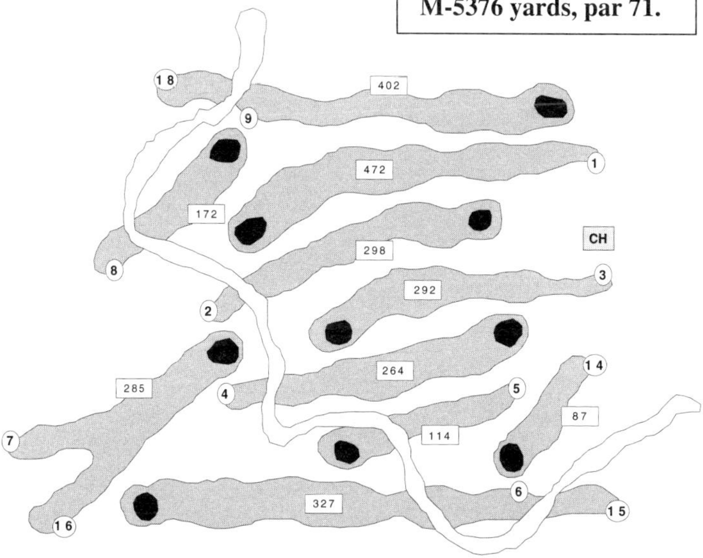

Orion Greens Golf Course (public, 9 hole course)

61525 Fargo Lane; Bend, OR 97702
Phone: (541) 388-3999. Fax: (541) 318-8538. Web: none.
Manager: Judy Lattig. Superintendent: Rich Colantino.
Rating/Slope: C 63.2/100; M 58.8/95; 95; W 58.8/93. **Course record:** 26.
Green fees: $24/$15 all week long; no other special rates M/C, VISA.
Power cart: $19/$10. **Pull cart:** $3/$2. **Trail fee:** $10/$5.
Reservation policy: call the pro shop for advance reservation policies.
Winter condition: the golf course is open all year long, weather permitting.
Terrain: flat (easy walking). **Tees:** grass. **Spikes:** soft spikes required.
Services: club rentals, snack bar, restaurant, beer, wine, putting green.
Comments: This facility is well kept. Greens are medium in size and are well bunkered. Great views of the surrounding countryside abound from nearly every tee. If you are looking for a change of pace Orion Greens Golf Course is sure to please. The golf course is in excellent condition most of the year. Good walking golf course that is great for the first time or senior golfer. Worth a trip.

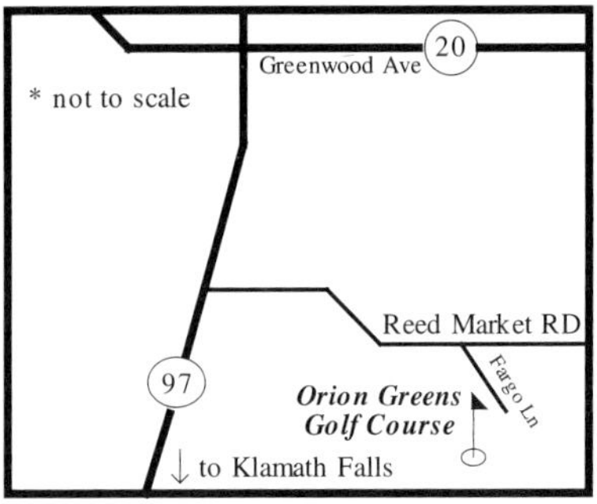

Directions: take Highway 97. Go east on Reed Market Road. Proceed 1.5 miles to Fargo Lane. Turn right on Fargo Lane and follow this to the golf course which will be on your right hand side. Look for signs from Highway 97 in Bend, Oregon to the golf course. The way is well marked.

Course Yardage & Par:
White tees: 2075 yards, par 31. **Gold tees: 1939 yards, par 31.** **Red tees: 1738 yards, par 31.**

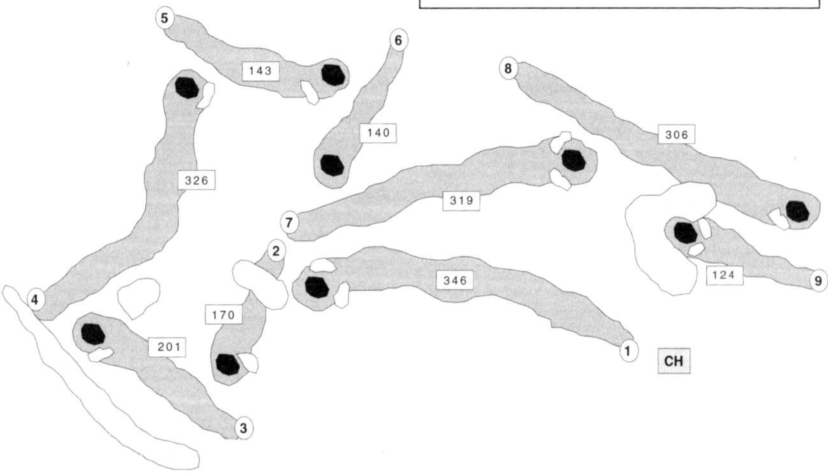

Oswego Lake Country Club (private, 18 hole course)

20 Iron Mountain Boulevard: P.O. Box 508; Lake Oswego, OR 97034
Phone: (503) 635-3659. Fax: (503) 636-4362. Web: none.
Pro: Brent Murray, PGA. Superintendent: Bob Sensman.
Rating/Slope: T 72.2/130; C 70.4/132; M 69.1/124; W 71.3/127. **Record:** 62.
Green fees: private club members & guests only; reciprocates; no credit cards.
Power cart: private club. **Pull cart:** private club. **Trail fee:** not allowed.
Reservation policy: for members and guests only. Call 2 days in advance.
Winter condition: the golf course is open all year long, damp conditions.
Terrain: very hilly. **Tees:** all grass. **Spikes:** soft spikes only please.
Services: lessons, snack bar, restaurant, lounge, beer, wine, liquor, pro shop, lockers, showers, driving range, putting & chipping greens, club memberships.
Comments: The golf course is noted for the many picturesque golf holes it has. Course can play very tough at times with large well bunkered greens.

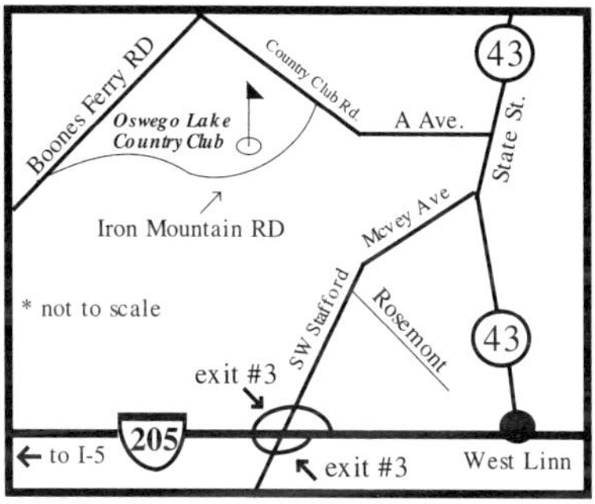

Directions: from I-5 take Hwy 217 exit into Lake Oswego. Take left on to Boones Ferry then a right onto Country Club. Take right onto Iron Mountain Blvd. The course will be on your right side. From I-205 exit to go north at either Pacific Hwy 43 Willamette Dr. or at SW Stafford and proceed north to State then turn left onto "A" Ave. to Country Club Rd.

Course Yardage & Par:

T-6557 yards, par 71.
C-6286 yards, par 71.
M-5910 yards, par 71.
W-5382 yards, par 73.

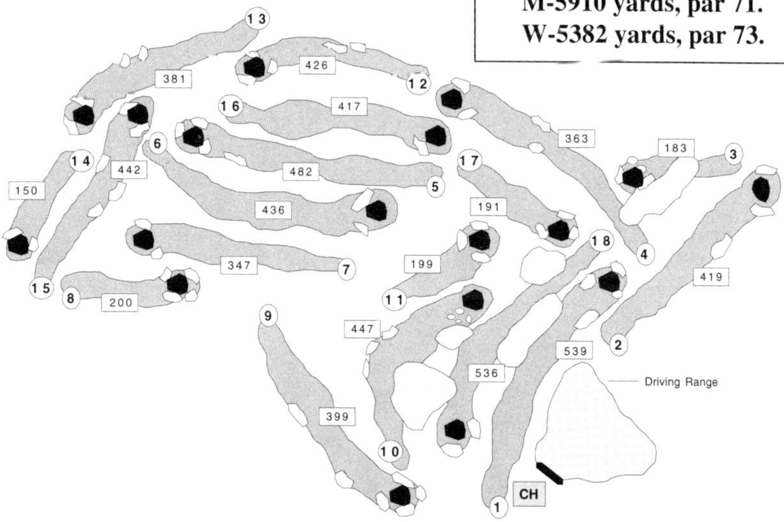

Pendleton Country Club (private, 18 hole course)

69772 Highway 395 South; Pendleton, OR 97801
Phone: (541) 443-4653. Fax: (541) 443-2323. Web: www.pendletoncc.com
Pro: Wayne Lovenz, PGA. Superintendent: Richard Matteson.
Rating/Slope: C 69.9/117; M 68.6/114; W 70.8/117. **Course record:** 63.
Green fees: private club members & guests only; reciprocates; M/C, VISA.
Power cart: $20. **Pull cart:** private club. **Trail fee:** private club.
Reservation policy: private club members & guests of members only.
Winter condition: the golf course is open all year long, weather permitting.
Terrain: flat (easy walking). **Tees:** grass. **Spikes:** soft spikes only.
Services: club rentals, lessons, snack bar, restaurant, lounge, beer, wine, liquor, beverages, pro shop, showers, driving range, putting green & chipping green.
Comments: course is well conditioned during the season. Lush fairways with small, mediuim to fast greens make this track a real bear from the back tees.

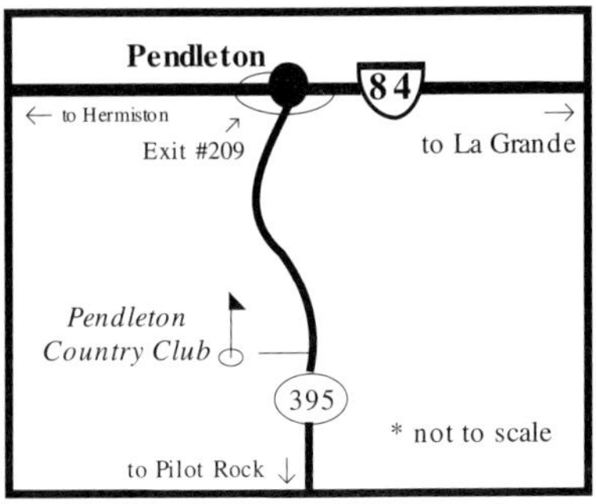

Directions: the golf course is located 8 miles south of Pendleton. From I-84 E&W take exit #209 to Highway 395. Follow Highway 395 for 7.7 miles to the golf course on your right hand side.

Course Yardage & Par:

C-6364 yards, par 72.
M-6088 yards, par 72.
W-5456 yards, par 74.

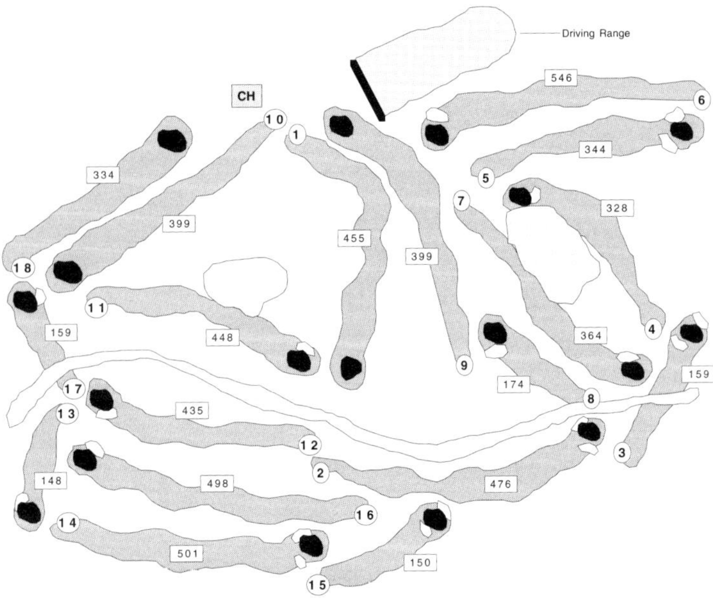

Persimmon Country Club (semi-private, 18 hole course)

500 SE Butler Road; Gresham, OR 97080
Phone: (503) 661-1800. Fax: (503) 667-3885. Web: persimmongolf.com
Pro: Stuart Smart, PGA. Superintendent: N/A.

Rating/Slope: C 71.9/136; M 69.1/118; W 72.0/126; W 68.0/120. **Record:** 63.
Green fees: Weekdays $60; Weekends $85 (fees include a cart); M/C, VISA
Power cart: included in fees. **Pull cart:** $4/$2. **Trail fee:** not allowed.
Reservation policy: 7 days in advance, 3 days in advance Fri.-Sun. for public.
Winter condition: the golf course open all year long, weather permitting.
Terrain: gently sloping. **Tees:** all grass. **Spikes:** soft spikes preferred.
Services: club rentals, lessons, swing analysis, outdoor practice cages, pro shop, club repair, driving range, grill room with beer & wine, lockers, putting green.
Comments: golf course designed by Bunny Mason with incredible views of the Cascade Mtns. Great golf course that will challenge you at every turn. This now able to play golf course is striving to become a private course in the near future.

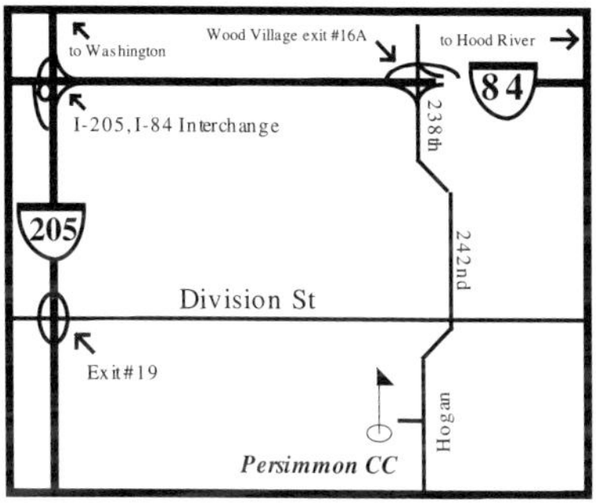

Directions: from I-84 take the Wood Village 16A exit and go south on 238th. 238th will become 242nd, then becomes Hogan Road. Proceed to the golf course which will be located on your right. The course is approximately 4.5 miles from your I-84 exit. Look for signs marking your way to the golf course.

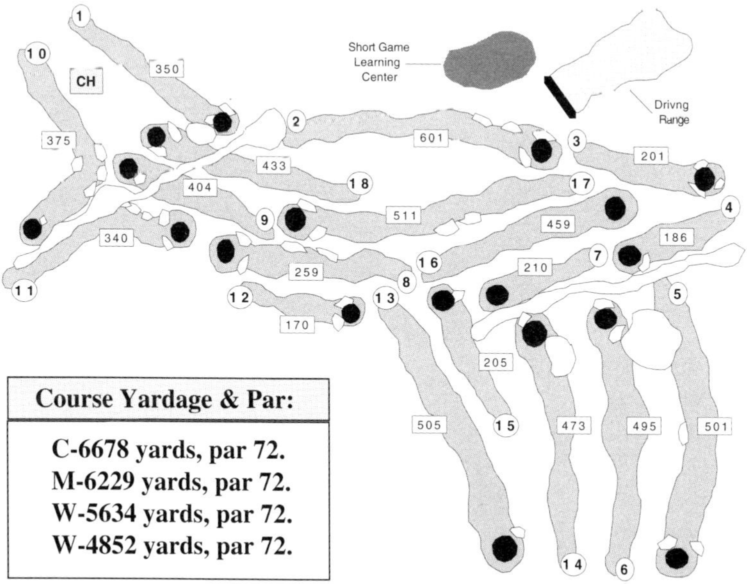

Course Yardage & Par:

C-6678 yards, par 72.
M-6229 yards, par 72.
W-5634 yards, par 72.
W-4852 yards, par 72.

Pine Hollow Golf Course (public, 9 hole course)

8-A South County Road; Tygh Valley, OR 97063
Phone: (541) 544-2035. Fax: (541) 544-2350. Web: none.
Owner: Irl Davis. Superintendent: Bev Gardner.
Rating/Slope: M 64.4/112; W 63.6/108. **Course record:** 30.
Green fees: $18/$10 all week long; M/C, VISA.
Power cart: $16/$8. **Pull cart:** $2.50. **Trail fee:** $3.
Reservation policy: reservations can be made up to 1 month in advance.
Winter condition: the golf course is open from April until October.
Terrain: flat, some hills. **Tees:** all grass. **Spikes:** soft spikes only.
Services: club rentals, lounge, beer, wine, limited pro shop, driving net, putting green, tournament planning, club memberships. **Comments:** this golf course was designed by Irl Davis and plays to a par of 34. The fairways are narrow in spots leaving the golfer little room off the tee. Dual tees are available for those wanting to play a full 18 hole round. Call ahead as some open play is restricted.

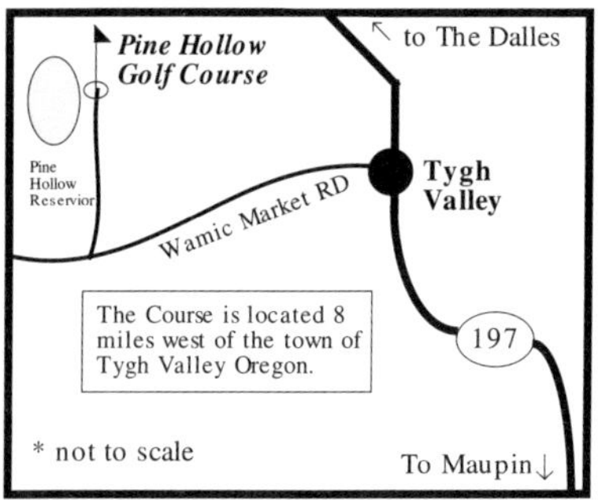

Directions: from Highway 197 turn westbound on Wamic Market Road when in the town of Tygh Valley. Proceed on Wamic Market Road to the Pine Hollow Reservoir. The course is located at the Pine Hollow Reservoir. Look for signs that are posted.

Course Yardage & Par:

M-2234 yards, par 34.
W-1954 yards, par 34.

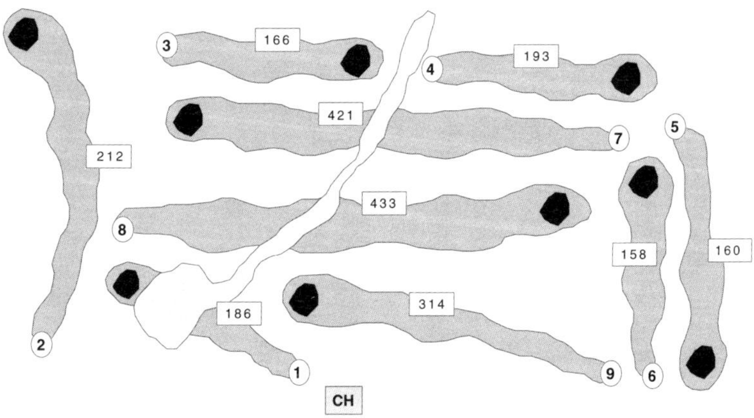

Pineway Golf Course (public, 9 hole course)

30949 Pineway Road; Lebanon, OR 97355
Phone: (541) 258-8815. Fax: none. Web: none.
Pros: Jim Glasser, Mickie Price. Superintendent: Jerry Johnson.
Rating/Slope: M 67.5/110; W 72.3/120. **Course record:** 64.
Green fees: W/D $23/$13; W/E $23/$13; Jr. & Sr. rates $17 (M-F); M/C, VISA.
Power cart: $20/$10. **Pull cart:** $2. **Trail fee:** $10/$5 for personal carts.
Reservation policy: yes, call 1 week in advance for your tee-times.
Winter condition: the golf course is open all year long, dry (drains very well).
Terrain: relatively hilly. **Tees:** all grass. **Spikes:** metal spikes permitted.
Services: club rentals, lessons, restaurant, lounge, beer, pro shop, snack bar, lockers, driving range, practice green. **Comments:** course is in great condition all year round. The terrain is up and down giving the golfer a wide variety of lies from the fairway. Dual tees offer you a different look when playing 18 holes.

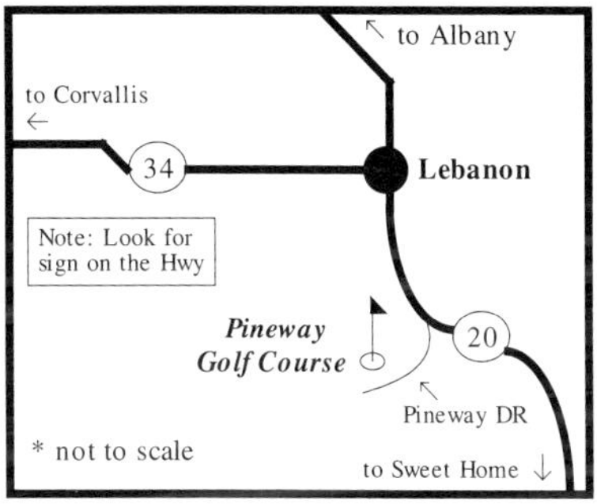

Directions: the golf course is located just off of Highway 20 4.3 miles southeast of Lebanon, Oregon. A sign will indicate the location of the golf course.

Course Yardage & Par:
M-2967 yards, par 36.
W-2960 yards, par 37.
Dual tees for 18 holes:
M-5927 yards, par 72.
W-5919 yards, par 74.

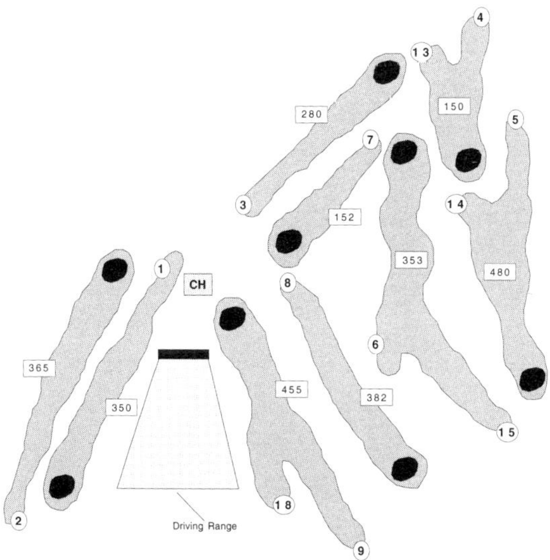

Pleasant Valley Golf Club (private, 18 hole course)

12300 SE 162nd Avenue; Clackamas, OR 97105

Phone: (503) 658-3101. Fax: (503) 658-7702. Web: pleasantvalleygolfclub.com

Pro: Derek Peterson, PGA. Superintendent: Paul Rozek.

Rating/Slope: C 71.2/129; M 68.8/125; W 66.5/114. **Course record:** 64.
Green fees: private club, members & guests of members only; reciprocates.
Power cart: private club. **Pull cart:** private club. **Trail fee:** not allowed.
Reservation policy: private club, members & guests of members only.
Winter condition: the golf course is open all year long, dry conditions.
Terrain: flat, some hills. **Tees:** all grass. **Spikes:** soft spikes preferred.
Services: club rentals, lessons, snack bar, restaurant, beer, liquor, pro shop, lockers, putting green. **Comments:** private club, members and guests only. The course is well conditioned and offers challenging golf. Great golf course. Fairways are tree lined and narrow in places. Greens are large and bunkered.

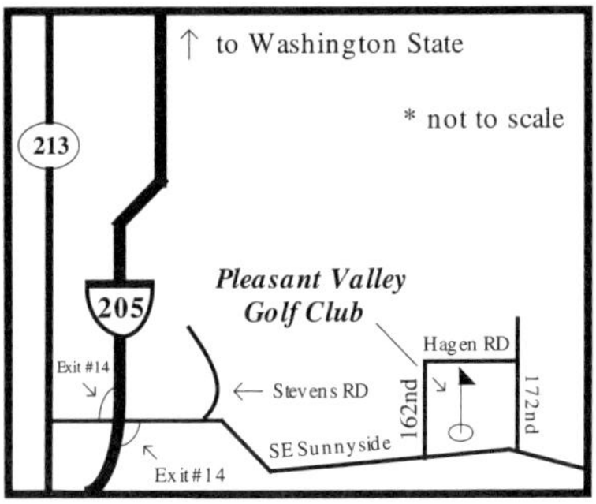

Directions: from Highway 205 exit eastbound on SE Sunnyside exit #14. Follow for 3.4 mi to 162nd and turn left for .5 mi to the golf course on your right. **Note:** sign indicating your turn.

Course Yardage & Par:
C-6593 yards, par 72.
M-6164 yards, par 72.
W-5410 yards, par 73.

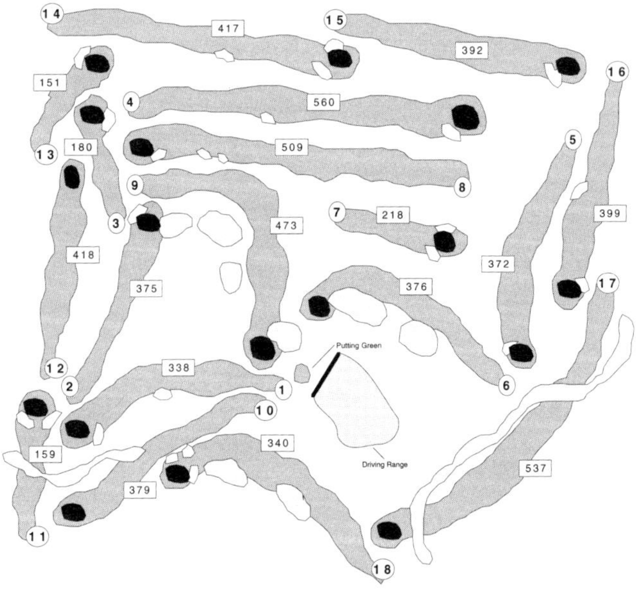

Portland Golf Club (private, 18 hole course)

5900 SW Scholls Ferry Road; Portland, OR 97225

Phone: (503) 292-2778. Fax: (503) 292-9177. Web: none.

Pro: Larry Lamberger Jr., PGA. Superintendent: Forest Goodling.

Rating/Slope: C 72.1/136; M 70.7/135; W 74.4/133. **Course record:** 64.

Green fees: private. Must be a guest of a member and be with the member.

Power cart: private club members only. **Pull cart:** private club members only.

Reservation policy: private club members and guests for members only.

Winter condition: the golf course is open all year long, damp conditions.

Terrain: relatively hilly. **Tees:** all grass. **Spikes:** soft spikes preferred.

Services: club rentals, lessons, snack bar, restaurant, lounge, beer, wine, liquor, beverages, pro shop, lockers, showers, driving range, putting & chipping greens.

Comments: Beautiful, old, historical golf course. Home to numerous past major tournaments, P.G.A. Championship, Ryder Cup, Western Open and the United State Senior Open. The golf course is rated #3 in the state of Oregon and is nothing short of spectacular. Excellent track that is rich in golf tradition.

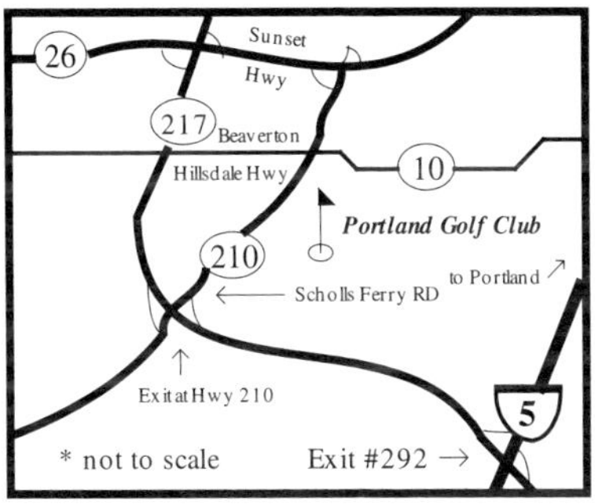

Directions: from I-5 take exit # 217. Follow SW Scholls Ferry Road and proceed 3 miles north to the golf course.

Course Yardage & Par:
C-6683 yards, par 72.
M-6323 yards, par 72.
W-5868 yards, par 73.

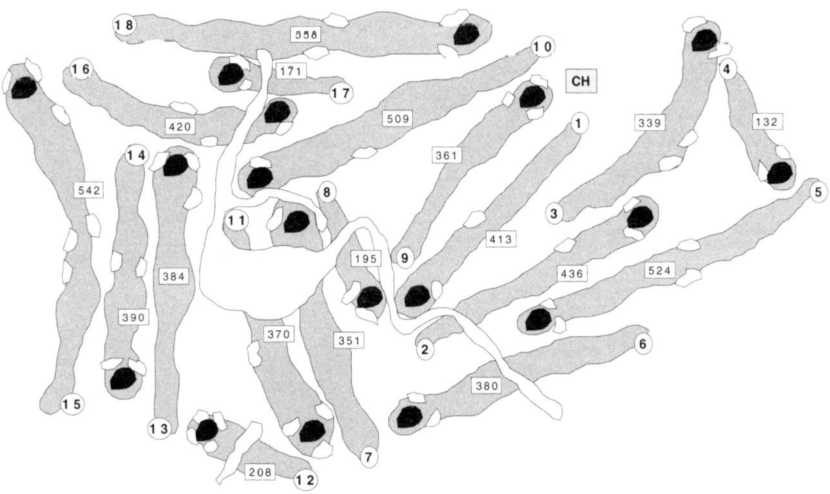

Portland Meadows Golf Course (public, 9 hole course)

901 North Schmeer Road; Portland, OR 97217

Phone: (503) 289-3405. Fax: none. Web: none.

Pro: teaching pro during the summer. Superintendent: none.

Rating/Slope: the golf course is not rated. **Course record:** 57.

Green fees: Monday's $7; Tuesday thru Friday $9; Sat., Sun. & holidays $10.

Power cart: none available. **Pull cart:** $2. **Trail fee:** not allowed.

Reservation policy: advance tee-time reservations are not needed or required. The course opens at 7am Saturday, Sunday & holidays. 8:30am Tuesday-Friday.

Winter condition: the golf course is open from May 1st to September 30th. The course is closed Monday through Friday during the months of October to April.

Terrain: flat (easy walking). **Tees:** grass. **Spikes:** metal spikes permitted.

Services: club rentals, snack bar, beer, driving range, lessons, limited pro shop.

Comments: Unusual setting. Greens are small, postage stamp type style. Very few hazards come into play off the tee or on your approach shots. The golf course is situated in the center of the Portland Meadows horse racing track.

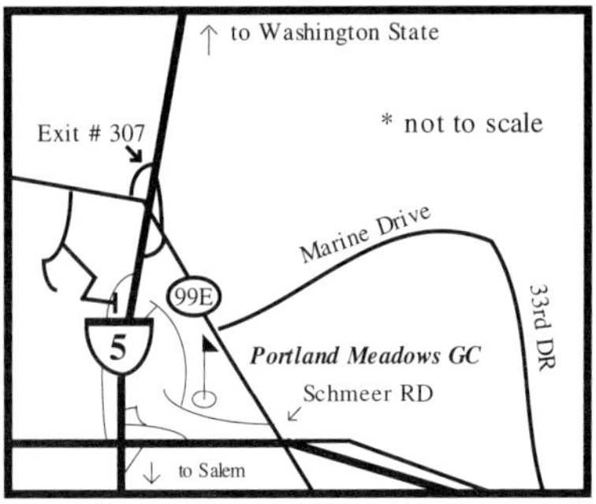

Directions: from I-5 N&S take exit # 306B (Delta Park). Turn left at the stop sign on North Victory Boulevard. Get in the right hand lane. Curve to the right for 1/2 mile to North Schmeer Road. The golf course will be located .2 miles ahead to your left at the race track. **Note:** Look for the Portland Meadows race track and you will find the course.

Course Yardage & Par:

M-1983 yards, par 31.
W-1983 yards, par 35.

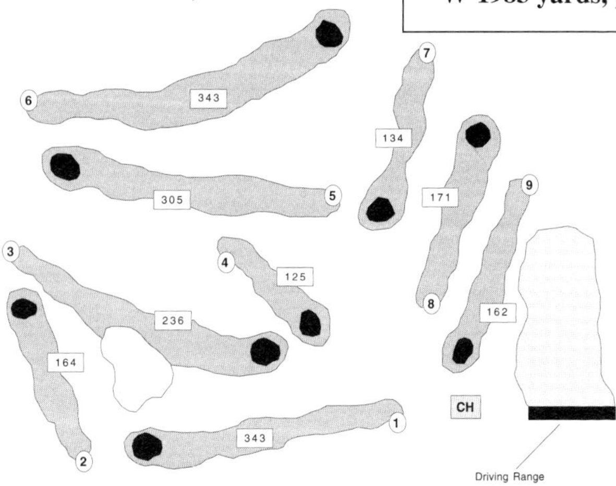

Prineville Golf & Country Club (private, 9 hole course)

7120 NE Ochoco Hwy; Prineville, OR 97754
Phone: (541) 416-2061. Fax: same as phone. Web: none.
Pro: Mark Payne, PGA. Superintendent: Danny Mays.
Rating/Slope: M 64.0/115; W 66.8/117. **Course record:** 58.
Green fees: private club members only, reciprocates; M/C, VISA.
Power cart: private club. **Pull cart:** private club. **Trail fee:** private club.
Reservation policy: private club members only, reciprocates call in advance.
Winter condition: the golf course is open all year long, dry (drains very well).
Terrain: flat, some slight hills. **Tees:** all grass. **Spikes:** soft spikes required.
Services: club rentals, lessons, snack bar, restaurant, lounge, beer, wine, liquor, pro shop, showers, driving range, putting & chipping greens, club memberships.
Comments: in excellent condition April through September. The golf course is very beautiful, tricky but fair. Separate tees for 18 hole play. Good course.

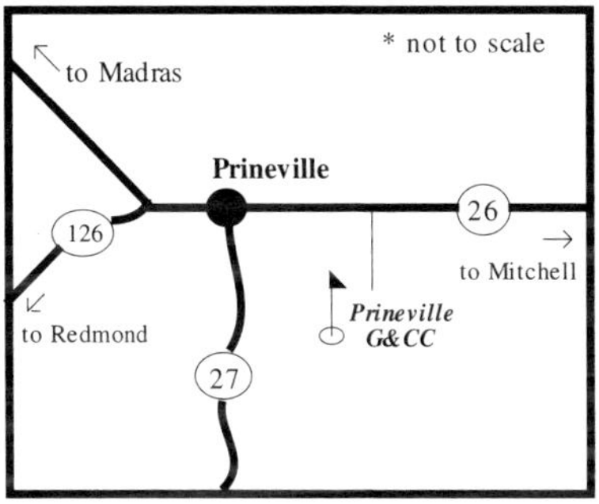

Directions: the golf course is located 3 miles east of Prineville, Oregon off of Highway 26. Look for a sign just past milepost 23 marking your entrance to the Country Club.

Course Yardage & Par:
M-2525 yards, par 33.
W-2268 yards, par 34.
Dual tees for 18 holes:
M-4959 yards, par 65.
W-4662 yards, par 68.

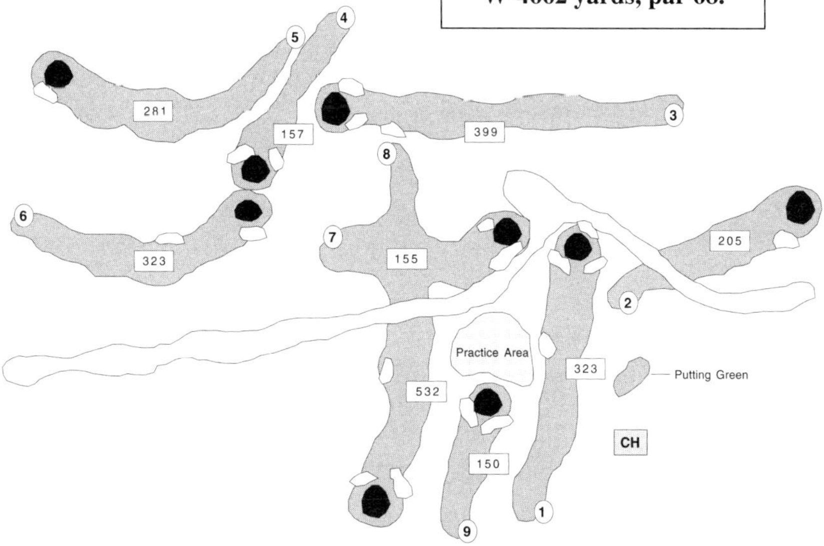

Pronghorn Golf Club (Tom Fazio Course, private, 18 holes)

NE of Bend Oregon off the Powell Butte Highway; Bend, OR 97702
Phone: information call 800-541-9424. Web-site: www.pronghornclub.com
Pro: to be determined. Superintendent: to be determined. Record: N/A.
Rating/Slope: The golf course will be rated at the time of the opening.
Green fees: private club, members and guests only; VISA, M/C, AMEX.
Power cart: private club. **Pull cart:** private club. **Trail Fee:** private club.
Reservation policy: private club, members and guests of members only.
Winter condition: to be determined upon opening.
Terrain: gentle rolling hills. **Tees:** bentgrass. **Spikes:** soft spikes required.
Services: club rentals, lessons, snack bar, restaurant, lounge, beer, wine, liquor, pro shop, showers, driving range, putting & chipping greens, caddie program, swimming and tennis facilities, golf academy center, golf club memberships.
Comments: this new Tom Fazio designed golf course promises to be one of the private golf clubs in the state. The course will feature rolling terrain and distinctive bunkering on most of the holes. Fairways are surrounded by desert landscape, natural wildlife and native Juniper trees. Course to open in 2003-2004.

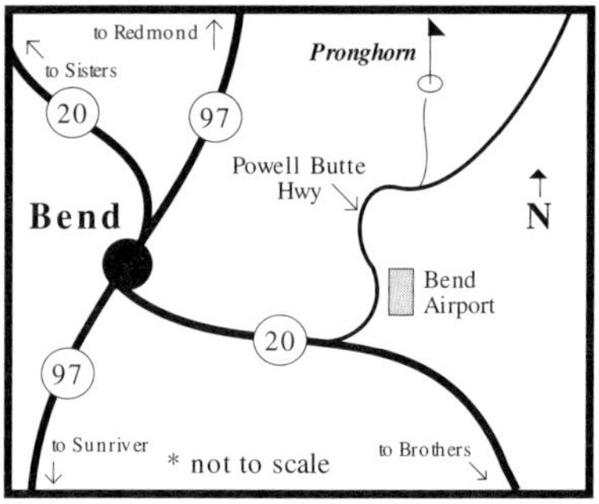

Directions: from Hwy 97 in Bend turn east on Hwy 20 (Central Oregon Hwy) toward Brothers. Follow Hwy 20 to the Powell Butte Hwy where you will turn left. Proceed on Hwy 20 on the Powell Butte Hwy past the Bend Airport (right side) until you reach the entrance to Pronghorn which will be located on your left a few miles ahead. Look for signs.

Pronghorn Golf Club (Jack Nicklaus Course, resort, 18 holes)

NE of Bend Oregon off the Powell Butte Highway; Bend, OR 97702
Phone: information call 800-541-9424. Web-site: www.pronghornclub.com
Pro: to be determined. Superintendent: to be determined. Record: N/A.
Rating/Slope: The golf course will be rated at the time of the opening.
Green fees: resort course, to be determined open opening; VISA, M/C, AMEX.
Power cart: to be determined. **Pull cart:** to be determined. **Trail Fee:** N/A.
Reservation policy: resort course, to be determined open opening.
Winter condition: to be determined upon opening of the resort.
Terrain: gentle rolling hills. **Tees:** bentgrass. **Spikes:** soft spikes required.
Services: club rentals, lessons, snack bar, restaurant, lounge, beer, wine, liquor, pro shop, showers, driving range, putting & chipping greens, caddie program, swimming and tennis facilities, golf academy center, golf club memberships.
Comments: the resort course designed by Jack Nicklaus will feature a traditional desert style course that will fit into the natural surroundings. The resort is due to open sometime in 2003 or 2004. Promises to be a great golfing venue.

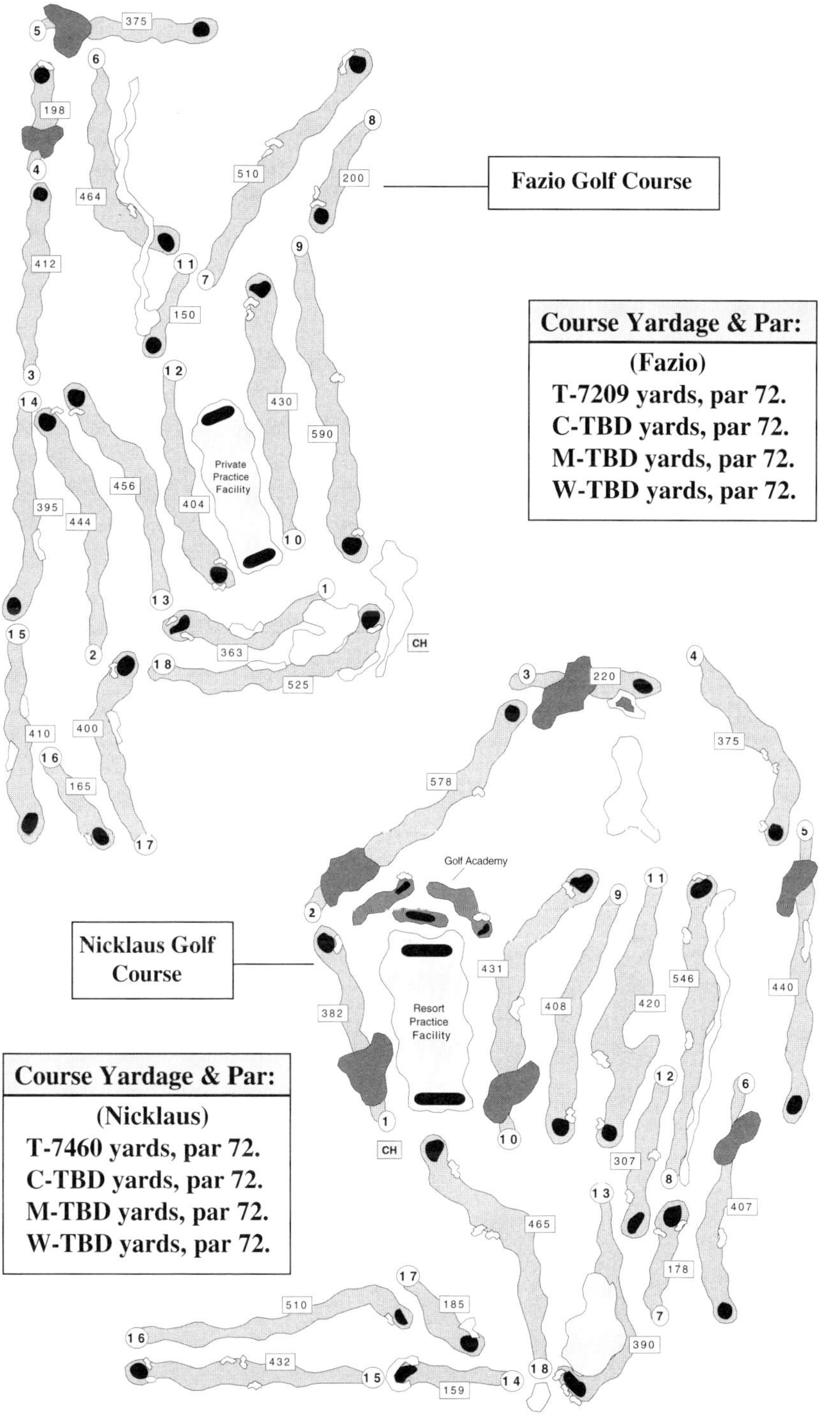

Course Yardage & Par:

(Fazio)
T-7209 yards, par 72.
C-TBD yards, par 72.
M-TBD yards, par 72.
W-TBD yards, par 72.

Course Yardage & Par:

(Nicklaus)
T-7460 yards, par 72.
C-TBD yards, par 72.
M-TBD yards, par 72.
W-TBD yards, par 72.

Pumpkin Ridge Golf Club (Ghost Creek) (semi-private, 18 holes)

12930 Old Pumpkin Ridge Road; North Plains, OR 97113
Phone: (503) 647-4747 or (503) 647-9977 or 1-888-594-GOLF.
Fax: (503) 647-2002. Web-site: www.pumpkinridge.com
Pro: Ben Hay, PGA. Superintendent: Bill Webster. Course record: 65.
Rating/Slope: T 73.8/139; C 71.4/135; M 69.1/132; W 70.0/128.
Green fees: Monday thru Thursday $95; Friday thru Sunday & Holidays $120; Off season rates available October thru May; VISA, M/C, AMEX, DIN, DIS.
Power cart: $18 per person. **Pull cart:** $5. **Trail Fee:** not allowed.
Reservation policy: call ahead up to 30 days in advance for your tee times.
Winter condition: the golf course is open all year long. Very dry conditions.
Terrain: gentle rolling hills. **Tees:** bentgrass. **Spikes:** soft spikes in summer.
Services: club rentals, lessons, restaurant,pro shop, driving range, group outings.
Comments: ranked #22 in *Golf Digest's* top 100 golf courses in the U.S. Robert Cupp Design. Pumpkin Ridge was host to the 1996 U.S. Amateur and the 1997 U.S. Womens Open Championship. This could quite possibly the nicest golf facility in the state of Oregon. Include this course on your must play list.

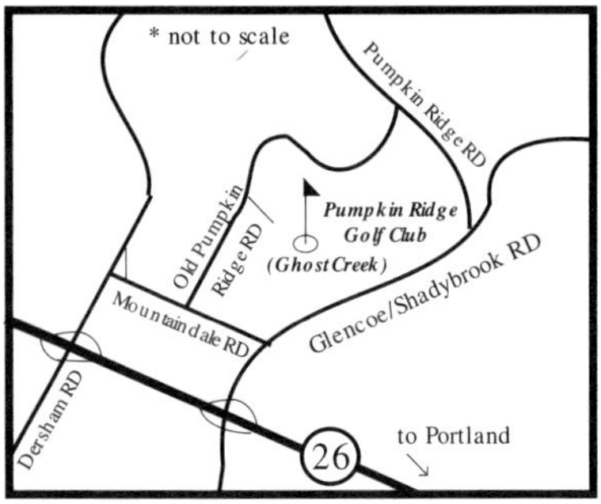

__Directions:__ From Hwy 26 (Sunset Hwy) take Dersham exit #55. Proceed north for .3 miles, take right onto Mountaindale Rd., proceed east for 1.0 miles, take a left onto Old Pumpkin Ridge Rd. Proceed for .5 miles to the entrance on your right.

Pumpkin Ridge Golf Club (Witch Hollow) (private, 18 holes)

12930 Old Pumpkin Ridge Road; North Plains, OR 97113
Phone: (503) 647-4747 or 647-2500. Fax: (503) 647-2002.
Web-site: www.pumpkinridge.com
Pro: Ken Jack, PGA. Superintendent: Bill Webster. Course record: 64.
Rating/Slope: T 75.2/143; C 72.7/142; M 70.2/140; W 72.0/134.
Green fees: private club. Members and guests of members only; M/C, VISA.
Power cart: private club. **Pull cart:** private club. **Trail Fee:** private club.
Reservation policy: private club members and guests of members only.
Winter condition: the golf course is open all year long. Dry conditions.
Terrain: flat, some hills. **Tees:** bentgrass. **Spikes:** soft spikes in summer.
Services: club rentals, lessons, restaurant, beer, wine, pro shop, driving range.
Comments: ranked #72 in *Golf Digest's* best 100 in the U.S. Robert Cupp design. The course sports bentgrass tees, fairways and greens. Pumpkin Ridge was host to the 1996 U.S. Amateur and hosted the 1997 U.S. Womens Open Championship. A true gem that is nothing short of spectacular. Great course.

Ghost Creek

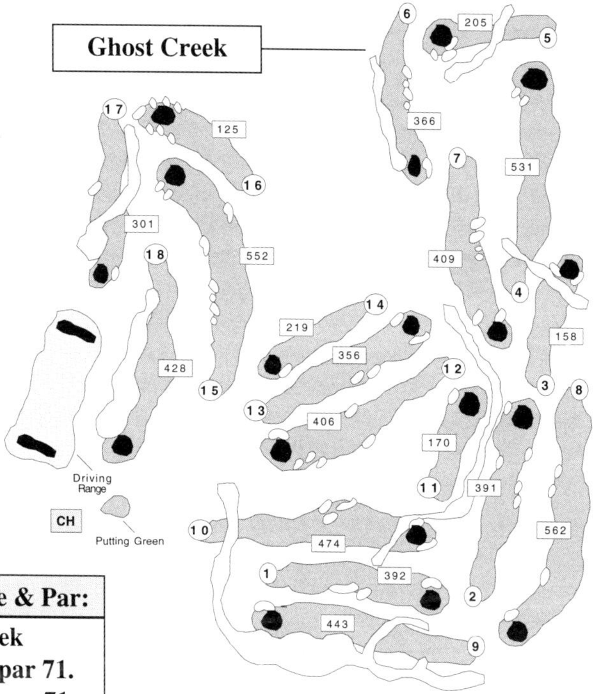

Course Yardage & Par:

Ghost Creek
T-6839 yards, par 71.
C-6451 yards, par 71.
M-5956 yards, par 71.
W-5206 yards, par 71.

Witch Hollow

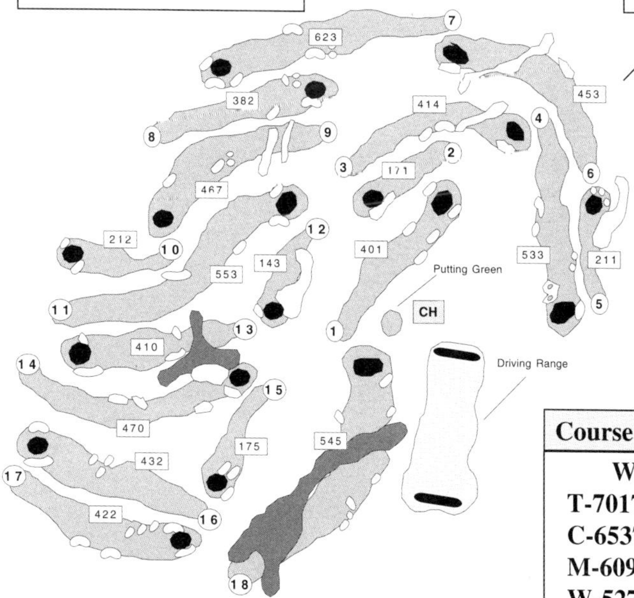

Course Yardage & Par:

Witch Hollow
T-7017 yards, par 72.
C-6537 yards, par 72.
M-6095 yards, par 72.
W-5270 yards, par 72.

Quail Point Golf Course (public, 9 hole course)

1200 Mira Mar; Medford, OR 97504
Phone: (541) 857-7000. Fax: (541) 857-7074. Web: www.quailpointgolf.com
Pro: Peggy Atwwod, LPGA. Superintendent: Paul Winterbottom.
Rating/Slope: C 69.4/122; M 68.2/119; W 68.8/121. **Course record:** 30.
Green fees: $22/$14 before 3pm; $18/$12 after 3pm; all day rates are available Senior day on Tuesdays and Thursdays $16/$10; M/C, VISA.
Power cart: $20/$12. **Pull cart:** $3/$2. **Trail fee:** not allowed.
Reservation policy: please call 7 days in advance to schedule tee-times.
Winter condition: the golf course open all year long, weather permitting.
Terrain: relatively hilly. **Tees:** all grass. **Spikes:** soft spikes required.
Services: club rentals, lessons, snack bar, pro shop, driving range, putting green.
Comments: This challenging nine hole course opened in August of 1993. The golf course offers resort conditions year round. Water comes into play on 6 holes. The hilly terrain makes this course play longer than yardage indicates.

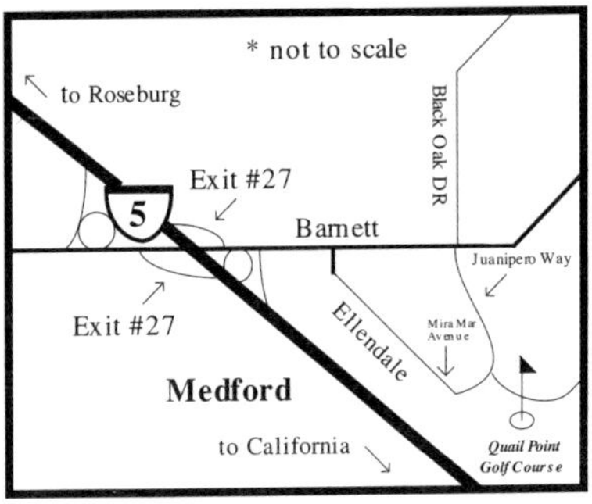

Directions: From I-5 N&S take exit #27 in Medford to Barnett Road. Travel east to Ellendale, turn right on Ellendale and then follow this to the golf course.

Course Yardage & Par:

C-3034 yards, par 35.
M-2901 yards, par 35.
W-2437 yards, par 35.

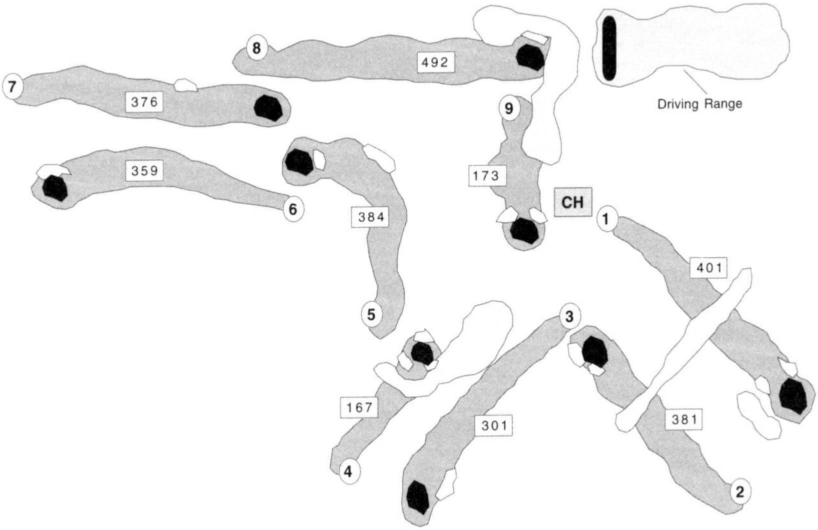

Quail Run Golf Course (public, 9 hole course)

16725 Northridge Drive; P.O. Box 4279; Sunriver, OR 97707
Phone: (541) 536-1303; 1-800-895-GOLF. Fax: (541) 536-1076.
Pro: Bill Martin. Superintendent: Rich Murphy. Web: none.
Rating/Slope: C 73.4/135; M 71.8/130; M 70.2/125; W 71.0/128. **Record:** 33.
Green fees: $40/$24 all week long; $35/$20 off season rates; M/C, VISA.
Power cart: $13/$7.50 per rider. **Pull cart:** $3/$2. **Trail fee:** $10.
Reservation policy: you may call up to 6 months in advance for your tee times.
Winter condition: the golf course is closed December through February.
Terrain: flat, some undulations. **Tees:** grass. **Spikes:** soft spikes required.
Services: club rentals, lessons, coffee shop, beer, wine, pro shop, driving range, putting green. **Comments:** Very scenic golf course with views of Mt. Bachelor and the surrounding area. Great 9 hole course to play when vacationing in Central Oregon. Voted the #2, 9 hole course in the country in 2001 by *Golf Digest*.

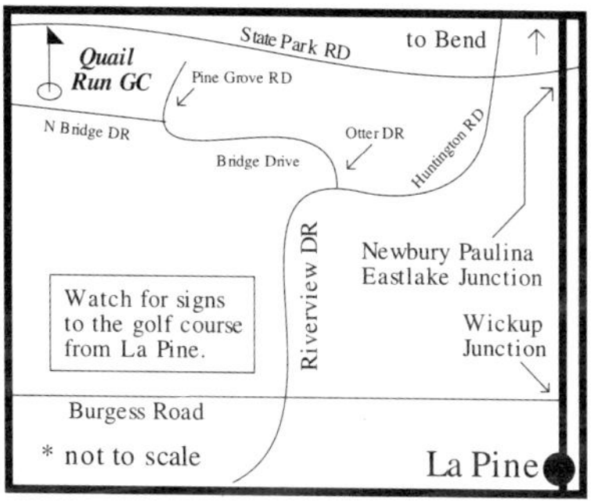

Directions: the golf course is located 9.6 miles south of Sunriver Oregon off of Highway 97. Turn right on the Newbury Paulina/Eastlake Junction. Go across the railroad tracks and follow signs to the golf course. Look for signs marking your way to the golf course from Hwy 97.

Course Yardage & Par:

C-3512 yards, par 36.
M-3185 yards, par 36.
M-3023 yards, par 36.
W-2707 yards, par 36.

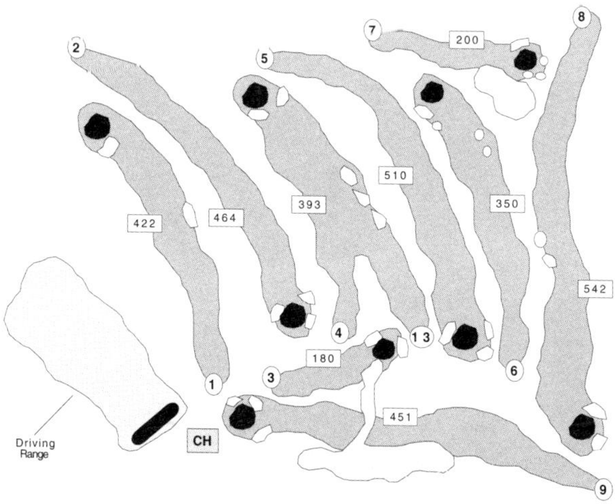

Quail Valley Golf Course (public, 18 hole course)

12565 NW Aerts Road; P.O. Box 200; Banks, OR 97106
Phone: (503) 324-4444. Fax: (503) 324-7500. Web: www.quailvalleygolf.com
Pro: Doug Hixson, PGA. Superintendent: Rusty Feltman.
Rating/Slope: C 71.1/119; M 69.5/114; W 71.0/128. **Course record:** 64.
Green fees: Monday-Thursday $32/$16; Friday-Sunday & Holidays $38/$19 Early Bird Specials Monday thru Thursday before 9am $26/$13; M/C, VISA.
Power cart: $24/$12. **Pull cart:** $3/$1.50. **Trail fee:** not allowed.
Reservation policy: please call the pro shop 7 days in advance for tee times.
Winter condition: the golf course open, weather permitting. Dry conditions.
Terrain: mounded. **Tees:** all grass. **Spikes:** soft spikes April thru October.
Services: fully stocked pro shop, club rentals, lessons, snack bar, driving range, putting & chipping greens. **Comments:** A beautiful golf course that is worth a special trip. Four lakes, 12 surface acres of water, 600 small trees, and 44 bunkers will challenge your golfing skill at every turn. A must play track.

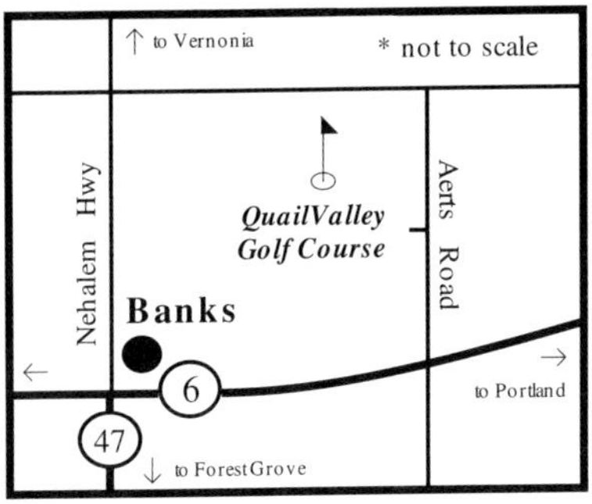

Directions: From Portland, Oregon take highway 26 westbound to Highway 6. Exit onto Highway 6 and proceed to NW Aerts Road, (just 1.5 miles from Highway 26). Turn right on NW Aerts Road and proceed to the golf course. Look for signs marking your way to the golf course.

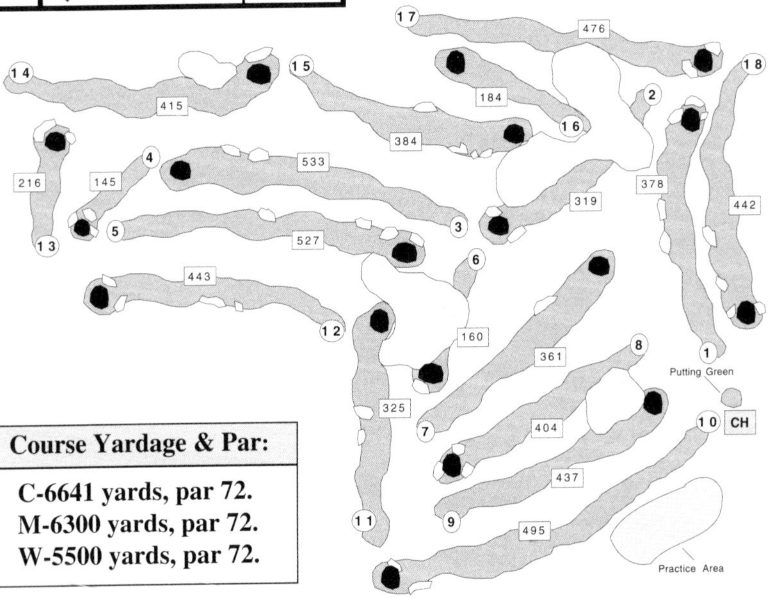

Course Yardage & Par:
C-6641 yards, par 72.
M-6300 yards, par 72.
W-5500 yards, par 72.

Ranch Hills Golf Club (public, 9 hole course)

26710 South Ranch Hills Road; Mulino, OR 97042
Phone: (503) 829-5666. Fax: none. Web: none.
Owners: Dewey & Dinene Wyatt.
Rating/Slope: M 65.0/108; W 68.8/108. **Course record:** 28 nine/59 eighteen.
Green fees: W/D $24/$12; W/E $26/$14; Sr. rates W/D's only; no credit cards.
Power cart $24/12. **Pull cart:** $4/$2. **Trail fee:** $5 per 9, for personal carts.
Reservation policy: yes, please call up to 3 days in advance for tee-times.
Winter condition: the golf course is open all year long, wet conditions.
Terrain: flat (easy walking). **Tees:** all grass. **Spikes:** metal spikes permitted.
Services: club rentals, snack bar, beer, wine, limited pro shop, putting green, driving range. **Comments:** Milk Creek wanders throughout this nine hole golf course putting an emphasis on accuracy off the tee. Golf course can play very tight at times with trees coming into play on many of the holes.

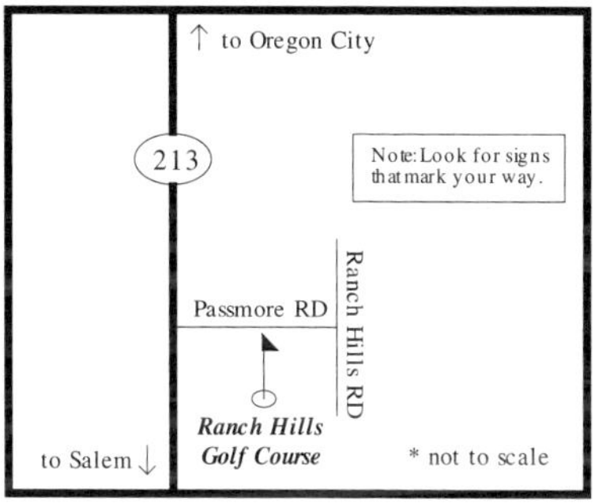

Directions: from Highway 213 S turn left on Passmore Road. Proceed straight ahead for 1/4 mile to the golf course. From Highway 213 N turn right on Passmore Road. Make sure you look for a sign marking your way to the course.

Course Yardage & Par:

C-2895 yards, par 36.
M-2838 yards, par 36.
W-2636 yards, par 37.

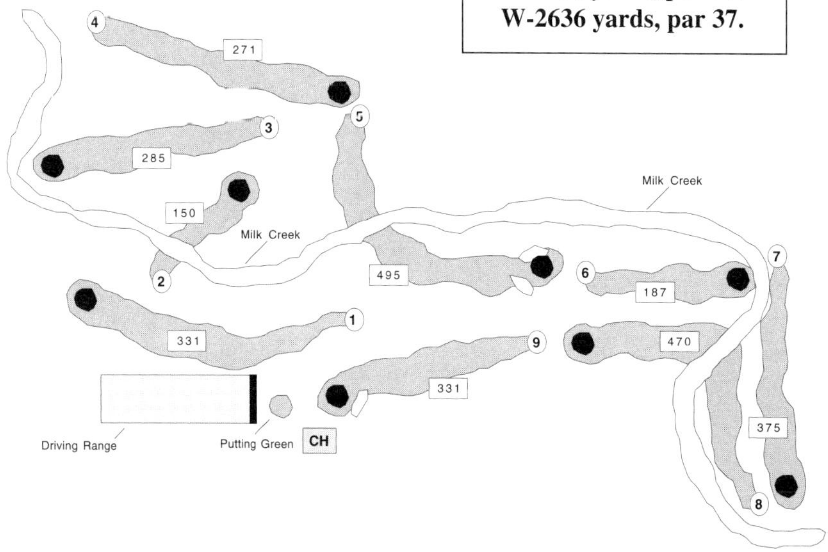

Reames Golf & Country Club (private, 18 hole course)

4201 Highway 97 South; Klamath Falls, OR 97603
Phone: (541) 884-7446. Fax: (503) 884-1435. Web: none.
Pro: Rick Verbarendse, PGA. Superintendent: Rich Flink.
Rating/Slope: C 70.7/119; M 69.4/117; W 71.0/117. **Course record:** 65.
Green fees: private club, members & guests only; reciprocates; M/C, VISA.
Power cart: private club. **Pull cart:** private club. **Trail fee:** private club.
Reservation policy: yes, 1 week in advance for members and guests only.
Winter condition: the golf course is open all year, weather permitting, good.
Terrain: flat, some hills. **Tees:** all grass. **Spikes:** soft spikes only.
Services: club rentals, lessons, restaurant, lounge, beer, wine, beverages, pro shop, lockers, showers, putting & chipping greens, driving range.
Comments: this is an outstanding golf facility. Large well bunkered greens and tree-lined fairways make this course a good test of your game. Landing area's are small in certain parts of the course putting emphasis on shot placement. If you get a chance to play Reames Golf &Country Club be sure not to pass it up.

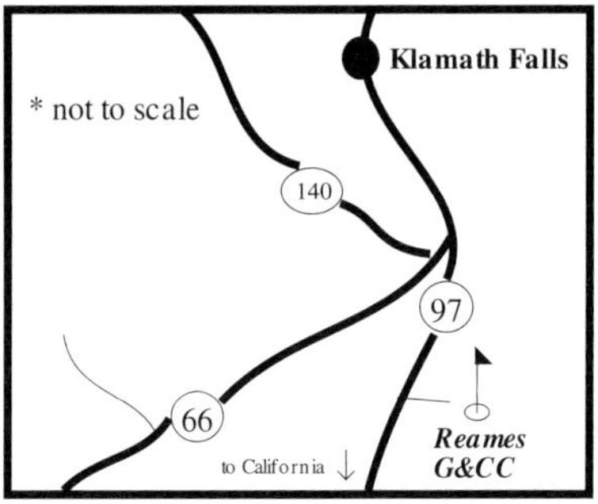

Directions: the golf course is located off Highway 97 south of Klamath Falls. You can see the golf course from the Highway. You will turn east to get to the clubhouse from Highway 97.

Course Yardage & Par:
C-6679 yards, par 72.
M-6371 yards, par 72.
W-5655 yards, par 74.

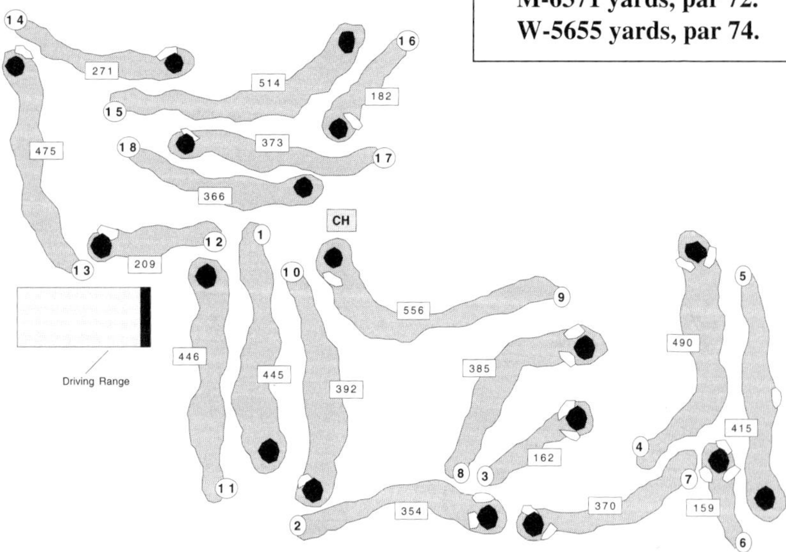

Red Mountain Golf Course (public, 9 hole course)

324 Mountian Greens Lane; Grants Pass, OR 97526
Phone: (541) 479-2297. Fax: (541) 476-9441. Web: none.
Owners: Brad & Kris Vandehey. Superintendent: Brad Vandehey.
Rating/Slope: the golf course is not rated. **Course record:** 54.
Green fees: $12/$7; Monday through Friday you can play all day for $15.
Power cart: $5 per nine holes. **Pull cart:** $1. **Trail fee:** $3 for personal carts.
Reservation policy: T-times on a 1st come 1st served basis. Walk-ons welcome.
Terrain: flat, some hills. **Tees:** all grass. **Spikes:** metal spikes permitted.
Services: club rentals, beer, beverages, snack bar, pro shop, putting green.
Comments: formerly Shoestring Golf Course this executive tract sports tree lined fairways and challenging golf. This family run course is a bright spot on the southern Oregon golf scene. Worth a trip if you have time for a quick nine.

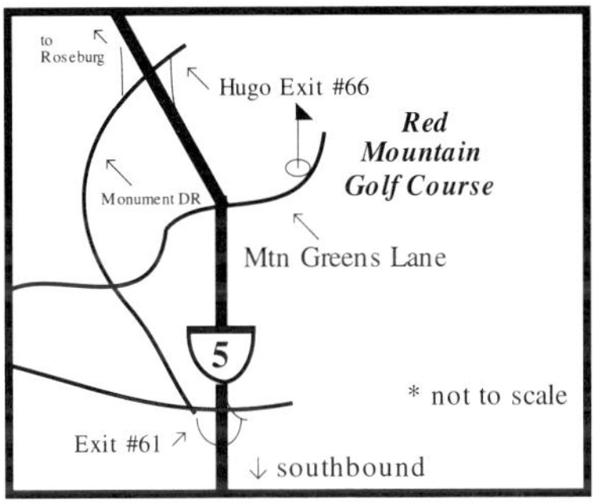

Directions: From I-5 N&S take the Merlin or Hugo exit. Proceed to Monument Drive. Follow to Potts Way. Turn east and follow this to the course.

Course Yardage & Par:

Blue tees-1049 yards, par 27.
White tees-1265 yards, par 30.
Dual tees for 18 holes:
Blue tees-2314 yards, par 57.
White tees-2314 yards, par 57.

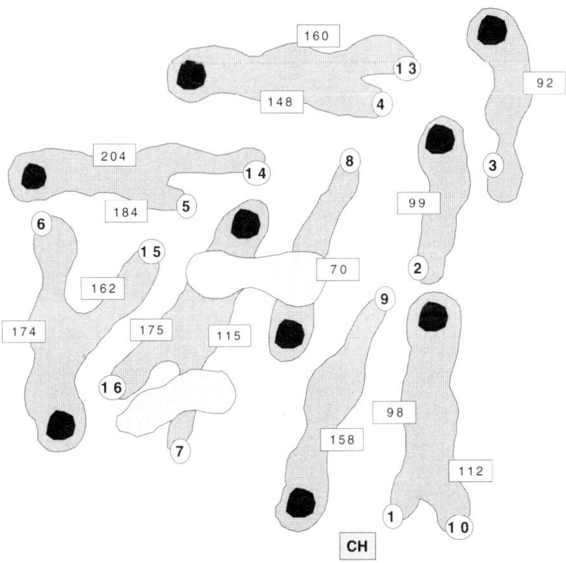

Redtail Municipal Golf Course (public, 18 hole course)

8200 Scholls Ferry Road; Beaverton, OR 97008
Phone: (503) 646-5166. Fax: (503) 646-5167. Web: www.golfredtail.com
Pro: Mark Bolton, PGA. Superintendent: John Standard.
Rating/Slope: T 74.4/135; C 72.5/132; M 70.4/124; W 73.3/131. **Record:** 65.
Green fees: W/D $37/$19; W/E & Holidays $39/$20 (peak season rates listed) Jr. & Sr. rates are available; off season rates are available; VISA, M/C.
Power cart: $24/$12. **Pull cart:** $3/$2. **Trail Fee:** $4 for personal carts.
Reservation policy: yes, please call up to 6 days in advance for your tee-time.
Winter condition: the golf course is open all year long. Dry conditions.
Terrain: flat, some hills. **Tees:** all grass. **Spikes:** soft spikes preferred.
Services: club rentals, lessons, restaurant, lounge, pro shop, driving range, putting & chipping greens. **Comments:** this golf course has totally been renovated for the 2000 golfing season. The new longer layout features better drainage, large well bunkered greens and water coming in to play on many holes.

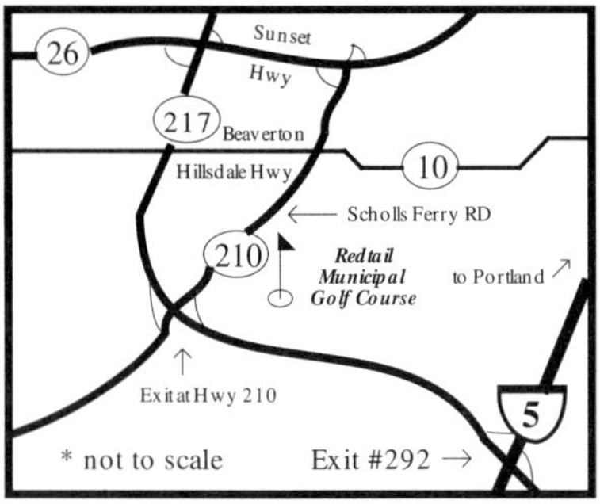

Directions: from Hwy 217 exit at the Progress exit. Go left on SW Hall Blvd. Take first left at the light after proceeding over the overpass onto Scholls Ferry Rd. Go for .3 miles to the course on the right. Signs are posted at your turns.

Course Yardage & Par:
T-7107 yards, par 72.
C-6682 yards, par 72.
M-6267 yards, par 72.
W-5746 yards, par 72.

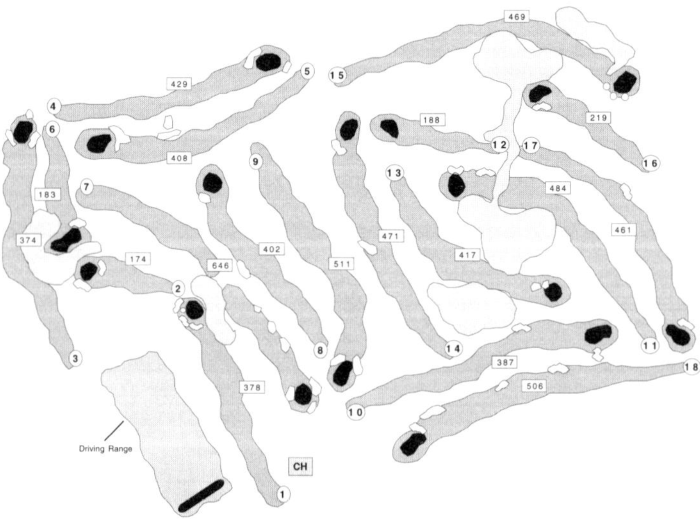

Resort at the Mountain (public, 27 hole course)

68010 E Fairway Avenue; Welches, OR 97067
Phone: (503) 622-3151 or call 1-800-669-GOLF for reservations.
Fax: (503) 622-5641. Web-site: www.theresort.com
Pro: Bob Turnquist, PGA. Supt.: Tony Lasher. Course record: 64.
Green fees: Mon.-Thur. $37/$22; Fri.-Sun. $48/$25; M/C, VISA, AMEX, DIS.
Power cart: $30/$18. **Pull cart:** complimentary. **Trail fee:** not allowed.
Reservation policy: yes, please call 2 weeks in advance, maximum non guests.
Winter condition: the golf course is open all year long. Fair conditions.
Terrain: flat, some hills. **Tees:** all grass. **Spikes:** soft spikes preferred.
Services: club rentals, lessons, snack bar, restaurant, lounge, beer, wine, liquor, pro shop, lockers, showers, driving range, complete resort. **Comments:** These 27 holes wander through an alpine setting. The facility has a excellent resort tied to the golf course for those wanting to take a golfer's vacation. Good course.

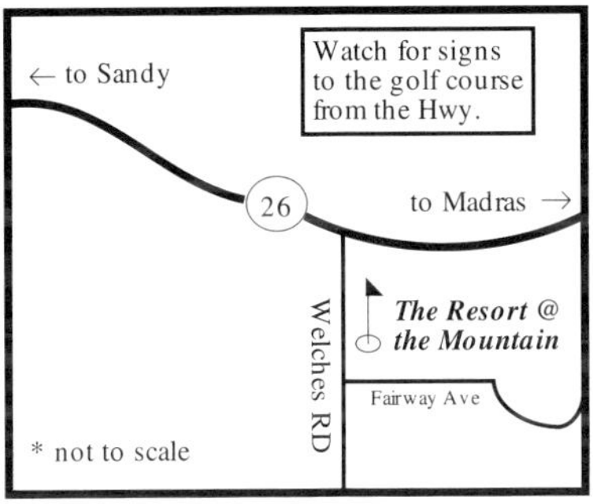

Directions: from Highway 84 proceed east to the Woodvillage exit to Hwy 26. Proceed east to Welches, Oregon. South on Welches Road to the golf course.

Rating/Slope:
Thistle/Foxglove: M 68.3/122; W 67.1/114.
Foxglove/Pine Cone: M 70.7/128; W 68.5/119.
Pine Cone/Thistle: M 69.4/122; W 66.0/109.

Course Yardage & Par:

Thistle Nine:
M-2956 yards, par 36. W-2238 yards, par 37.
Fox Glove Nine:
M-3106 yards, par 36. W-22539 yards, par 37.
Pine Cone Nine:
M-3299 yards, par 34. W-2427 yards, par 34.

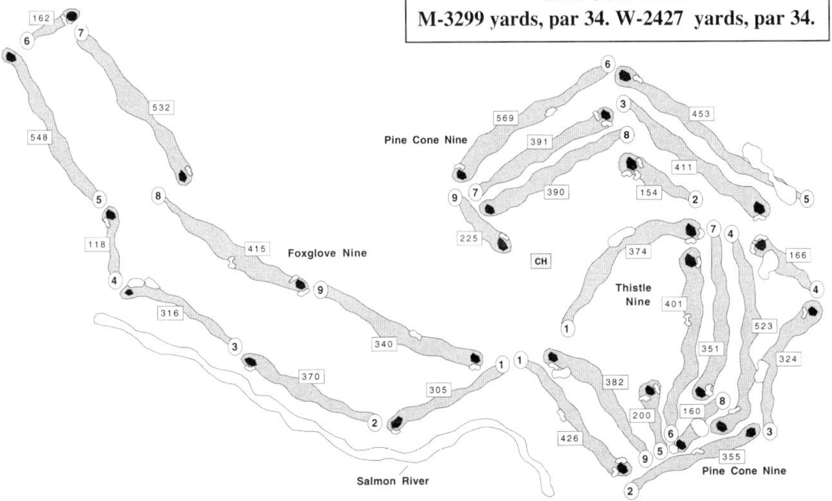

Riveridge Golf Course (public, 18 hole course)

3800 North Delta; Eugene, OR 97408
Phone: (541) 345-9160. Fax: (541) 345-1202. Web: none.
Pros: Ric Jeffries, PGA, Al Mundle, PGA. Supt.: Steve Bletscher.
Rating/Slope: C 68.6/118; M 67.4/111; W 69.6/119. **Course record:** 63.
Green fees: Mon.-Fri. $30 with soft spikes; Sat.-Sun. $32 with soft spikes. the pro shop sells them. Sr. rates (Monday through Friday); M/C, VISA.
Power cart: $24/$13. **Pull cart:** $2. **Trail fee:** personal carts not allowed.
Reservation policy: yes, please call 7 days in advance for your tee-times.
Winter condition: the golf course is open all year long, weather permitting.
Terrain: flat, some hills. **Tees:** all grass. **Spikes:** soft spikes preferred.
Services: club rentals, lessons, snack bar, beer, pro shop, driving range, putting & chipping greens. **Comments:** the course has a covered and lighted driving range. The golf course is kept in excellent condition and is worth a stop if in the area. Complete practice facility with putting green, chipping green and bunkers.

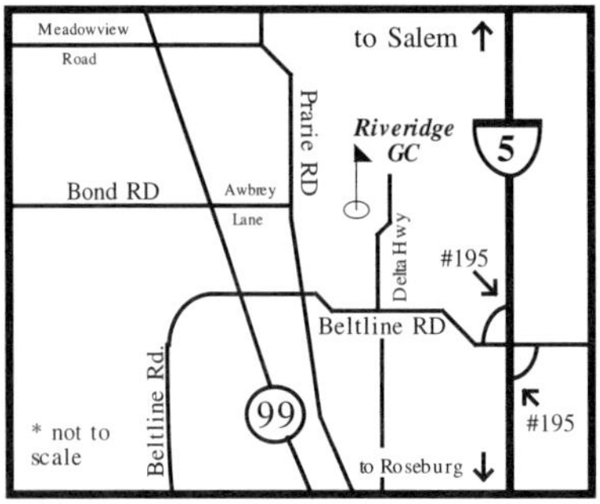

Directions: from I-5 N&S take (exit 195) go west on Beltline to Delta Highway. Go north on Delta Highway for 1.5 miles to the golf course which will be located on your left hand side of the road. Look for signs marking your way to the golf course.

Course Yardage & Par:

C-6318 yards, par 71.
M-6007 yards, par 71.
M-5560 yards, par 71.
W-5197 yards, par 71.

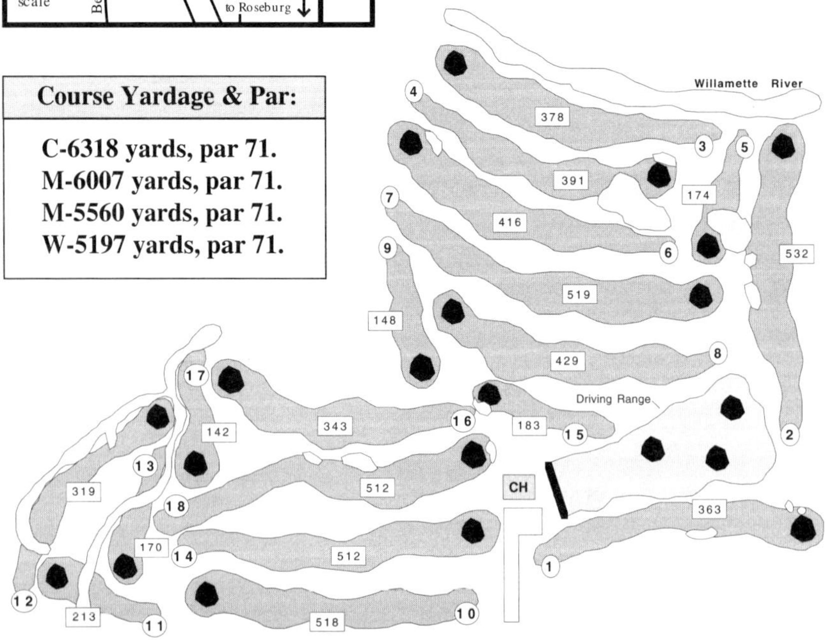

River's Edge Golf Resort (public, 18 hole course)

400 Pro Shop Drive; Bend, OR 97701

Phone: (541) 389-2828. Fax: (541) 389-0249. Web: www.riverhouse.com

Pro: Zach Swoffer, PGA. Superintendent: Leann Brousseau.

Rating/Slope: C 72.0/134; M 71.2/131; M 69.9/127; W 71.2/136. **Record:** 68.
Green fees: $49/$28 all week long; winter and Jr. rates; M/C, VISA.
Power cart: $28/$18. **Pull cart:** $3/$2. **Trail fee:** personal carts not allowed.
Reservation policy: public 1 week ahead. Hotel guests w/ room confirmation.
Winter condition: the course is open all year long depending upon conditions.
Terrain: hillside course. **Tees:** all grass. **Spikes:** soft spikes preferred.
Services: club rentals, lessons, snack bar, beer, wine, pro shop, driving range.
Comments: 2 different nines one narrow and short. The other is longer and more open. Very scenic with picturesque waterfalls and serene surroundings. This course will challenge you at every turn. Good central Oregon track.

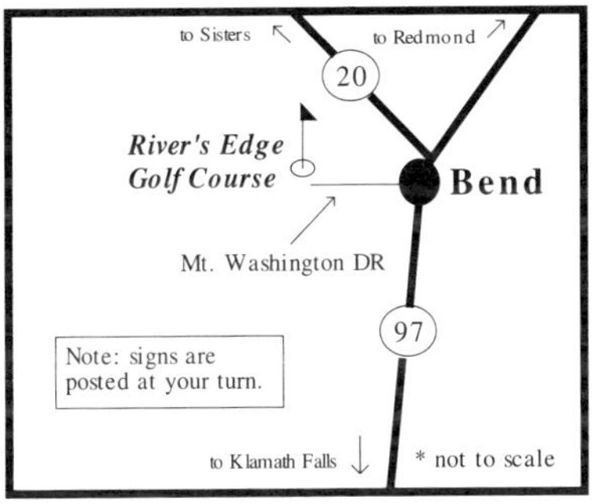

Directions: from Hwy 97, turn into Mt. Washington Drive at the south end of the Riverhouse Motor Inn. Course will be 1 mile ahead. Course located at the north end of Bend. Look for signs at your turn.

Course Yardage & Par:

C-6683 yards, par 72.
M-6440 yards, par 72.
M-6128 yards, par 72.
W-5381 yards, par 73.

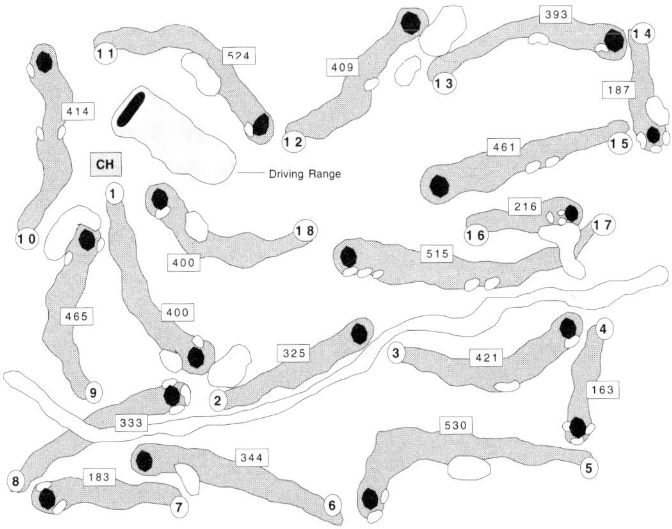

Riverside Golf & Country Club (private, 18 hole course)

8105 NE 33rd Drive; Portland, OR 97211
Phone: (503) 282-7265. Fax: (503) 282-1383. Web: none.
Pro: Pat Sutton, PGA. Superintendent: Tom Christy.
Rating/Slope: C 72.7/135; M 71.8/130; M 70.8/129; W 74.0/132. **Record:** 65.
Green fees: private club, members & guests of members only; M/C, VISA.
Power cart: private club. **Pull cart:** private club. **Trail fee:** not allowed.
Reservation policy: private club, members & guests of members only.
Winter condition: the golf course is open all year long. Fair conditions.
Terrain: flat. **Tees:** all grass. **Spikes:** no metal spikes March to September.
Services: club rentals, lessons, restaurant, lounge, beer, wine, liquor, pro shop, lockers, showers, driving range, putting & chipping greens, club memberships.
Comments: Mature trees abound at this picturesque course. One of Portland's best private clubs. Course plays very tough in places. Excellent golf course.

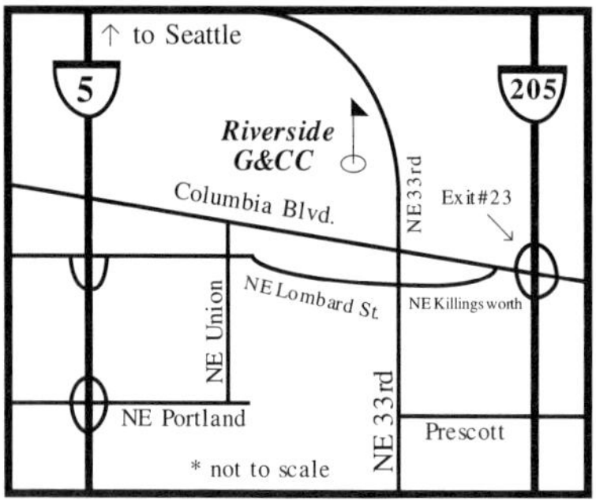

Directions: from I-5 take the Columbia Street exit and go eastbound to NE 33rd. Turn left to the course. From I-205 take the Columbia St. exit and go westbound for 2 miles to NE 33rd. Turn right.

Course Yardage & Par:
C-6624 yards, par 72.
M-6393 yards, par 72.
M-6075 yards, par 72.
W-5738 yards, par 73.

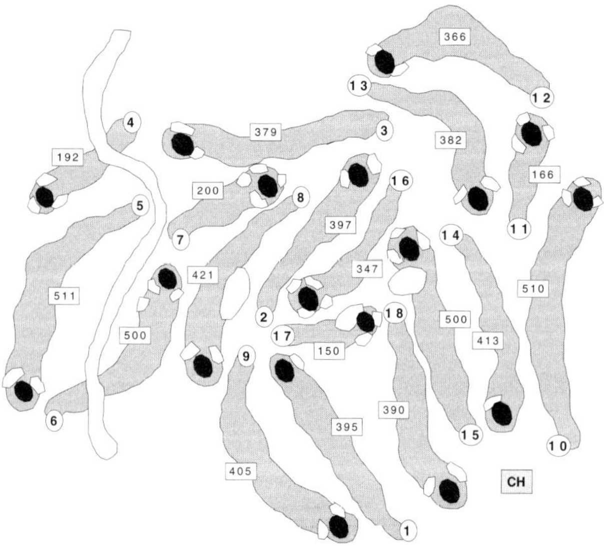

Riverwood Golf Course (public, 9 hole course)

21050 SE Riverwood Road; Dundee, OR 97115

Phone: (503) 864-2667. Fax: (503) 864-2660. Web: none.

Pro: Gregory C. Brown, PGA. Superintendent: Earl Brown.

Rating/Slope: M 68.6/124; W 68.0/115. **Course record:** 65.

Green fees: W/D $23/$13; W/E & Holidays $24/$14; Jr. & Sr. rates (M-F).

Power cart: $20/$10. **Pull cart:** $2. **Trail fee:** $45 for 9 holes.

Reservation policy: yes, please call for your tee-times 7 days in advance.

Winter condition: the golf course is open all year long, damp conditions.

Terrain: flat (easy walking). **Tees:** all grass. **Spikes:** soft spikes only.

Services: club rentals, lessons, snack bar, beer, wine, pro shop, driving range.

Comments: Course is flat and very easy to walk. This course was built in 1932 and displays many mature trees. Recent improvements make for a challenging 9 hole round. Greens are medium in size and have some green-side bunkers.

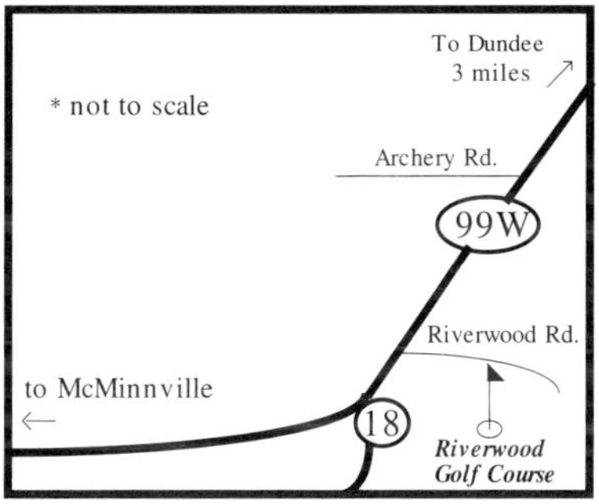

Directions: the golf course is located 1 mile off of Hwy 99W. After traveling 3 miles on Hwy 99W look for Riverwood Road. Turn right to the golf course. Look for a sign on the east side of the highway. The golf course located south of Newburg Oregon.

Course Yardage & Par:

M-2861 yards, par 35.
W-2483 yards, par 35.
Dual tees for 18 holes:
M-5805 yards, par 71.
W-5205 yards, par 71.

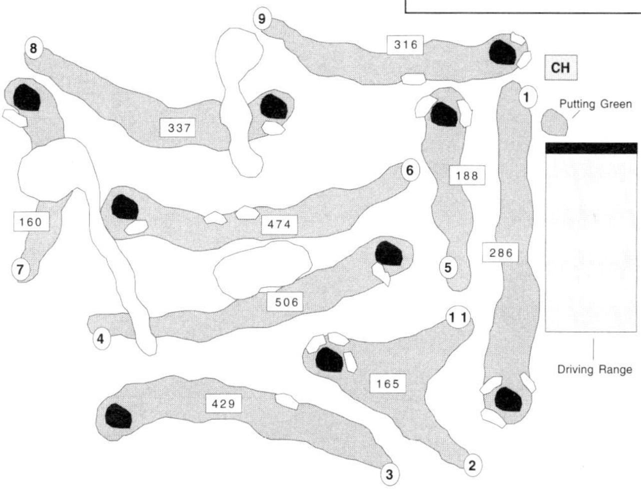

Rock Creek Country Club (private, 18 hole course)

5100 NW Neakahnie; Portland, OR 97229
Phone: (503) 645-1101. Fax: (503) 645-1755. Web: none.
Pro: Chuck DaSilva, PGA. Superintendent: Robert Wilkinson.
Rating/Slope: C 72.7/131; M 71.2/128; W 71.7/121. **Course record:** 63.
Green fees: private, members only; reciprocates; no credit cards.
Power cart: available. **Pull cart:** available. **Trail fee:** no charge.
Reservation policy: private club, members and guests of members only.
Winter condition: the golf course is open all year long. Dry conditions.
Terrain: flat, some rolling terrain. **Tees:** grass. **Spikes:** soft spikes preferred.
Services: club rentals, lessons, restaurant, lounge, beer, wine, liquor, pro shop, lockers, showers, driving range, putting and chipping greens, club memberships.
Comments: A quiet and beautiful private club nestled throughout the Rock Creek neighborhood of Portland. The tree-lined fairways, ponds and greenside bunkers provide a challenge to all levels of golfers. Excellent golf course.

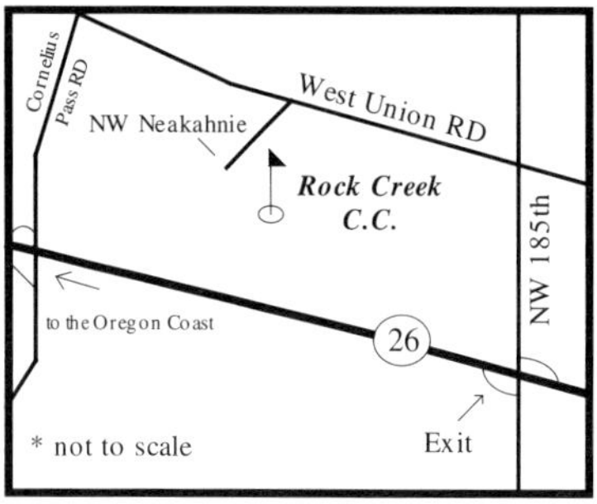

__Directions:__ from I-5 exit on Highway 26 (Sunset Highway West). Go 10 miles to 185th. Turn northbound on 185th and proceed approximately 1.1 miles to the West Union Road Intersection. Turn left and travel westbound for .5 miles to Neakahnie and the golf course.

Course Yardage & Par:

C-6700 yards, par 72.
M-6391 yards, par 72.
W-5476 yards, par 74.

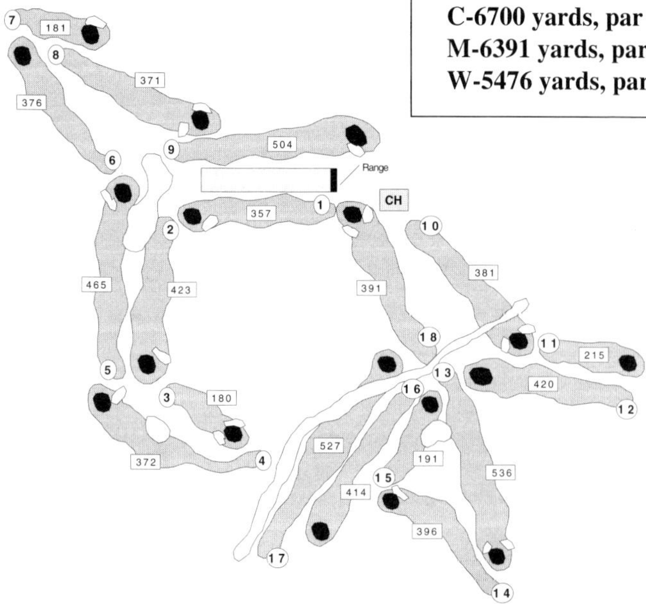

Rogue Valley Country Club (private, 27 hole course)

2660 Hillcrest Road; Medford, OR 97504

Phone: (541) 772-4050. Fax: (541) 776-0960. Web: www.rvcc.com

Pro: Jim Wise, PGA. Superintendent: Ken Johnson.

Rating/Slope: Course #1: C 71.4/123; M 69.9/122; W 69.7/122. **Record:** 63.
Green fees: private club, members and guests only; reciprocates ; M/C,VISA.
Power cart: private club. **Pull cart:** private club. **Trail fee:** private club.
Reservation policy: private club, members and guests only.
Winter condition: the golf course is open all year long, weather permitting.
Terrain: flat, some hills. **Tees:** all grass. **Spikes:** no metal spikes in summer.
Services: club rentals, lessons, snack bar, restaurant, lounge, beer, wine, liquor, beverages, pro shop, lockers, showers, driving range, putting & chipping greens.
Comments: Host of the Southern Oregon Golf Championship. Great private golf course that has large, well bunkered greens and fairly wide fairways.

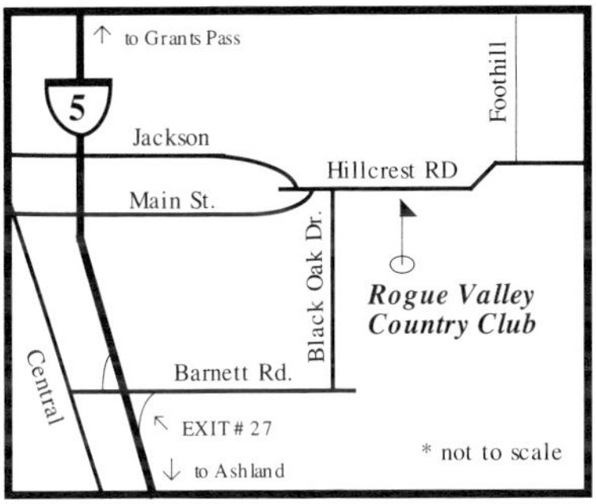

Directions: from I-5 take the Barnett exit. Travel east on Barnett to Black Oak Rd, turn left. Proceed straight to Hillcrest Rd. Turn right on Hillcrest Road to the course.

Course Yardage & Par:

Course #1
T-6666 yards, par 72.
C-6353 yards, par 72.
M-5980 yards, par 72.
W-5283 yards, par 72.

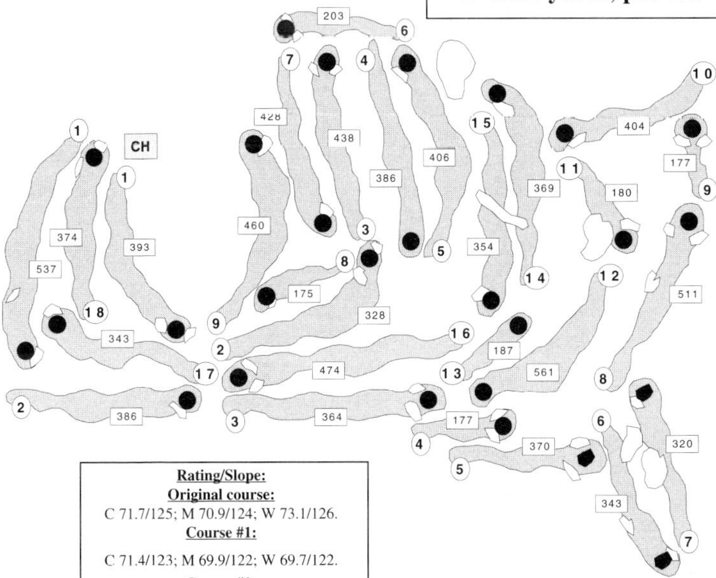

Rating/Slope:
Original course:
C 71.7/125; M 70.9/124; W 73.1/126.
Course #1:
C 71.4/123; M 69.9/122; W 69.7/122.
Course #2:
C 70.8/123; M 69.2/116; W 73.1/126.

Rose City Golf Course (public, 18 hole course)

2200 NE 71st Avenue; Portland, OR 97213
Phone: 292-8570 for Tee-times or (503) 253-4744. Fax: (503) 255-8189.
Pro: Hank Childs, PGA. Superintendent: Jim Heck. Web: none.
Rating/Slope: C 70.9/118; M 69.2/115; W 74.4/122; W 71.6/111. **Record:** 61.
Green fees: Mon.-Thur. $20/$10; Friday-Sun. & Hol. $22/$11; Jr. & Sr. rates.
Power cart: $25/$13. **Pull cart:** $3/$2. **Trail fee:** $4/$2 for personal carts.
Reservation policy: yes, call six days in advance or visit a week in advance.
Winter condition: the golf course is open all year long. Dry (drains well).
Terrain: flat, some hills. **Tees:** all grass. **Spikes:** metal spikes permitted.
Services: club rentals, lessons, snack bar, restaurant, beer, wine, pop, pro shop, putting green, club memberships. **Comments:** Beautiful old clubhouse surrounded by mature trees. Fairways are tree-lined and can be a factor off of the tee. Water comes into play 4 holes and greens are well guarded by bunkers. Greens can generally be found in excellent condition throughout the year. Good public track that can get very busy during the summer months.

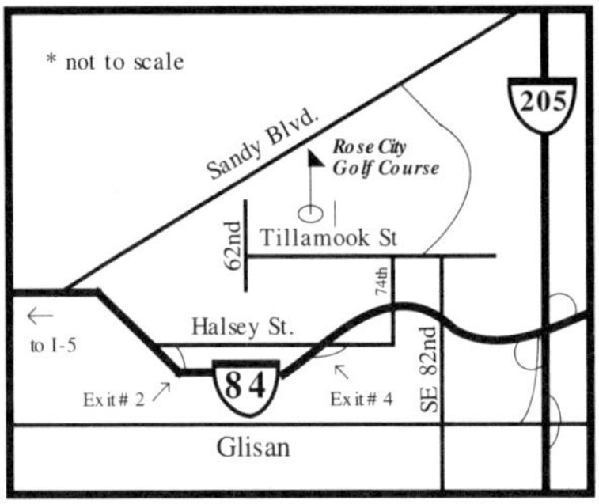

Directions: from I-84 eastbound take exit #4 (68th Avenue) and travel straight on NE Hasley Street for .3 miles to NE 74th. Turn left on 74th and proceed .3 miles to Tillamook. Turn left, the golf course will be on your right hand side. Look for signs.

Course Yardage & Par:
C-6455 yards, par 72.
M-6166 yards, par 72.
W-5619 yards, par 74.

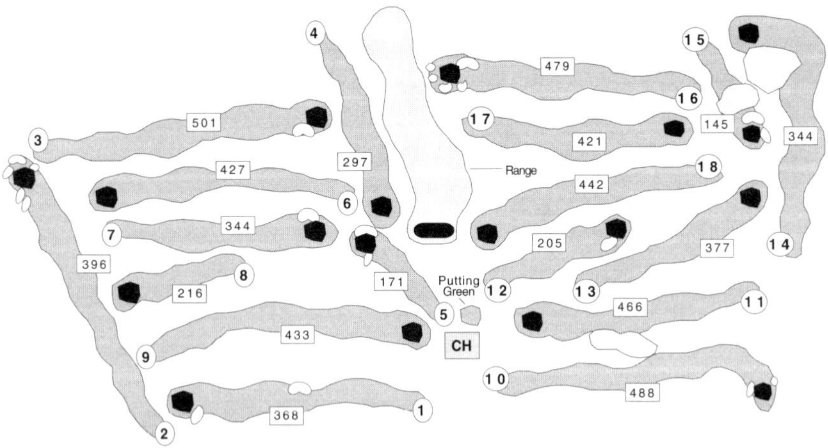

Roseburg Country Club (private, 18 hole course)

5051 NW Garden Valley Road; Roseburg, OR 97470
Phone: (541) 672-4041. Fax: (541) 672-6411. Web: roseburgcountryclub.com
Pro: Brian Sackett, PGA. Superintendent: Barry Adams.
Rating/Slope: C 70.0/124; M 68.5/120; W 71.4/126. **Course record:** 62.
Green fees: private club, members & guests of members only; reciprocates.
Power cart: $25. **Pull cart:** $2.50. **Trail fee:** N/A.
Reservation policy: private club, members can call up to 7 days in advance.
Winter condition: the golf course is open year round.
Terrain: some hills, flat areas. **Tees:** all grass. **Spikes:** soft spikes only.
Services: club rentals, lessons, snack bar, restaurant, lounge, pro shop, lockers, showers, driving range, putting & chipping greens, swimming pool.
Comments: Medium length course with well bunkered, undulating greens. The fairways are tree-lined with narrow landing area's. The pro states that "no one ever tears this course up". Excellent country club with a relaxed look and feel.

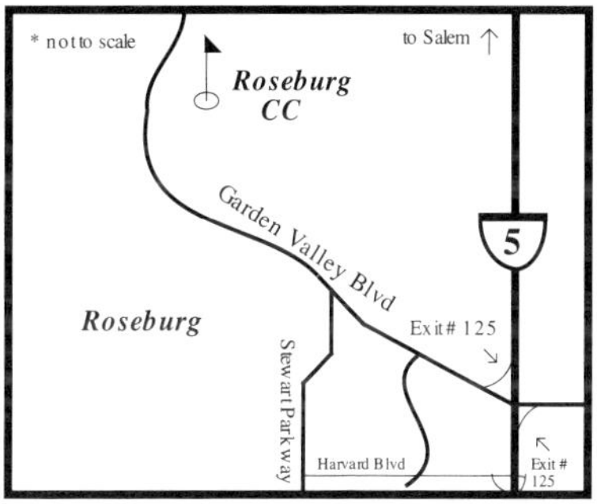

<u>Directions:</u> from I-5 take exit #125 at Roseburg (Garden Valley). Travel west for 4.5 miles on NW Garden Valley Road to the golf course which will be on your right hand side. Look for a sign at the turn.

Course Yardage & Par:
C-6450 yards, par 72.
M-6109 yards, par 71.
W-5518 yards, par 72.

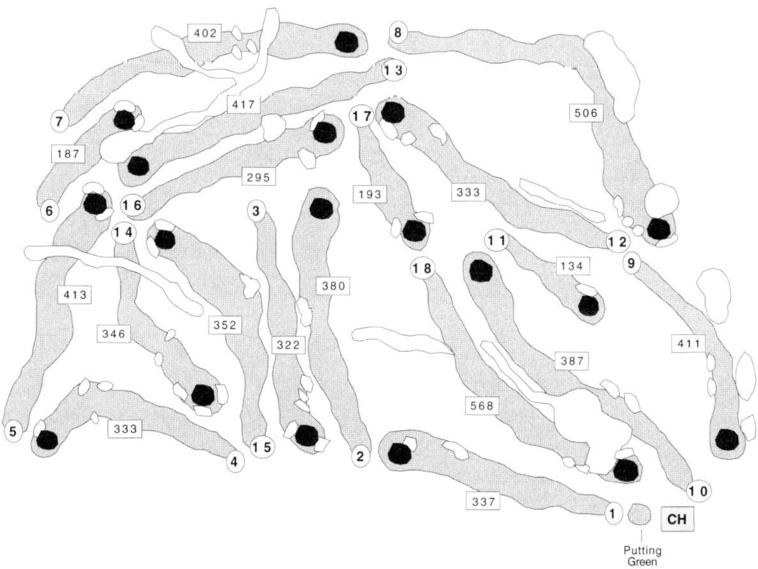

Round Lake Resort (public, 9 hole course)

4000 Round Lake Road; Klamath Falls, OR 97601
Phone: (541) 884-2520. Fax: (541) 884-2520. Web: none.
Manager: Rod Gatley. Superintendent: none.
Rating/Slope: the golf course is not rated. **Course record:** 25.
Green fees: $14/$9 all week long; student & Sr. rates; M/C, VISA.
Power cart: none available. **Pull cart:** $1.50. **Trail fee:** no charge.
Reservation policy: you may call up to seven days in advance for tee-times.
Winter condition: course is open March or April depending on the weather.
Terrain: flat (easy walking). **Tees:** all grass. **Spikes:** metal spikes permitted.
Services: club rentals, snack bar, beverages, pro shop, RV parking.
Comments: the golf course offers discount greens fee rates for people who are staying at the RV park. This short course has trees lining the fairways but is fairly wide open. Greens are small leaving you a real test at scoring from the fairway. The course sports one lake and a stream that runs through 2 holes.

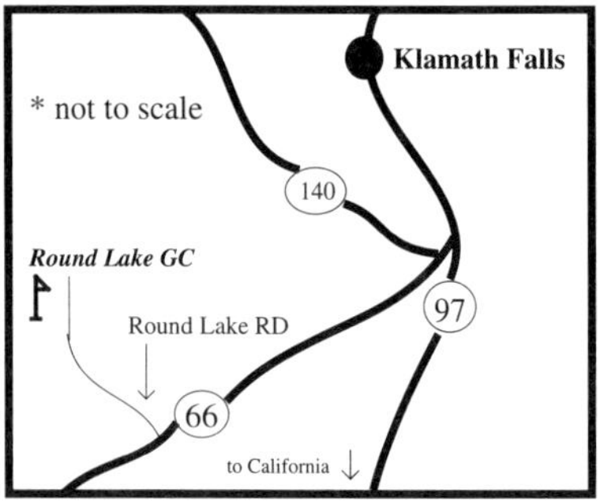

<u>**Directions:**</u> from Hwy 97 take Hwy 66 (Ashland Highway) to Round Lake Road. The golf course is located approximately 3.5 miles up Round Lake Road. The golf course will be located on your right hand side. Look for signs marking your way to the golf course.

Course Yardage & Par:
M-1645 yards, par 30.
W-1645 yards, par 30.

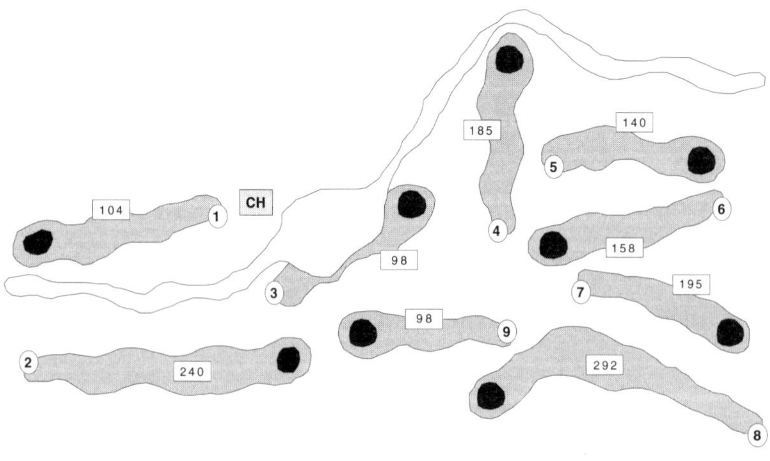

Running Y Ranch Resort (resort, 18 hole course)

5790 Coopers Hawk Road; Running Y, OR 97601
Phone: (541) 880-5580 or call toll free 1-888-850-0261.
Fax: (541) 850-5581. Web-site: www.runningy.com
Pro: Jim Skaugstad, PGA. Manager: Stuart Wooly. Supt.: Chad Morris.
Rating/Slope: T 73.2/131; C 71.5/125; M 68.0/111; W 66.4/120. **Record:** 64.
Green fees: $65/$40 all week long (peak season); M/C, VISA, AMEX, DIS.
Power cart: $36/$26. **Pull cart:** $4/$2. **Trail fee:** personal carts not allowed.
Reservation policy: you may call up to 2 weeks in advance for tee-times. Golf packages may call well in advance to book tee times. No time limit.
Winter condition: the golf course is open all year depnding on the weather.
Terrain: flat, some rolling hills. **Tees:** all grass. **Spikes:** soft spikes only.
Services: club rentals, snack bar, beer, wine, pro shop, driving range, putting green, practice bunker, 18 hole putting course. **Comments:** this Arnold Palmer designed golf course is nothing short of spectacular. Greens are large, firm and undulated. Fairways are wide, giving the golfer room off the tee to move the tee shot. *Golf Digest* ranked Running "Y" as the "best new affordable golf course in the nation" making it worth every penny of the $65 green fee. A must play.

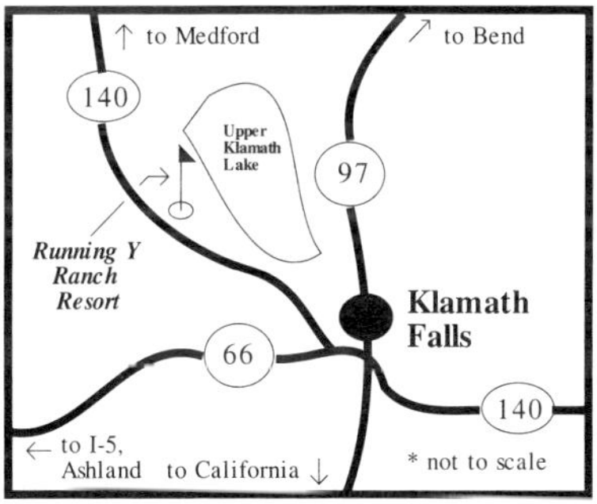

Directions: the golf course is located off of Hwy 140, 7.5 miles west of Klamath Falls, Oregon. Look for signs that are posted off of Hwy 140 directing you to the golf resort entrance.

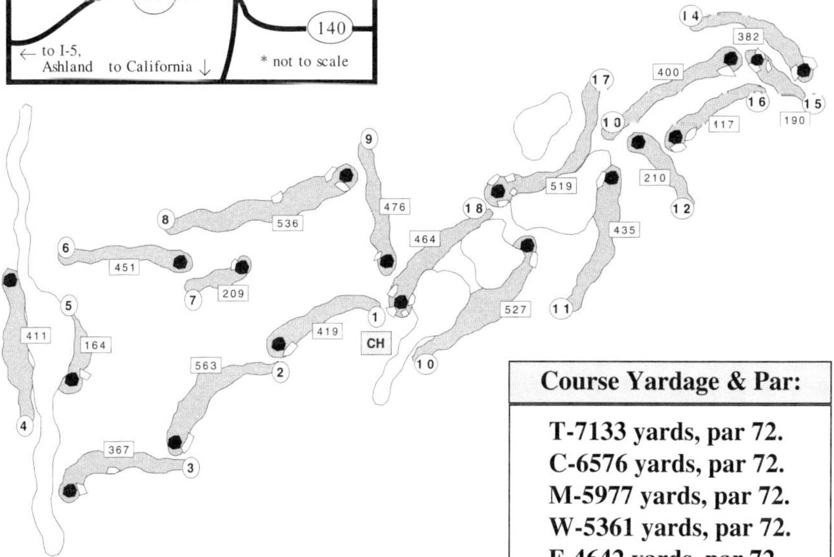

Course Yardage & Par:

T-7133 yards, par 72.
C-6576 yards, par 72.
M-5977 yards, par 72.
W-5361 yards, par 72.
F-4642 yards, par 72.

Sah-Hah-Lee Golf Course & Driving Range (public, 18 holes)

17104 SE 130th Avenue; Clackamas, OR 97015
Phone: (503) 655-9249, 655-3215 (range). Fax: (503) 655-0970.
Pro: Don Otto, PGA. Superintendent: Bud Lisac. Web: www.sah-hah-lee.com
Rating/Slope: the golf course is not rated. **Course record:** 47.
Green fees: W/D $14/$8; W/E $16/$9; Jr. & Sr. rates (M-F) $11/$6.50.
Power cart: none. **Pull cart:** $3/$1.50. **Trail fee:** personal carts not allowed.
Reservation policy: call 1 week in advance, 7 days a week for tee-times.
Winter condition: the golf course is open all year long. Excellent drainage.
Terrain: flat (easy walking). **Tees:** all grass. **Spikes:** soft spikes only.
Services: club rentals, lessons, snack bar, beer, pop, pro shop, driving range.
Comments: great par 3 layout, you will use every iron in your bag. Excellent driving range and practice facility for those wanting to practice their games.

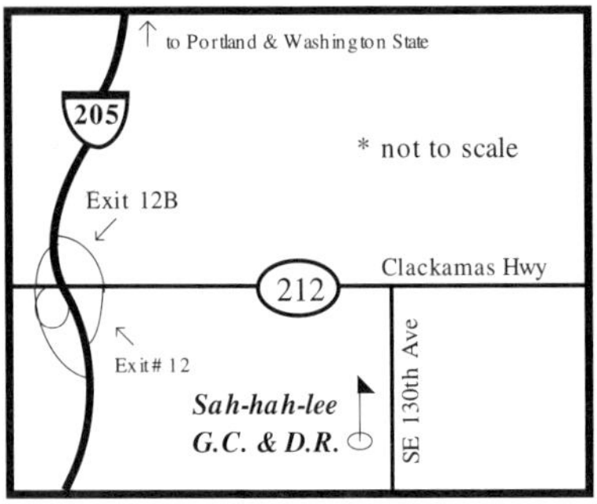

__Directions:__ from I-205 northbound & southbound exit at Highway 212 going eastbound. Proceed to SE 130th Avenue and head southbound to the golf course. Look for signs to the golf course.

Course Yardage & Par:
M-2477 yards, par 54. **W-2294 yards, par 54.**

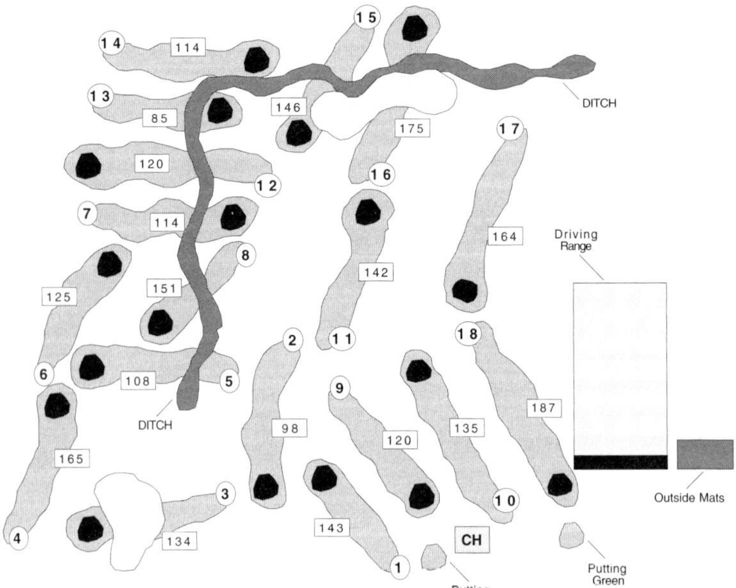

Saint Helens Golf Course (public, 9 hole course)

57246 Hazen Road; Warren, OR 97053
Phone: (503) 397-0358. Fax: (503) 397-1408. Web: none.
Pro: Jeff Stirling, PGA. Superintendent: Jeff Stirling.
Rating/Slope: M 68.8/122; W 71.4/116. **Course record:** 65.
Green fees: W/D $19/$10; W/E $25/$14; Sr. rates $17/$9 (M-F); M/C, VISA.
Power cart: $24/$12. **Pull cart:** $2. **Trail fee:** $12/$6 for personal carts.
Reservation policy: yes, please call 7 days in advance for your tee-times.
Winter condition: the golf course is open all year long, weather permitting.
Terrain: flat, some hills. **Tees:** all grass. **Spikes:** soft spikes preferred.
Services: club rentals, snack bar, beer, wine, pro shop, practice range.
Comments: Course has challenging greens and lush fairways. The varied terrain gives the golfer a wide variety of lies from the fairway. The course can usually be found in fair shape in the summer months. Not a bad walking golf course.

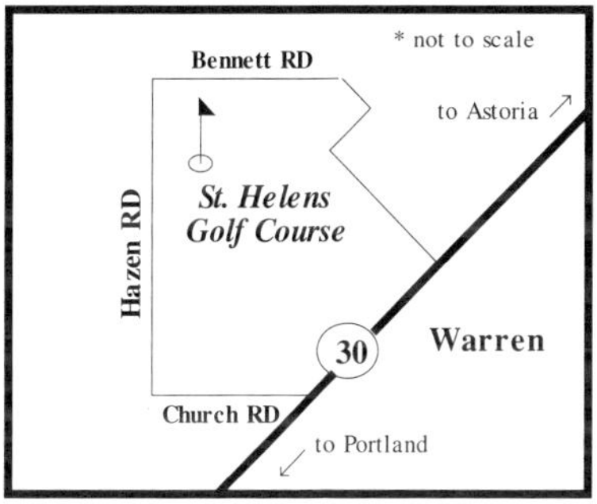

Directions: from Highway 30 go west on Church Road for 1.5 miles. At Hazen Road turn right. The golf course is located .5 miles ahead on your right hand side. **Note:** Look for signs marking the way to the course from the highway.

Course Yardage & Par:
M-2934 yards, par 36.
W-2663 yards, par 36.
Dual tees for 18 holes:
M-6003 yards, par 71.
W-5503 yards, par 73.

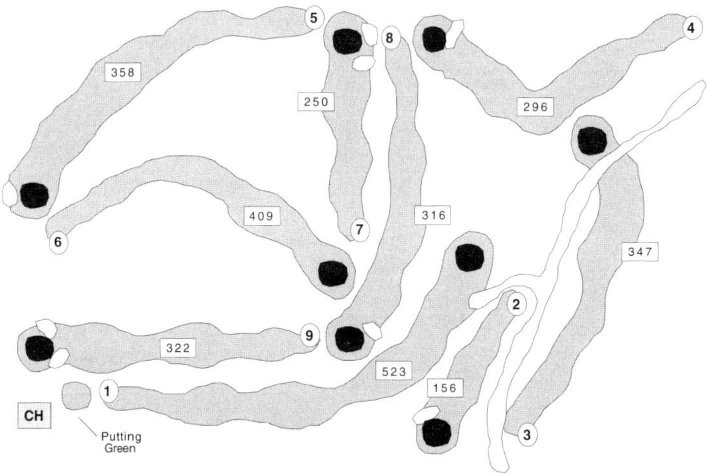

Salem Golf Club (semi-private, 18 hole course)

2025 Golf Course Road South; Salem, OR 97302
Phone: (503) 363-6652. Fax: (503) 315-1080. Web: none.
Pro: Len Collett, PGA. Superintendent: Mike O'Neill.
Rating/Slope: C 68.7/116; M 68.0/114; W 68.8/116. **Course record:** 64.
Green fees: $40/$20 all week long; call for special rates; M/C, VISA.
Power cart: $24/$12. **Pull cart:** $2. **Trail fee:** personal carts not allowed.
Reservation policy: you may call 7 days in advance for your tee-times.
Winter condition: the golf course open all year long. Fair conditions.
Terrain: flat, some hills. **Tees:** all grass. **Spikes:** metal spikes permitted.
Services: club rentals, lessons, covered driving range, snack bar, restaurant, beer, wine, pro shop. **Comments:** club was established in 1928. Beautiful old colonial style clubhouse in a picturesque setting. Visitors are welcome with restricted tee-times so be sure to call ahead. Excellent course that is worth a trip.

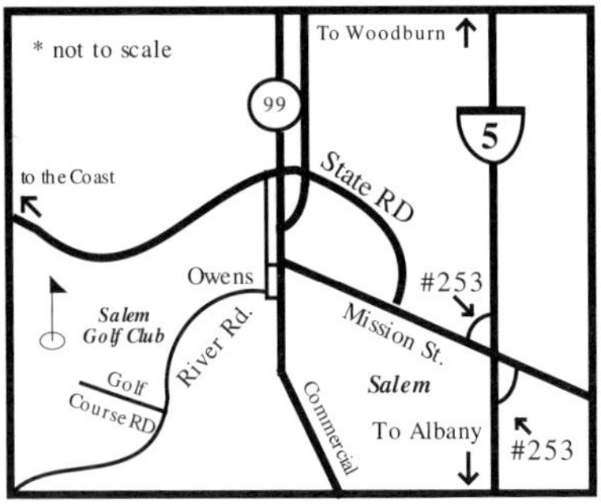

Directions: from I-5 N take the Parkway exit #248 and proceed north on Commercial to Owens. Turn left on Owens which turns into River Road. Course located 1.9 miles ahead. From I-5 S take the North Santiam exit #253 (Mission St.). Proceed west on Mission to Commercial turn left. Proceed to Owens and turn right, Owens turns into River Road. Course located 1.9 miles ahead on the right hand side.

Course Yardage & Par:
C-6200 yards, par 72; M-5939 yards, par 72; W-5163 yards, par 72.

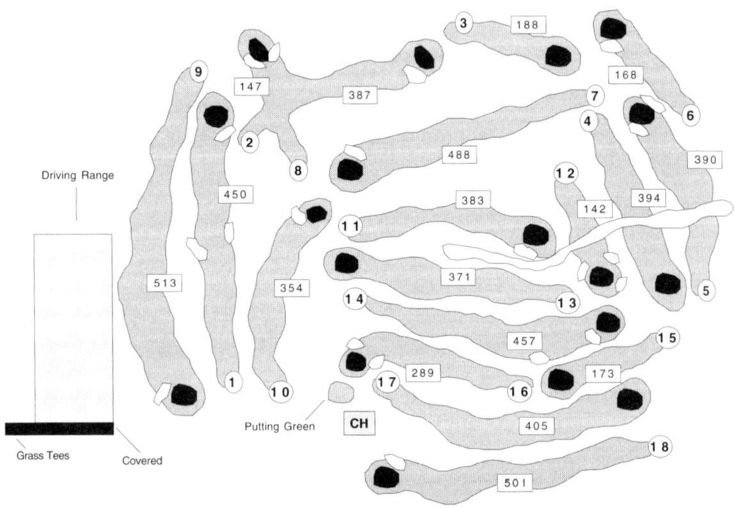

Salemtowne Golf Club (private, 9 hole course)

2900 Oakcrest Drive NW; Salem, OR 97304
Phone: (503) 362-2215. Fax: none. Web: none.
Manager/Superintendent: Gary Schafer.
Rating/Slope: C 55.9/82; M 55.0/79; W 58.5/86. **Course record:** 25.
Green fees: private club, members and guests of members only.
Power cart: none. **Pull cart:** none. **Trail fee:** personal carts are not allowed.
Reservation policy: private club, members and guests of members only.
Winter condition: the golf course is open all year long weather permitting, dry.
Terrain: flat, some hills. **Tees:** all grass. **Spikes:** metal spikes permitted.
Services: full service private golf club, beverages, putting & chipping greens.
Comments: The golf course is well manicured with excellent greens. The golf course sports many greenside bunkers that will challenge any level of golfer. The course is fairly flat and easy to walk giving the golfer a relaxed round.

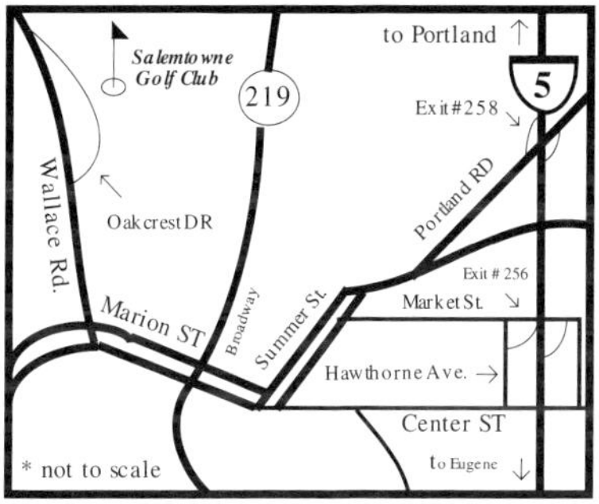

Directions: from I-5 take exit #256 (Market Street Silverton). West on Market Street for 1.6 miles to Summer Street. Turn left on Summer Street and proceed .5 miles to Marion Street. Turn right on Marion St. As you approach the bridge stay right and follow signs for Edgewater Street, Dayton (Highway 221). Proceed for 3.4 miles to Oakcrest Drive. Turn right. The pro shop will be on your left hand side.

Course Yardage & Par:
M-1690 yards, par 30. **W-1657 yards, par 32.**

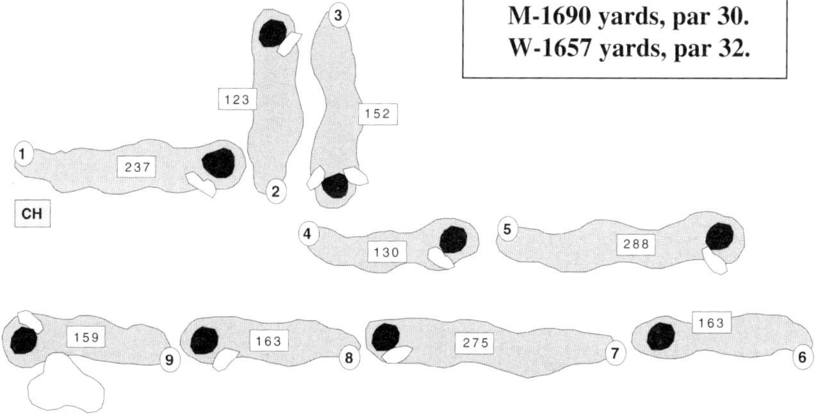

Salishan Golf Links (resort course, 18 hole course)

Highway 101; P.O. Box 118; Gleneden Beach, OR 97388
Phone: (541) 764-3632, 1-800-890-0387. Fax: (541) 764-2264.
Pro: Mark Swift, PGA. Supt.: Ryan Bancroft. Web: www.salishan.com
Rating/Slope: C 72.3/132; M 70.4/130; W 72.3/128. **Course record:** 66.
Green fees: $75/$45; lower rates lodge guests; seasonal rates; M/C, VISA, DIS.
Power cart: $25/$20. **Pull cart:** $5/$3. **Trail fee:** personal carts not allowed.
Reservation policy: yes, please call up to 2 weeks in advance for tee times.
Winter condition: the golf course is open all year long. Damp conditions.
Terrain: flat, some hills. **Tees:** all grass. **Spikes:** soft spikes June-September.
Services: club rentals, lessons, restaurant, beer, wine, pro shop, driving range, full service accommodations, putting & chipping greens, 18 hole putting course.
Comments: the golf course was selected as one of the top resort courses in America by *Golf Digest* in 1992. Very challenging 18 hole layout built in the rugged Scottish tradition of golf. Greens are well bunkered and fast. Fairways are tree-lined and can be narrow on certain holes. Excellent facility that is worth the price of admission when visiting the scenic Oregon coast.

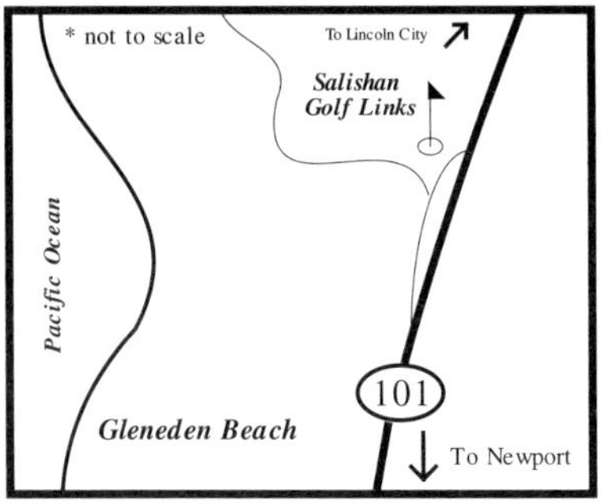

Directions: from I-5 take Ocean Beaches Highway to Highway 101. The golf course is located just south of Lincoln City in the town of Gleneden Beach on the west side of Highway 101. Look for signs marking your turn to the golf course.

Course Yardage & Par:
C-6453 yards, par 72.
M-6203 yards, par 72.
W-5389 yards, par 72.

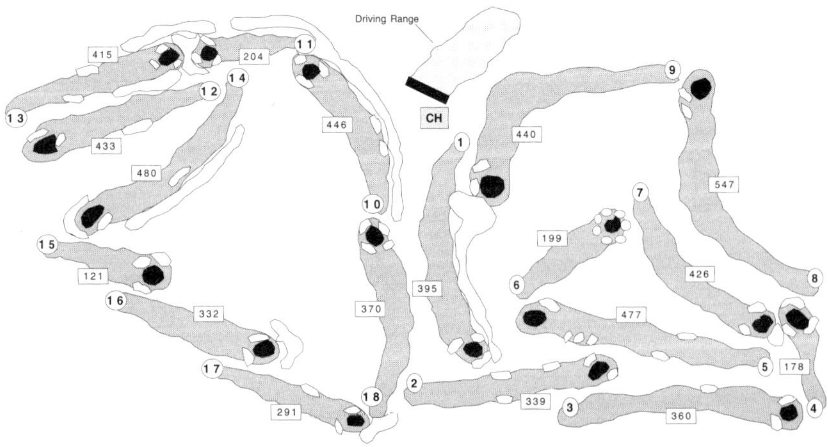

Salmon Run Golf & Resort (semi-private, 18 hole course, 9 hole executive)

99040 South Bank Chetco River Road; Brookings, OR 97415
Phone numbers: (541) 469-4888 or 1-877-423-1234.
Fax: (541) 469-4889. Web-site: www.salmonrun.net
Manager: Felix Claveran. Superintendent: N/A.
Rating/Slope: C 70.6/129; M 68.8/121; W 70.6/129; F 61.8/97. **Record:** 68.
Green fees: W/D $42; W/E $52; seasonal rates; M/C, VISA, DIS.
Power cart: $25/$13. **Pull cart:** $3. **Trail fee:** personal carts not allowed.
Reservation policy: yes, please call up to 30 days in advance for tee times.
Winter condition: the golf course is open all year long. Damp conditions.
Terrain: flat, some hills. **Tees:** all grass. **Spikes:** soft spikes preferred.
Services: club rentals, lessons, restaurant, beer, wine, liquor, pro shop, driving range, full service accommodations, putting & chipping greens, lounge.
Comments: this newer course opened for play in late 1999 and is spectacular. The layout is fantastic with water or bunkers coming in to play on nearly every hole. The course uses the natural surroundings to create a very competitive, championship caliber layout. The resort has just added a 9 hole executive course measuring 1310 yards and plays to a par of 34. Good track that is worth the trip.

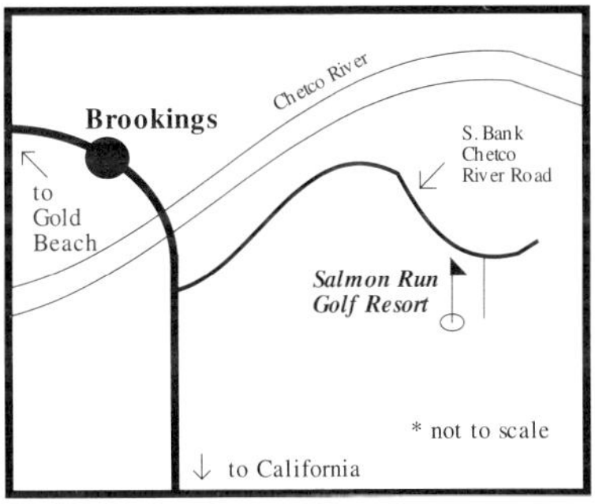

Directions: take Hwy 101 N&S to Brookings, Oregon. When in Brookings take the South Bank Chetco River Road exit (off 101 eastbound). Follow this road for 2.7 miles to the golf course.

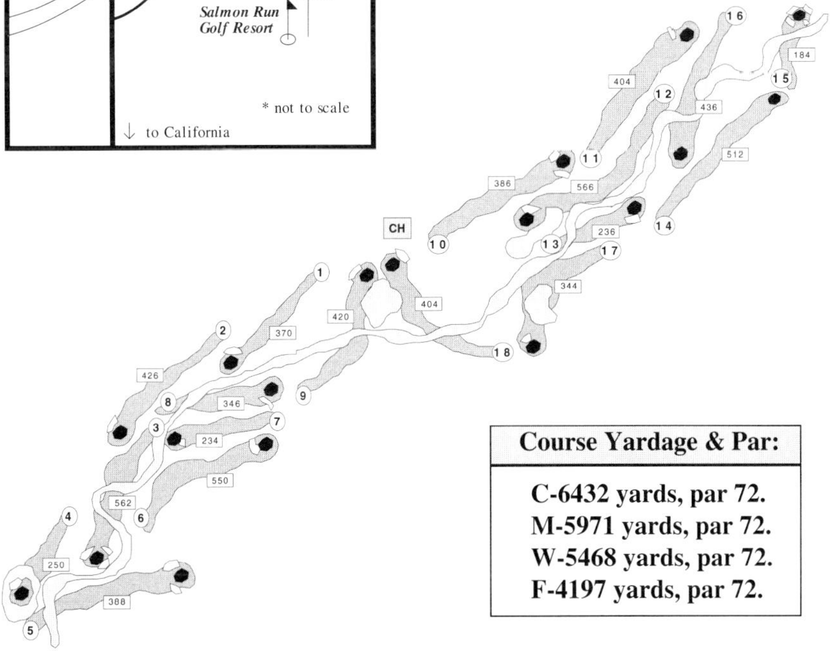

Course Yardage & Par:
C-6432 yards, par 72.
M-5971 yards, par 72.
W-5468 yards, par 72.
F-4197 yards, par 72.

Sandelie Golf (public, 18 hole course)

28333 SW Mountain Road; West Linn, OR 97068
Phone: (503) 655-1461. Fax: none. Web: none.
Owner: Jan Kaiser. Superintendent: Dave McRabbie.
Rating/Slope: M 67.3/112; W 69.8/112. **Course record:** 65.
Green fees: W/D $22/$11; W/E $24/$12; Sr. rates on W/D's; no credit cards.
Power cart: power carts are not available. **Pull cart:** $2. **Trail fee:** $4.
Reservation policy: please call in 7 days in advance for tee-times.
Winter condition: the golf course is closed January1st to March 15th.
Terrain: flat, some hills. **Tees:** all grass. **Spikes:** soft spikes preferred.
Services: club rentals, snacks, beverages, small pro shop.
Comments: fair conditioned golf course set back in the country among rolling hills and tree lined fairways. Greens are large with few hazards fronting them. The course does have some water that the golfer will have to contend with.

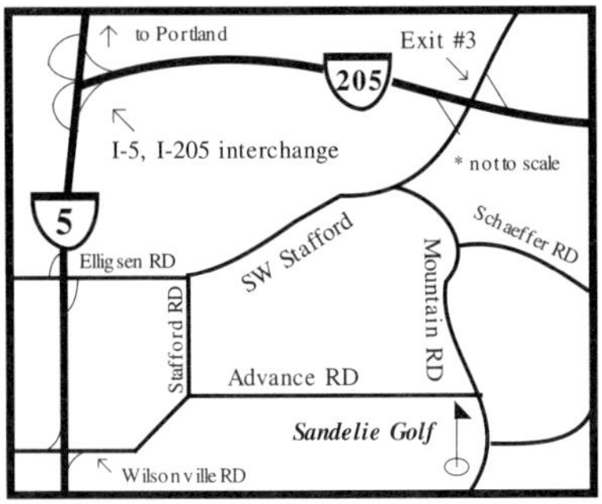

Directions: from I-205 N&S take exit #3 (Stafford Road). Travel south on Stafford Road for .8 miles to SW Mountain Road. Turn left. The course is located 3.3 miles ahead on your right.

Course Yardage & Par:

M-5894 yards, par 70.
W-5406 yards, par 72.

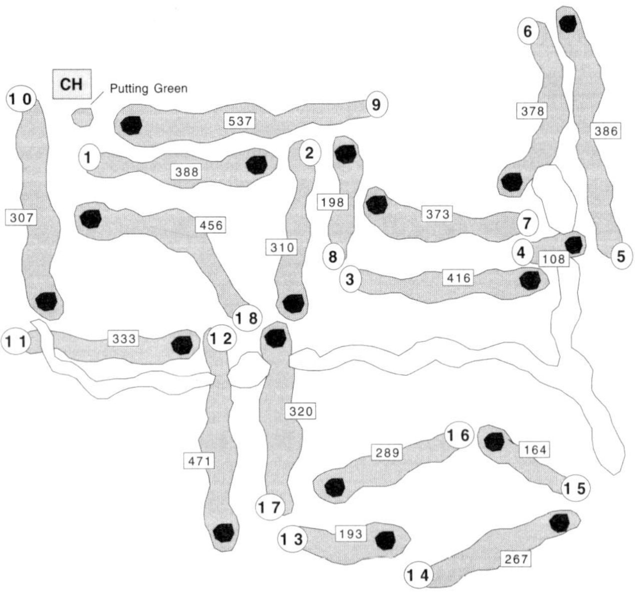

Sandelie West 9 (public, 9 hole course)

3030 SW Advance Road; Wilsonville, OR 97070
Phone: (503) 682-2022. Fax: none. Internet: none.
Owner: Jan Kaiser. Superintendent: Dave McRabbie.
Rating/Slope: the golf course is not rated. **Course record:** 64.
Green fees: W/D $22/$11; W/E $22/$11; no credit cards.
Power cart: power carts are not available. **Pull cart:** $2. **Trail fee:** $4.
Reservation policy: please call in 7 days in advance for tee-times.
Winter condition: the golf course is open February 15th thru October 1st.
Terrain: flat, some hills. **Tees:** all grass. **Spikes:** soft spikes preferred.
Services: club rentals, snacks, beverages, small pro shop, puting green.
Comments: this is a 9 hole golf course that was designed by William Kaiser and opened for play in 1996. Greens are bentgrass and medium to small in size and have few hazards fronting them. Water comes into play on a few holes but is not much of a factor. Fair conditioned golf course that is closed during the winter.

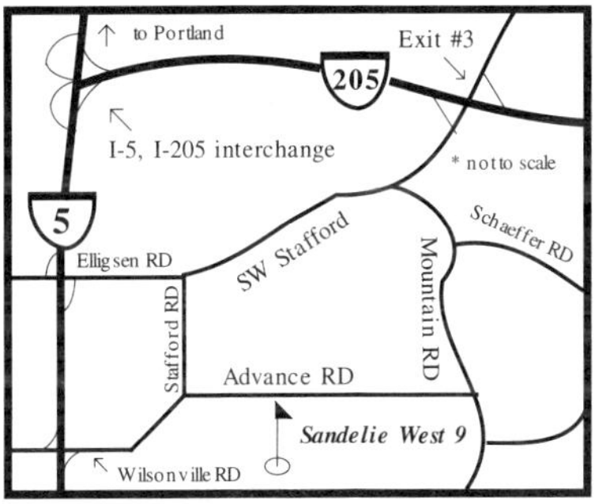

Directions: from I-205 N&S take exit #3 (Stafford Road). Travel south on Stafford Road for .8 miles to SW Mountain Road. Turn left. Proceed 3.3 miles to Advance Road where you will turn right. Proceed for 1.1 miles to the golf course on your left hand side.

Course Yardage & Par:
M-3150 yards, par 36. **W-2714 yards, par 36.**

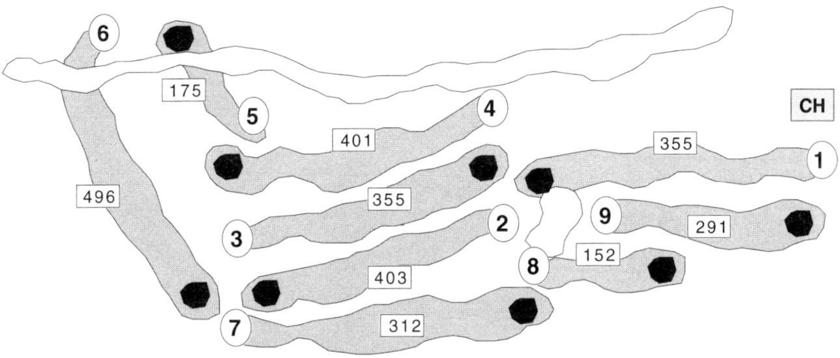

...Golf Links (public, 18 hole course)

...reet; Florence, OR 97439

...1) 997-1940 or call 1-800-917-4653. Fax: (541) 997-2010.

Pro: ... Rannon, PGA. Supt.: Darrell Fields. Web: www.sandpines.com

Rating/Slope: T 74.9/130; C 72.7/128; M 70.4/121; W 72.7/129. **Record:** 67.
Green fees: $59 summer rates; $35 winter rates; M/C, VISA, AMEX.
Power cart: $26/$18. **Pull cart:** $4. **Trail fee:** personal carts not allowed.
Reservation policy: you may call up to 14 days in advance for tee-times.
Winter condition: the golf course open all year long. Very dry conditions.
Terrain: flat, some small hills. **Tees:** grass. **Spikes:** metal spikes permitted.
Services: club rentals, lessons, snack bar, beer, pro shop, driving range.
Comments: a newer Rees Jones design, this golf course is built on the Oregon sand dunes. The course is a links style course where water comes into play on three holes. The course was voted best new public course in the United States for 1993 by *Golf Digest*. Be sure to include Sandpines in any vacation to OR.

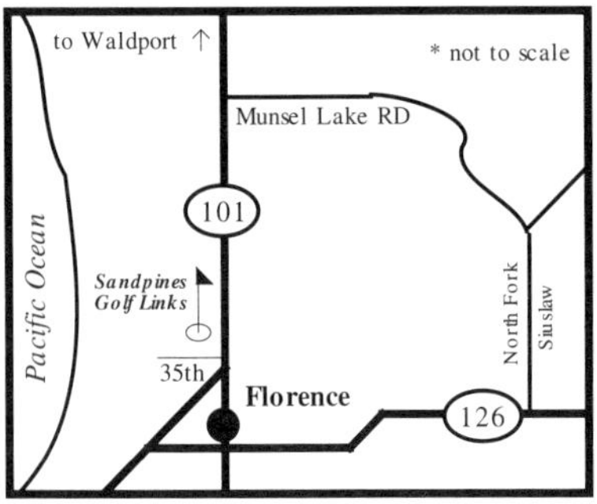

Directions: From Highway 101 turn west on 35th street to the golf course. The course is located in the north city limits. Look for signs marking your way to the golf course the way is well marked.

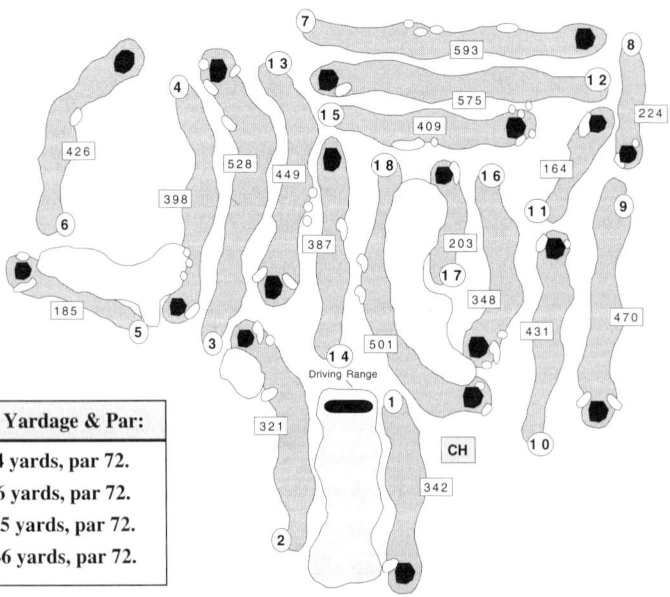

Course Yardage & Par:
- **T-6954 yards, par 72.**
- **C-6536 yards, par 72.**
- **M-6085 yards, par 72.**
- **W-5346 yards, par 72.**

Santiam Golf Club (public, 18 hole course)

8724 Golf Club Road SE; P.O. Box 207; Stayton, OR 97383
Phone: (503) 769-3485. Fax: none. Web: none.
Pro: Jeff Cunningham, PGA. Superintendent: Tim Halfman.
Rating/Slope: C 69.9/123; M 68.8/119; W 72.2/122. **Course record:** 63.
Green fees: $28/$16 all week long; M/C, VISA; Sr. rates $23/$14.
Power cart: $24/$12. **Pull cart:** $2. **Trail fee:** $15/$8 for personal carts.
Reservation policy: yes, please call 7 days in advance for weekends, holidays.
Winter condition: the golf course is open all year long. Dry, drains very well.
Terrain: flat (easy walking). **Tees:** grass. **Spikes:** metal spikes permitted.
Services: club rentals, lessons, snack bar, restaurant, lounge, beer, wine, liquor, driving range, putting & chipping greens. **Comments:** Course is a good test of golf with lots of trees, water and creeks to challenge any golfer. Good walking course that is popular with the locals. This course can get very busy in summer.

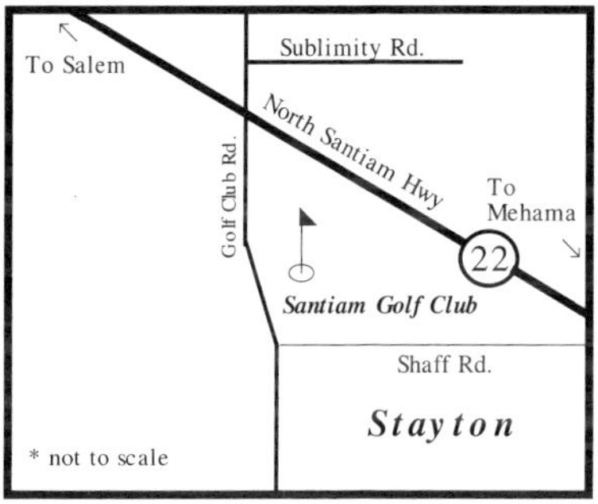

Directions: from I-5 take the Stayton exit. Travel approximately 12 miles eastbound on Highway 22 to the course. The golf course is located on the south side of Highway 22. **Note:** be sure to look for the sign to the golf course from the Highway marking your turn to the clubhouse.

Course Yardage & Par:
C-6387 yards, par 72.
M-6157 yards, par 72.
W-5697 yards, par 75.

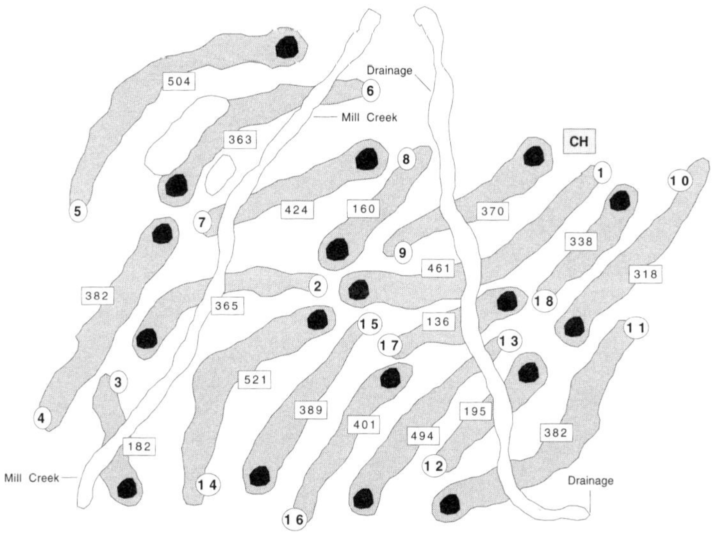

Seaside Golf Course (public, 9 hole course)

451 Avenue U; Seaside, OR 97138
Phone: (503) 738-5261. Fax: (503) 738-3822. Web: none.
Manager/Pro: Wayne Fulmer. Superintendent: Wayne Fulmer.
Rating/Slope: M 63.8/105; W 67.4/110. **Course record:** 28.
Green fees: Mon.-Thur. $19/$11; Friday-Sunday $24/$12; M/C, VISA, DIS.
Power cart: $24/$12. **Pull cart:** $2. **Trail fee:** $5 for personal carts.
Reservation policy: not required, course is run on a first come first served basis.
Winter condition: the golf course is open all year long, wet conditions.
Terrain: flat (easy walking). **Tees:** grass. **Spikes:** metal spikes permitted.
Services: club rentals, snack bar, restaurant, lounge, beer, wine, liquor, pro shop.
Comments: easy to walk and friendly track. Course located on the fantastic Oregon coast. The Necamicum River runs through the whole golf course and is a major factor. Fair public course that is great for quick 9 hole golf fix.

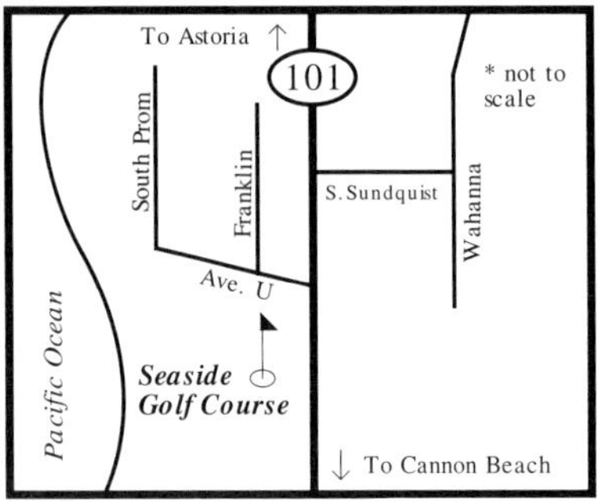

Directions: from Highway 101 turn west on Avenue U. The golf course will be located on your left hand side. (The golf course is located at the south end of the town of Seaside Oregon). The golf course can be seen from Highway 101.

Course Yardage & Par:
M-2593 yards, par 35. **W-2593 yards, par 35.**

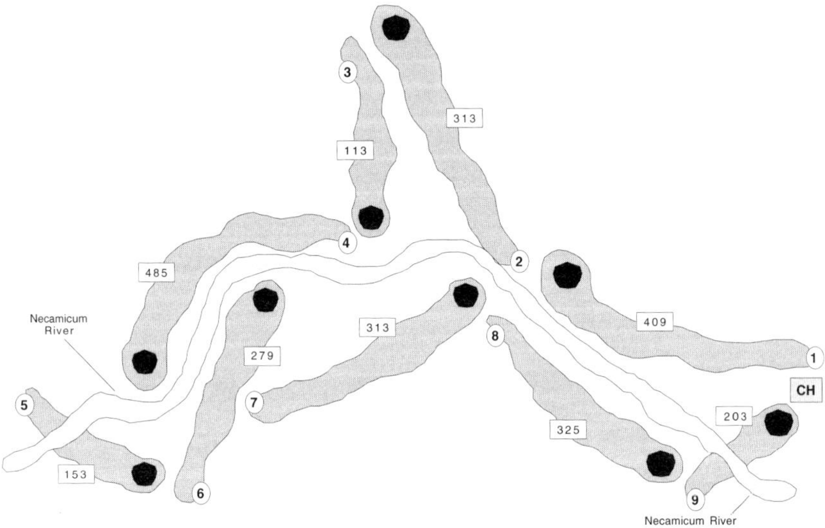

Senior Estates Golf & Country Club (private, 18 hole course)

1776 Country Club Drive; Woodburn, OR 97071
Phone: (503) 981-0189. Fax: (503) 982-5144. Web: none.
Pro: Jim White, PGA. Superintendent: Tim O'Larey.
Rating/Slope: M 65.5/100; W 67.7/109. **Course record:** 63.
Green fees: private club members & guests only; reciprocates; M/C, VISA.
Power cart: private club. **Pull cart:** private club. **Trail fee:** not allowed.
Reservation policy: private club, members & guests of members only.
Winter condition: the golf course is open all year long. Wet conditions.
Terrain: very flat. **Tees:** all grass. **Spikes:** metal spikes permitted.
Services: club rentals, lessons, restaurant, beer, wine, pro shop, putting green.
Comments: Easy walking golf course. The course is well taken care of. Very popular senior course with many retirement homes around the layout. You may call the golf pro to check tee-time availablity for outside play.

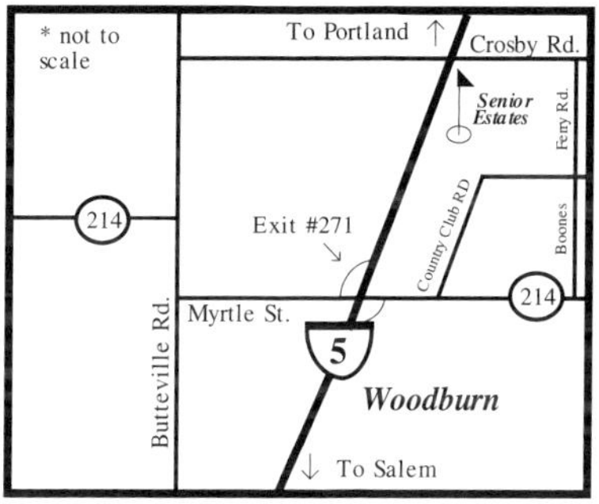

__Directions__: From I-5 take the Woodburn exit. Travel east on Newberg Hwy for .5 miles to Country Club Dr. Turn left. Follow for .3 miles to the course entrance on your right.

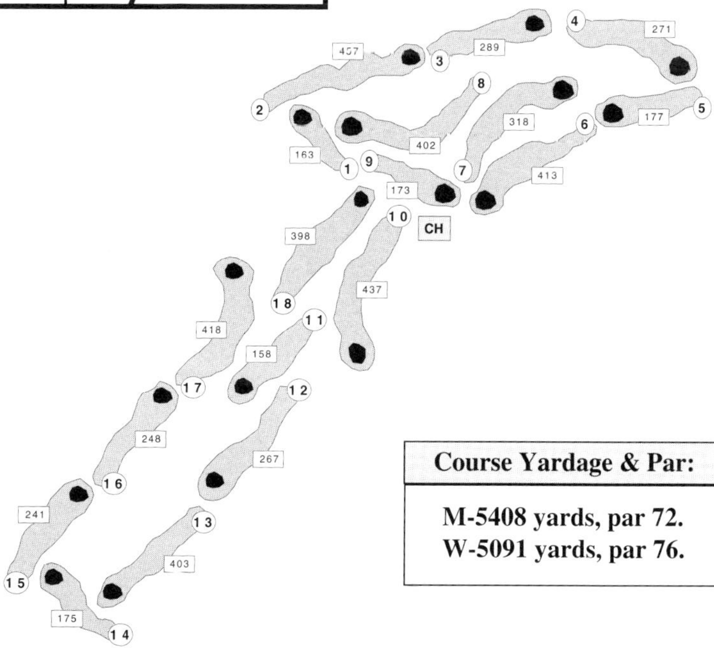

Course Yardage & Par:
M-5408 yards, par 72.   **W-5091 yards, par 76.**

Shadow Hills Country Club (private, 18 hole course)

92512 River Road; Junction City, OR 97448
Phone: (541) 998-8441. Fax: (541) 998-6779. Web: www.shadowhillscc.com
Pro: Mark Keating, PGA. Superintendent: Randy Marshall.
Rating/Slope: C 73.7/124; M 72.5/128; M 71.4/119; W 70.5/123. **Record:** 65.
Green fees: private, members & guests only, reciprocates; M/C, VISA.
Power cart: private club. **Pull cart:** private club. **Trail fee:** not allowed.
Reservation policy: reciprocates please call 2 days in advance for tee-times.
Winter condition: the golf course is open all year long weather permitting.
Terrain: flat (easy walking). **Tees:** all grass. **Spikes:** no metal spikes.
Services: lessons, restaurant, lounge, beer, wine, liquor, beverages, pop, shop, showers, lockers, driving range, putting & chipping greens, club memberships.
Comments: Course is noted for the lush fairways and some of the best greens in Oregon. The course sports a great deal of water and many greenside bunkers.

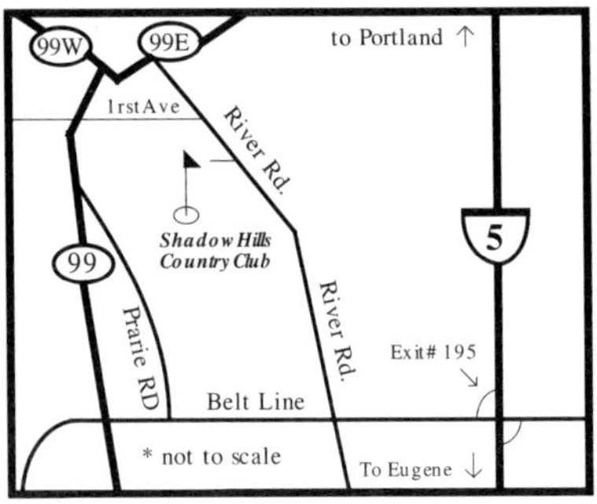

__Directions:__ from I-5 N&S take exit #195 and travel west on Beltline to River Road. Travel northbound on River Road. The golf course is about 10 minutes from here. From Highway 99 travel eastbound on River Road to the golf course.

Course Yardage & Par:
C-6926 yards, par 72.
M-6718 yards, par 72.
M-6430 yards, par 72.
W-5296 yards, par 72.

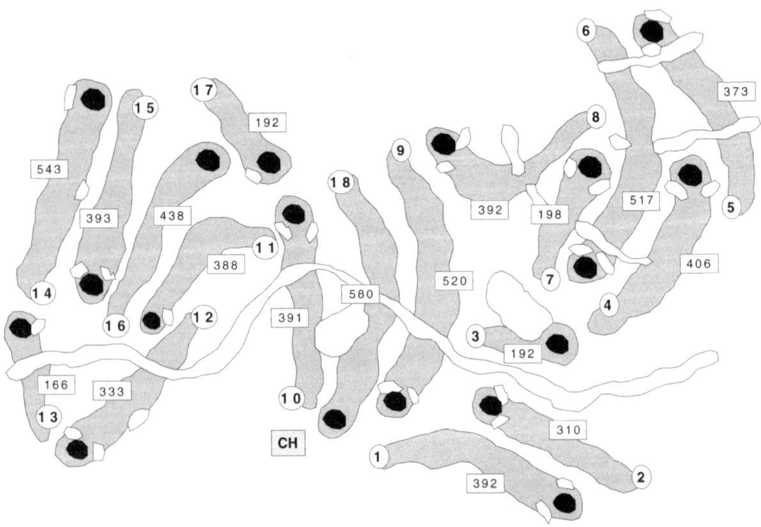

Shield Crest Golf Course (semi-private, 18 hole course)

3151 Shield Crest Drive; Klamath Falls, OR 97603

Phone: (541) 884-1493. Fax: (541) 884-8946. Web: sheildcrestgolfcourse.com

Pro: Scott Wise. Superintendent: Eric Moen.

Rating/Slope: C 71.8/117; M 70.4/116; M 68.8/12; W 68.2/116. **Record:** 64.
Green fees: $35/25 all week long; (Sr. rates Mon.-Thur.); M/C, VISA, DIS.
Power cart: $24/$14. **Pull cart:** $3. **Trail fee:** personal carts not allowed.
Reservation policy: yes, please call 24 hours in advance for your tee-times.
Winter condition: the golf course is open all year long weather permitting.
Terrain: flat, some hills. **Tees:** all grass. **Spikes:** soft spikes required.
Services: club rentals, lessons, restaurant, lounge, beer, wine, liquor, pro shop, driving range. **Comments:** Water hazards and undulating greens make this well kept golf course a real challenge. Greens can be very difficult to read at times. Good semi-private track that is located in a beautiful area of southern Oregon.

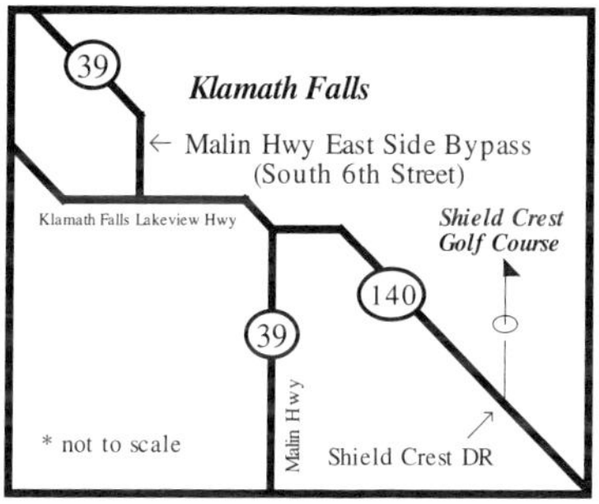

Directions: the golf course is located on the southeast side of town. If you are coming from the north on Hwy 97 take the Alameda Bypass and proceed through town to Hwy 140. At Highway 140 go east toward Lakeview to the golf course. From Highway 140 go eastbound to Lakeview. The golf course is located 1 mile beyond Merrill, Lakeview Junction.

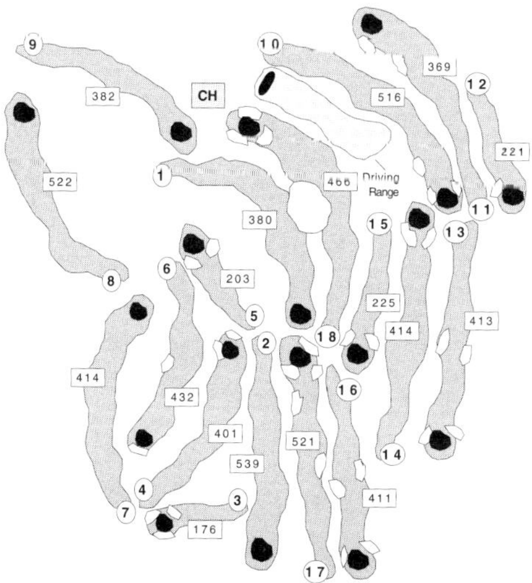

Course Yardage & Par:
C-7005 yards, par 72; M-6637 yards, par 72; W-5464 yards, par 72.

Spring Hill Country Club (private, 18 hole course)

155 Country Club Lane; Albany, OR 97321
Phone: (541) 928-5454. Fax: (541) 926-0332. Web: none.
Pro: Bill Raschko, PGA. GM: Tom Coburn. Superintendent: Matt Peltier.
Rating/Slope: C 71.4/129; M 68.8/122; W 69.9/128. **Course record:** 63.
Green fees: private club members & guests only; reciprocates.
Power cart: private club. **Pull cart:** private club. **Trail fee:** private club.
Reservation policy: call up to 1 week in advance for tee-times. Members only.
Winter condition: the course is open all year long weather permitting, damp.
Terrain: flat, some hills. **Tees:** all grass. **Spikes:** soft spikes preferred.
Services: club rentals, lessons, restaurant, lounge, beer, wine, liquor, pro shop, lockers, showers, driving range, putting & chipping greens, club memberships.
Comments: Course has many mature trees that come into play on several holes. Excellent greens and lush fairways are the trademark of this club. Good track.

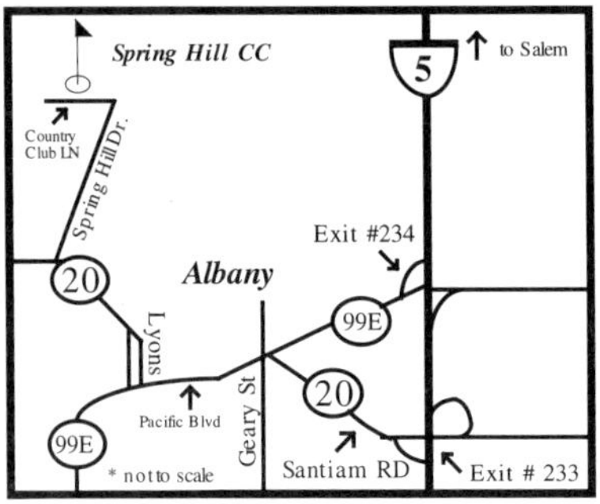

Directions: from I-5 N&S take exit #233 (Santiam Highway 20) and go west to the Lyons Street (Highway 20) exit. Proceed through town over the bridge and take your first right on Springhill Drive. Go to the Country Club LN turn left to course.

Course Yardage & Par:
C-6432 yards, par 72.
M-6145 yards, par 72.
W-5461 yards, par 73.

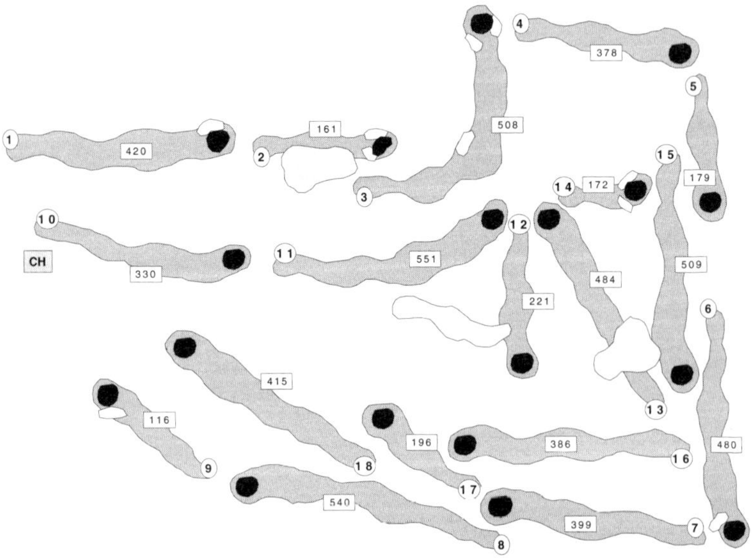

Springfield Country Club (private, 18 hole course)

90333 Sunderman Road; Springfield, OR 97478
Phone: (541) 747-2517. Fax: (541) 747-4225. Web: www.sccgolf.org
Pro: Fadel Nahle, PGA. Superintendent: Andre Paquet.
Rating/Slope: C 70.2/121; M 68.8/122; W 69.9/128. **Course record:** 63.
Green fees: private club, members & guests of members only.
Power cart: private club. **Pull cart:** private club. **Trail fee:** private club.
Reservation policy: yes, 1 day in advance for members & guests only.
Winter condition: the golf course is open all year long. Damp conditions.
Terrain: relatively hilly. **Tees:** all grass. **Spikes:** metal spikes permitted.
Services: club rentals, lessons, restaurant, lounge, beer, wine, pro shop, lockers, showers, driving range. **Comments:** Golf course plays longer than the yardage indicates. Tough greens and several ponds make this golf course a challenge. A private course that has a golf tradition look and feel. Excellent golf course.

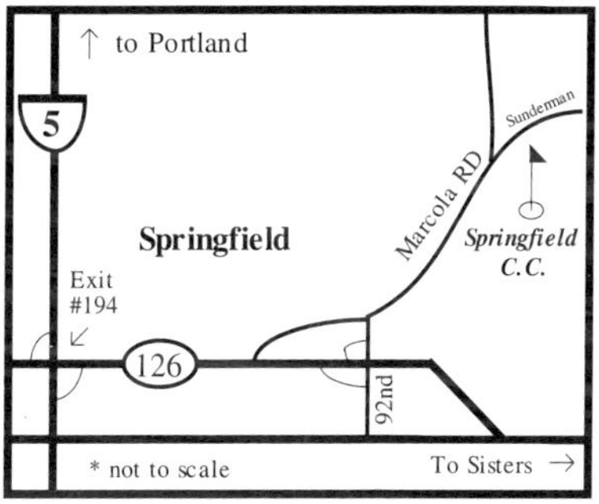

Directions: from I-5 N&S take exit # 194 (Highwey 126) and go eastbound to the 2nd exit (42nd). Turn left on 42nd and proceed northbound to Marcola Road. Turn right on Marcola Road and proceed 5 miles to Sunderman. At Sunderman turn right to the golf course.

Course Yardage & Par:
C-6341 yards, par 71.
M-5949 yards, par 71.
W-5443 yards, par 73.

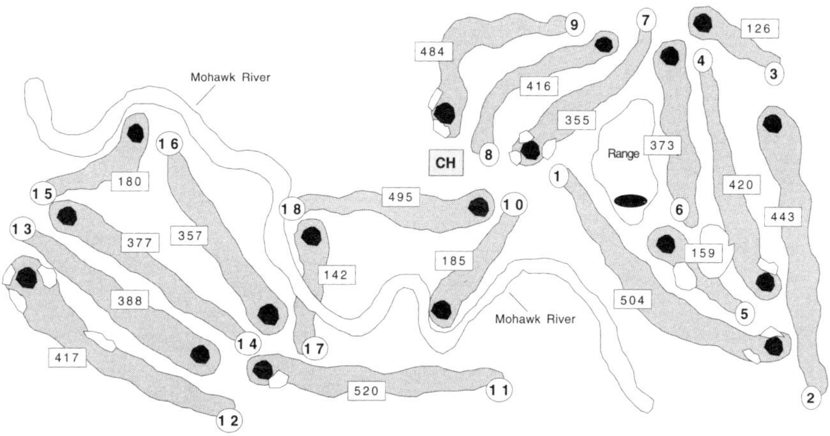

Springwater Golf Course (public, 9 hole course)

25230 South Wallens Road; Estacada, OR 97023
Phone: (503) 630-4586. Fax: none. Web: none.
Owners: Pat & Vickie O'Meara. Superintendent: Max Williams
Rating/Slope: M 67.9/120; W 72.8/116. **Course record:** 32.
Green fees: W/D $21/$10; W/E & Hol. $23/$11.50; Sr. & Jr. rates (M-F).
Power cart: $20/$10. **Pull cart:** $2. **Trail fee:** $4.50 for 9 holes.
Reservation policy: yes, call up to 3 to 5 days in advance for tee times.
Winter condition: the golf course is open all year long. Dry (drains well).
Terrain: relatively hilly. **Tees:** grass. **Spikes:** metal spikes permitted.
Services: club rentals, snack bar, beer, wine, pro shop, putting/chipping greens.
Comments: The golf course is noted for being very playable during the winter months. Two sets of tees will offer you a different look for those wanting to play a full 18 holes. Greens are medium to large with few hazards fronting them.

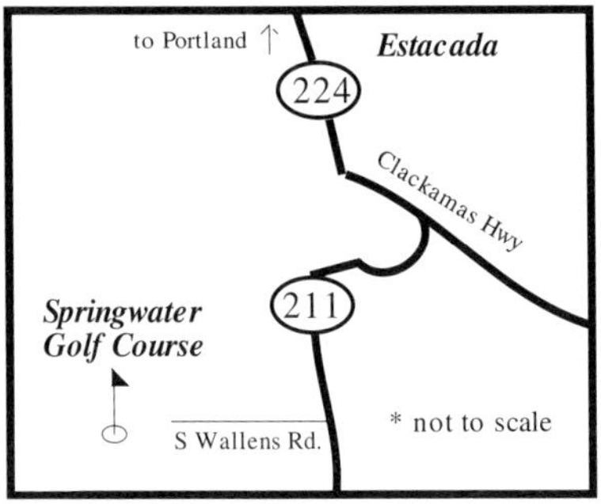

__Directions:__ from Highway 224 exit toward Springwater in Estacada onto Highway 211. From Highway 211 turn right on Wallens Road. Cross over Springwater Road. The course is located on the left hand side of Wallens Road. The course is located 4 miles south of Estacada. Look for signs.

Course Yardage & Par:

M-3003 yards, par 36.
W-2479 yards, par 36.
__Dual tees for 18 holes:__
M-6204 yards, par 72.
W-5355 yards, par 73.

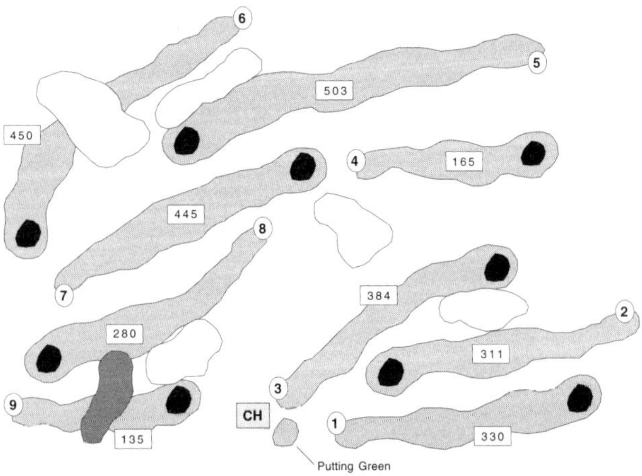

Stewart Meadows (public, 9 hole course)

1801 South Holly Street; Medford, OR 97501
Phone: (541) 770-6554. Fax: none. Web: www.stewartmeadows.com
Pro: Dan Coughlin, PGA. Superintendent: Rod Smith.
Rating/Slope: M 66.8/114; W 66.8/115. **Course record:** 65.
Green fees: $22/$15; Jr. rates, Sr. rates Mondays/Thursday's only $15/$10.
Power cart: $10/$6 per person. **Pull cart:** $2/$1. **Trail fee:** not available.
Reservation policy: please call 7 days in advance for your tee times.
Winter condition: the golf course is open all year long weather permitting.
Terrain: flat (easy walking). **Tees:** all grass. **Spikes:** soft spikes preferred.
Services: club rentals, lessons, snack bar, beer, wine, pro shop, driving range, putting & chipping greens. **Comments:** A good golf course that is beautifully mounded and landscaped. Ponds, bunkers, and a creek makes for a challenging 9 holes of golf. The course will soon sport two set of tees for those wanting to play a different 9 on the second time around. This golf course opened in July of 1994 and has fast become a local favorite. Worth a trip if you are in the area.

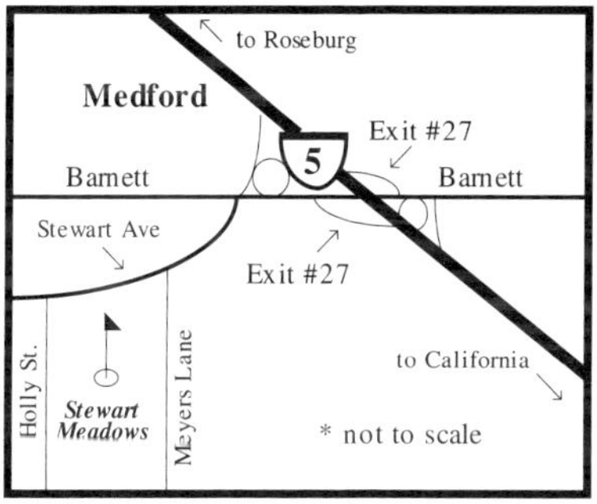

Directions: From I-5 N&S take the Barnett Street exit to South Medford. Cross Barnett Street to Stewart Avenue. Proceed until you reach Holly Street. Turn left on Holly Street. The course is located on the left hand side of Holly Street. Look for signs to the golf course.

Course Yardage & Par:
C-3000 yards, par 36.
M-2858 yards, par 36.
W-2580 yards, par 36.

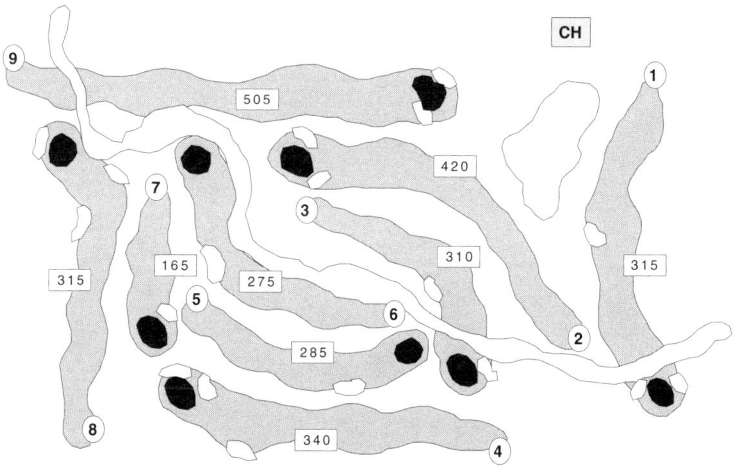

Stewart Park Golf Course (public, 9 hole course)

1005 Stewart Parkway; Roseburg, OR 97470

Phone: (541) 672-4592. Fax: (541) 464-0770. Web: none.

Pro: Pat Huffer, PGA. Superintendent: Mel Ganger.

Rating/Slope: M 69.8/114; W 72.1/127. **Course record:** 64.

Green fees: W/D $17.50/$10.50; W/E $20/$12.50; Sr. rates (M-F); M/C, VISA.

Power cart: $19/$11. **Pull cart:** $4/$2.50. **Trail fee:** call for price.

Reservation policy: yes, call 1 week in advance for your tee-times.

Winter condition: the golf course is open all year long. Fair conditions.

Terrain: flat, some rolling hills. **Tees:** all grass. **Spikes:** soft spikes preferred.

Services: club rentals, snack bar, beer, wine, pro shop, driving range.

Comments: Monthly discounted rates available. Water hazards, bunkers and mature trees make this course a challenge. The terrain is up and down and gives the golfer a wide variety of lies from the fairway. Great nine hole track.

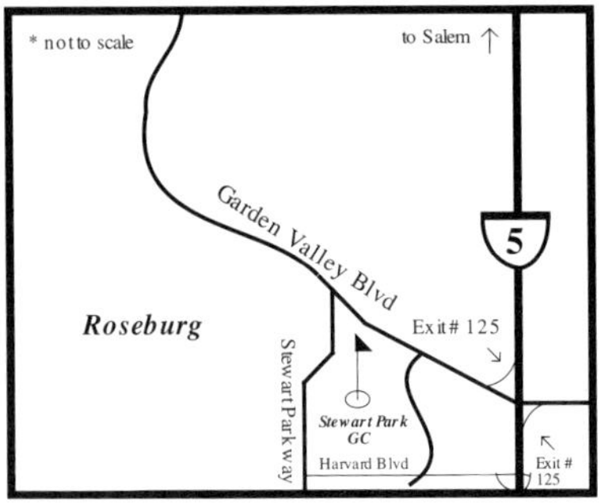

Directions: from I-5 N&S take the City Center exit (#124) and travel westbound. Turn right on Stewart Parkway to the golf course. The golf course will be located on your right hand side. Look for signs that are posted at your turns.

Course Yardage & Par:

M-2954 yards, par 35.
W-2835 yards, par 37.

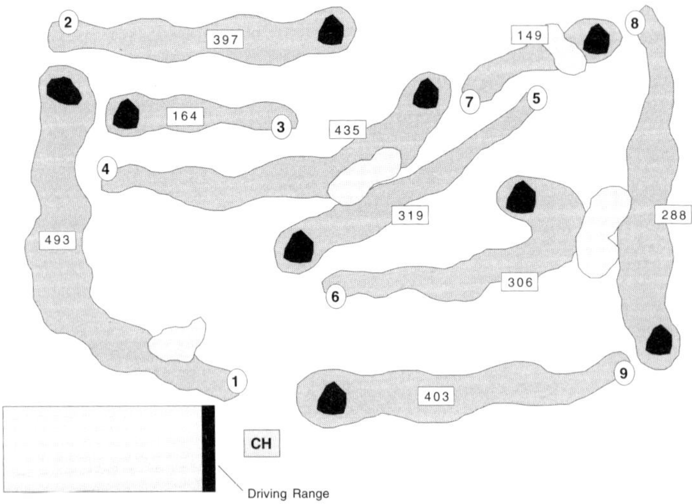

Stone Creek Golf Club (public, 18 hole course)

14603 South Stoneridge Drive; Oregon City, OR 97045

Phone: (503) 518 4653. Fax: (503) 518-3299. Web: stonecreekgolfclub.net

Pro: Doug, Suse, PGA. Superintendent: David Phipps

Rating/Slope: T 72.4/125; 70.3/122; 67.7/118; W 69.0/120. **Course record:** 64.
Green fees: Monday thru Thursday $35; Friday thru Sunday $39; M/C, VISA.
Power cart: $13/$8 per rider. **Pull cart:** $4. **Trail fee:** not allowed.
Reservation policy: 7 days in advance in person, 6 days in advance by phone.
Winter condition: the golf course is open all year long. Excellent conditions.
Terrain: flat, some hills. **Tees:** all grass. **Spikes:** soft spikes required.
Services: club rentals, lessons, deli, beer, wine, pro shop, driving range, putting and chipping greens, beverage cart in season, corporate tournament tent.
Comments: generally flat, Stone Creek offers a nice mix of golf holes, with the front nine winding over relatively open meadows, and the back nine holes lined by towering firs. This is first public golf course built by PGA tour player Peter Jacobsen. Put this golf course on your must play list. Excellent winter course.

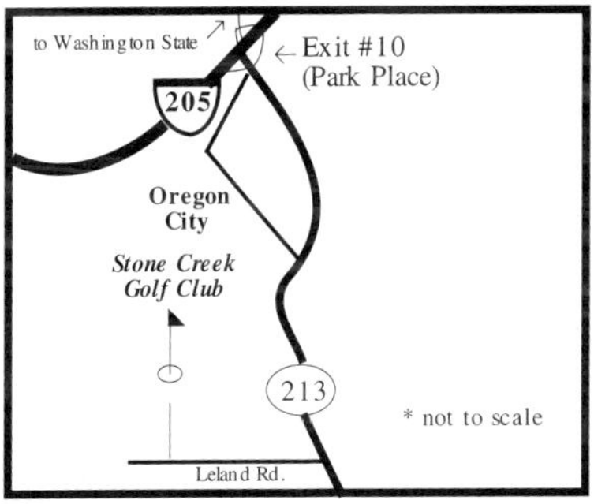

Directions: from I-205 N&S take exit #10 Park Place to Hwy 213. Proceed 6 miles south on Hwy 213 to Leland Rd. Turn right, proceed to Stoneridge Dr. turn right on Stoneridge Dr. to the golf course.

Course Yardage & Par:
T-6873 yards, par 72.
C-6525 yards, par 72.
M-5999 yards, par 72.
W-5191 yards, par 72.

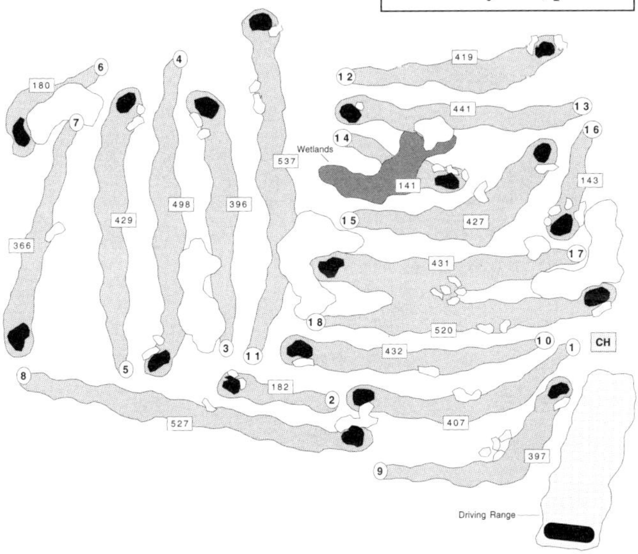

Stone Ridge Golf Club (public, 18 hole course)

500 East Antelope Road; Eagle Point OR 97524
Phone: (541) 830-GOLF (4653). Fax: (541) 830-4654. Web: none.
Pro/General Manager: Pat Akins, PGA. Superintendent: Casey Arden.
Rating/Slope: T 71.8/135; C 70.3/127; M 67.6/121; W 68.2/118. **Record:** 65.
Green fees: W/D $25/$15; W/E & Holidays $30/$20; ask for special rates.
Power cart: $20/$10. **Pull cart:** $2. **Trail fee:** $10 for personal carts.
Reservation policy: public can call up to 1 week in advance for tee times.
Winter condition: the course is open all year long. Course conditions are good.
Terrain: flat, some moderate hills. **Tees:** grass. **Spikes:** soft spikes preferred.
Services: club rentals, lessons, snack bar, beer, wine, pro shop, driving range.
Comments: Set within the breathtaking tranquility of the Rogue Valley, Stone Ridge captures the true essence of Southern Oregon Golf more than any other. Stone Ridge received the #1 public course in Oregon State with green fees under $50. In 2001 the golf course received a "four star rating" from *Golf Digest*.

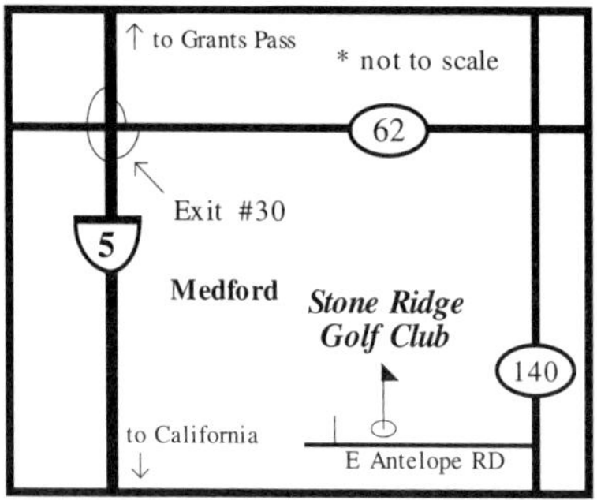

Directions: from I-5 N&S take exit #30. Proceed eastbound on Hwy 62. Proceed for 6 miles to Hwy 140 and turn right. Proceed 3 miles to East Antelope Road. turn right. Proceed 1/4 mile to the golf course entrance. Look for signs.

Course Yardage & Par:
T-6738 yards, par 72. **C-6312 yards, par 72.** **M-5834 yards, par 72.** **W-4986 yards, par 72.**

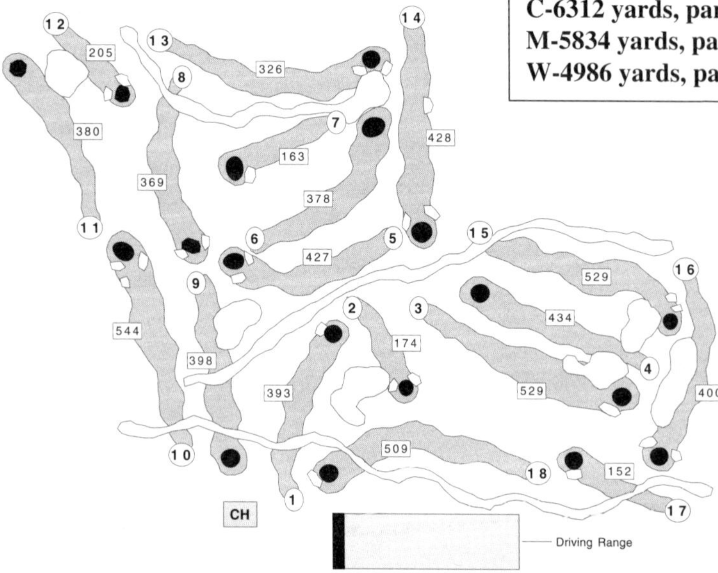

Summerfield Golf & Country Club (semi-private, 9 holes)

10650 SW Summerfield Drive; Tigard, OR 97224
Phone: (503) 620-1200. Fax: none. Web: none.
Pro: Bill Houston, PGA. Superintendent: none.
Rating/Slope: M 62.0/102; W 65.8/105. **Course record:** 29.
Green fees: $24/$12 all week long; no special rates; no credit cards.
Power cart: $20/$10. **Pull cart:** $2. **Trail fee:** personal carts are not allowed.
Reservation policy: public times after mens & ladies club play. 2 days ahead.
Winter condition: the golf course is open all year long. Wet conditions.
Terrain: flat, some hills. **Tees:** all grass. **Spikes:** metal spikes permitted.
Services: club rentals, pro shop, lessons, beverages, putting & chipping greens.
Comments: Course is situated among beautiful homes and club house. The golf course is moderately flat so it is very easy to walk. Few hazards come into play off the tee but most of the greens are small in size and fronted by bunkers.

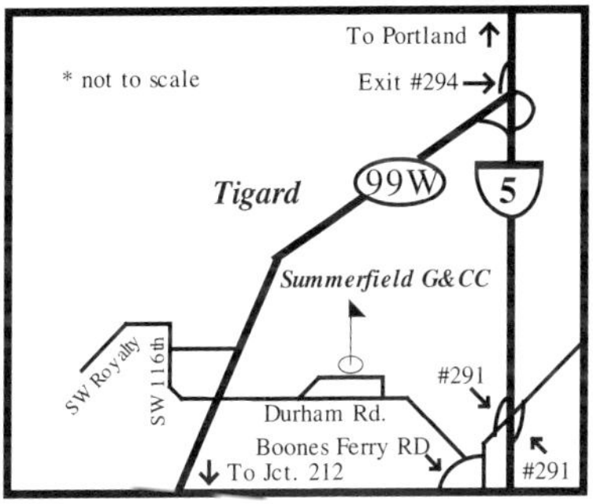

__Directions:__ from I-5 N&S take Highway 99 W exit. Travel south through King City. Turn left on SW Durham. Take the first left at the light on SW Summerfield Drive. Stay right for .5 miles to the golf course which will be located on your right.

Course Yardage & Par:

M-2320 yards, par 33.
W-2231 yards, par 33.
__Dual tees for 18 holes:__
M-4673 yards, par 66.
W-4452 yards, par 66.

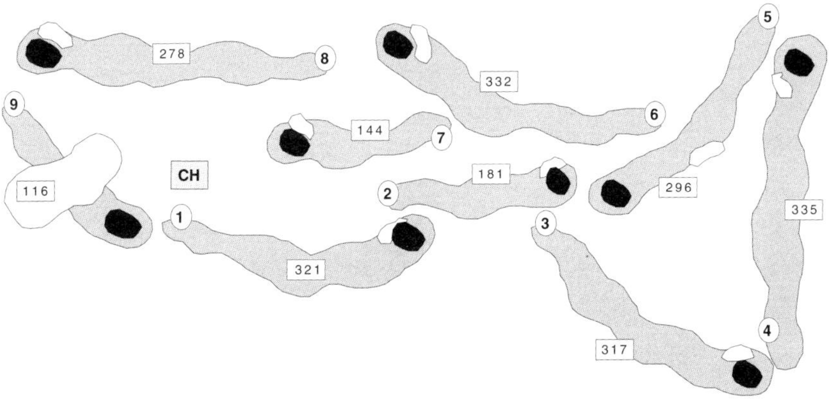

Sunriver Resort (Meadows, resort, 18 hole course)

Highway 97; P.O. Box 3609; Sunriver, OR 97707
Phone: (541) 593-3750 or 1-800-962-1769. Fax: (541) 593-4678.
For Tee-times call: (541) 593-4402. Web-site: www.sunriver-resort.com
Pro: Tim Blasins, PGA. Superintendent: Steve Walz.
Rating/Slope: C 72.9/131; M 71.0/132; M 68.1/123; W 69.8/127. **Record:** 68.
Green fees: W/D $90; W/E $100; lower rates for guests; M/C, VISA, AMEX.
Power cart: $15 person. **Pull cart:** $5. **Trail fee:** not allowed.
Reservation policy: resort guests at reservation time, public 2 days in advance.
Winter condition: the golf course is closed from November 1st to April 14th.
Terrain: flat, some hills. **Tees:** all grass. **Spikes:** soft spikes only.
Services: club rentals, lessons, snack bar, restaurant, lounge, beer, wine, pro shop, driving range, putting green. **Comments:** the Meadows was designed by acclaimed architect John Fought, with the towering Mount Bachelor as its backdrop. Featuring bent grass tees and greens and Fought's dramatic use of directional and fore-bunkers, Meadows serves up ample challenges for all. Four sets of tees on each hole make this a user friendly course for all levels.

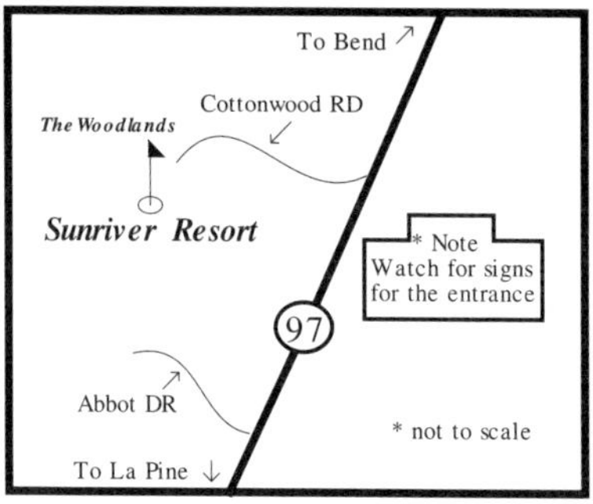

<u>**Directions:**</u> the golf course is located approximately 15 miles south of Bend, Oregon off of Hwy 97. Look for signs on Hwy 97 that direct you to the turn. You will turn west off the Hwy. Signs are posted within the resort directing you to each of the golf courses.

Sunriver Resort (Woodlands, resort, 18 hole course)

Highway 97; P.O. Box 3609; Sunriver, OR 97707
Phone: (541) 593-3750 or 1-800-962-1769. Fax: (541) 593-3733.
For Tee-times call: (541) 593-4402. Web-site: www.sunriver-resort.com
Pro: Jon Noack, PGA. Superintendent: Jared Jeffries.
Rating/Slope: C 73.1/136; M 69.2/117; W 71.2/132. **Record:** 63.
Green fees: W/D $90; W/E $100; lower rates for guests; M/C, VISA, AMEX.
Power cart: $15 per person. **Pull cart:** $5. **Trail fee:** not allowed.
Reservation policy: resort guests through reservation number, public 2 days.
Winter condition: the golf course is closed from November 1st to April 14th.
Terrain: flat, some hills. **Tees:** all grass. **Spikes:** soft spikes only.
Services: club rentals, lessons, snack bar, beer, pro shop, driving range, tennis, swimming, full resort facility. **Comments:** designed by Robert Trent Jones II. Rated in *Golf Digest's* top 25 resort courses in America. With its abundance of water and numerous outcroppings of lava rock, Woodlands places a premium on club selection and accuracy. This is one of the Northwest's finest golf courses.

Meadows

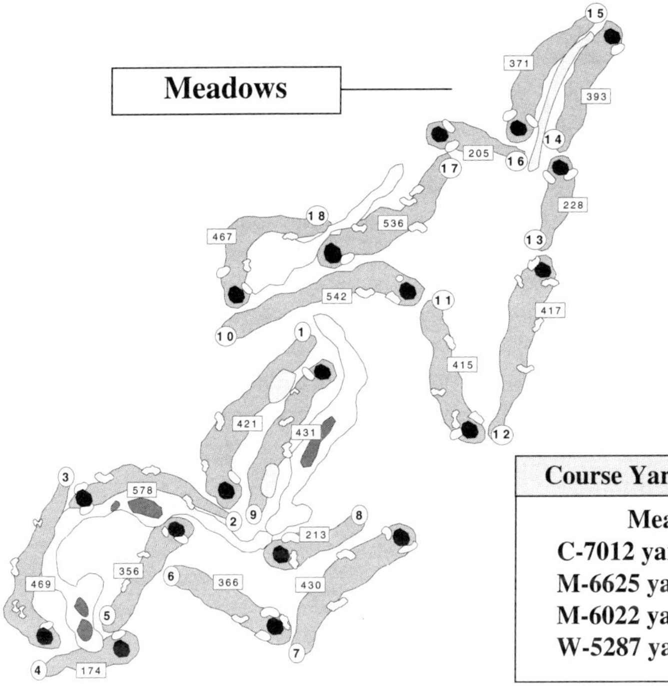

Course Yardage & Par:

Meadows
C-7012 yards, par 71.
M-6625 yards, par 71.
M-6022 yards, par 71.
W-5287 yards, par 71.

Woodlands

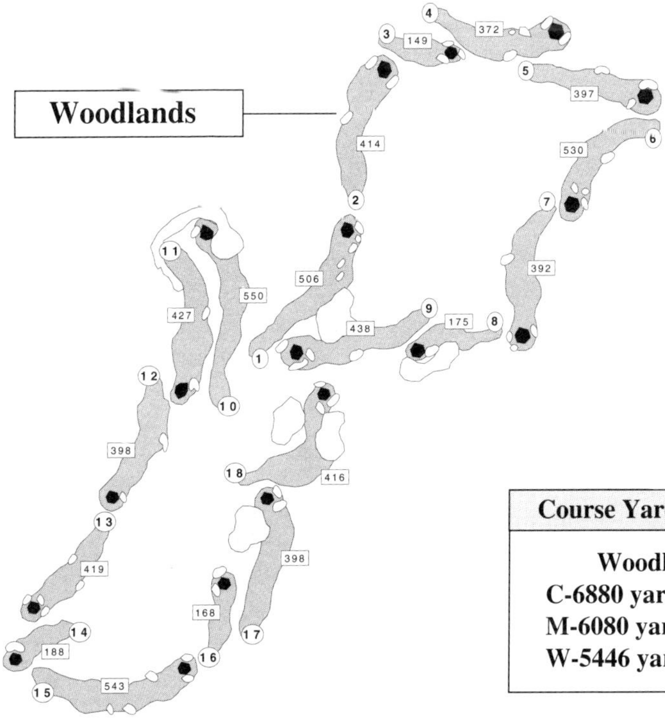

Course Yardage & Par:

Woodlands
C-6880 yards, par 72.
M-6080 yards, par 72.
W-5446 yards, par 72.

Sunset Bay Golf Course (public, 9 hole course)

11001 Cape Arago Highway; Coos Bay, OR 97420
Phone: (541) 888-9301. Fax: (541) 888-2881. Web: none.
Manager: Rosalie Hyatt. Superintendent: Larry Hyatt.
Rating/Slope: M 66.8/105; W 68.6/108. **Course record:** 31.
Green fees: W/D $18/$10; W/E $19/$11; Jr. rates; M/C, VISA.
Power cart: $22/$12. **Pull cart:** $2/$1. **Trail fee:** personal carts not allowed.
Reservation policy: not needed. Tee-times are on a first come first served basis.
Winter condition: the golf course is open all year long. Dry (drains very well).
Terrain: flat, some hills. **Tees:** all grass. **Spikes:** metal spikes permitted.
Services: club rentals, snack bar, beverages, pro shop, putting/chipping greens.
Comments: Course opened in 1969, and was designed by John Zoller, winner of the 1990 Ross Award for Golf Course architecture. "One of the most interesting courses anywhere" states *Golf Oregon Magazine*. The course is planning to expand to 18 holes in the near future. This course is worth a special trip.

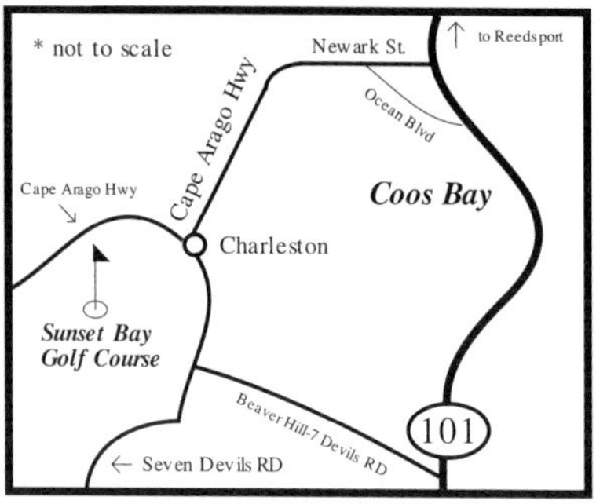

Directions: the golf course is located in the Charleston Recreation Area, 12 miles west of Coos Bay, it adjoins Sunset Bay State Park. From Highway 101 follow the signs to Charleston, State Parks, Ocean Beaches, and the golf course. Look for signs marking your way to the golf course.

Course Yardage & Par:

Yellow/Blue tees: 3020 yards, par 36.
White/Red tees: 2609 yards, par 36.
Dual tees for 18 holes:
Yellow/Blue tees: 6055 yards, par 72.
White/Red tees: 5415 yards, par 72.

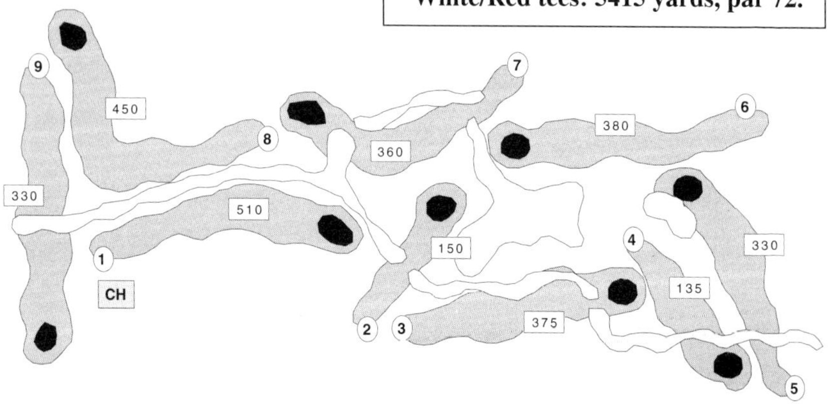

Sunset Grove Golf Club (public, 9 hole course)

41615 NW Osterman Road; Forest Grove, OR 97116
Phone: (503) 357-6044. Fax: none. Web: none.
Owner: Joan Abarno. Superintendent: Chip Abarno.
Rating/Slope: M 67.6/114; W 70.4/115. **Course record:** 63.
Green fees: W/D $18/$10; W/E $22/$11; Jr. & Sr. rates (M-F); M/C, VISA.
Power cart: $22/$11. **Pull cart:** $2. **Trail fee:** personal carts not allowed.
Reservation policy: yes, call for reservations, they advised them in summer.
Winter condition: the golf course is open all year long. Dry (drains well).
Terrain: flat, easy walking. **Tees:** all grass. **Spikes:** soft spikes preferred.
Services: club rentals, snack bar, beer, wine, pop, pro shop, putting green.
Comments: the golf course is very dry during the winter months so if you are looking for a course to play in wet weather try Sunset Grove. The golf course is wide open and plays to an intermediate level. Greens are fairly large. The golf course is easy to walk and is a favorite for the senior or first time golfer.

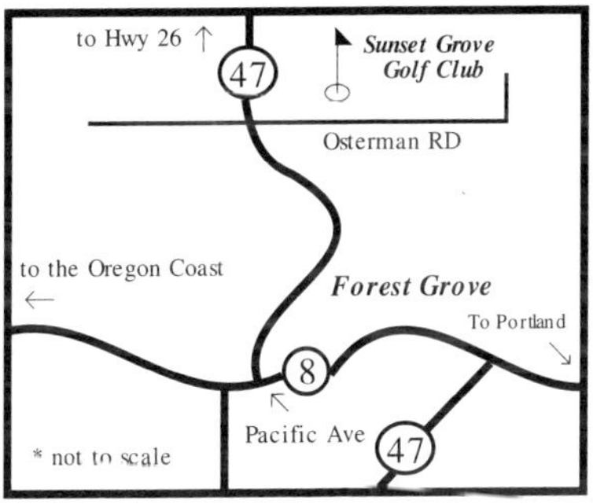

Directions: the golf course is located between Banks and Forest Grove, Ore. From Portland take Highway 26 west to Highway 6, then cut off to Highway 47 south. The golf course is located on the east side of Highway 47. Look for signs.

Course Yardage & Par:
M-2849 yards, par 36.
W-2715 yards, par 37.
Dual tees for 18 holes;
M-5564 yards, par 72.
W-5430 yards, par 74.

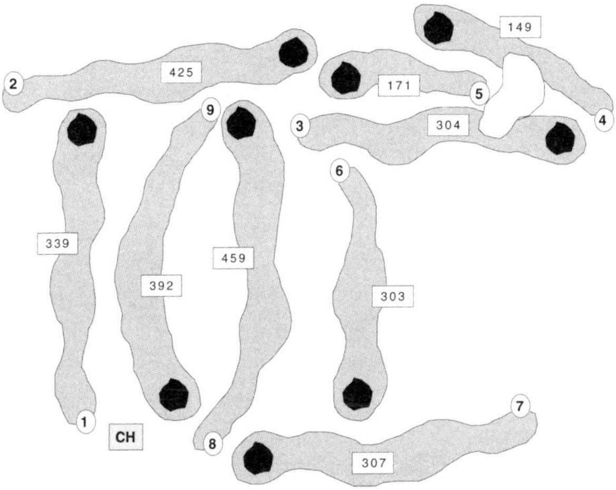

The Reserve Vineyards & G.C., North Course (semi-private)

4805 S.W. 229th Avenue; Aloha, OR 97007 (18 hole Course)
Phone: (503) 649-8191. Fax: (503) 848- 3425. Web: www.reservegolf.com
Pro: Chris Rogers, PGA. Superintendent: Eric Peterson.
Rating/Slope: T 72.8/136; C 70.7/126; M 68.3/116; W 70.4/121. **Record:** 68.
Green fees: the golf course operates on a seasonal rate basis. Call ahead.
Power cart: $20. **Pull cart:** yes. **Trail fee:** not allowed.
Reservation policy: you may call ahead up to 14 days in advance.
Winter Condition: the course is considered dry and open all year long.
Terrain: flat, some hills. **Tees:** all grass. **Spikes:** soft spikes only.
Services: club rentals, lessons, lounge, restaurant, snack bar, beer, wine, liquor, pro shop, driving range, state of the art practice facility, putting/chipping green.
Comments: this facility is one of the premier golf complexes in the Pacific Northwest. Designed for golfers who appreciate the game and tradition. The Cupp course is more open with many water hazards and rolling mounds. Both courses wind along the Gordon and Butternut Creeks. Worth a special trip

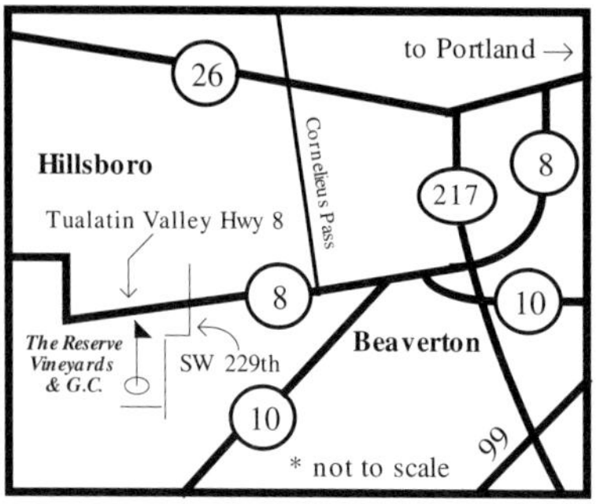

Directions: from Highway 26 East and West. Exit at Hwy 8 the (Tualatin Valley Highway 8) exit. Proceed on Hwy 8 the Tualatin Hwy until you reach SW 229th. At SW 229th you will turn left. Proceed on SW 229th to the golf course. Look for signs that are posted along the way.

The Reserve Vineyards & G.C., South Course (semi-private)

4805 S.W. 229th Avenue; Aloha, OR 97007 (18 hole Course)
Phone: (503) 649-8191. Fax: (503) 848- 3425. Web: www.reservegolf.com
Pro: Chris Rogers, PGA. Superintendent: Eric Peterson.
Rating/Slope: T 74.1/132; C 72.3/130; M 69.3/124; 70.3/126.
Green fees: the golf course operates on a seasonal rate basis. Call ahead.
Power cart: $20. **Pull cart:** yes. **Trail fee:** not allowed.
Reservation policy: you may call ahead up to 14 days in advance.
Winter Condition: the course is considered dry and open all year long.
Terrain: flat, some hills. **Tees:** all grass. **Spikes:** soft spikes only.
Services: club rentals, lessons, lounge, restaurant, snack bar, beer, wine, liquor, showers, lockers, pro shop, driving range, state of the art practice facility.
Comments: designed by award winning architects John Fought and Robert Cupp the golf experience at The Reserve promises to be unique. The Fought course is the more traditional of the two, there are numerous sand bunkers, dramatic terrain changes, and many older established tree stands. The winery theme is located throughout the architecture of both courses.

Course Yardage & Par:
The North Course
Gold-6845 yards, par 72.
Blue-6344 yards, par 72.
White-5846 yards, par 72.
Red-5199 yards, par 72.

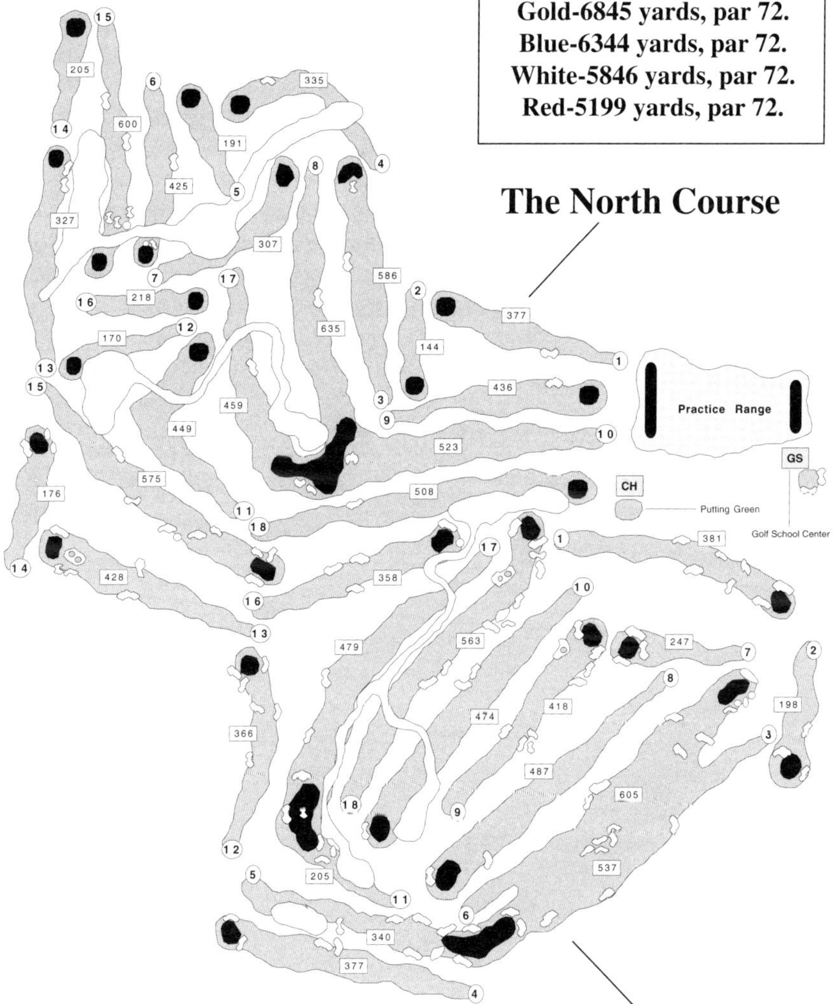

The South Course

Course Yardage & Par:
The South Course
Gold-7172 yards, par 72.
Blue-6809 yards, par 72.
White-6201 yards, par 72.
Red-5189 yards, par 72.

Tokatee Golf Club (public, 18 hole course)

54947 McKenzie Highway; Blue River, OR 97413
Mailing address: P.O. Box 989; Eugene, OR 97440
Phone: (541) 822-3220, 800 452-6376. Fax: (541) 822-6094. Web: tokatee.com
Pro: Dan King, PGA. Superintendent: Bill Masten. Course record: 63.
Rating/Slope: BK 72.3/126; BL 69.6/121; W 67.8/118; R 67.8/109.
Green fees: $37/$20 all week long; off season rates; VISA, M/C.
Power cart: $28/$18. **Pull cart:** $4/$3. **Trail fee:** $12 for personal carts.
Reservation policy: yes, call up to 30 days in advance for your tee-times.
Winter condition: the course is closed from November 15th to February 1st.
Terrain: flat, some hills. **Tees:** all grass. **Spikes:** soft spikes preferred.
Services: club rentals, coffee shop, beer, pro shop, driving range, lessons.
Comments: the facility has been rated in the top 25 of *Golf Digests* "America's Best Public Golf Courses" in 1989, 93, 95, 96 and also in 1997. A nice surprise in Oregon that is a joy to play anytime. This golf course is worth a special trip.

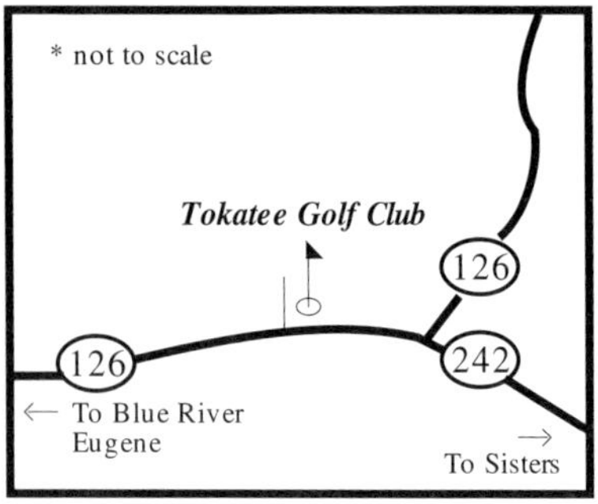

Directions: the golf course is located 47.5 miles east of Eugene, Oregon on Highway 126 (near Blue River). From Highway 126 the golf course is located 7 miles east of the Blue River exit. Look for signs.

Course Yardage & Par:
Black tees: 6842 yards, par 72.
Blue tees: 6245 yards, par 72.
White tees: 5951 yards, par 72.
Red tees: 5018 yards, par 72.

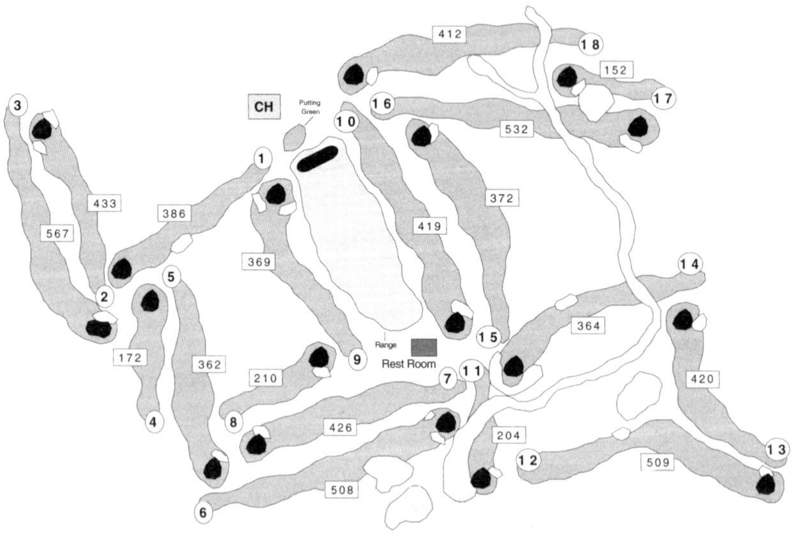

Top O'Scott Golf Course (public, 18 hole course)

12000 SE Stevens Road; Portland, OR 97266

Phone: (503) 654-5050. Fax: (503) 654-0377. Web: toposcottgolf.com

Pro: Scott Nash, PGA. Superintendent: Pat Hamlin.

Rating/Slope: C 62.7/103; M 62.1/102; W 61.5/96. **Course record:** 58.

Green fees: Mon.-Thur. $19/$11; Fri.-Sun. $21/$12; Jr. & Sr. rates; M/C, VISA.

Power cart: $22/$11. **Pull cart:** $4/$2. **Trail fee:** $5/$3 for personal carts.

Reservation policy: yes, for weekends, holidays. Please call up to 7 days ahead.

Winter condition: the golf course is open all year long. Damp conditions.

Terrain: flat, some hills. **Tees:** all grass. **Spikes:** metal spikes permitted.

Services: club rentals, lessons, discount pro shop, driving range, putting green.

Comments: tree lined fairways and tricky greens make this course a challenge. Beautiful views of the Portland area and surrounding country side from the east and south. Good course for those wanting to spend a relaxing day on the links.

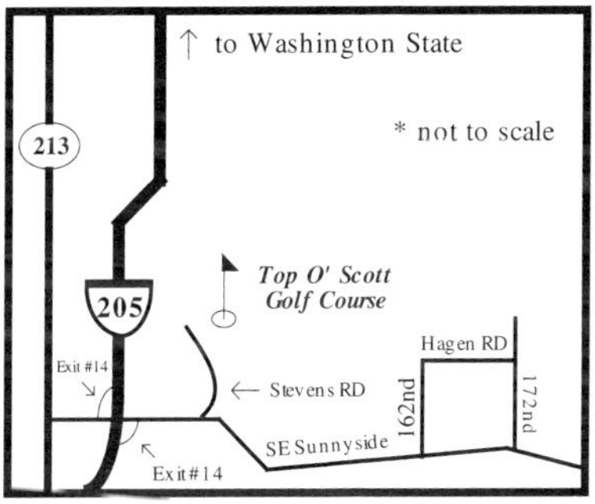

Directions: from I-205 southbound exit at exit #14 (Sunnyside Road) and travel eastbound. Take first left on Stevens Road go 1/4 mile up Stevens Road. The golf course is located across from the New Hope Church on Stevens Road.

Course Yardage & Par:

M-4890 yards, par 68.
W-4605 yards, par 70.

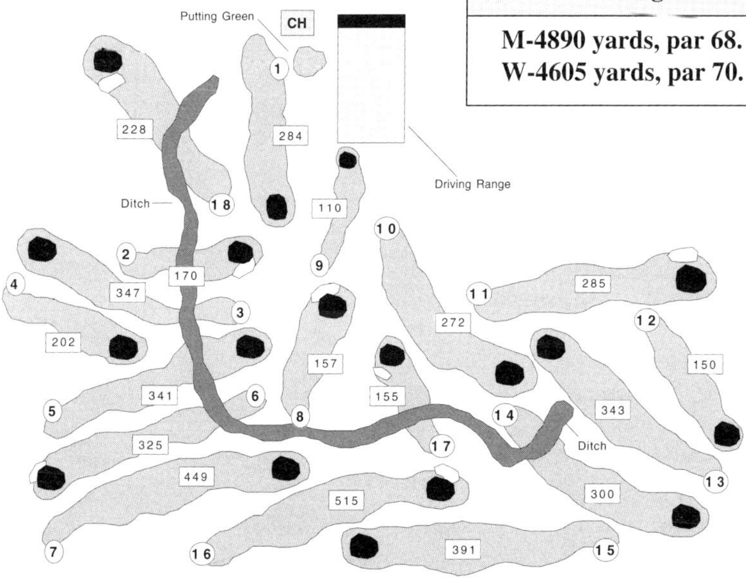

Trysting Tree Golf Club (public, 18 hole course)

34028 Electric Road; Corvallis, OR 97333
Phone: (541) 752-3332. Fax: (541) 754-3550. Web: none.
Pro: Sean Arey, PGA. Superintendent: Pat Doran.

Rating/Slope: T 73.1/127; C 71.4/127; M 69.2/119; W 70.7/117. **Record:** 64.
Green fees: $30/$16; Oregon College students $15/$10; Jr. rates.
Power cart: $24/$12. **Pull cart:** $3. **Trail fee:** $10 for personal carts.
Reservation policy: yes, call up to 1 week in advance for your tee-times.
Winter condition: the golf course is open all year long. Dry (drains very well).
Terrain: flat, some hills. **Tees:** all grass. **Spikes:** metal spikes permitted.
Services: club rentals, lessons, snack bar, beverages, pro shop, driving range, putting & chipping greens. **Comments:** Beautiful Scottish links style golf course with mounds and swales throughout the golf course. Water and bunkers are the major factor at this course. Be sure not to pass on a chance to play this course.

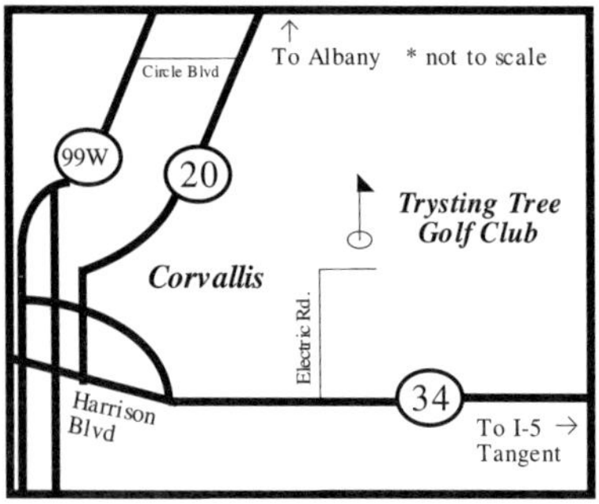

__Directions:__ from I-5 N&S take the exit for Highway 34 westbound toward the city of Corvallis. Proceed for 9 miles. Turn right on Electric Road to the golf course. The golf course is located on the north side of the road. Look for signs marking your way to the golf course.

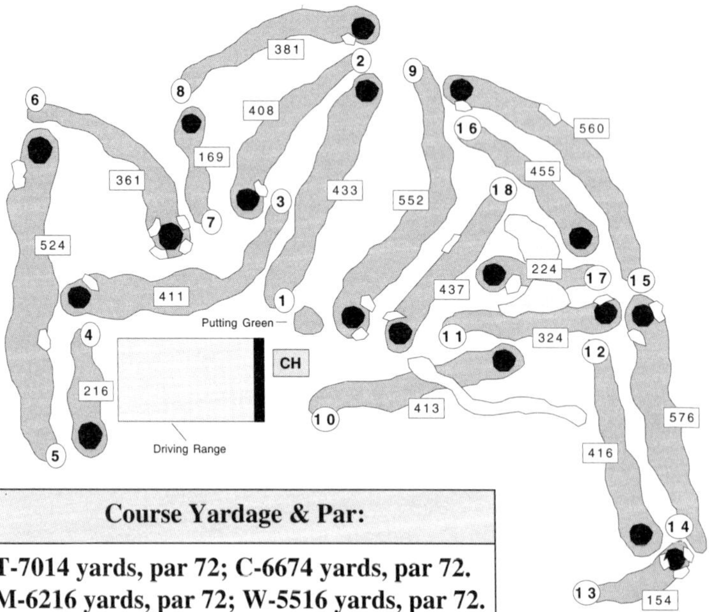

Course Yardage & Par:

T-7014 yards, par 72; C-6674 yards, par 72.
M-6216 yards, par 72; W-5516 yards, par 72.

Tualatin Country Club (private, 18 hole course)

9145 SW Tualatin Road; PO Box 277; Tualatin, OR 97062
Phone: (503) 692-4620. Fax: (503) 691-9871. Web: tualatincountryclub.com
Pro: Jim Nicol, PGA. Superintendent: Randy Shults.
Rating/Slope: C 71.2/126; M 68.6/120; W 70.9/122. **Record:** 63.
Green fees: private club, members & guests of members only; M/C, VISA.
Power cart: private club. **Pull cart:** private club. **Trail fee:** members only.
Reservation policy: private club members & guests of members only.
Winter condition: the golf course is open all year long. Dry conditions.
Terrain: flat, some hills. **Tees:** all grass. **Spikes:** no metal spikes in summer.
Services: club rentals, lessons, snack bar, catering, restaurant, pro shop.
Comments: this well conditioned private course is spectacular at every turn. The fairways are narrow and tree-lined. Greens are medium in size and have bunkers fronting most of them. This course is a must play if you ever get the chance.

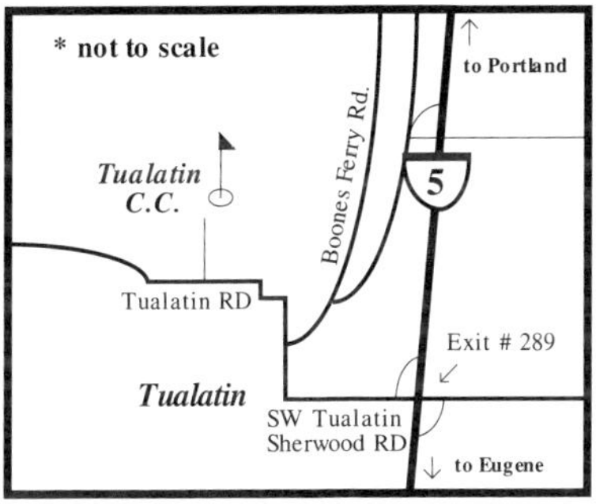

Directions: from I-5N take exit #289 (Tualatin). Turn left over the freeway. Take the first left on SW Tualatin Sherwood Rd. go .5 miles to Boones Ferry Rd. Turn right. Proceed .3 miles to SW Tualatin. Turn left on SW Tualatin. Travel .4 miles to the entrance, turn right.

Course Yardage & Par:
C-6611 yards, par 72; M-6054 yards, par 72. M-5843 yards, par 72; W-5468 yards, par 72.

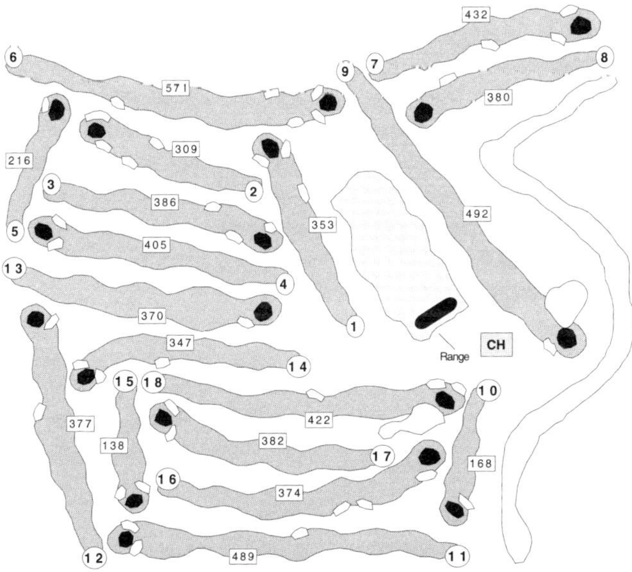

Umatilla Golf Course (public, 18 hole course)

705 Willamette Street; Umatilla, OR 97882
Phone: (541) 922-3006. Fax: (541) 922-5311. Web: none.
Pro: Todd Demarest, PGA. Superintendent: Joe Matzen.
Rating/Slope: M 69.1/115; W 73.5/122. **Course record:** 62.
Green fees: W/D $18/$10; W/E $22/$11; Jr. rates; M/C, VISA, DISCOVER.
Power cart: $24/$12. **Pull cart:** $3/$2 **Trail fee:** 10/$5 for personal carts.
Reservation policy: weekends yes call ahead. Weekdays first come first served.
Winter condition: the golf course is open all year long. Dry, course drains well.
Terrain: flat (easy walking). **Tees:** grass. **Spikes:** no metal spikes permitted.
Services: club rentals, lessons, restaurant, snack bar, lounge, beer, wine, liquor, beverages, pro shop, putting green/chipping greens, lodging at the nearby motel.
Comments: challenging 18 hole layout that offers the golfer wide fairways and large greens. The course is flat and easy to walk. Great golf course for seniors.

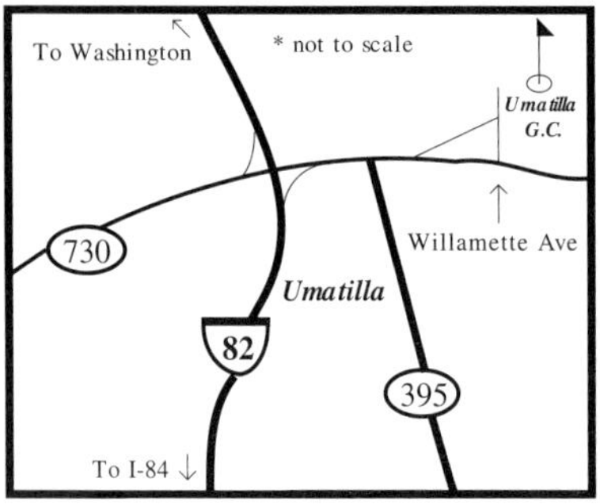

Directions: from I-84 E&W exit at the Irrigon/Umatilla exit. Proceed eastbound for 14.5 miles through the Umatilla city center. The golf course will be located 2 miles ahead. The way to the golf course is well marked with signs along your way. Course is located at the Nendel's Resort.

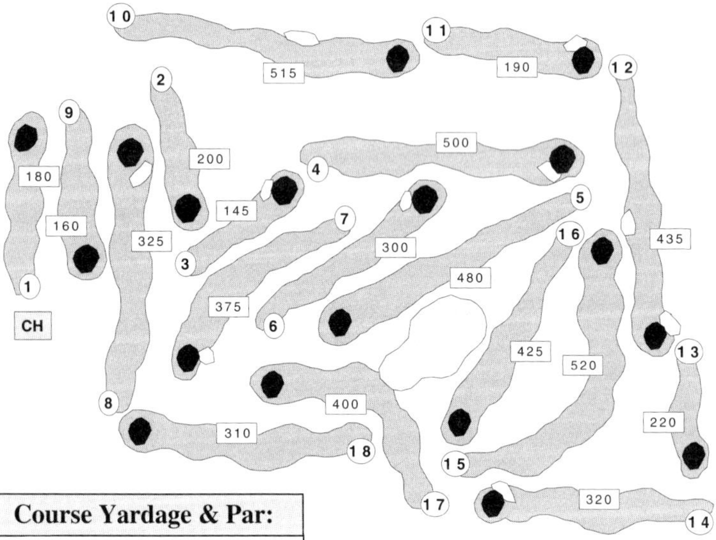

Course Yardage & Par:

M-5975 yards, par 70.
W-5940 yards, par 71.

Valley Golf Club (public, 9 hole course)

345 Hines Boulevard, P.O. Box 96; Hines, OR 97882
Phone: (541) 573-6251. Fax: none. Web: none.
Manager: Pete Jacobs. Superintendent: Joe Rubio.
Rating/Slope: M 68.4/106; W 72.4/118. **Course record:** 33.
Green fees: W/D $18/$12; W/E $22/$15; VISA, M/C.
Power cart: $20/$10. **Pull cart:** $2. **Trail fee:** $7 for personal carts.
Reservation policy: not necessary. Tee-times on a first come first served basis.
Winter condition: the golf course is open all year long. Dry (drains well).
Terrain: flat (easy walking). **Tees:** all grass. **Spikes:** soft spikes only.
Services: club rentals, snack bar, beverages, showers, pro shop, putting green.
Comments: Course is well conditioned and easy to walk. The golf course is fairly long and can play tough when you stray from the fairway. Fairways are on the large size with wide landing area's. Greens are medium in size and have few hazards fronting them. Dual tees are available for those wanting to play 18 holes.

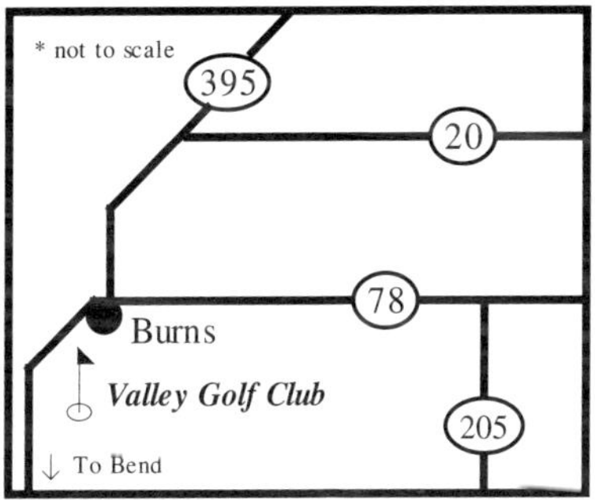

Directions: the golf course is located between the intersections of Highway 395 and Highway 20, in the town of Hines Oregon. The golf course is right off of Highway 395. Look for signs marking your way to the golf course.

Course Yardage & Par:

M-3190 yards, par 36.
W-3190 yards, par 38.
Duals tees for 18 holes:
M-6405 yards, par 72.
W-6405 yards, par 72.

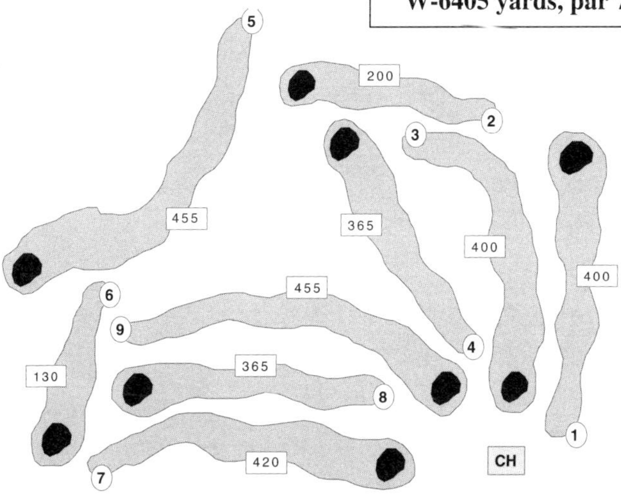

Vernonia Golf Club (public, 18 hole course)

15961 Timber Road E; Vernonia, OR 97064
Phone: (503) 429-6811. Fax: (503) 429-6811. Web: none.
Manager: Fred Fulmer III. Superintendent: Bob Zavales.
Rating/Slope: C 68.6/120; M 67.2/117; W 69.8/114. **Course record:** 63.
Green fees: W/D $20/$12; W/E $25/$14; Jr./Sr. rates (M-F); M/C, VISA.
Power cart: $24/$12. **Pull cart:** $2. **Trail fee:** $6 for personal carts.
Reservation policy: yes, call 7 days in advance for weekends and holidays.
Winter condition: the golf course is open all year long. Dry (good drainage).
Terrain: flat, some hills. **Tees:** all grass. **Spikes:** metal spikes permitted.
Services: club rentals, lessons, snack bar, beer, wine, pro shop, putting green.
Comments: course was established in 1928. The golf course is situated in a very scenic, quiet, rural setting along the Nehalem River. It is located only 45 minutes from downtown Portland. Vernonia has expanded its layout to 18 holes. The layout features small to medium sized greens and tree lined fairways.

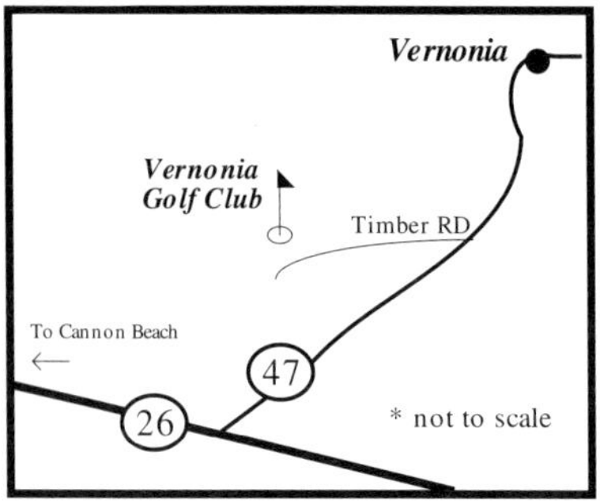

Directions: from Highway 26 westbound from Portland to Highway 47 (Vernonia exit). Proceed for 14 miles. Turn left on Timber Road. Proceed for 1 mile. The golf course will be located on your right hand side. Look for signs at your turns.

Course Yardage & Par:

C-5763 yards, par 70.
M-5490 yards, par 70.
M-5116 yards, par 70.
W-5116 yards, par 74.

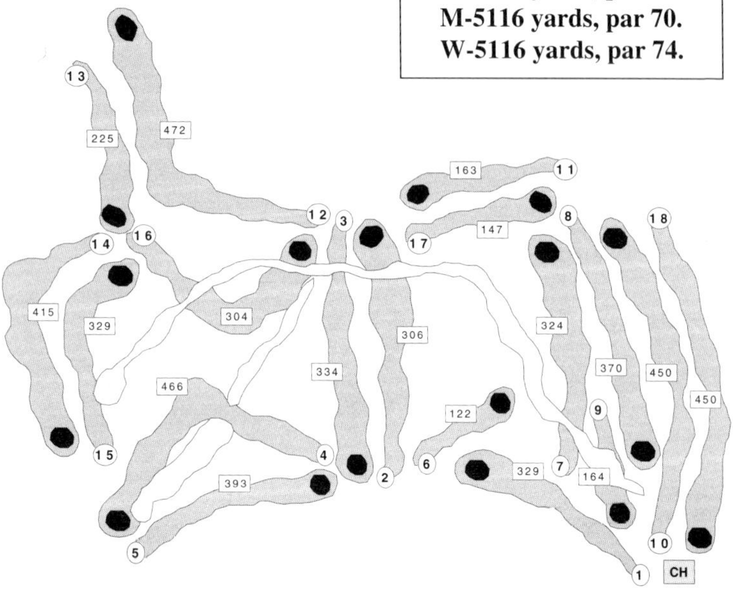

Veterans Administration Domiciliary G.C. (private, 9 holes)

Domiciliary Golf Course; White City, OR 97503
Phone: (541) 826-2111. Fax: (541) 826-3322. Web: none.
Golf Shop Director: Ron Riddle. Superintendent: none.
Rating/Slope: the golf course is not rated. **Course record:** 29.
Green fees: course is for patients and staff of the domiciliary. Play allowed for outpatients along with their guests as long as they have proper paperwork.
Power cart: no charge. **Pull cart:** no charge. **Trail fee:** no charge.
Reservation policy: Private club members, guests and patients only.
Winter condition: the course is open all year long weather permitting.
Terrain: flat (easy walking). **Tees:** grass. **Spikes:** metal spikes permitted.
Services: all services provided by the Veterans Administration, putting green.
Comments: Golf course is one of the finest recreational standpoints of the White City Domiciliary Recreation Program. No public play is allowed.

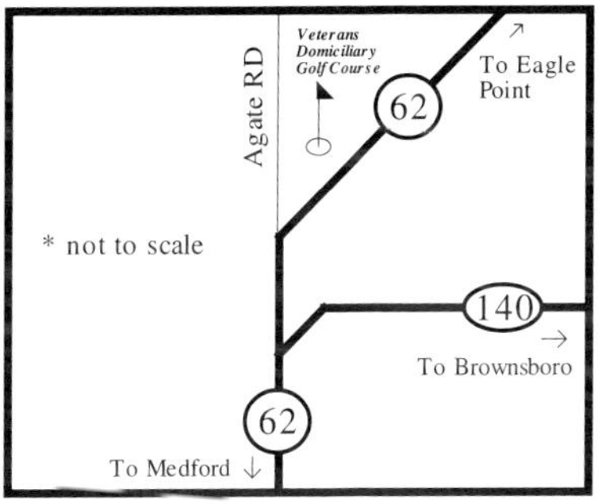

Directions: the golf course is located northeast of Medford off of Highway 62.

Course Yardage & Par:
White tees: 2018 yards, par 33. **Blue tees: 2018 yards, par 33.**

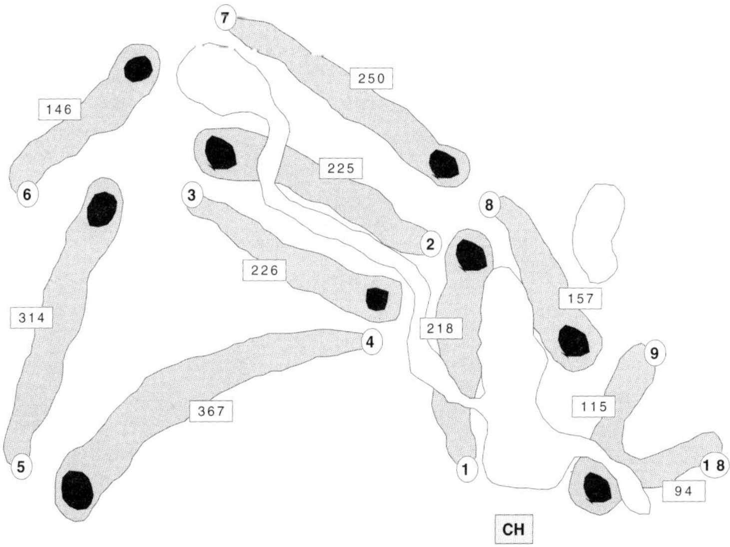

Waverley Country Club (private, 18 hole course)

1100 SE Waverley Drive; Portland, OR 97222
Phone: (503) 654-9509. Fax: (503) 654-4571. web: none.
Pro: John Wells, PGA. Superintendent: John Alexander.
Rating/Slope: C 71.2/128; M 70.1/125; W 73.8/130. **Course record:** 65.
Green fees: private club; members only; no outside play permitted.
Power cart: yes. **Pull cart:** yes. **Trail fee:** no personal carts are allowed.
Reservation policy: members & guests of members only.
Winter condition: the golf course is open all year long. Dry conditions.
Terrain: flat, some hills. **Tees:** grass. **Spikes:** soft spikes preferred.
Services: private club, restaurant, pro shop, lounge, showers, lockers, driving range (members only), putting & chipping greens, club memberships.
Comments: Course is rich with tradition and character. One of the finest courses in the state of Oregon. Host of many major tournaments throughout the years.

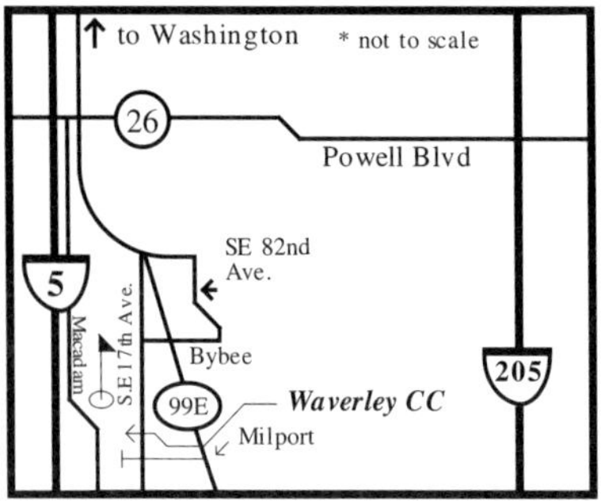

Directions: from Highway 99E (McLoughlin Blvd), take Highway 224 exit and travel westbound to 17th. Turn right (north). Proceed to Waverly Drive. At Waverly Drive turn left to the golf course. Look for a small sign at the turn.

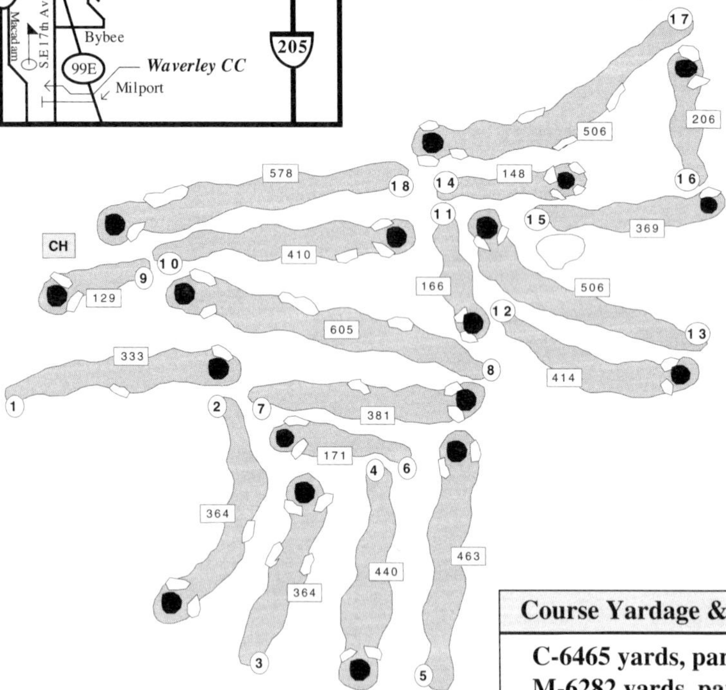

Course Yardage & Par:

C-6465 yards, par 70.
M-6282 yards, par 72.
W-5875 yards, par 72.

Widgi Creek Golf Club (semi-private, 18 hole course)

18707 Century Drive; Bend, OR 97702

Phone: (541) 382-4449. Fax: (541) 385-7094. Web: www.widgi.com

Pro: Mark Roberts, PGA. Superintendent: Jerry Palmerton.

Rating/Slope: T 71.9/134; C 69.7/128; M 66.7/118; W 67.4/119. **Record:** 65.
Green fees: Monday-Thursday $59/$45; Friday-Sunday & Holidays $85/$65; off season rates in spring and fall; Jr. rates and twlight rates; M/C, VISA.
Power cart: $14/$9 per person. **Pull cart:** $5/$3. **Trail fee:** members only.
Reservation policy: yes, public can call 30 days in advance with credit card.
Winter condition: the golf course is closed during the winter months.
Terrain: flat, some hills. **Tees:** all grass. **Spikes:** soft spikes only.
Services: club rentals, lessons, restaurant, beer, wine, pro shop, driving range.
Comments: championship course designed by Robert Muir Graves. The golf course borders the Deschutes National Forest. A challenging, beautiful track. If you are vacationing in the central Oregon area be sure to visit Widgi Creek.

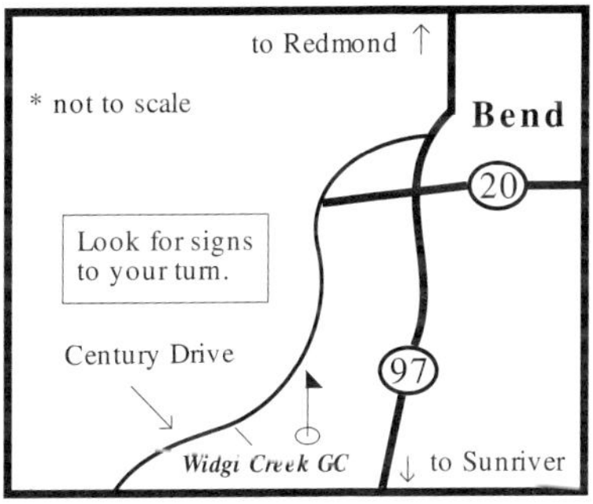

<ins>Directions</ins>: from Hwy 97 in Bend follow to Mt. Bachelor, Cascade Lakes. The course is located 5 miles west of Bend on the way to Mt. Bachelor on Century Dr./Cascade Lakes Highway. The course will be located on your left as you approach from Bend. Look for signs to the golf course.

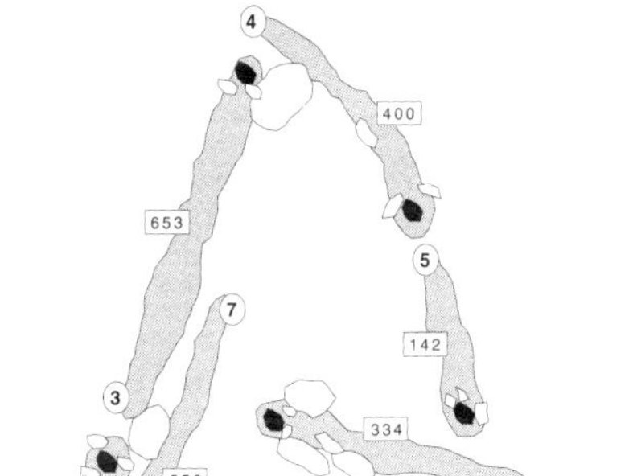
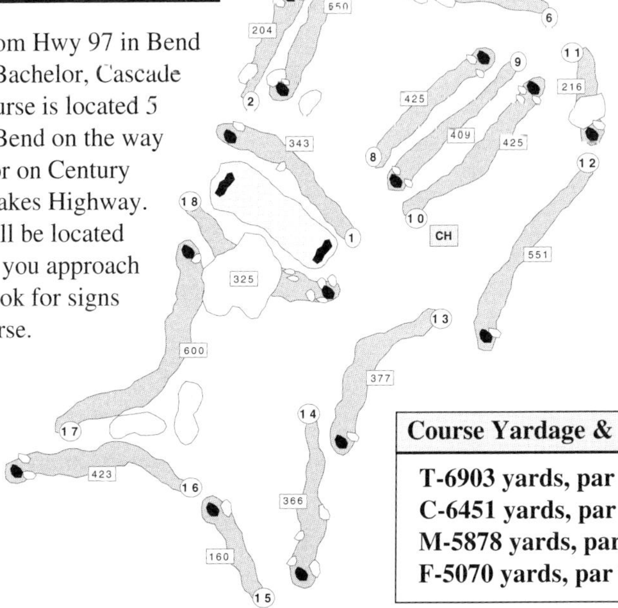

Course Yardage & Par:

T-6903 yards, par 72.
C-6451 yards, par 72.
M-5878 yards, par 72.
F-5070 yards, par 72.

Wild Horse Resort Golf Course (resort, 18 hole course)

72787 Highway 331; Pendleton, OR 97801
Phone: (541) 276-5588. Fax: (541) 276-5888. Web: wildhorseresort.com
Pro: Laine J. Wortman, PGA. Superintendent: Sean Hoolehan.
Rating/Slope: T 74.4/129; C 71.6/128; M 69.4/123; W 72.9/126. **Record:** 63.
Green fees: W/D $27/$15; W/E $32/$18; M/C, VISA, DIS, AMEX.
Power cart: $26/$17. **Pull cart:** $3. **Trail fee:** personal carts not allowed.
Reservation policy: please call in advance for all tee-times. No time limit.
Winter condition: the golf course open, weather permitting. Dry winter course.
Terrain: flat, some hills. **Tees:** all grass. **Spikes:** soft spikes only.
Services: club rentals, lessons, snack bar, restaurant, pro shop, driving range.
Comments: this John Steidel designed layout is a championship caliber course. The layout features extensive mounding, large undulating greens and well bunkered fairways laced with water. Worth a trip if in the Pendleton area.

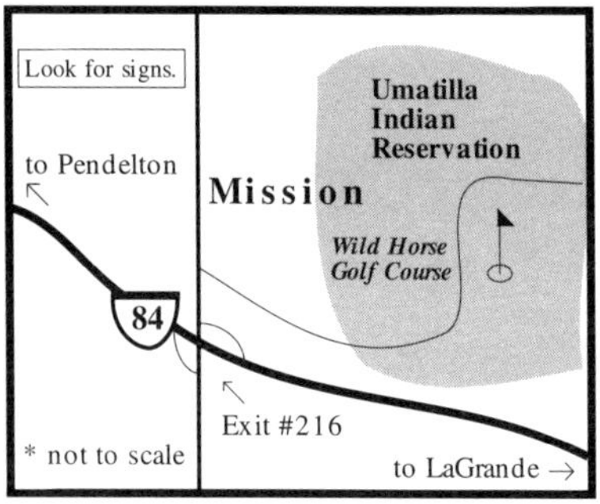

Directions: from I-84 East & West take exit #216 and head north towards the Umatilla Indian Reservation. The golf course is located 1 mile north of I-84 on the Indian Reservation.

Course Yardage & Par:

T-7112 yards, par 72.
C-6647 yards, par 72.
M-6150 yards, par 72.
F-5718 yards, par 72.

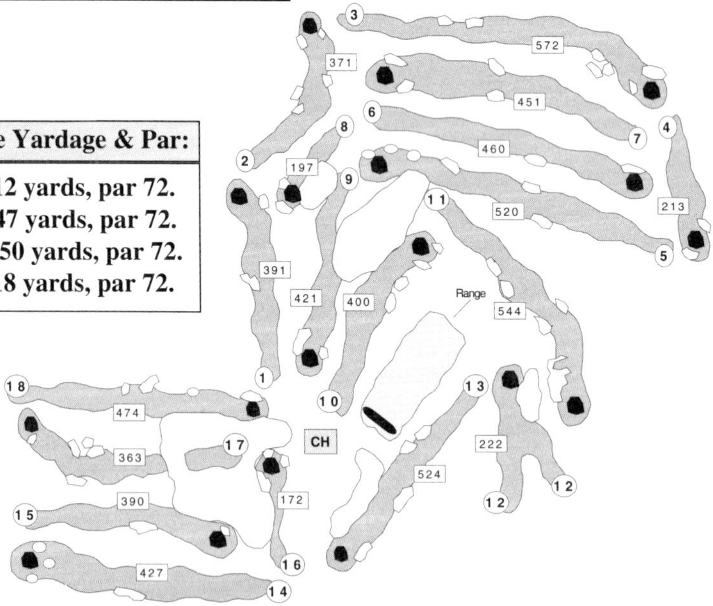

Wildwood Golf Course (public, 18 hole course)

21881 NW Saint Helens Road; Portland, OR 97231
Phone: (503) 621-3402. Fax: (503) 621-1056. Web: none.
Owners: Bill & Kay O'Meara. Superintendent: Bill O'Meara.
Rating/Slope: C 69.1/115; M 68.3/113; W 72.4/120. **Course record:** 66.
Green fees: W/D $22/$12; W/E $26/$14. M/C, VISA, AMEX.
Power cart: $20/$10. **Pull cart:** $3/$2. **Trail fee:** $5 for personal carts.
Reservation policy: call 7 days in advance for your tee-time reservations.
Winter condition: the golf course is open all year long. Drains fairly well.
Terrain: flat, some hills. **Tees:** grass. **Spikes:** soft spikes only April-Sept.
Services: club rentals, pro shop, driving range, restaurant, putting green.
Comments: friendly family run course. This golf course sports three creeks running through it. Great place to host a casual golf tournament or outing.

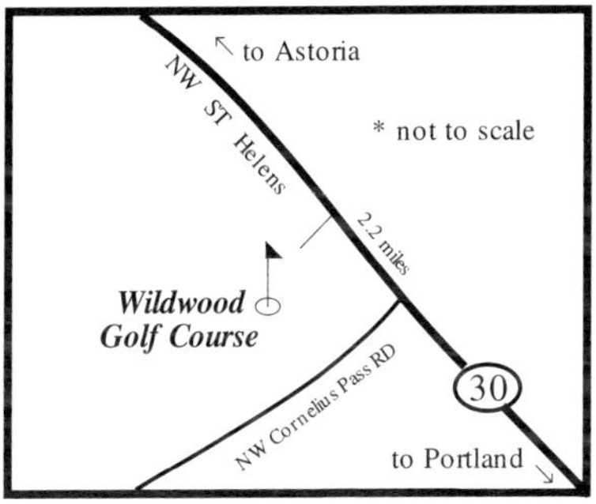

__Directions:__ The golf course is located right off of Hwy 30, 2 miles west of the Cornelius Pass turnoff. The course will be located on the west side of Hwy 30.

Course Yardage & Par:

C-5797 yards, par 72.
M-5806 yards, par 72.
W-5035 yards, par 72.

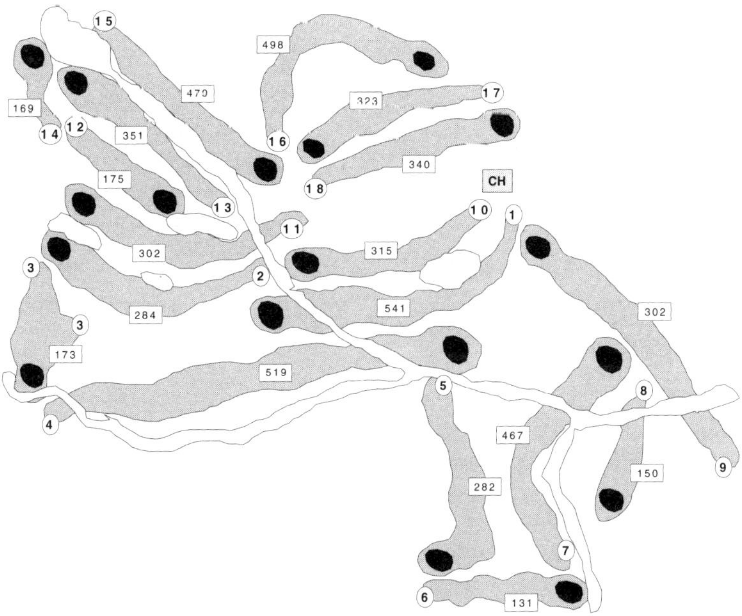

Willamette Valley Country Club (private, 18 hole course)

900 Country Club Place; Canby, OR 97013
Phone: (503) 266-2102. Fax: (503) 266-4389. Web: willamettevalleycc.com
Pro: Danny Moore, PGA. Superintendent: Larry Rashko. Record: 65.
Rating/Slope: T 73.7/137; C 70.7/134; M 70.7/134; M 69.4/126; W 72.1/127.
Green fees: private club; reciprocates with other private clubs; M/C, VISA
Power cart: private club. **Pull cart:** private. **Trail fee:** private club.
Reservation policy: public tee-times are not allowed. Private members only.
Winter condition: the golf course is open all year long weather permitting, dry.
Terrain: flat. **Tees:** all grass. **Spikes:** no metal spikes April-October.
Services: pro shop, restaurant, lounge, showers, driving range, putting green.
Comments: Course has tree lined fairways and well conditioned greens. Good private facility. Almost all of the greens are guarded by greenside bunkers. The course can play very tight at times putting emphasis on accuracy off the tee.

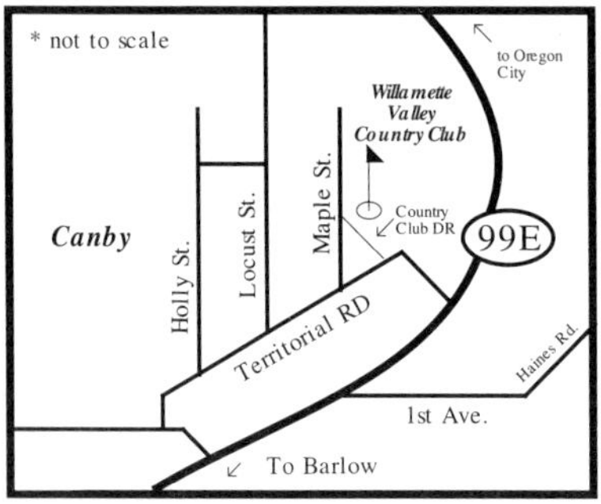

Directions: From Portland take I-5 south. Take exit 282A, Canby/Hubbard. Turn left at the first light onto Arndt Rd. Proceed straight at the 4 way stop. Proceed for about 4 miles (road curves and becomes Knights Bridge Road). Come to the 4 way stop, go straight. Come to the next stop, go left on N Holly. Turn right on NE Territorial Road. Turn left on Maple St. the golf course will be on your right.

Course Yardage & Par:

T-6944 yards, par 72.
C-6668 yards, par 72.
M-6410 yards, par 72.
M-6076 yards, par 72.
W-5478 yards, par 72.

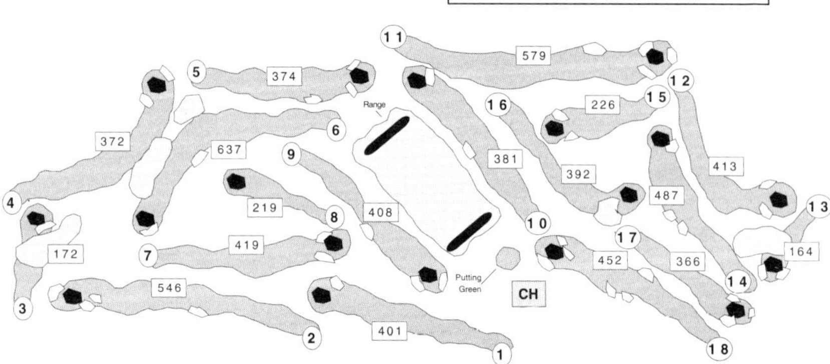

Willow Creek Country Club (semi-private, 9 hole course)

53726 Highway 74; P.O. Box 64; Heppner, OR 97836
Phone: (541) 676-5437. Fax: (541) 676-5437. Web: none.
Pro: Craig Holland. Superintendent: Jiggs Bowman.
Rating/Slope: M 58.2/82; W 58.3/82. **Course record:** 26.
Green fees: $15/$10 all week long; $20 all day rate; no credit cards are allowed.
Power cart: $20/$10. **Pull cart:** $2. **Trail fee:** no trail fee.
Reservation policy: not needed. T-times are on a first come first served basis.
Winter condition: the golf course is open all year long. Damp conditions.
Terrain: flat some hills. **Tees:** all grass. **Spikes:** soft spikes only.
Services: club rentals, candy, beverages, small pro shop, putting green.
Comments: Short, well kept course that lets you practice your iron play. Good walking course that does not play very long. Great for the senior golfer.

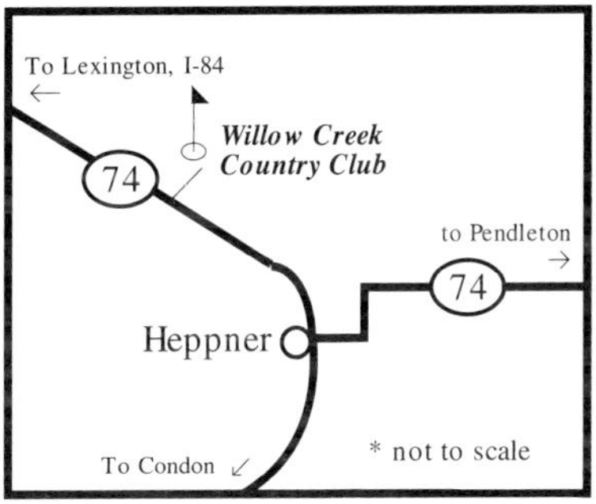

__Directions:__ the golf course is located 1.1 miles NW of Heppner Oregon off of Hwy 74. The golf course is located on the west side of the Highway. Look for signs to the golf course that are posted on the Highway.

Course Yardage & Par:
M-1724 yards, par 30. **W-1705 yards, par 30.** **__Dual tees for 18 holes:__** **M-3416 yards, par 60.** **W-3353 yards, par 60.**

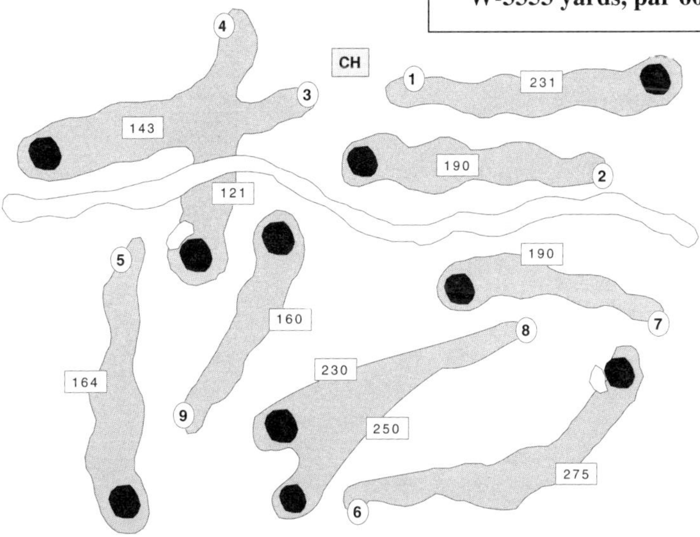

Wilson's Willow Run Executive G. C. (semi-private, 9 holes)

Physical address: West end Wilson's Lane; Boardman, OR 97818
Mailing address: 78873 Tom's Camp Road; Boardman, OR 97818
Phone: (541) 481-4381. Fax: (541) 481-3343. Web: none.
Manager: Hope Phillips. Superintendent: Gordon Lienau.
Rating/Slope: M 59.0/88; W 57.4/85. **Course record:** 57.
Green fees: W/D $10/$7; W/E $12/$8; no credit cards are accepted.
Power cart: $17/$9. **Pull cart:** $2/$1. **Trail fee:** $7/$4.
Reservation policy: tee times are on a first come, first served basis.
Winter condition: open all year. Club house closed December 1st to March 1st.
Terrain: flat (easy walking). **Tees:** all grass. **Spikes:** metal spikes permitted.
Services: club rentals, vending machines, putting green, beginner course.
Comments: Very challenging short "easy" course with water hazards and trees. Course also features "The Wedge" beginners course and practice area. ($1, complimentary prior to tee time.) Course closed Mondays except holidays.

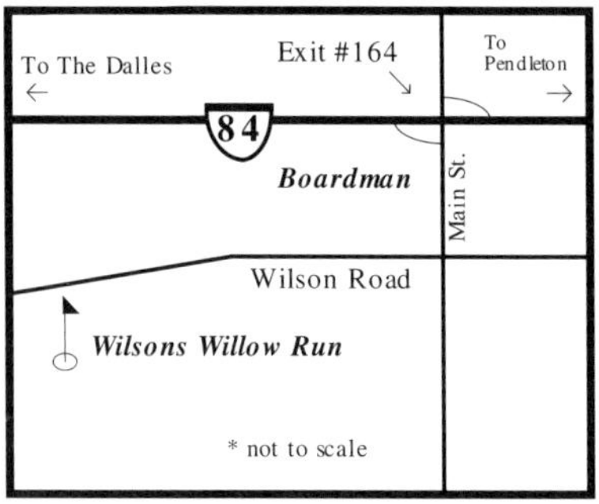

Directions: from I-84 take the Boardman exit #164. Turn left (south) 1 mile to Wilson Road. Turn right (west) and proceed 3 miles to the golf course.

Course Yardage & Par:

M-1803 yards, par 31.
W-1803 yards, par 32.
Dual for tees 18 holes:
M-3742 yards, par 62.
W-3742 yards, par 64.

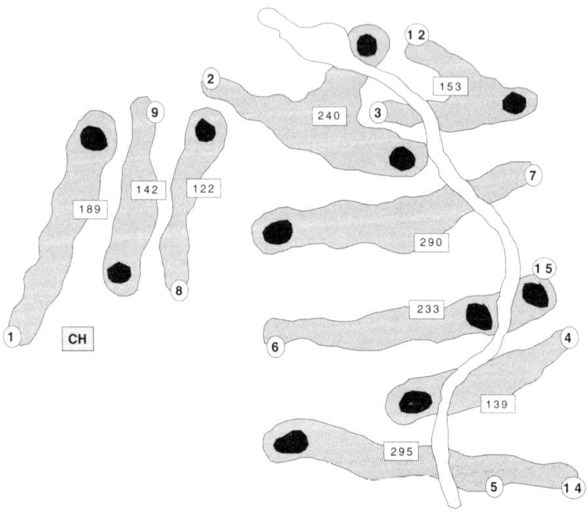

Woodburn Golf Club (public, 9 hole course)

Highway 214 West; Woodburn, OR 97071
Phone: no phone listed. Fax: none. Web: none.
Pro: none available. Superintendent: none.
Rating/Slope: the golf course is not rated. **Course record:** 31.
Green fees: $4/$3 annual fees $75; husbands & wives $85; no credit cards.
Power cart: none. **Pull cart:** none. **Trail fee:** no charge for personal carts.
Reservation policy: self service. Times are on a first come first served basis
Winter condition: the golf course is open all year long. Very wet conditions.
Terrain: flat (easy walking). **Tees:** all grass. **Spikes:** metal spikes permitted.
Services: very limited services, putting green, picnic table.
Comments: Mens club plays on Wednesday morning. Ladies club plays on Thursday morning. One of the last courses in the northwest to have sand greens. The course can be very wet during the winter months. Very rustic golf course.

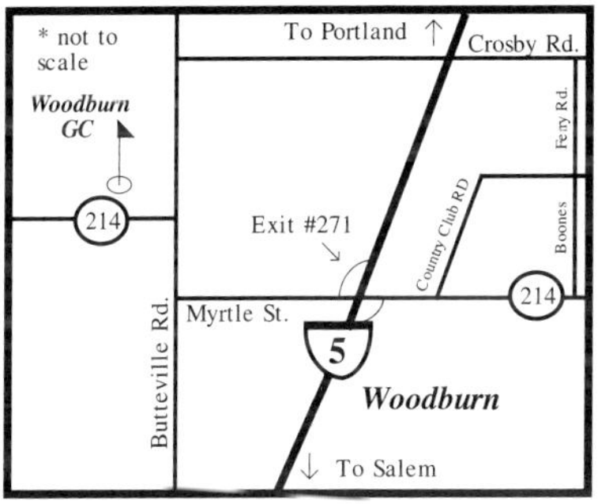

Directions: from I-5 north & south take the Woodburn exit. Go westbound on Highway 214 for 1.9 miles. The golf course will be on your right hand side.

Course Yardage & Par:
M-2592 yards, par 34. **W-2570 yards, par 36.**

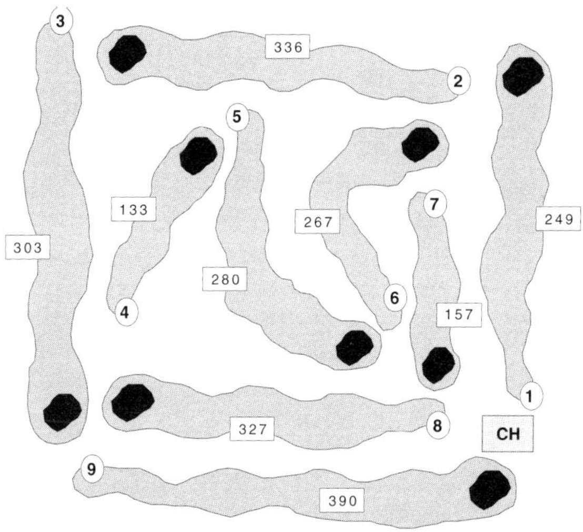

82nd Avenue Golf Center
2806 NE 82nd; Portland, OR 97220
(503) 253-0902. Pro: John Bowen, PGA.
Hours: Monday through Friday 9am-10pm, Saturday & Sunday 7am-10pm.
Lights: yes. **Covered:** yes. **Putting & chipping:** yes.
Services: club re-grip and re-finishing, lessons, International Golf pro shop.
Directions: I-205 N&S take airport exit and travel westbound to 82nd. Turn left on 82nd and proceed to the driving range.

Albertson Golf Range
33575 Toyas Lane; Seaside, OR 97138
(503) 717-0623. Pro: none.
Hours: 10am to sunset all week long.
Lights: no. **Covered:** yes. **Putting & chipping:** yes.
Services: lessons, club repair, pro shop, snacks.
Directions: the driving range is located on Highway 101, 2 miles north of the Gearhart Junction on the east side of the highway.

All Golf at Beaverton
16251 SW Jenkins Road; Beaverton, OR 97006
(503) 626-2244. Manager: Sheri Okazaki.
Hours: W/D's 9am-10pm, W/E's 9am-10pm all year round.
Lights: yes. **Covered:** yes. **Putting & chipping:** yes.
Services: grass tees, mini golf, lessons, pro shop, deli, club repair, practice bunker. **Directions:** from Hwy 217 take the Walker Road exit. Head west turn left on Cedar Hills Road. Proceed to Jenkins turn right. Proceed to the range.

Caddieshack Driving Range
5201 State Street; Salem, OR 97301
(503) 581-7045. Pro: Jim Hynds, PGA.
Hours: 8:30am to dusk all week long.
Lights: no. **Covered:** yes. **Putting & chipping:** yes.
Services: lessons, pro shop, snack bar, rentals.
Directions: from I-5 take the Center St. exit and travel east. At Lancaster turn right and follow to State St. Turn left on State St. and proceed to the range.

Chip Shot Driving Range
14189 South Union Mills Road; Mulino, OR 97042
(503) 829-4653. Pro: unavailable.
Hours: seasonal hours. Please call the range for details.
Lights: no. **Covered:** yes. **Putting & chipping:** yes.
Services: lessons, club repair, pro shop, sand bunker, snacks.
Directions: from I-205 N&S take exit 10 to Hwy 213 south. Go south for 6 miles to Union Mills Road. Turn left. Range will be on the right.

Cordon Road Driving Range
4205 Cordon Road NE; Salem, OR 97302
(503) 362-3694. Pro: Mike Dwyer, PGA.
Hours: seasonal hours depending upon the time of year.
Lights: no. **Covered:** yes. **Putting & chipping:** yes.
Services: lessons, club repair, pro shop, sand bunker, snacks.
Directions: the driving range is located 1/2 mile north of the Silverton Road and Cordon Road intersection.

Dino's Driving Range
21661 Beavercreek Road; Oregon City, OR 97045
(503) 632-3986. Owner: Dino Marasigan.
Hours: W/D's 9am-dusk; W/E's 8am-dusk.
Lights: no. **Covered:** yes. **Putting & chipping:** yes & bunker.
Services: pro shop, four teaching pros, lessons, food, custom golf clubs, club repair, regripping. **Directions:** I-205 N&S take exit #10 (Park Place). Go south on Highway 213. Turn left at Beavercreek Road. (3rd light). Range ahead.

Eagle Driving Range
63977 Imnaha Highway; Joseph, OR 97946
no phone number listed. Pro: none available.
Hours: 7am to 8pm; March-November.
Lights: yes. **Covered:** no. **Putting & chipping:** yes, with practice bunker.
Services: lessons. **Directions:** the driving range is located 1/2 mile out of Joseph, Oregon on the north side of the Imnaha Highway.

Eagle View Golf Center
off of Highway 730; McNary, OR 97882
(541) 922-9787. Pro: Todd Sprong.
Hours: please call for hours summer hours.
Lights: none. **Covered:** none. **Putting & chipping:** putting only.
Services: lessons, small pro shop.
Directions: the range is located in the town of McNary Oregon off of Hwy 730.

Grants Pass Golf Center
2540 NW Vine Street, Grants Pass, OR 97526
(541) 479-9500. Pro: none.
Hours: 9am to 8pm (the range hours change in the winter months).
Lights: yes. **Covered:** yes. **Putting & chipping:** yes.
Services: club rentals, lessons, club repair, pro shop.
Directions: from I-5 southbound take the first Grants Pass exit (last going northbound). Turn right at the first light. Proceed to Vine Street and then turn right on Vine Street.

High Desert Golf Range
20420 Robal Lane; Bend, OR 97701
(541) 389-3919. Pro: Bob Garza.
Hours: 7am to 9pm, hours may vary during the winter months.
Lights: yes. **Covered:** yes. **Putting & chipping:** yes.
Services: lessons, snack bar, pro shop.
Directions: the range is located between Hwy's 20 & 97 just north of the Mountain View Mall.

Highway 58 Golf Range
34455 Highway 58; Eugene, OR 97405
(541) 741-1119. Pro: unavailable.
Hours: open daylight hours only. Seven days a week.
Lights: no. **Covered:** yes. **Putting & chipping:** yes.
Services: lessons, snack bar, pro shop.
Directions: from I-5 N&S exit to Highway 58. Proceed eastbound on Highway 58 to the driving range on the left hand side of the Highway.

Lone Pine Village Driving Range
355 Lone Pine Drive; The Dalles, OR 97058
(541) 298-2800. Manager: Tom Condon.
Hours: hours vary depending upon season.
Lights: yes. **Covered:** yes. **Putting & chipping:** yes.
Services: club repair, lessons, pro shop.
Directions: from I-84 E&W exit at the Junction for Hwy 197. Turn northbound off of the exit. The driving range is located on your left hand side.

Raymax Golf Center
3707 Eberlein; Klamath Falls, OR 97603
(541) 884-1094. Pro: Hal Greene.
Hours: range open from dawn to dusk.
Lights: no. **Covered:** yes. **Putting & chipping:** yes.
Services: lessons, pro shop.
Directions: the driving range is located in Klamath Falls on Eberlein Street.

Tee to Green Driving Range
10805 South E Street; La Grande, OR 97850
(541) 963-2648. Pro: none available.
Hours: range hours will vary depending upon the season.
Lights: no. **Covered:** yes. **Putting & chipping:** yes, practice bunker.
Services: lessons, small pro shop.
Directions: from I-84 E&W take exit #261 Hwy 82. Follow northeast bound to McAlister Road where you will turn right. Proceed to Mt. Fanny Ave. Turn right and proceed to South East Street. Turn right again and proceed to the range.

Trails End Golf Center
1107 Abernethy Road; Oregon City, OR 97045
(503) 723-6811. Pro: none.
Hours: hours vary depending upon the season.
Lights: yes. **Covered:** yes. **Putting & chipping:** yes.
Services: club repair, snack bar, pro shop, lessons.
Directions: from I-205 N&S take exit #10 (Hwy 213). Proceed southbound on Hwy 213 (Cascade Hwy S) to Abernethy Road where you will turn right. The range will located on your right hand side.

Tualatin Island Greens
20400 SW Cipole Road; Tualatin, OR 97062
(503) 691-8400. Pro: Todd Andrews, PGA.
Hours: hours vary depending upon the season.
Lights: yes. **Covered:** yes & heated stalls. **Putting & chipping:** yes.
Services: club repair, 18 hole putting course, snack bar, pro shop, lessons.
Directions: from I-5 N&S exit #289 going west on Tualatin-Sherwood Road for 3 miles to Cipole Road. Turn northbound on Cipole Road to the range.

Wacker's Hollow
240 Suncrest Road; Talent, OR 97540
(541) 535-3600. Pro: none.
Hours: open daylight hours.
Lights: no. **Covered:** no. **Putting & chipping:** yes.
Services: club repair, lessons.
Directions: from I-5 N&S take exit #21 west bound. Go to Rogue River Parkway turn right. Proceed to Suncrest Road and turn right. Proceed to range.

Westside Driving Range
6050 Highway 22; Independence, OR 97351
(503) 364-3615. Owner: Paul Cheney.
Hours: open daylight hours.
Lights: no. **Covered:** yes. **Putting & chipping:** yes.
Services: club repair, lessons, pro shop, sand trap.
Directions: the range is located between Salem and Independence Oregon right off of Hwy 22. Look for the signs.

A & A Custom Golf
4803 SW 76th; Portland, Oregon; (503) 292-3711
Services: club repair, custom clubs, refinishing.

A Hole in One Golf Shop
2300 NE Division; Bend, Oregon; (541) 388-7537
Services: club repair, custom clubs, club refinishing, swing analysis.

Caplan Sportsworld
625 SW 4th & Morrison; Portland, Oregon; (503) 226-6467
Services: retail golf store, custom clubs.

Cascade Custom Golf
18370 SW Tualatin Valley Hwy; Beaverton, Oregon; (503) 848-0224
Services: club repairs, custom clubs, club refinishing.

Cascade Yamaha
2045 NE Highway 20; Bend, Oregon; (541)388-0770
Services: golf cart sales and service.

Club Crafters
1020 Green Acres Road; STE 2; Eugene, Oregon; (541) 343-2222
Services: club repairs, custom clubs, club refinishing.

Custom Clubs by Roger
106 NW F Street; Grants Pass, Oregon; (541) 471-0557
Services: club repair, custom clubs, refinishing.

Custom Clubs by Stu
17110 NE Halsey Street; Portland, Oregon; (503) 255-8280
Services: club repair, custom clubs, refinishing.

DOT Golf Center
8604 SW Hall Boulevard; Beaverton, Oregon; (503) 643-5984
Services: excellent retail golf store, club repair, custom clubs, club refinishing.

DOT Golf Center
12412 NE Halsey Street; Portland, Oregon; (503) 408-1215, 1-800-554-6539
Services: excellent retail golf store, club repair, custom clubs, club refinishing

Eagle Golf
3020 Cleopatra Circle; Medford, Oregon; (541) 772-1859
Services: club repair, custom clubs, club refinishing.

Farwest Golf of Central Oregon
900 SE Wilson Avenue #H; Bend, Oregon; (541) 388-2029
Services: golf cart sales and service.

Farwest Industrial Vehicles
4110 NE Columbia Blvd; Portland, Oregon; (503) 282-6022
Services: golf cart sales and service.

Foltz's Valley Golf Service
5239 Table Rock Road; Central Point, Oregon; (503) 664-3971
Services: club repair, custom clubs, refinishing, custom fitting, used clubs.

Gillette & Weiler Golf Shop
301 Catherine Avenue; Milton Freewater, Oregon; (541) 938-6411
Services: retail golf shop.

Golf City
1052 NE 3rd Street; Bend, Oregon; (503) 389-3919
Services: club repair, custom clubs, club refinishing.

Golf Headquarters
10215 SW Parkway; Portland, Oregon; (503) 297-1808
Services: club repair, club refinishing, retail merchandise, large pro shop.

Golf Headquarters
9515 SE 82nd Avenue; Portland, Oregon; (503) 771-4742
Services: club repair, club refinishing, retail merchandise, large pro shop.

Golf Shop
840 SW 1st Avenue; Portland, Oregon; (503) 228-0330
Services: retail golf store, club repair, club refinishing, retail merchandise.

International Discount Golf
2806 NE 82nd; Portland, Oregon; (503) 253-0902
Services: retail store, lessons, club fitting, driving range.

International Discount Golf
2065 SW 185th Avenue; Hillsboro, Oregon; (503) 629-8845
Services: retail store, lessons, club fitting.

International Discount Golf
11493 SE 82nd Avenue; Portland, Oregon; (503) 659-6020
Services: retail store, lessons, club fitting.

International Discount Golf
9160 SW Hall Blvd. Suite B; Tigard, Oregon; (503) 598-1200
Services: retail store, lessons, club fitting.

Jack Beaudoin's Golf Shop
1455 Burnside Street; Gresham, Oregon; (503) 666-4653
Services: retail store, club fitting.

Kim's Indoor Golf Shop
8305 SE Powell Blvd.; Portland, Oregon; (503) 771-7489
Services: indoor golf course.

Lady Golf
5123 SW Macadam Avenue; Portland, Oregon; (503) 223-9100
Services: womens golf supplies.

Missing Link
1935 S Highway 97; Redmond, Oregon; (541) 923-3426
Services: club repair, custom clubs, club refinishing

Northwoods
7410 SW Macadam; Portland, Oregon; (503) 245-1910
Services: club repair, custom clubs, club refinishing.

Oregon Custom Golf Clubs
16377 Inverurie Road; Lake Oswego, Oregon; (503) 635-8861
Services: custom clubs.

Pacific Northwest Yamaha
1600 NE 25th Avenue #B; Hillsboro, Oregon; (503) 647-5001
Services: golf cart sales & services.

Parfection
1293 NE 3rd; Bend, Oregon; (541) 389-3499
Services: club repair, custom clubs, club refinishing, lessons, retail store.

Pop's Golf Shop
18321 SE McLoughlin Blvd.; Portland, Oregon; (503) 659-7551
Services: club repair, custom clubs, club refinishing.

Portland Golf Academy
8103 NE Killingsworth; Portland, Oregon; (503) 253-4653
Services: club repair, custom clubs, club refinishing, lessons.

Albany: Golf Club of Oregon, Spring Hill Country Club
Aloha: The Reserve Vineyards & Golf Club
Ashland: Oak Knoll Public Golf Course
Astoria: Astoria Golf & Country Club
Aurora: Langdon Farms Golf Club
Baker City: Baker Golf Club
Bandon: Bandon Dunes (Dunes, Pacific), Bandon Face Rock Golf Course
Banks: Quail Valley Golf Course
Beaverton: All Golf at Beaverton, Redtail Golf Course
Bend: Awbrey Glen G.C., Bend G. & C.C., Black Butte Ranch, Broken Top Club, Crosswater, High Desert Golf Range, Lost Tracks G.C., Mountain High Golf Course, Orion Greens Golf Course, Pronghorn, River's Edge Golf Resort, Sunriver Resort (Woodlands, Meadows), Widgi Creek Golf Club
Blue River: Tokatee Golf Club
Boardman: Wilson's Willow Run Executive Golf Course
Boring: Greenlea Golf Course, Mountain View Golf Course
Brookings: Salmon Run Golf Club
Canby: Frontier Golf Course, Willamette Valley Country Club
Cave Junction: Illinois Valley Golf Club
Christmas Valley: Christmas Valley Golf Course
Clackamas: Pleasant Valley Golf Club, Sah-Hah-Lee Golf Course & D.R.
Condon: Condon Golf Course
Coos Bay/North Bend: Coos Country Club, Kentuck, Sunset Bay Golf Course
Cornelius: Forest Hills G.C., Pumpkin Ridge (Ghost Creek & Witch Hollow)
Corvallis: Corvallis C.C., Golf City, Marysville G.C., Trysting Tree G.C.
Cottage Grove: Hidden Valley Golf Course, Middlefield Village G.C & D.R.
Creswell: Emerald Valley Golf Club.
Crooked River Ranch: Crooked River Ranch Golf Course
Dallas: Cross Creek Golf Course, Dallas Golf Course
Dundee: Riverwood Golf Course
Eagle Creek: Eagle Creek Golf Course
Eagle Point: Eagle Point Golf Course, Stone Ridge Golf Course
Echo: Echo Hills Golf Course
Enterprise: Alpine Meadows Golf Course
Estacada: Springwater Golf Course
Eugene: Coburg Hills G.C., Eagles #275 G.C., Eugene C.C., Fiddlers Green, Highway 58 D.R., Laurelwood G.C., Oakway G.C., Riveridge Golf Course
Florence: Ocean Dunes Golf Links, Sandpines
Forest Grove: Sunset Grove Golf Club
Fossil: Kinzua Hills Golf Club
Gearhart: Gearhart Golf Links, Highlands at Gearhart
Gladstone: Children's Course
Glenden Beach: Salishan Golf Links
Gold Beach: Cedar Bend Golf Club

Gold Hill: Laurel Hill Golf Course
Grants Pass: Applegate Golf, Colonial Valley Golf Course, Dutcher Creek Golf Course, Grants Pass G.C., Grants Pass Golf Club, Red Mountain G.C.
Gresham: Gresham Golf Course, Persimmon Country Club
Heppner: Willow Creek Country Club
Hines: Valley Golf Club
Hillsboro: Kilarney West Golf Club, McKay Creek Golf Course, Meriwether National Golf Club, Orenco Woods Golf Club
Hood River: Hood River Golf & Country Club, Indian Creek Golf Course
Independence: Eola Hills Golf Course, West Side Driving Range
Island City: La Grande Country Club
John Day: John Day Golf Club
Joseph: Eagle Driving Range
Junction City: Shadow Hills Country Club
Keizer: McNary Golf Club
King City: King City Golf Course
Klamath Falls: Harbor Links G.C., Raymax D.R., Reames G. & C.C., Round Lake Resort, Running Y Ranch Resort, Sheild Crest Golf Course
La Grande: La Grande Country Club, Tee to Green Driving Range
La Pine: Quail Run Golf Course
Lakeview: Lake Ridge Golf Course
Lake Oswego: Lake Oswego Golf Course, Oswego Lake Country Club
Lebanon: Mallard Creek Golf Course, Pineway Golf Course
Lincoln City: Lakeside Golf & Racquet Club
Lyons: Elkhorn Valley Golf Club
McMinnville: Bayou Golf Club, Michelbook Country Club
Madras: Nine Peaks Golf Course
Manzanita: Manzanita Golf Course
McNary: Eagle View
Medford: Bear Creek Golf Course, Cedar Links Golf Club, Quail Point Golf Course, Rogue Valley Country Club, Stewart Meadows
Milton-Freewater: Milton-Freewater Golf Course
Mission: Wild Horse Golf Course
Mollala: Arrowhead Golf Club
Monroe: Diamond Woods Golf Course
Mount Angel: Evergreen Golf Club
Mulino: Chip Shot Driving Range, Ranch Hills Golf Club
Myrtle Creek: Myrtle Creek Golf Course
Myrtle Point: Coquille Valley Elks Golf Club
Neskowin: Hawk Creek Golf Course, Neskowin Beach Golf Course
Newport: Agate Beach Golf Course
North Bend: Kentuck Golf Course
Oakridge: Circle Bar Golf Club
Ontario: Country View, Ontario Golf Club

Oregon City: Dino's Driving Range, Oregon City Golf Club, Stone Ridge Golf Club, Trail's End Golf Center
Pendleton: Pendleton Country Club, Wild Horse Golf Course
Portland: All Golf @ Beaverton, Broadmoor Golf Course, Claremont Golf Club, Columbia Edgewater C.C., Colwood National G.C., Dino's D.R., Eastmoreland Golf Course, 82nd Ave. Golf Center, Glendoveer Golf Course (East & West), Heron Lakes Golf Club (Great Blue & Greenback), Portland G.C., Portland Meadows G.C., Redtail G.C., Riverside G.&C.C., Rock Creek C.C., Rose City G.C., Top O'Scott G.C., Waverly C.C., Wildwood G.C.
Prineville: Meadow Lakes Golf Course, Prineville Golf & Country Club
Redmond: Eagle Crest Resort (Mid-Iron Course, Resort Course, Ridge Course), Greens at Redmond, Juniper Golf Course, Pronghorn
Reedsport: Forest Hills Country Club
Roseburg: Roseburg Country Club, Stewart Park Golf Course
Salem: Auburn Center G.C., Battle Creek G.C., Caddieshack D.R., Cordon Road D.R., Cottonwood Lakes G.C. & D.R., Creekside G.C., Illahe Hills C.C., McNary G.C., Meadowlawn G.C., Salem Golf Club, Salemtowne Golf Club
Seaside: Albertson Driving Range, Seaside Golf Course
Seneca: Bear Valley Meadows Golf Course
Sisters: Aspen Lakes Golf Club, Black Butte Ranch
Springfield: McKenzie River Golf Course, Springfield Country Club
Stayton: Santiam Golf Club
Sunriver: Crosswater, Sunriver Resort (North Woodlands, South Meadows)
Sutherlin: Oak Hills Golf Club
The Dalles: Lone Pine Village Driving Range, The Dalles Country Club
Tigard: King City Golf Course, Summerfield Golf & Country Club
Tillamook: Alderbrook Golf Course, Bay Breeze G.C. & D.R.
Toledo: Olalla Valley Golf Course.
Troutdale: McMenamins Pub Course
Tygh Valley: Pine Hollow Golf Course
Tualatin: Tualatin Country Club, Tualatin Island Greens
Umatilla: Umatilla Golf Course
Union: Buffalo Peak Golf Club.
Vernonia: Vernonia Golf Club.
Waldport: Crestview Hills Golf Course
Walterville: McKenzie River Golf Course
Warm Springs: KAH-NEE-TA Resort
Warren: Saint Helens Golf Course
Warrenton: Astoria Golf & Country Club
Welches: Resort at the Mountain
West Linn: Sandelie Golf, Sandelie West 9, Oregon Golf Club
White City: Veterans Administration Domiciliary Golf Course
Wilsonville: Charbonneau Golf & Country Club
Woodburn: Senior Estates, O.G.A. Members Course, Woodburn G.C.

Oregon State Regional Map

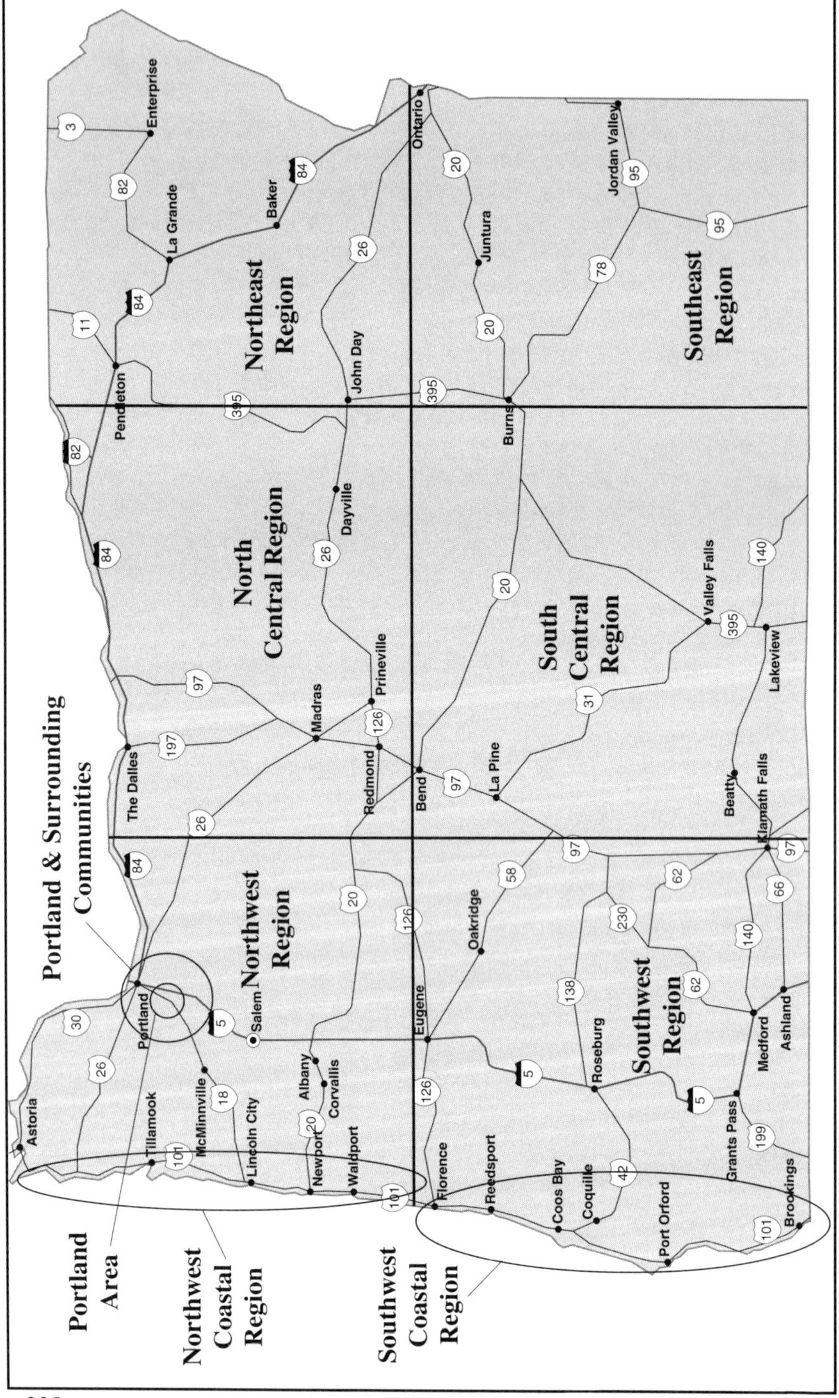

North Central Region

Aspen Lakes Golf Club
Black Butte Ranch (Big Meadow, Glaze Meadow)
Condon Golf Course
Crooked River Ranch Golf Course
Dalles Country Club, The
Eagle Crest Resort (Resort, Ridge, Mid-Iron Courses)
Eagle View Golf Center
Echo Hills Golf Course
Greens at Redmond
High Desert Golf Range
Hood River Golf & Country Club
Indian Creek Golf Course
Juniper Golf Club
KAH-NEE-TA Resort
Kinzua Hills Golf Club
Lone Pine Village Driving Range
McKenzie River Golf Course
Meadow Lakes Golf Course
Nine Peaks Golf Course
Northwest Aluminum Golf Course
Pine Hollow Golf Course
Prineville Golf & Country Club
Resort at the Mountain
Tokatee Golf Club
Umatilla Golf Course
Willow Creek Country Club
Wilson's Willow Run Executive Golf Course

Northeast Region

Alpine Meadows Golf Course
Baker Golf Club
Buffalo Peak Golf Course
John Day Golf Club
La Grande Country Club
Milton-Freewater Golf Course
Pendleton Country Club
Tee to Green Driving Range
Wild Horse Golf Course

Northwest Costal Region

Agate Beach Golf Course
Albertson Golf Range
Alderbrook Golf Course

Astoria Golf & Country Club
Bay Breeze Golf & Driving Range
Crestview Hills Golf Course
Gearhart Golf Links
Hawk Creek Golf Course
Highlands at Gearhart
Lakeside Golf & Fitness Club
Manzanita Golf Course
Neskowin Beach Golf Course
Olalla Valley Golf Course
Salishan Golf Links
Seaside Golf Course

Northwest Region

Arrowhead Golf Club
Auburn Center Golf Club
Battle Creek Golf Course
Bayou Golf Club
Caddieshack Driving Range
Chip Shot Driving Range
Cordon Road Driving Range
Corvallis Country Club
Cottonwood Lakes Golf Course & Driving Range
Creekside Golf Club
Cross Creek Golf Course
Dallas Golf Club
Diamond Woods Golf Course
Eagles #275 Golf Course
Eola Hills Golf Club
Elkhorn Valley Golf Club
Evergreen Golf Club
Frontier Golf Course
Golf City
Golf Club of Oregon
Illahe Hills Country Club
Mallard Creek Golf Course
Marysville Golf Course
McNary Golf Club
Meadowlawn Golf Club
Michelbook Country Club
O.G.A. Members Course
Pineway Golf Course
Ranch Hills Golf Club
Riverwood Golf Course

Saint Helens Golf Course
Salem Golf Club
Salemtowne Golf Club
Santiam Golf Club
Senior Estates Golf & Country Club
Shadow Hills Country Club
Spring Hill Country Club
Springwater Golf Course
Sunset Grove Golf Club
Trysting Tree Golf Club
Vernonia Golf Club
Westside Driving Range
Willamette Valley Country Club
Woodburn Golf Club

Portland Area

Broadmoor Golf Course
Claremont Golf Club
Columbia Edgewater Country Club
Colwood National Golf Club
Eastmoreland Golf Course
Glendoveer Golf Course (East & West Courses)
Heron Lakes Golf Club (Great Blue, Greenback Courses)
Portland Golf Club
Portland Meadows Golf Course
Riverside Golf & Country Club
Rock Creek Country Club
Rose City Golf Course
Top O'Scott Golf Course
Waverley Country Club
Wildwood Golf Course

Portland & Surrounding Communities

82nd Avenue Golf Center
All Golf at Beaverton
Charbonneau Golf & Country Club
Children's Course
Dino's Driving Range
Eagle Creek Golf Course
Forest Hills Golf Course
Greenlea Golf Course
Gresham Golf Course
Killarney West Golf Club
King City Golf Course

Lake Oswego Golf Course
Langdon Farms Golf Club
McKay Creek Golf Course
McMenamins Pub Course
Meriwether National Golf Club
Mountain View Golf Course
Oregon City Golf Club
Oregon Golf Club
Orenco Woods Golf Club
Oswego Lake Country Club
Persimmon Country Club
Pleasant Valley Golf Club
Pumpkin Ridge Golf Club (Ghost Creek & Witch Hollow Courses)
Quail Valley Golf Course
Redtail Municipal Golf Course
Sah-Hah-Lee Golf Course & Driving Range
Sandelie Golf
Sandelie West 9
Stone Creek Golf Club
Summerfield Golf & Country Club
The Reserve Vineyards & Golf Club
Trail's End Golf Center
Tualatin Country Club
Tualatin Island Greens

South Central Region

Awbrey Glen Golf Club
Bend Golf & Country Club
Broken Top Club
Christmas Valley Golf Course
Crosswater (at Sunriver Resort)
Harbor Links Golf Course
Lakeridge Golf & Country Club
Lost Tracks Golf Club
Mountain High Golf Course
Orion Greens Golf Course
Pronghorn Golf Club
Quail Run Golf Course
River's Edge Golf Resort
Sunriver Resort (Meadows & Woodlands Courses)
Widgi Creek Golf Club

Southeast Region

Bear Valley Meadows Golf Course

Country View
Eagle Driving Range
Ontario Golf Club
Valley Golf Club

Southwest Coastal Region

Bandon Dunes (The Dunes Course, Pacific Dunes Course)
Bandon Face Rock Golf Course
Cedar Bend Golf Club
Coos Country Club
Coquille Valley Elks Golf Club
Forest Hills Country Club
Kentuck Golf Course
Ocean Dunes Golf Links
Salmon Run Golf & Resort
Sandpines Golf Links
Sunset Bay Golf Course

Southwest Region

Applegate Golf
Bear Creek Golf Course
Cedar links Golf Club
Circle Bar Golf Club
Colonial Valley Golf Course
Dutcher Creek Golf Course
Eagle Point Golf Course
Emerald Valley Golf Club
Eugene Country Club
Fiddler's Green Golf Course & Driving Range
Grants Pass Golf Center
Grants Pass Golf Club
Hidden Valley Golf Course
Highway 58 Golf Range
Illinois Valley Golf Club
Laurel Hill Golf Course
Laurelwood Golf Course
Middlefield Village Golf Course & Driving Range
Myrtle Creek Golf Course
Oak Hills Golf Club
Oak Knoll Public Golf Course
Oakway Golf Course
Quail Point Golf Course
Raymax Golf Center
Reames Golf & Country Club

Southwest Region Continued

Red Mountain Golf Course
Riveridge Golf Course
Rogue Valley Country Club
Roseburg Country Club
Round Lake Resort
Running Y Ranch Resort
Shield Crest Golf Course
Springfield Country Club
Stewart Meadows
Sewart Park Golf Course
Stone Ridge Golf Course
Veterans Adminstration Domiciliary Golf Course
Wacker's Hollow

Pick's by Dan is a segment in all our books giving you an idea of the author's favorite golf courses that the public is allowed to play within a given state. The courses are listed in alphabetical order and in no order of preference. All courses have comments listed by each of them giving you an idea of how they made it on the "courses that the public can play list". I hope you find the list enjoyable to read and somewhat informative when planning your next golfing vacation to the state of Oregon.

Dan's favorite golf courses the public can play:

Aspen Lakes Golf Club, page 18. *One of central Oregon's best-kept secrets. Aspen Lakes will be even better when they expand to 27 holes.*
Bandon Dunes, pages 23-24. *Simply put, the finest 36 hole golf facility in the state of Oregon, possibly the nation. Bandon Dunes has been awarded so many "best of awards" that if I listed them all here I would run out of room. Lodge is spectacular, golf is unforgettable and all right next to the Pacific Ocean. Be sure to play these magnificent courses. Expensive but well worth it.*
Black Butte Ranch, pages 32-33. *Great family golf destination. Our family has vacationed here for years. Nothing but "sun and fun". In addition to 36 holes of championship golf the ranch offers a varity of activities for all ages. Be sure to visit the western theme town of Sisters just 7-8 miles up the road.*
Buffalo Peak Golf Club, page 36. *Out of the way surprise in Eastern Oregon that has gotten better every year it has been open. Excellent value.*
Crooked River Ranch G.C., page 55. *Great value in a beautiful setting. Be sure to take advantage of any special offers the course may be having.*
Diamond Woods Golf Course, page 60. *Family built, owned and operated diamond Woods offers wonderful golf at affordable prices.*
Eagle Crest Resort pages 63-65. *Three excellent courses to choose from. The kids love the mid-iron course. Great stay and play resort.*
Eastmoreland Golf Course, page 68. *One of the finest public courses in the state of Oregon. Well run pro-shop and a beautiful clubhouse to boot.*
Elkhorn Valley Golf Club, page 70. *A little out of the way but well worth the drive. Course conditions are excellent during the summer months.*
Gearhart Golf Links, page 79. *Just a great golf venue. What is better than playing golf on the coast of Oregon. A must play!*
Greens @ Redmond, page 86. *Want a change of pace? This course is pure fun and relaxing. We always play here every time we are in Central Oregon.*
Golf Club of Oregon, page 83. *A public track with a very friendly atmosphere. Greens are excellent and I love green fees around $30.*
Heron Lakes Golf Course, pages 90-91. *Play all 36 holes in one day! This could be my favorite courses in the state of Oregon. Great public course that has a good driving range and an excellent pro shop.*
Indian Creek Golf Course, page 97. *Good bang for the buck at Indian Creek. This course is much improved and will not disappoint.*

Langdon Farms Golf Club, page 109. *Well run facility that is sure to please. They are on the cover this year. Need I say more?*
Lost Tracks Golf Club, page 112. *This course improves each and every year and should be a part of any Central Oregon golf vacation.*
Mallard Creek Golf Course, page 113. *Worth every penny of the $45 green fee. Challenging for the low handicapper but forgiving for the average player. Be sure to take advantage of off season play specials.*
Meadow Lakes Golf Course, page 120. *Drive a little and play the entire day. One of my favorite courses to play while on vacation. Very affordable!*
Ocean Dunes Golf Links, page 135. *Great course to play while on the Oregon Coast. Excellent "bang for the buck golf course".*
Pumpkin Ridge (Ghost Creek), pages 154-155. *Voted in the top 100 golf courses in the nation. This 36 hole (one private course and one semi-private course) facility is spectacular and well maintained. Worth a special trip anytime of year. Put this on your must play list when in the Portland area.*
Quail Run Golf Course, page 157. *Voted as the #2, 9 hole course in the nation. I can tell you this, "Quail Run Run will not disappoint you".*
Redtail Golf Course, page 162. *Good value for your dollar at this public track located near Portland.*
River's Edge Golf Resort, page 165. *Tough and hilly but the views of Bend and the surrounding mountain ranges are spectacular. Take a cart!*
Running Y Ranch Resort, page 173. *Arnold Palmer designed a gem near Klamath Falls. A joy to play for all levels of golfers.*
Sandpines Golf Links, page 182. *One of my favorite Oregon Coast golf courses. Be sure to stay and play all day long.*
Stone Creek Golf Club, page 193. *New course that has location, location, location along with affordable green fees for the public golfer. Good course.*
Stone Ridge Golf Course, page 194. *Set in the Rogue Valley this spectacular course received a "four star rating" from Golf Digest magazine. Be sure to put this track on your must play list if traveling the I-5 corridor.*
Sunriver Resort (Meadows) (Woodlands) pages, 196-197. *Two resort courses to choose from. 36 holes of great golf surrounded by a very popular summer and winter vacation spot. Great place to bring the family to. You can even play Crosswater if you are staying at the lodge.*
The Reserve Vineyards, pages 200-201. *This is the public golfer's country club even though both courses are semi-private and restrict some of their tee times. The Reserve Vineyards offers everything a golfer could ever want. Excellent greens, spectacular grounds, and first rate golf.*
Widgi Creek Golf Club, page 211. *Another Central Oregon Gem. Ski in the morning at Mount Bachelor and play golf in the afternoon (usually in the month of June only). Being both an avid skier and golfer it does not get any better than this.*
Wild Horse Golf Course, page 212. *Out of the way golf course that can be a delight to play (if the wind is not blowing).*

In the eighteen years of writing golf books and doing golf research I have played golf with some very interesting people along the way but no one as fun and interesting as my friend Warren. You may know him better from ski world fame and his fifty plus years of producing ski films and making us laugh. Warrens love for skiing is only surpassed by his love for golf these days. This story is about one of our mis-adventures.

"THREE INCHES OF RAIN IS PAR"

The slap, slap, of the windshield wipers emphasized that it was going to be a really miserable day to be playing golf. It further substantiated my personal belief that golf is as dumb as skiing, but is for older people. I had made the arrangements a month ago and the two people I was going to play with had set the day aside in their busy schedule of corporate life. Since both of them are good golfers, I felt I could learn something if I hacked my way around 18 holes with them. What I learned is that the more I play golf the dumber I am when I try and play 18 holes while it is raining a half inch of cold rain an hour and the snow level is down to 2,000 feet and I am playing at about fifteen hundred feet above sea level.

My friends assured me when they made the reservation that the course is never crowded on Tuesday. It turned out that we were the only three people in this part of the world who were insane enough today, to wade around this particular golf course.

Several times, the slowly flowing water was up over the floorboards of our golf cart, but by that time I didn't even bother lifting my feet out of the muddy water, because on the first hole I was walking toward where my ball stuck a little way up out of a large puddle. This is where the clay topsoil has the tenacity of a five-foot octopus and it sucked my right shoe right off. By the time I got it back on, my sock was the color of the muddy clay and I started to doubt my theory that if a scratch golfer will play in this kind of weather, there must be something I can learn from him.

I learned that we laughed at how hard it is to try and hit a golf ball that is always half under water, no matter where it stops rolling on the fairway. Winter rules notwithstanding, we had to move the ball as much as a hundred feet from what would be considered the drop zone to get a spot dry enough where we could put the ball on grass and have enough room to get some sort of a hold with our spikes in the deep sticky clay.

I forgot to mention that before I left the clubhouse I got nailed for the price of a pair of waterproof pants and a waterproof windbreaker. What I really should have bought was a facemask, a snorkel and a pair of swim fins. When the club pro loaned me his waterproof hat and his waterproof glove I sort of realized that he knew something I didn't know. The hat worked the best because when I stood over the ball, the rain was really pouring off of the hat brim and all I had to do was to figure out where to line up the flowing water in relation to the ball. Maybe Golf Magazine could offer a tip of the month about lining up your hat-brim, rain-drippings with the ball.

Most of the sand traps were two thirds full of water so we played winter rules and took a drop on the sandy edge of the miniature lake. When we sloshed into the clubhouse to thaw out before starting the back nine holes I almost bought my own pair of Northwestern golf goulashes. These are fourteen-inch high rubber boots with golf spikes on the bottom. I can see how they might normally really work on rainy day like this, but some of the running water today would have come right over the top of them.

Bob, Dan, and I were laughing so much at the dumbness of our first nine holes that we decided to keep right on playing. However, Dan knew the course a lot better than either of us and he magically skipped a hole and in the driving rain and the low-lying clouds, Bob and I had no idea where we were. As we approached the green on what we thought was the third hole of the back nine, it turned out to be the green for the ninth hole. We had been sloshing around in this rain for two and a half hours so far so when our tour conductor, Dan said, "how does a cup of coffee sound to the two of you" we didn't even bother finishing that ninth hole for the second time.

The clubhouse restaurant was closed for the day because of lack of customers. However we did play on our own private golf course that day and the green fee was only $18.00 a person. Oh, and I have to add to that my cost of a waterproof windbreaker, a pair of waterproof pants, and a pair of goulashes with golf spikes in the doubtful chance that some other time in my life, I just might be dumb enough to get into a situation where I can't phone in sick when it's raining a half an inch an hour.

By: Warren Miller ©

MAC PRODUCTIONS ORDER FORM

Quantity			Subtotal
	Golfing in Arizona	10/2003	
______	1st Edition	*$16.95 ea*	__________
	Golfing in British Columbia	4/2003	
______	1st Edition	*$16.95 ea*	__________
	Golfing in Hawaii	5/2003	
______	1st Edition	*$12.95 ea*	__________
	Golfing in Idaho & Montana	5/2003	
______	3rd Edition	*$12.95 ea*	__________
	Golfing in Nevada	10/2003	
______	1st Edition	*$12.95 ea*	__________
	Golfing in Oregon	4/2003	
______	12th Edition	*$12.95 ea*	__________
	Golfing in Washington	4/2003	
______	17th Edition	*$14.95 ea*	__________

Shipping & Handling Charges
Add $5 for the first book and .50 for each additional book for shipping & handling. __________

WA Residents Add 8.4% State Sales Tax __________

Total Enclosed __________

Paying by credit card please include card number below.

Expiration date: ____/____ MasterCard ☐ VISA ☐

Send Check or Money order to:
MAC Productions
P.O. Box 84
Duvall, WA 98019 USA

(Canadian residents please send US funds only)

MAC Productions
Golf Guides Since 1986

Send Books to:

____
Name of Recipient

____
Address

____
City, State or Province, zip or postal code